F. R. Leavis

F. R. LEAVIS
Essays and Documents

edited by
Ian MacKillop & Richard Storer

Sheffield
Academic Press

© 1995, Sheffield Academic Press

Published by Sheffield Academic Press
Mansion House, 19 Kingfield Road,
Sheffield s11 9as, England

Typeset by Carnegie Publishing
18 Maynard Street, Preston

Printed on acid-free paper in Great Britain
by Bookcraft, Midsomer Norton, Somerset

British Library Cataloguing in Publication Data
A catalogue record for this book is available
from the British Library

ISBN 1-85075-564-7

Contents

Introduction

F. R. Leavis was born in Cambridge in 1895. This volume is intended to mark his centenary.

It is also intended to address a situation which we as editors have become increasingly aware of while working on Leavis over the last five years – one writing a biography, *F. R. Leavis: A Life in Criticism* (Allen Lane: The Penguin Press, 1995), and the other ('supervised' by the first) writing a Ph.D thesis on '"English", Education and the University: The Work and Significance of F. R. Leavis'. It seems clear that Leavis is by no means a forgotten figure. He remains controversial in the sense that mention of his name or influence can still provoke surprisingly strong reactions or fierce debate (to announce 'Leavis' as one's topic is to generate certain polarized expectations, even apprehensions). At the same time it is generally recognized that Leavis is an unavoidable topic for anyone who wants to understand the history and theory of English criticism in this century. He has become a landmark – an essential reference-point, and most essential as such perhaps for those intent on setting off in a new direction. Readers of Terry Eagleton's *Literary Theory: An Introduction*, for example, start their journey of discovery by being told that they are 'card-carrying Leavisites, whether they know it or not'. Yet references to Leavis tend to rely on a remarkably limited and – as it turns out – often quite *un*reliable body of supposed 'knowledge'. In approaching Leavis the eye is always drawn to the same few details: certain topics, passages and events which compose a convenient figure. But there are other threads in the tapestry which are rarely noticed and which have faded almost to the point of invisibility. The purpose of this book is to restore some texture to the discussion of Leavis – some more attention to the unregarded details, and quite simply some more texts to the reader.

The instance of neglect we have had particularly in mind in preparing this book has to do with our understanding of Leavis as a teacher. Everyone knows this about Leavis – not just that he was an inspiring university teacher but that he somehow begot generations of inspiring school teachers who acted as his missionaries ('Despising research, he sent them into the schools . . .').[1] That seems to be all we know and all we need to know. But what does it mean to be a university teacher – or what did it mean for Leavis and for his students? And how does it differ from being a 'literary critic', which was how Leavis identified himself in his writing? Leavis actually devoted a great deal of thought to the question of how these potentially divergent functions should be productively related, and the minor classic *Education and the University* (1943) was his answer. He was uncomfortable with the label 'teacher': 'if one's concern is essentially with literature one doesn't think of oneself as "teaching". One thinks of oneself as engaged with one's students in the business of criticism.'[2] The teacher in this sense 'doesn't find himself holding back his subtlest insight and his most adventurous thought because they are not suitable for communication to first-year men' while the student 'needs to feel . . . that in the matter of his work and its significance he belongs to a community that is implicitly collaborative'.[3] But Leavis also had great respect and admiration for the teaching profession (the 'school-masters' as he less than accurately called them), as is evident from *Scrutiny*. In 'Keynes, Spender and Currency-Values' in June 1951 he quoted Roy Harrod's description of Keynes as 'determined not to relapse into salaried drudgery' and observed sarcastically that 'the rejected "salaried drudgery" was university teaching.'[4] It is interesting to note that the same issue of *Scrutiny* contained an article on 'Matthew Arnold: Her Majesty's Inspector'.

It is an important start to grasp Leavis's particular interpretation of the role of the university English teacher. But we should ask how this worked out in practice. Indeed it is particularly relevant to ask this of a foundational figure like Leavis now, in the mid-1990s, when changes in Higher Education are forcing 'English' departments to think through (not without considerable anguish) issues of literary pedagogy and classroom practice. What did Leavis and his students actually do while they were 'engaged . . . in the business of criticism'? Was it a discussion – or a monologue? How and what exactly did the students learn? Individual learning experiences tend to be locked away in data either personal to the point of privacy or austerely institutional. But our contributors help to reconstruct some aspects of the teaching situation which Leavis and his students shared, by providing both personal accounts and documentary evidence. We have encouraged all our contributors to the 'Biographical' section to include as much detail as possible about their experiences of being taught by Leavis, and the 'Education in the University' section is devoted to various documents related to his teaching practice. Charles Page, for example, analyses the handouts around which Leavis improvised his 'Appreciation and Analysis' lectures for the English Faculty. And Charles Winder's notes from Leavis's Downing College seminars provide a rare and interesting opportunity to approach the history of education from the point of view of what the student heard rather than what the teacher said. It is with Downing that Leavis's role as a teacher is particularly associated. He held classes for his college students – seeing one 'year' at a time, which usually meant about a dozen Downing undergraduates plus some regular visitors. But it is important to note that through much of the time Leavis was Director of Studies at Downing his students also attended weekly 'super-visions' – one or two at a time with a supervisor, usually a youngish recent graduate – at which a weekly essay was discussed (*not* read out). And the classes themselves were held three or four times a week through much of Leavis's career. There were also the Faculty lectures – including those given by Leavis himself. If there was a monologue, then, it must be set in the context of several different layers of teaching event. The density and variety of teaching in the Downing system was probably greater than that furnished elsewhere in Cambridge. Was this brainwashing? The charge could only be made in Britain where the weekly contact hour is still the norm. The documentary evidence of the way Leavis selected and organized material suggests that he didn't think of his students as passive. He presented them with a series of carefully structured exercises which encouraged them to develop and test hypotheses – in other words, actually to think and learn. As he put it in *Education and the University*, 'literature is desolatingly vast': 'It is absurd that last year's schoolboy should be flung into a wilderness of books and abandoned to his own resources . . . There is no doubt a function for some lectures, but even if lectures were no better than they commonly are, the lecture-method could not provide what the student needs. It is plain, on the other hand, that the method of planned and prepared discussion, involving concerted reading and some written work, is capable of most fruitful applications.'[5]

We make no apology, then, for including in this book a considerable amount of the sort of material that often does not survive a student's departure from university – reading lists, examination papers and so on. These are after all the papers that really fashion what students do – or as one of Leavis's key influences, Alexander Meiklejohn, put it: 'Nothing is more revealing of the purpose underlying a course of study than the nature of the examination given at its close.'[6] It is not just in relation to pedagogical issues, however, that we think it is important to collate the more un-promising or unlikely miscellaneous data. As part of this book we have taken the opportunity to include some of the more unusual but interesting research that has been done on Leavis recently (William Baker's study of Leavis's annotations, for example, in Chapter Two) and we are grateful to our contributors for all the occasional or frankly anecdotal material they have provided. Anecdotes about Leavis, of course, have never been in short supply, and a lively oral tradition seems to have grown up around him quite early in his career. We hesitate to declare some of the more bizarre versions of 'Leavis' we have come across for fear of adding another link to the chain of Chinese whispers. There is the Leavis who is supposed to have banned Indian students from his class on Keats's 'Ode to a Nightingale'. There is the Leavis who is supposed to have taught in his dressing-gown. And whose works were written by Q. D. Leavis. There is the Leavis who banned the works of Dickens from the reading-lists of 'at least two universities'; Leavis gnawing at an 'Attlee-like' pipe; Leavis whose *Great Tradition* 'corrupted more readers than a thousand television book programmes'. None of these is true – or at least none of them is verifiable. But they all say something about the way people have wanted to talk about Leavis, and as such they are historical data of a kind, worth capturing in print. The most important thing perhaps is not to be satisfied with these limiting mythic constructions of Leavis but to continue to ask questions about the historical realities behind the anecdotes.

It might have been expected that we would use this Introduction to make a forceful case *for* Leavis *against* something else. If we haven't done so, it is partly for reasons of space, partly also because of the difficulty of completing the opposition. Leavis against 'theory'? Leavis against 'cultural studies'? Leavis against 'mass higher education'? We would rather offer this book as an aid towards clarifying the different contexts in which a case *for* Leavis might be made. With this in mind we are particularly glad to be able to include essays by Barry Cullen and Gary Day, which explore ways of affirming the value of Leavis's criticism in relation to post-structuralism and philosophy. Michael Black's thorough survey of Leavis's dealings with Lawrence represents some of the strengths of the traditional Leavisian agenda.

We hope this book will focus more attention on what Leavis actually wrote and what he actually did, and we have tried to make more material of this kind available to be focused on. But there is one aspect of the historical Leavis we cannot represent, and that is the *voice* – commented on by almost everyone who heard him. There are a few tape recordings of Leavis speaking. The best is a 45-minute tape of him reading, mostly from Eliot's *Four Quartets* and 'Ariel' poems, which was made by Philip Brockbank some time after Leavis took up his Visiting Professorship at the University of York. Brief interesting remarks are made between the poems. After reading Parts II and III of 'Little Gidding' Leavis breaks off to talk briefly about Eliot: 'I gulp at the *terza rima* passage which I admire so much. I'm taken aback, every now and then, by remembering *things he said to me.*' Leavis's capacity for an unemphatic, yet singing, manner of delivery remained in the memory of many. His voice was professionally described by a BBC producer, R. E. Keen, in a standard transmission report in September 1949: 'Quiet, rather flat voice with East Anglian vowels, which sounds somewhat monotonous and pleasant.' But hardly anything of Leavis was broadcast. He proposed a series of radio talks before the war, but nothing came of it, partly because of his own suspicions. After the war he gave three talks in September 1949, November 1955 and September 1956, which survive as transcripts in the BBC Written Archives Centre at Caversham Park. As far as we know there is only one voice-recording interview. In 1957 the Canadian writer and critic Nathan Cohen recorded a short (10-minute) interview with Leavis for the Canadian Broadcasting Corporation: the tape was later found by Robert Fothergill in the CBC Archives. The interview has an interesting edge because Leavis is aware that his interviewer comes from outside what he (Leavis) calls a 'very tight little island'. To understand contemporary English literature and criticism, he says, 'the first order of fact that anyone from outside ought to know something about is sociological. One must know something about the set-up, the social set-up of the literary world. As I've remarked to you privately already, this is a very tight little island and

a very small body, a very small core of writers command.' At one point
Nathan Cohen asks Leavis what he believes are the essential qualities a
critic should bring to bear in the evaluation of a work. 'I don't know'
Leavis replies politely. 'I think the answer is intelligence, I don't see what
else one can say.'

Leavis's lecture at the 1968 Cheltenham Festival of Literature, 'T. S.
Eliot and the Life of English Literature', was also recorded and can be
heard (by appointment) at the National Sound Archive. One other public
lecture taped – highly suitable in subject-matter – was 'Reading Out
Poetry', delivered at the Queen's University, Belfast, in May 1972. This
includes readings from Eliot, Shakespeare (*Othello*), Hopkins, Pope (*The
Dunciad*) and Thomas Hardy. As Leavis approached the platform on this
occasion, his friend Professor G. S. Singh asked if he minded being
recorded. Leavis murmured that he didn't – so long as the recording was
for Singh's use only. Singh honourably never consented to having the
recording put into circulation, though a transcript was made.

The end of this lecture is rather striking, and worth noting in Leavis's
centenary year. He was certainly nervous of 'reading out poetry' to an
audience of about a thousand people and concluded thus: 'Well, I won't
say more, I'm so grateful to have got to the end without any calamitous
– at least, I hope without any calamitous – breakdown. But I do apologize
about stumbles and so on; they were quite inevitable. But now I'll stop
and apologize for going on so long. I hadn't realized how long the thing
had taken.'

We are grateful to the Executors of the Leavis estate for their permission
to quote extracts from Leavis's published work. We would also like to
thank the Society of Authors, as Literary Representative of the Estate of
A. E. Housman, for permission to reproduce two poems in Chapter 6;
and Laurence Pollinger Ltd and the Estate of Frieda Lawrence Ravagli,
for permission to reproduce the poem 'Piano'.

We would also like to thank Gina Dobbs of Random House UK
Limited for permission to consult and quote from the Bodley Head and
Chatto & Windus Archives; and Michael Bott, the Keeper of the Archives
at the University of Reading, for his friendly help in this matter.

We are grateful to all our contributors, and to those who contributed other material and information; particularly Marjorie Glick, Peter Harcourt, Mrs Peggy Kinch, John Haffenden, D. F. Rowe, R. T. Jones, Norman Guilding, and Robert Jefford. We would also like to thank Professor Michael Hattaway for his help as Head of the Department of English Literature, University of Sheffield.

Notes on Contributors

William Baker is Professor of English, Northern Illinois University. He is editor of *George Eliot-George Henry Lewes Studies*. He is, with John Kimber and Maurice Kinch, author of *F. R. Leavis and Q. D. Leavis: An Annotated Bibliography* (1989).

Michael Black is Fellow of Clare Hall, Cambridge. Joined Cambridge University Press in 1951: responsible for its English list at the time of the re-issue of *Scrutiny*. Publishing sponsor and member of editorial board of the Cambridge Edition of the Letters and Works of D. H. Lawrence. He is author of *D. H. Lawrence: The Early Fiction*, of *D. H. Lawrence: The Early Philosophical Works,* of a study of *Sons and Lovers* ('Landmarks in World Literature': Cambridge University Press), and editor of a new edition of *The White Peacock* for Penguin Books.

Barry Cullen is the course head of BA English at Middlesex University. He has written on I. A. Richards and Cambridge criticism, and recently on Leavis as an 'anti-philosopher'. He is shortly to publish a book on Leavis as a literary thinker.

Gary Day researched and taught at University of Wales, Cardiff and is Senior Lecturer in Critical and Cultural Theory at De Montfort University, Bedford. He is editor of and contributor to *The British Critical Tradition* (1993) and has recently completed a Ph.D thesis on F. R. Leavis.

Keith Dobson was born in Hull, educated at Paisley Street and Scarborough Boys' High School. From 1939 to 1940 he taught English and History at Scarborough College, then from 1945 English, History and German at the High Pavement Grammar School (later Sixth Form College), Nottingham.

Patrick Kennard Harrison, C.B.E., won an Exhibition to Downing College in 1946. He went up in 1949, taking English and Social Anthropology. He served in the Scottish Office until 1968 when he became Secretary of the Royal Insitute of British Architects. From 1989 he was Project Secretary of the Building Museum Project.

Eric McCormick, born in Taihape, North Island, New Zealand. A leading

New Zealand cultural historian, he is author of a biography of the painter Frances Hodgkins, *The Expatriate* (1954) and Alexander Turnbull, business and patron of the arts. He has also written studies of Abel Tasman, of the painter Eric Lee-Johnson, of Omai, the first Polynesian to visit Britain, and, in his eighty-third year, Charles Brown, the friend of John Keats. His life's work has been the analysis of his country's two cultures, Polynesian and European.

Ian MacKillop is a Senior Lecturer in English Literature at the University of Sheffield. He is the author of *The British Ethical Societies* (Cambridge University Press, 1986) and *F. R. Leavis: A Life in Criticism* (Allen Lane, The Penguin Press, 1995). He edited *Delta* from 1961 to 1973.

Charles Page was formerly Lecturer at the University of Exeter, a specialist in modern literary criticism and art history.

Neil Roberts is a Senior Lecturer in English Literature at the University of Sheffield. He has published books on George Eliot and on Ted Hughes. His latest book is *The Lover, the Dreamer and the World: The Poetry of Peter Redgrove* (1994).

Richard Storer is Lecturer in English at Trinity and All Saints, a College of the University of Leeds. His PhD thesis, completed at the University of Sheffield, was on F. R. Leavis, 'English' and Higher Education.

Charles Winder is Head of English at Bolton School, Lancashire.

PART I

Bibliographical

Leavis as Critic of New Poetry: Uncollected Reviews

Although F. R. Leavis made a number of collections of his published articles and reviews during his lifetime, and sanctioned several others, the complete list of items that remained uncollected at his death is surprisingly long, and has not been shortened much by later volumes. Looking down the list there are one or two intriguing items (Leavis's review of a book on the relationship between John Stuart Mill and Harriet Taylor, for example)[1] but in most cases it seems clear that these miscellaneous items were passed over because they dealt with themes and opinions that were well enough aired in other collected pieces. One group, however, that stands out as a more coherent body of work and remains under-represented in existing collections, is formed by Leavis's occasional reviews of modern poetry between 1927 and 1941. These pieces all belong with *New Bearings in English Poetry* (1932), the book that established Leavis's career as a critic, but they cover a much broader range of contemporary reference than that book. Leavis was in fact a much more energetic – if not exactly enthusiastic – critic of contemporary poetry, in the years immediately before and after the publication of *New Bearings,* than he seems to have wanted to recall when he came to write his 'Retrospect' for the new edition in 1950. Developments in modern English poetry after Eliot, he declared then, had not been 'of such a kind as I should care to write about at length':

> Actually, I think the history of English poetry since then has been depressing in the extreme . . . Some four or five years ago, on the reopening of relations between this country and France, I was asked by the visiting *conseil de redaction* of a French review what, looking back, I could report as having happened in English poetry during the previous ten years. The question was a disconcerting one . . . All I could find

to say was: 'Yeats has died, and Eliot has gone on.' And that seems to
me an epitome of the years that have passed since I took my note of
the 'new bearings' and reported the signs of promise.[2]

It makes more sense to interpret Leavis's reply as an epitome of the years
to come, in terms of his narrowing interests and lack of engagement with
any post-war poets. But 'Yeats has died, and Eliot has gone on' does not
do justice to Leavis's investment in poetry-reviewing before the war. He
may not have been particularly impressed by anyone except Eliot and
Yeats, but he was prepared to read and discuss ('write about at length')
contemporary work by many others, as the uncollected reviews show.
The aim of this chapter is not to attempt a detailed analysis of Leavis's
occasional poetry criticism in this period – though obviously there are
some interesting issues to follow up – but simply to make more of the
data available by sampling some of the reviews, many of which have
become relatively difficult to track down to their original source and are
unlikely ever to be reprinted in full.

Leavis's earliest reviews were all written for *The Cambridge Review*. Two
early reviews of poetry were of volumes by Edmund Blunden. The first
of these, on *Retreat*, was later incorporated into *New Bearings in English
Poetry* and thus constitutes the earliest published section of that book.
Leavis cut several sentences from his review in the later version, including
his description of Blunden as 'a genuine poet who understood and really
cared about his themes' and his reference to 'the pang of memory, the
sense of exile, the yearning after the irrevocable' that were 'more directly
expressed' in *Retreat*.[3] From his second review, of *Near and Far*, Leavis
only recycled a few lines in *New Bearings* and omitted this conclusion:

> So we are the apter to murmur when his verse offers difficulties; for
> the occasional knots and clutterings can hardly point for justification to
> a packed and complex sensibility. Indeed, they result, rather, from a
> lack of drive. But commonly Mr Blunden does not invite us to look
> for more than the quiet, reminiscent pleasure he can give.[4]

'Quiet' is the right word for these earlier short pieces. Leavis's review of
Cambridge Poetry 1929, however, was more substantial and provocative –
and should be read in conjunction with 'T. S. Eliot – A Reply to the
Condescending' published three weeks earlier in the same journal.[5] Leavis
used the review as a way of developing his critique of the Victorian poetic
tradition and celebrating Eliot's counter-influence. Student anthologies

were usually 'depressing' because 'all these apprentices, who are interested enough in poetry to be at considerable pains to write some, show themselves to be imitating models, and working under influences, that must frustrate any gifts they may have. The conventions, the techniques, and the preconceptions of "the poetic", coming down from the last century are manifested in these anthologies as none the less blighting for a growing looseness and debility.' This time, however, Cambridge had succeeded in breaking the mould:

> It is time now to say that *Cambridge Poetry, 1929*, is not in the least depressing: on the contrary, I find it cheering, as I have found no other anthology of modern verse. For, whatever its faults and weaknesses, they are not of the old hope-destroying kind: it betokens a decisive throwing-off of the fatal conventions and preconceptions. Georgianism, which was never alive, is now well on the way to being forgotten. Squirearchy, which once held paralysing sway, is dead. For it is not mere rebellion, mere 'modernist' intransigence, that *Cambridge Poetry, 1929* exhibits: Sitwellism counts for very little in it, and E. E. Cummings is not there. (See, for contrast, *Oxford Poetry, 1928*, which favours also the most debile of 'traditional' verse). It is the nature and direction of the 'modernising' that makes the Cambridge book so encouraging.

Despite this overview, Leavis did not spare the 'faults and weaknesses' of individual contributors – in particular, he made great play with John Davenport's reliance on Eliot as a model:

> But although Mr Davenport has carefully imitated some of Mr Eliot's habits of movement, he has found Mr Eliot's essential rhythm beyond him. Hence an amusing discrepancy between the explicit burden of *Dying Gladiator* and its tone and movement. It is no use Mr Davenport's telling us that Time

> > has lopped
> > from their fierce mouths the brazen trumpets'
> > > tongues
> > so that this dull world dances to no tune

> or that the poet walks

> > . . . fearful, sadly, dumb;
> > Cruelly cold and barren in this dark

and fecund month that heaves and swells with life,
standing against an anaesthetic sky,

(like a patient etherized upon a table?): we cannot believe him. The
gusto with which he elaborates his disillusion is too infectious. For Mr
Davenport is a young Romantic, of a kind not new in literary history,
venting his fine energy in embroideries upon themes from Mr Eliot.
His opening passage, with its vague suggestiveness (so unlike anything
of Mr Eliot's), is a romantic manifesto. His habit of mind betrays itself
in his quite unironical (and probably quite unconscious) recourse to
Keats –

through the dark verdure of my fading thought,

and to Swinburne –

in the dim hollows of the dark earth's womb.
(With sadder than the Niobean womb,
And in the hollow of her breasts a tomb.)

And when the end approaches

Annihilation, like a courtesan,
solicits earnestly my waning strength.

very appropriately in the Grand Style. Whether Mr Davenport will be
able to do anything by himself is impossible to guess from this poem.
But it is very much more interesting to read than a Georgian excercise,
and at least took skill and intelligence to put together.

This review is also interesting for Leavis's first – and very favourable –
response to William Empson:

When we come to William Empson we find something that we must
take very seriously. There is nothing parasitic about his work. But
although he does not borrow from Mr Eliot, it is clear that he knows
Mr Eliot's criticism, or, at any rate, has profited by the ideas that Mr
Eliot has put into currency. For it is Mr Eliot who has indicated the
right place of the Seventeenth Century in the English tradition, and
suggested that the modern poet would do well to study the metaphysicals . . . [here Leavis quoted six lines from 'Arachne'] . . . It is plain
that Mr Empson knows his Donne. But I hasten to disavow the
suggestion that he is derivative. He is an original poet who has studied
the right poets (the right ones for him) in the right way. His poems

have a tough intellectual content (his interest in ideas and the sciences, and his way of using his erudition, remind us of Donne – safely), and they evince an intense preoccupation with technique. These characteristics result sometimes in what seems to me an unprofitable obscurity, in faults like those common in the Metaphysicals. But Mr Empson commands respect. Three of his poems, *To An Old Lady*, *Villanelle*, and *Arachne*, raise no doubt at all in me: there is a compelling drive behind them. I look forward to seeing more of Mr Empson's work.

Leavis quoted the same lines from 'Arachne' in the Epilogue to *New Bearings in English Poetry*, and his comments there are generally similar – as they are also in the essay 'Poetry and the Modern World': nevertheless each piece has been substantially rewritten.

There were no new Empsons to be discovered in *Cambridge Poetry 1930* – only more imitations of Eliot. Leavis singled out J. Bronowski's poem 'Betrayal':

Mr Bronowski is, no doubt, tired of being told that he is parasitic upon Mr Eliot . . . But it has to be said again. He has clearly put much brainwork into his verse, but brainwork alone will not make poetry. He is at liberty to borrow for his method from Mr Eliot, but more is needed than method, and what more than method Mr Bronowski offers comes mainly from Mr Eliot. That is what is meant by saying that he is parasitic. The number of reminiscences, more or less disguised, is so great that it disposes of the poem merely to point them out, for Mr Bronowski has done nothing with them; he has merely summoned them to do his work for him. Indeed, there is a damning number that does not need pointing out; the reader will be quick to recognize, again and again, *Gerontion*, *The Love-song of J. Alfred Prufrock*, *Portrait of a Lady*, *Rhapsody on a Windy Night*, and *The Waste Land*. So that even if Mr Bronowski contended that he was doing something justifiable with *The Hollow Men* in

> Between the shaven armpits
> the patent leather
> between the woodwind and the saxophone

we should hardly be impressed. Indeed, we are so affected by the emptiness of the poem and by the swarm of ghosts that haunt it that we are apt, perhaps, to detect ghosts unfairly. Such is the state of mind Mr Bronowski has induced in us. It is so plain that he has nothing of

his own to offer, and that the names and symbols he introduces are
dead counters.

This review also included a brief reference to Malcolm Lowry – 'Mr
Lowry's *For Nordahl Grieg Ship's Fireman* exhibits a curious mixture of
Whitman and D. H. Lawrence, and is in the kind of free verse that is
hardly verse' – and to Hugh Sykes Davies, whose 'preoccupation with
typography makes it difficult for the reader to take him seriously'.[6]

Leavis's first publication in *The Spectator* was a letter in April 1932,
commenting on a review of *New Bearings*. It was followed in May 1932
(perhaps as a result of this intervention) by 'Poetry-Lovers, Prosody and
Poetry', a short review of the work of ten different poets.[7] What makes
this almost unique among Leavis's reviews is that none of the names was
at all significant in terms of critical recognition – or was ever referred to
again in Leavis's work. Leavis was reviewing in *Fiction and the Reading
Public* mode: he took for granted that none of the works achieved the
reality of 'poetry', and turned the review into an opportunity to speculate
on the existence of different audiences for verse:

> There is, for example, probably a large public that could read *The Little
> Drum* with pleasure. This does not amount to critical commendation:
> the writer is qualified for popularity by an ability to pass from fervent
> Christian sentiment to fervent patriotic sentiment without a sense of
> change, and by a corresponding technical *naiveté*. But it is with unmixed
> satisfaction that one recognizes how widely *Golden Wedding* might give
> pleasure – *might*, if there were still a popular audience for verse. For
> *Golden Wedding* is straightforward narrative and description by a writer
> genuinely interested in his themes. There was once a wide public for
> such work, but now that we are all educated it has disappeared; and
> the absence at this level of a public for verse is bad for poetry in
> general . . .
> . . . the tradition is lacking. And so Professor Julian Huxley, who has
> practised verse from his youth, and who laudably refuses to divorce the
> poet from the scientist, has not even begun to recognize any technical
> problems. Yet it seems reasonable to suppose a man of his combined
> interests might, if there had been to-day anything analogous to the
> seventeenth-century tradition, have amused himself in verse with some-
> thing more than merely personal profit. But it is possible for the
> cultivated to-day to remain unaware that anything has happened in
> poetry since (say) Matthew Arnold. Of this traditionalism that means

the death of tradition Mr R. C. Trevelyan's technical experimenting is more impressive evidence than Professor Huxley's technical conservatism.

Mr Trevelyan's dealings with technique are also essentially of the prize-poem kind. Technique for him, that is, has nothing to do with the problem of realizing a personal sensibility. Yet he has been able to give a large part of an arduous life to its study – as the late Poet Laureate did. Indeed, Mr Trevelyan, as his *Note on Metre* avows, is of the school of Robert Bridges. And what may be said of *The Testament of Beauty* may, perhaps, be said without offence of Mr Trevelyan's experiments: the technique that derives from a study of prosody is not the technique that concerns the critic of poetry. For prosody, dealing with rhythm as a matter of syllables abstracted from meaning, deals in unprofitable abstractions, and is an academic game.

Leavis deliberately omitted any reference to W. H. Auden from *New Bearings*. As he later explained, he had been impressed by *Paid on Both Sides*, but 'it seemed impossible to offer an account of it that shouldn't have the effect of taking away more than it granted, so in the end I said nothing.'[8] He had reviewed Auden elsewhere, however. Two unsigned reviews by Leavis, of Auden's *Poems* in 1931 and *The Orators* in 1932 have been identified by John Haffenden and collected in *Auden: The Critical Heritage*. Leavis's preoccupation in both is with the difficulty of the poems. He complained in 1931 that 'although we can sense his general meaning, it requires a kind of effort to discover the exact relevance of his allusions which, even when we are sure of having done so, destroys the possibility of real enrichment.'[9] He introduced *The Orators* with a similar observation:

> Mr Auden's first book of poems has already won him a reputation; yet it is safe to say that no reader put the book down with a comfortable sense of having understood. The present book makes no easier reading, and, since Mr Auden obviously has unusual gifts, it becomes important to examine into the nature of the difficulty; for snobism (such as attends upon every cult) is fickle, and will desert a writer after having encouraged his faults. We expect some measure of difficulty in modern verse; indeed we are suspicious when we find none. But now that fashion has come to favour modernity there is a danger that difficulty may be too easily accepted. The publishers of *The Orators*, on the dust-cover, have almost an air of boasting that their author is obscure. Yet the general nature of what he has to say is plain enough, and the obscurity of the particulars seems to a great extent weakness . . . The opening piece of prose,

'Address for a Prize Day', is very good, but the standard of precision and coherence introduced here in the part is not maintained generally. Mr Auden seems apt to set down too readily as final what comes, on the tacit plea that modern poetry has vindicated the right to demand hard work from the reader. But we demand of the poet that he should have done his share, and in Mr Auden's case we are not convinced. Too often, instead of complexity and subtlety, he gives us a blur; and again and again it is evident that he has not taken enough trouble to make his private counters effective currency. One gathers assurance to put the judgment in this way from the signs, here and there, that he does not know just how serious he is . . .

Leavis conceded nevertheless that Auden's bad habits were associated with 'a certain strength that makes Mr Auden's work remarkable. His imagination tends to the creation of myth. The hints he drops lead one to dream of a representative modern English poem – such as it seems extravagant to hope for.' On this theme the review ended with a brief notice of another poem and one of Leavis's scattered references to James Joyce:

To-morrow will be Different, by Daniel George, is (to quote the epigraph from Hawthorne):

'The journal of a human heart from a single day in ordinary circumstances. The lights and shadows that flit across it, its internal vicissitudes' –

– the sincerest form of flattery, then: Ulysses in verse. But Mr Joyce's prose is more like poetry than Mr George's verse, and both verse and heart are simple.

Leavis's consolidated his view of Auden – and of the new poets of the 1930s – in 'This Poetical Renascence', an important essay, collected in For Continuity, which shows a much more impressive engagement with the contemporary scene than the unfortunate 'epilogue' to New Bearings, devoted mostly to praise of Ronald Bottrall. He reformulated and developed his views further in the three articles entitled 'English Letter' which he contributed to Poetry: A Magazine of Verse, the Chicago journal edited by Harriet Monroe. This was Leavis's first opening in America, and it seems quite a prestigious one, confirming his status as a leading critic of contemporary poetry (Ezra Pound had been the journal's original 'foreign correspondent'). Leavis began by taking mild issue with Eliot:

An interview in an American paper I have seen reports Mr Eliot as saying that the most interesting young English poets today are W. H. Auden, Stephen Spender, Louis Macneice and Ronald Bottrall. Whether the report is correct or not, the selection – at any rate, the first three names – would seem reasonable to the average English reader who believes in having a contemporary poetry; though he might, perhaps, protest that Mr Eliot had left out Day Lewis. I had better say at once that I find only Auden and Bottrall interesting, and that I am sure that what is most interesting in Auden's published work is hardly read.[10]

Leavis then went on to outline his diagnosis of 'the state of critical journalism in this country' before returning to the status of the new poets – including Auden – whom he characterized as 'Neo-Georgian':

. . . the country in which no public could be marshalled (a few hundreds would have sufficed) to support an organ as lively in its seriousness as *The Calendar* is one in which a general feeling that we ought to have modern poets doesn't help much to produce them. Such a feeling produced the Georgian movement, and, if there is no more quickening of critical intelligence than seems likely at present to be tolerated, the new movement represented by *New Signatures*, *New Country* and *New Verse* will turn out to be not essentially different from the old.

As with the Georgians there was as a rule not much reason for distinguishing one from another, so with the 'pylon-poets' (the label suggests what has replaced Nature and country place-names – suggests well enough the corporate attitude towards contemporary civilization, though it would be hard, I imagine, to convey to Americans the odd and very common blend of Communism and Public School). Stephen Spender, it is true, has individual characteristics to justify the distinction accorded him, in current valuation, along with W. H. Auden – except that I cannot see that they make him a poet. But here my judgment is at odds with Mr Eliot's (if he is correctly reported).

Of Auden's talent, however, there can be no question. It was manifested, as a matter of fact, before the 'movement' was assembled and in ways that hardly suggest the later associations. *Paid on Both Sides*, the 'charade' that appeared in *The Criterion* two or three years ago, was obviously the product of a strongly individual sensibility and a subtle mind, and if it was technically very immature, it was not the less promising for that. But prosperous development, it was plain, would involve arduous wrestling with problems of technique, and to expect this of a young poet in the absence of a critical reception and a critical environment is to expect too much. At any rate, *The Orators*, which came out a year ago, showed no signs of such wrestling. It is extremely difficult, with a difficulty very largely of the wrong kind; yet it was almost everywhere acclaimed (by critics who were clearly puzzled by it) as an event in the history of English poetry. An artist who under these conditions does nevertheless develop must have unusual strength of character as well as of intelligence. That Auden has indeed rare gifts anyone may quickly be convinced by reading the opening prose-piece in *The Orators*, entitled *Address for a Prize-day*. Even in the propagandist and satiric trifles he tosses off something of his distinction appears, but it is a pity that it should be as one of the Neo-Georgians that he is becoming current.

In his second 'English Letter' Leavis speculated on the possibility that Auden and Spender might be awarded Gold and Silver medals for their contributions to British poetry. The only obvious representative of 'modern' criticism on the awarding committee was I. A. Richards, but he would probably find he had become an establishment figure. Leavis noted the recent publication of Auden's *Dance of Death*: 'It confirms the judgment that he has been encouraged by his reception to write far too easily.'[11] He also mentioned volumes by Siegfried Sassoon, Herbert Read and Yeats:

Siegfried Sassoon's *The Road to Ruin* and Herbert Read's *The End of a War* are in the same series. Sassoon writes much as he did a decade ago, and one hopes he may be widely read by his own class. Read's criticism of war is very much more subtle; on this theme, whether in verse or prose, he always commands profound respect and one can at times almost take his rare seriousness and integrity for poetic talent.

Yeats's latest volume appeared, of course, on both sides of the Atlantic. *The Winding Stair* contains nothing as good as the best of *The Tower*, but in no volume published during the year on this side by any of his juniors were gift and achievement so undeniable. The commonplaces of reviewing stressed the greatness of the later Yeats for, roughly speaking, the right reasons, and in this, perhaps, we have something as nearly approaching evidence of an effective change of taste in the past decade as we shall find.

Sassoon and Read featured again in 'Auden, Bottrall and Others' published in *Scrutiny* the following month. Leavis assigned them to the category of writers who were not poets but were 'in some way interesting: they may be read seriously as attempting to express sensibilities of our time in verse':

> This applies, for instance, to Mr Herbert Read's little book, distinguishing it decisively from the companion one by Mr Siegfried Sassoon (though this is not to say that Mr Sassoon's verses may not have, in certain social *milieux*, their function). One judges Mr Sassoon to be indubitably sincere; but when one speaks of Mr Read's 'sincerity,' one means a great deal more by the attribution. One has in mind a certain fine tension, a certain unmistakable effort to realize, and to fix with precision, representative subtleties of intimate personal experience. And yet, while intensely respecting Mr Read (as always when war is his theme), I cannot say that I think *The End of a War* successful poetry. The intended subtle complexity of feeling (the intention is obvious enough) does not seem to me realized in the verse; it is not acted, done, given, in concrete particularity and compelled upon the reader, but pointed to, for his acquiescent and too general recognition.
>
> . . . one is certainly looking in modern verse for something distinctively modern – a modernity, say, of 'approach' and 'treatment,' and the modernity of approach and treatment that doesn't manifest itself in technique invites a comment of the form of that just passed on Mr Read: a comment, that is, on the gap between intention and realization. What one is looking for is a handling of words that registers a pressure of sensibility, and a sensibility that is not decidedly of its time will hardly be of a kind to exert a commanding pressure – to have that peculiar individual intensity that manifests the poet. Verse that falls short of exhibiting such an intensity may still be interesting.[12]

Edwin Muir also fell into this category of being modern but not a poet: '*Variations on a Time Theme* is hardly poetry; it is rather a poetic meditation *upon* certain modern themes – one might almost say "essay about them" . . . the theme is always pointed to rather than grasped and presented.' As Leavis's title implied, of the ten poets reviewed only Auden and Bottrall were the genuine article: 'they demand criticism at an altogether different level from the others – as indubitable talents, capable, on a convincing measure of proof, of expressing sensibilities of our time in poetry.' But Leavis was still only interested in discussing Auden's *Paid on Both Sides* in detail. He used some comments by Empson to develop a comparison:

> Mr Auden's strength, then, is to have just what Mr Empson appears to lack: a profound inner disturbance; a turbid pressure of emotions

from below; a tension of impulsive life too urgent and shifting to permit him the sense of intellectual mastery. As a poet he is too immediately aware of the equivocal complexity of his material and too urgently solicited by it, to manipulate it with cool insistence into firm definition and deliberately coherent elaboration. He has nevertheless achieved enough in the matter of technique to impress upon the reader a highly individual sensibility.

Leavis's review of Bottrall was also a restatement of his view of Pound:

The influence of the *Cantos*, apparent in the versification and in other ways, seems to me . . . wholly deplorable. Bottrall is drawn towards Pound for reasons that should work the other way: no poet, I think, has much of profit to teach him whose technique is not a matter of delicate response to inner pressure, and whose technical problems are not pre-eminently problems of organizing experience and persuading sensibility to definition. It is the Pound of *Mauberley* whose beneficent influence appears in the verse of *The Loosening and Other Poems* – where (it is a significant fact) there is nothing that looks much like Pound.

That first volume of Bottrall's has not had nearly the attention it deserves: its due representation in a critical anthology of the best modern work would be very impressive. If, however, the present volume contains much less that gives me anything like unqualified satisfaction, that is not to say that Bottrall has retrogressed; he is attempting something much more difficult.

Leavis was clearly struggling with a sense of disappointment in Bottrall. Nevertheless he managed to work up to a positive conclusion, identifying 'something in Bottrall that is fundamentally a strength: a certain moral energy, a *naiveté* (if this term may be used to denote a virtue), that, along with such intelligence and acquisitiveness, makes one hopeful of his development.'

In his final 'English Letter', published the following year, Leavis again discussed the new poets – this time analysing them in terms of 'the English Public School tradition':

I am not at all surprised that Day Lewis should be popular; I was, however, surprised when Malcolm Cowley in *The New Republic* distin-guished him as the pre-eminently intellectual member of the group. (It is nevertheless true too that, on this side, the *New Statesman* critic signalized *A Time to Dance*, Day Lewis's recent long poem, as having the same order of importance as *The Waste Land*.) Day Lewis's virtues are those of the English Public School tradition. He stands for healthy-mindedness (*mens sana in corpore sano*), sporting courage and generosity ('Why do we all, seeing a Red, feel small?') and the team-spirit. That a sense of social responsibility should emerge with such insistence from the Public School ethos is (I refer to the group in general) an interesting and probably important fact. But Leftward leanings, however preferable one may find them to those of Kipling and Newbolt, do not of themselves turn simple healthy-minded sentiments and energies into poetry . . .

Spender has brought out his *Vienna* since I last referred to him in these pages. My estimate of him remains what it was. I cannot see that he is more significantly talented than Rupert Brooke; indeed, he seems to me to be a poet and modern in much the same way as Brooke was in his time. Auden I still find the one significant talent of the group. He too has a pronounced Public School accent, which is very noticeable in the play that he has been writing this past year with Christopher Isherwood, and that Faber & Faber are just bringing out. *The Dog Beneath the Skin* is very lively and amusing and should be a great success when the Group Theatre produces it next autumn. It is a more satisfactory thing than *The Dance of Death*, Auden's earlier dramatic experiment. But it too suffers from a radical uncertainty – it does not succeed in being as serious as it means to be. The satire of contemporary society does not strike one as being any more securely based than the uneasy enlightenment now current in 'Bloomsbury.' The uncertainty manifests itself in the contrast between the touch of Gilbert and Sullivan in some parts, and the seriousness (too dependent on *The Rock*, perhaps – the study of Eliot is in any case apparent) of the choruses. Where we are particularly invited to demand proof of a mature outlook, what we get is sentimentality. The vision, in fact, in spite of the unmistakable distinction of talent and intelligence, and the will to escape the limitations of upbringing and social environment, is Public School.[13]

Hugh MacDiarmid, whom Leavis reviewed in December 1935, represented a possible alternative to this tradition:

It is a great tribute to Hugh Macdiarmid to say that we find nothing either amusing or offensive in his characteristic attitude, which is that of the inspired Poet – the nobly indignant genius – of the Romantic tradition. But 'Romantic' is an unfortunate word if it suggests the usual self-dramatizing vanity, the petty egotism enjoying its *saeva indignatio*, the feminine gush of stoic pride and self-pity. Macdiarmid exhibits a truly fine disinterestedness and convinces us that we have here rare character if not rare genius. This disinterestedness, this character, this profound seriousness, distinguishes him again from the better-known of the young Left-wing poets. The title-poem, *Second Hymn to Lenin*, is sufficiently a success to deserve inclusion in the ideal anthology (which would be a very small one) of contemporary poetry.[14]

But this was clearly only a passing interest: Leavis's review was less than a page long. Indeed he seems generally to have lost interest in new poetry after 1935. His later reviews were mostly revaluations of reputations established in the 1920s. In June 1935 he reviewed the *Selected Poems* of Marianne Moore, introduced by T. S. Eliot:

I am forced to conclude either that Mr Eliot is specially advantaged by familiarity with the background of Miss Moore's poems and, perhaps, by having heard her own rendering and elucidation of them, or else that, if I am intellectual at all, it is very much less than moderately. For I have worked hard at them, applying myself to most of the book again and again at different sittings, and there is not one poem of which I can confidently say that I see the point . . . I hope to be assured and convinced that I have been obtuse.[15]

Eliot would have proved himself a better guide, Leavis suggested in 1937, if he had directed critical attention towards Isaac Rosenberg instead.[16]

In 1939, in retrospective mood, Leavis returned to the theme of thwarted development, reviewing the case of Edward Thomas:

As a poet, of course, he got his jog from Robert Frost, and wrote his poetry at the very end of his life when in the army (the relief with which he surrendered himself to the purpose provided by the war is significant). This poetry is devoted almost wholly to expressing the characteristic unhappiness of his life, and has corresponding limitations of the kind that D. W. Harding indicates. Yet there it is, a fine and unique, if decidedly limited, poetry; the particular thing it is – and it expresses a representative kind of modern experience – conditioned by that particular history of the poet. A happy Edward Thomas might have written no poetry at all. And yet it is hard to believe that the man who wrote a poetry so original and fine could not, with better luck, have produced something less negative in its essential attitudes – for there is an obvious sense in which 'negative' applies to his actual work. It is perhaps a tribute to the positive virtue of this 'negativeness' that the Group – the post-Eliot Group – have not co-opted him into their bosom along with 'Wilfrid' and 'Kathy'. And it is worth noting that Georgian taste, though he has perhaps suffered from having made his début in Georgian pastoral company, didn't take to him. Harold Monro, for instance, could see nothing in his work.[17]

In the same number of *Scrutiny* Leavis also pronounced on Hart Crane:

Crane's ambition, it is clear, was possible because of his lack of all qualification for it: having no glimpse or notion of any principles of order, he was able to take a rhapsodically vatic Whitmanesque warmth as sufficient for the undertaking, which justified itself by its very magnitude.

   That the America of the 1920s should have produced a Hart Crane is not surprising. What is surprising is the critical respect the legend commands. For the question is not, as one would gather from American criticism, At what point does Crane fall short? but, Why should he enjoy any reputation at all – as a poet, that is? At any rate, I cannot see that, apart from his conviction of genius and his confidence, he had any relevant gift.[18]

Leavis's 1941 review of 'East Coker' in *The Cambridge Review* marks the beginning of the end of his career as a poetry reviewer. Eliot was 'our only living great poet' and after this he became (with the exception of one essay on Yeats) more or less the only modern poet Leavis was interested in writing about – over thirty years later he was still preoccupied with 'Four Quartets'. And yet in 1941 'East Coker' was a new work, and Leavis was attempting a 'due placing' of it for the first time:

East Coker, which is much less difficult than *Burnt Norton* (some things in which I don't altogether understand) must, I think, be judged to be another success . . . It has in it, I think, less of the positive in motion and attitude than any other poem of Mr Eliot's. The satire (if that is the right word) of the admirable *Coriolan* poems, the manner of which is represented in a passage of *East Coker*, has much more about it that is positive. At one point there is a brief reminder of the manner of *The Journey of the Magi*, which poem in prevailing tone, comes as near to *East Coker* as any of the earlier poems does. But the negativeness of *East Coker* is more complete and profound, and this poem, the comparison makes us note, lacks the dramatic frame of *The Journey of the Magi*. It is, in fact, very much in the nature of a directly personal meditation, so that we can hardly help relating the mood to that of the valedictory editorial of *The Criterion*. Nor can we help relating to the mood the looseness of organization, or the absence of complexity, that makes *East Coker* so much easier to read than *Burnt Norton*.

But it is not fair to close without noting that what the poem offers is humility . . . something other, it may be insisted, than a mere negative. Still, the due placing, in relation to the rest of Mr Eliot's poetry, of *East Coker* judged as a poem seems to me what I have indicated.[19]

'Something other . . . than a mere negative.' One would like to feel able to apply this formula to Leavis himself – to what he offered, as a writer, and how we regard it now. The early reviews are at least a welcome reminder that, however his views may have hardened and narrowed later, he did at one stage find something more to say about the poetry of his own time than 'Yeats has died, and Eliot has gone on.'

Leavis as Reader of *Daniel Deronda*

Leavis's bibliographers record three published items focusing primarily on George Eliot's last novel, *Daniel Deronda:* (a) an essay published in *Scrutiny* in 1946, which then formed the last part of the chapter on Eliot in *The Great Tradition* (1948)[1]; (b) an essay published in *Commentary* in 1960, which was then reprinted as the Introduction to a 1961 Harper Torchbook edition of the novel[2]; and (c) an essay published posthumously, in 1982, as 'Gwendolen Harleth'.[3] The primary concern of this essay is not to offer a comparative analysis of these different responses, but to catalogue some of Leavis's markings in his copy of *Daniel Deronda* – markings which do not belong to the period after 1960 but do relate to essays (a) and (b) above.

In 1960 Leavis gave his marked copy of *Daniel Deronda* (Blackwood new edition, 1878) to Brian Worthington, one of his students at Downing College, Cambridge, who recalls that Leavis 'said he'd been given a new US paperback [the Harper Torchbook edition] and so didn't need his copy'. According to Brian Worthington, who has other books from the library of F. R. and Q. D. Leavis in his possession, the marginal linings in his Blackwood edition of *Daniel Deronda* are 'representative' of the way in which F. R. Leavis annotated his books. There are no detailed marginal comments, all but two of the innumerable markings throughout the volume are in pencil, and they take the form of underscorings, perpendicular lines, and hieroglyphics, including a non-capitalized 'x', 'E!', 'W', and more frequently the number '60', which might refer to a quotable quote. There are also the initials 'JA', 'DHL', 'HJ', 'GE', which in their context evidently stand for Jane Austen, D. H. Lawrence, Henry James, and George Eliot. The text is heavily scored: almost every chapter is marked in some way, and Leavis also made notes on the front and end papers. The analysis that follows will approach this material by several different routes: it will start by reviewing Leavis's frequent use of the

marginal note 'GE', and then go on to examine Leavis's notes on the
front and end papers, using these as a guide to corresponding annotations
in the main body of the text.

Marginal 'GE'

The letters 'GE' are found in the margin of 44 different pages of Leavis's
copy of *Daniel Deronda*.[4] The letters evidently refer in some way to George
Eliot's presence in her narrrative – that is 'the George Eliot predominant'
Leavis speaks of in his *Commentary* essay (xvi). In many cases, Daniel
Deronda himself is the subject of narrative concern. Leavis notes 'GE' in
the right-hand margin against this sentence, for example: 'His imagination
had so wrought itself to the habit of seeing things as they probably appeared
to others, that a strong partisanship, unless it were against an immediate
oppression, had become an insincerity for him' (p. 271: Chapter 32).

On three occasions Leavis uses 'GE' to identify Eliot as the source of
epigraphs or mottoes to chapters in *Daniel Deronda*. Leavis correctly
attributes epigraphs to Chapters 18 and 38 to George Eliot's hand. He
seems less certain about the authorship of the epigraph to the final chapter
of the novel,writing 'GE?' in his right-hand margin (p. 609: Chapter 70).
The epigraph is George Eliot's. Leavis's question mark may refer specifically
to her use of 'one' in the epigraph, 'our' and 'us' in its second sentence.
Similarly, Leavis's placing of 'GE' in the right-hand margin alongside the
second stanza of her epigraph to Chapter 18 (p. 145) suggests that he
particularly identifies the 'She' in these lines with Eliot.

Narrative pronoun usage does seem to prompt Leavis's marginal 'GE'.
For example, the last sentence of the final paragraph of Chapter 32 reads:
'The admirable arrangements of the solar system, by which our time is
measured, always supply us with a term before which it is hardly worth-
while to set about anything we are disinclined to' (p. 283). In his right-hand
margin Leavis writes 'GE 60' against this. In the right-hand margin by
the brief three-sentence conclusion to Chapter 35 (p. 323) he writes '60
GE'. In Chapter 55 Grandcourt's drowning is conveyed through Deronda's
experience as he takes 'his evening walk' on the quay at Genoa. Attention
has focused on a boat which is drifting out at sea, and there is speculation
on the quayside: 'a Frenchman who had no glass would rather say that it
was *milord* who had probably taken his wife out to drown her, according
to the national practice – a remark which an English skipper immediately

commented on in our native idiom (as nonsense which – had undergone a mining operation), and further dismissed by the decision that the reclining figure was a woman' (p. 516). Leavis's left-hand margin, the words from 'an English skipper' to 'and further', contain his 'GE 60'.

Leavis's 'GE' is also found by passages of authorial intrusion when the author uses 'we'. In Chapter 7 the comparison of 'Goodness' to nature and harvest prompts Leavis's 'GE': 'Goodness is a large, often a prospective word; like harvest, which at one stage when we talk of it lies all underground, with an indeterminate future' (p. 48).

There are occasions in Leavis's marginalia in which 'GE' is used for comparative purposes. For instance, in Chapter 45, lines from an Italian nationalist song reverberate in Daniel Deronda's mind: 'they seemed the very voice of that heroic passion which is falsely said to devote itself in vain when it achieves the godlike end of manifesting unselfish love. And that passion was present to Deronda now' (p. 420). This provokes Leavis, in his left-hand margin, to note 'GE cf WBY'. The initials – which I take to be those of W. B. Yeats – are placed by the translation of Leopardi's lines: 'Do none of thy children defend thee? Arms! bring me arms! alone I will fight, alone I will fall.'

It is perhaps surprising that only one instance is found in Leavis's markings of a comparative reference to George Eliot and George Henry Lewes. And Leavis's marginal 'GHL GE', when it occurs, is perhaps an obvious example of their association at work. At Genoa Gwendolen becomes more and more estranged from her husband. She and Grandcourt are not 'some couple, bending, cheek by cheek, over a bit of work done by the one and delighted in by the other . . . reckoning the earnings that would make them rich enough for a holiday among the furze and heather' (p. 504: Chapter 54). In his left-hand margin Leavis writes Lewes's initials 'GHL' and underneath them 'GE'.

Leavis's 'GE' is by no means reserved for narrative in which Deronda is the focus of attention. Sometimes Gwendolen is the subject. For instance, at the conclusion to Chapter 7 she reacts negatively to Rex's advances. George Eliot writes: 'if any one had asked her why she objected to love-making speeches, Gwendolen would have said laughingly, "Oh, I am tired of them all in the books." But now the life of passion had begun negatively in her. She felt passionately averse to this volunteered love' (p. 59). Leavis's marginal 'GE' against this passage clearly relates to the last two sentences of direct authorial narrative intrusion. A similar instance is seen when Gwendolen's thoughts appertaining to Grandcourt are described: 'True, he was not to have the slightest power over her (for Gwendolen had not considered that the desire to conquer is itself a sort of subjection)' (p. 77). Leavis's marginal 'GE' relates to the words in parenthesis. The annotative 'GE' is also found in many instances alongside passages in which Lush, Kalonymous, Hans Meyrick and Mirah are the narrative centre.

Annotations in front and end papers

The inside front paper opposite the half-title of Leavis's copy of *Daniel Deronda* contains just two annotations in red crayon: 'Chapt (1) XLIII' and underneath '(2) XLVI'. The first refers to the chapter in which Deronda discovers that Mordecai is Mirah's brother; the second, to the chapter in which he reveals to Mordecai that Mirah is still alive.

A more useful guide to Leavis's marking is found on the end papers. On the first page of the familiar 'New Publications' listing, Leavis notes 'date 530' – a reference to the opening sentence of Chapter 58, which on page 530 has, in the left-hand margin, the word 'date'. Dating tests were frequently given to Leavis's students and other Cambridge undergraduates. The sentence – 'Extension, we know is a very imperfect measure of things; and the length of the sun's journeying can no more tell us how far life has advanced than the acreage of a field can tell us what growths may be active within us' – no doubt appeared useful to Leavis for this purpose.

The final page of 'New Publications' contains what may well be a series of cross-references to relevant material within the novel. In the left-hand margin Leavis lists: 'Good prose analysis 29, 30, 36, 37.' These pages contain the opening eight paragraphs of Chapter 5, and the opening three paragraphs of Chapter 6. The ending of the lengthy cumulative opening sentence of Chapter 6 has Leavis's 'GE' in its left-hand margin. He also annotates '60 WX', followed by two vertical lines alongside the words 'one of the exceptional persons who have a parching thirst for a perfection undemanded by their neighbours.' The second sentence of the third paragraph – 'What she was clear upon was, that she did not wish to lead the same sort of life as ordinary young ladies did; but what she was not clear upon was, how she should set about leading any other, and what

were the particular acts which she would assert her freedom by doing'
(p. 37) – has, in the right-hand margin, Leavis's single vertical lining and
the letters 'JA' underlined – probably a comparative reference to Jane
Austen. Leavis wrote in the opening chapter of *The Great Tradition* (1948)
that George Eliot 'was capable of understanding Jane Austen's greatness
and capable of learning from her. And except for Jane Austen there was
no novelist to learn from – none whose work had any bearing on her
own essential problems as a novelist.' The letters 'JA' are found, perhaps
surprisingly, only on one other occasion in Leavis's annotation, and that
is on an otherwise heavily marked page (27) of Chapter 4.

To return to the end papers, the note 'Exams 133' clearly relates to
material in Chapter 16 and Deronda's problems with the Cambridge
examination system – an area not unfamiliar to Leavis. His note 'words
put together like dominos 224' draws attention to moments just prior to
Grandcourt's proposal to Gwendolen in Chapter 27, where Eliot comments
that 'the subtly-varied drama between man and woman is often such as
can hardly be rendered in words put together like dominoes, according
to obvious fixed marks' (p. 224). The opening sentence of the next long
paragraph – 'The little pauses and refined drawlings with which this speech
[Grandcourt's] was uttered, gave time for Gwendolen to go through a
dream of a life' – has Leavis's annotations in the left-hand margin 'anal.con-
crete' and 'fs' with '60' and a large 'X'. The paragraph concentrates on
Gwendolen's creation of illusions concerning her future existence with
Grandcourt: dreams which all too soon will collapse.

An author not usually associated with Leavis is named in the next
annotation on the final page of the 'New Publications' listing: 'Congreve
226 232'. Leavis writes 'Congreve' in the left-hand margin on p. 226
(Chapter 27) by the paragraph:

> 'And nothing that I don't like? – please say that, because I think I dislike
> what I don't like more than I like what I like,' said Gwendolen, finding
> herself in the woman's paradise where all her nonsense is adorable.

Leavis's 'C' is also found on p. 232, where there is an animated dialogue
between Gwendolen and her mother concerning the ring Grandcourt has
sent. Leavis's '60W' is found in the left-hand margin against the sentences:
'Suitors must often be judged as words are, by the standing and the figure
they make in polite society: it is difficult to know much else of them.
And all the mother's anxiety turned, not on Grandcourt's character, but

on Gwendolen's mood in accepting him'. In *The Great Tradition* Leavis indicates George Eliot's superiority to Congreve: 'Gwendolen's talk is really dramatic, correspondingly significant, and duly "placed".'[5]

To return again to Leavis's end paper notation, 'Prose! 272' is a reference to a lengthy cumulative sentence describing Deronda:

> He was ceasing to care for knowledge – he had no ambition for practice – unless they could both be gathered up into one current with his emotions; and he dreaded, as if it were a dwelling-place of lost souls, that dead anatomy of culture which turns the universe into a mere ceaseless answer to queries, and knows not everything, but everything else about everything – as if one should be ignorant of nothing concerning the scent of violets except the scent itself for which one had no nostril (p. 272: Chapter 32).

Leavis does not cite this in any of his essays on *Daniel Deronda*, so it is not clear what 'Prose!' means. The exclamation mark may indicate that he regarded this as an example of 'the worst prose', examples of which 'would take up more room than can be spared' in *The Great Tradition*.[6]

The annotation 'Gdt torpedo' clearly relates to: 'Already, in seven short weeks, which seemed half her life, her husband had gained a mastery which she could no more resist than she could have resisted the benumbing effect from the touch of a torpedo' (p. 317). This magnificent sentence Leavis, in his right-hand margin, marks 'i.60'. The end paper notation which follows it – 'The religious life 340' – similarly accompanies a word, or cluster of words, in the text. Deronda tells Gwendolen, 'The refuge you are needing from personal trouble is the higher, the religious life, which holds an enthusiasm for something more than our own appetites and vanities.' This sentence receives in Leavis's left-hand margin his evaluative 'm.pr.x', probably meaning 'medium prose' as distinct from 'good' or 'bad' prose (p.340). Gwendolen's guilt following Grandcourt's drowning is noted by Leavis in the end papers – the 'white, dead face 507' – and in the margin with his 'x'. This symbol is also used for a further group of words noted at the back of Leavis's copy – 'best society 109' – and in the right-hand margin of Chapter 14. Again, 'subdued fervour of sympathy' (p. 132), used to describe Deronda, is noted at the back as 'subdued fervour of symp.132', and underlined by Leavis in the text.

There are five more annotations to be found among the advertisements at the back of Leavis's edition (the square brackets indicate writing I have not been able to decipher):

Comedy
Vict. age
[ ] acceptance a duty 104
[ ] irony 166
Yearnings 563

Where Leavis gives page references these notes can be explicated. Thus '[ ] acceptance a duty 104' refers to Gwendolen's uncle's moral strictures found in Chapter 13 concerning her conduct towards Grandcourt. There is a single 'x' in the left-hand margin of page 166 (Chapter 20), where Mab informs Mirah: 'And I carry his signature in a little black-silk bag round my neck to keep off the cramp. And Amy says the multiplication-table in his name.' Assuming that this is the passage Leavis is referring to, it is difficult to find irony in it, unless 'little black-silk bag round my neck to keep off the cramp' is given manifold interpretations. 'Yearning' is a not infrequent word in George Eliot's fiction. In Chapter 63, when Daniel tells Mordecai and Mirah that he is a Jew, he is described as 'enjoying one of those rare moments when our yearnings and our acts can be completely one, and the real we behold is our ideal good' (p. 563). In Leavis's copy the line containing 'our yearnings' has his annotation 'x GE' in the right-hand margin.

The end flyleaf of Leavis's copy contains the following notation:

pp. 20, 21	Symb. 100, 115
p. 64 *	x irony 104
p. 199 *	
p. 290	[clue] & p. 245
374	moral stupidity 382
384	D's conscience
paraphrase 386	
characteristic moral formulation 401, 409, 468, 499, 502	
emotional theory 410	
psych 418	Enthusiast 427
B x & 448 cf D [ ] or [ ]	
Cf.LIV insp. in prose, arch [ ] after [fasting]	
Gd Gent. 506	
images of impartial sympathy 561, 565	

> I am determined to be happy – 18
> wit 27
> fem. touch 32
> reflect 78
> Grandcourt 81
> Gd image 89 99 102. 190 217 225 236 441 453
> lively venturesomeness of talk

Some of these notes are self-explanatory. For instance, the last one repeats a passage found on page 202, which is marked in Leavis's left-hand margin 'C60' with double lines. Similarly, 'I am determined to be happy' (p. 18) repeats Gwendolen's words, although in his left-hand margin Leavis notes 'Isabel Archer': in *The Great Tradition* he discusses at length the comparison between Gwendolen Harleth and Isabel Archer.

The listing of nine illustrations of 'gd' – that is, 'good' – images doesn't necessarily mean that the images receive marginal markings, and in some instances it is difficult to see what Leavis is referring to. The passages cited include: 'The young activity within her made a warm current through her terror' (p. 217), marked by Leavis in his right-hand margin; 'She seemed to herself to be, after all, only drifted toward the tremendous decision' (p. 225) marked with ';' and 'X' in the right-hand margin; 'Grandcourt's thoughts this evening were like the circlets one sees in a dark pool continually drying out and continually started again by some impulse from below the surface', marked in the left-hand margin with an 'i' (p. 236; the 'i' no doubt means 'image'); 'his negative mind was as diffusive as fog' (p. 441), marked in the right-hand margin with double lines, 'i' and '60'; 'bows, smiles, conversation, repartee, are mere honey-combs' (p. 453) also marked in the right-hand margin 'i'. To Leavis these are all self-evident examples of 'good images'.

The note 'characteristic moral formulation' and the page references given '401, 409, 468, 499, 502' all relate to Daniel Deronda. The first three concern Daniel's reactions to Mordecai, the last two his reactions to his mother. In the first reference, for example, which is to Chapter 42, Deronda views Mordecai as 'a man steeped in poverty and obscurity, weakened by disease, consciously within the shadow of advancing death, but living an intense life in an invisible past and future, careless of his personal lot, except for its possibly making some obstruction to a conceived good which he would never share except as a brief inward vision – a day afar off whose sun would never warm him . . .' (p. 401) In now very faded pencil in his right-hand margin of the page, Leavis writes 'Char.form' and in pencil still easily read, '60'.

Deronda and Mordecai also provide the foundation for the note 'emotional theory 410'. In the penultimate paragraph of Chapter 43, Deronda 'felt at one with this man [i.e. Mordecai] who had made a visionary selection of him: the lines of what may be called their emotional theory touched.' The words following the colon attract in the left-hand margin of Leavis's page his 'n'. The next two sentences are lined by him in the same margin with the note 'sig' (p. 410).

The annotation 'psych 418' on the end back paper relates to another set of relationships in the novel. George Eliot writes at the end of Chapter 44 that Grandcourt 'had no imagination of anything in her [Gwendolen] but what affected the gratification of his own will; but on this point he had the sensibility which seems like divination' (p. 418). This receives Leavis's marks '60' and 'ps' in the left-hand margin. Leavis's marginal 'Enthusiast 427' refers to Chapter 45 where Deronda tells Mrs Meyrick: 'Mordecai is an enthusiast: I should like to keep that word for the highest order of minds' (p. 427). Leavis highlights this with a line in his right-hand margin.

There are numerous annotations in the margins of Chapter 54, the chapter Leavis in his end paper refers to as a comparison: 'cf.LIV. insp. in prose'. The chapter focuses on the Grandcourt-Gwendolen yachting trip. George Eliot's revelation that

> He [Grandcourt] himself knew what personal repulsion was – nobody better: his mind was much furnished with a sense of what brutes his fellow-creatures were, both masculine and feminine; what odious familiarities they had, what smirks, what modes of flourishing their handkerchiefs, what costume, what lavender-water, what bulging eyes, and what foolish notions of making themselves agreeable by remarks which were not wanted (p. 504)

is lined by Leavis in the left-hand margin of his text, and at the foot of the page. Leavis writes twice the name of Henry James's 'Osmond' about whom he writes astutely in *The Great Tradition*. The third and fourth sentences of the fifteenth paragraph of the chapter, the paragraph beginning with the powerful words 'the embitterment of hatred' (p. 506) receive left-hand lining, the letter 'g' and the note 'abst. as prose'.

'Images of impartial sympathy 561, 565' are easier to explicate. Both are in Chapter 63 and concern Deronda. The first one is associated with

the sentence which begins: 'It was as if he had found an added soul in
finding his ancestry – his judgment no longer wandering in the mazes of
impartial sympathy . . .' (p. 561). Leavis places an 'X' by this in his
right-hand margin, with a '60'. The second does not contain the words
'impartial sympathy' but is associated with one or both of Leavis's annotations on page 565. Deronda tells Mordecai 'It is you who have given
shape to what, I believe, was an inherited yearning – the effect of brooding,
passionate thoughts.' In the right-hand margin Leavis writes a 'V' by this,
with an 'n'. In the same speech Deronda says to Mordecai, 'Since I began
to read and know, I have always longed for some ideal taste, in which I
might feel myself the heart and brain of a multitude – some social
captainship.' In the same margin Leavis again writes a 'V' and 'GE'.

'I am determined to be happy – 18' elucidates yet another of Leavis's
references to Henry James and to his characters which are speckled through
the annotations in this copy of *Daniel Deronda*. In the third chapter
Gwendolen informs her mother 'I am determined to be happy – at least
not to go on muddling away my life as other people do, being and doing
nothing remarkable' (p. 18). Leavis's left-hand margin has his '60 Isabel
Archer /\.' The note 'wit 27' refers to Eliot's description of Gwendolen:
'In the schoolroom her quick mind had taken readily that strong starch of
unexplained rules and disconnected facts which saves ignorance from any
painful sense of limpness' (p. 27: Chapter 4). In the right-hand margin
Leavis lines the passage, and places a 'v' against it. But there are other
more interesting annotations on the same page. The reference to Gwendolen as 'the princess in exile . . . in time of famine' receives Leavis's
marginal lining and the letter 'w'. The lines 'if she came into the room
on a rainy day when everybody else was flaccid and the use of things in
general was not apparent to them, there seemed to be a sudden, sufficient
reason for keeping up the forms of life' carry the letters 'JA' in the
right-hand margin – presumably a reference to Jane Austen, although these
lines are quoted with a Jamesian comparison in *The Great Tradition*. And
at the foot of the page Leavis writes and underlines the initials of a writer
who obsessed him 'DHL'. The Lawrentian associations are not apparent
unless they refer to Gwendolen's vitality in a 'room on a rainy day'.

Some of Leavis's finest observations in his first two essays on *Daniel
Deronda* are reserved for Klesmer and his impact on Gwendolen. 'Fem
touch 32' refers to his entrance and introduction to Gwendolen. 'Reflect

78' may well refer to the words at the end of Chapter 10: 'the unconquered Klesmer threw a trace of his malign power ever across her pleasant unconsciousness' (p. 78). 'Grandcourt 81' is probably a general reference to the dialogue between Gwendolen and Grandcourt at the Archery meeting in Chapter 11 (p. 81). Leavis writes in *The Great Tradition* that 'It is in the scene between Gwendolen and Grandcourt that George Eliot's mastery of dialogue is most strikingly exhibited. We have it in the brush that follows, in Chapter XI, in their being introduced to each other'.[7]

Wolfgang Iser argues that 'the critic's task is not to explain the text but rather its effects on the reader', and he sees 'the reader's experience of reading' as 'at the centre of the literary process'.[8] Descriptive examination of a great literary critic's markings in his copy of a novel can thus become an exercise in the implications of reader-response theory. Leavis's marked copy of the Blackwood single volume 'New Edition' of *Daniel Deronda* demonstrates the assiduity of attention he paid as a reader of George Eliot's last novel. His annotations, not unsurprisingly, contain elements crucial to his critical methodology: comparison with other authors; close attention to specific verbal detail; concern with authorial intrusion; moral preoccupation and valuation; discerning, and evaluating, the 'good' from the 'bad' or prosaic, etc. Perhaps the surprise is that Leavis's comments are not more detailed and wordy. He hardly writes a sentence whilst in the act of reading, confining himself to linings and other hieroglyphics. Leavis reserved his slightly lengthier annotations to his end papers, which have served as the main guide to this journey into his reading of *Daniel Deronda*. But Chapters 34, 62, 67, 68 are the only ones which do not contain markings. Leavis reads with pencil in hand ready to score anything that attracts his attention. Ideas, images, the aptness of a phrase, and the narrative stances associate with Leavis's critical method. The reading process becomes a continuum between immersion in another's text (Eliot's) and Leavis's own creativity, selecting and adapting what will be useful to him, or remembering what was useful to him or what remains in his mind from previous readings. The annotations are a conductor's, and a great conductor's at that, going through a great score. Leavis's is an individual reading. Examination and description of his markings in his copy allow participation in the private journey of a great critic, F. R. Leavis, as a reader of a great novel, *Daniel Deronda*.

Leavis and 'Gwendolen Harleth'

As Professor Baker suggests in 'Leavis as Reader of *Daniel Deronda*', Leavis's annotations to his 1878 copy of George Eliot's novel are interesting for their 'representative' status: they indicate the reading habits on which some of Leavis's most influential criticism was based. The pre-1960 annotations are also the prelude to a more unusual development later in his career. In 1974, Leavis was commissioned by The Bodley Head to prepare a drastically abridged version of *Daniel Deronda*, to be published as 'Gwendolen Harleth'. He completed the work for this project, and wrote an Introduction for it which has since been published. The abridged novel itself was never published, however, largely because The Bodley Head were unable to find an American or paperback publisher to share the costs of production.

The idea of separating *Daniel Deronda* into two parts and calling one of them 'Gwendolen Harleth' had been central to Leavis's critique of George Eliot's novel in *The Great Tradition*. He noted early on that the Deronda and Gwendolen plots 'stand apart, in fairly neatly separable masses' and concluded that 'as for the bad part . . . there *is* nothing to do but cut it away.' Leavis seemed to be offering this idea as a serious proposal to any interested publisher:

> there is, lost under that damning title, an actual great novel to be extricated. And to extricate it for separate publication as Gwendolen Harleth seems to me the most likely way of getting recognition for it. Gwendolen Harleth would have some rough edges, but it would be a self-sufficient and very substantial whole (it would by modern standards be a decidedly long novel). Deronda would be confined to what was necessary for his role of lay-confessor to Gwendolen, and the final cut would come after the death by drowning, leaving us with a vision of Gwendolen as she painfully emerges from her hallucinated worst conviction of guilt and confronts the day-light fact about Deronda's intentions.[1]

The good and bad parts of *Daniel Deronda* corresponded to Leavis's sense of a division running through all George Eliot's major works (except *Silas Marner*). There was 'the great George Eliot', the supremely intelligent and creative artist, and the 'idealizing' George Eliot, who identified too personally with Maggie Tulliver and her successors – Dorothea in *Middlemarch* and Daniel Deronda himself. The other novels also divided into good and bad parts, depending on which George Eliot had the writing hand: Leavis spoke of 'the live part' of *Felix Holt* and 'an unreduced enclave of the old immaturity' in *Middlemarch*. But it was only in *Daniel Deronda* that the parts were so obviously separable.

Leavis's basic diagnosis of George Eliot's 'case' remained unchanged in his 1960 essay on *Daniel Deronda*. But he now seemed ambivalent about the operation he had recommended. Reading *Daniel Deronda,* he suggested, we are unmoved by Deronda ('a mere emotionalized postulate') and 'can't help thinking of trying to separate off' *Gwendolen Harleth*. But it was better not to go beyond the 'thinking' stage. Referring back to his earlier, more concrete-seeming proposal, Leavis conceded that after re-reading the whole novel 'my already growing sense that the surgery of disjunction would be a less simple and satisfactory affair than I had thought has been reinforced . . . the admirer of George Eliot's genius, intent on a full appreciation, will demand the whole book, and will be right.'[2]

How did it come about, then, that fourteen years later Leavis decided to attempt the 'surgery of disjunction' after all? The background to the *Gwendolen Harleth* project can be partly traced from the relevant file in The Bodley Head Archives, now kept at Reading University. The project was not initiated by Leavis but by an editor at The Bodley Head, and was inspired by his first rather than his second essay. James Michie wrote to Leavis in October 1973:

> A month ago I read *Daniel Deronda* for the first time and I have just read the passage in *The Great Tradition* in which you discuss the book. What you say seems to me so just that I would like to try to persuade you to put your own suggestion into practice and produce an extricated *Gwendolen Harleth* with editorial linking passages where necessary. With your authority behind it *Gwendolen Harleth* could, I believe, win a new range of readers for George Eliot.

Leavis's initial response was cautious. He promised to consider Michie's suggestion, but he was preoccupied with completing the book that would eventually become *The Living Principle* – also he had not re-read *Daniel Deronda* since 1960. Michie succeeded in quickening his interest, however. Leavis reported in November 1973 that he had started re-reading the novel ('mainly between 5 and 7 in the morning') and was 'more than ever impressed by its distinction'. By the end of February 1974 he was confident that *Gwendolen Harleth* was viable and was ready to commit himself to the project. A formal agreement was then made: Leavis would provide The Bodley Head with a copy of the 1961 Torchbook edition of *Daniel Deronda* marked up with all the excisions and additions necessary to turn it into *Gwendolen Harleth* and would also provide a preface explaining and justifying the project. For copyright in the preface and adaptation, on delivery, he would receive a total fee of £1,000.

The agreement between Leavis and The Bodley Head specified delivery of the material by the end of 1974. But Leavis had already spent several months thinking his way into the project and lost no time now in completing it: he had submitted the Introduction and 'liberated' text by the end of April 1974. The editing task was made more straightforward by the conclusion he had already reached, in the course of re-reading *Daniel Deronda*, that a coherent and self-contained *Gwendolen Harleth* could be produced 'by mere excision' – without the addition of any editorial text. Even the excisions were fairly straightforward, since Leavis was reluctant to tamper with George Eliot's prose: he mostly carved away Chapters and blocks of Chapters rather than individual sentences or paragraphs. The new novel that emerged consisted of thirty-six Chapters from the original seventy that made up *Daniel Deronda*: I–XV, XXI–XXXI, the first nine paragraphs of XXXII, XXXV, XLIV, XLV (later cut), XLVIII, LIV–LVII, LXIV, LXV, and parts of LXIX. This encompassed almost all of Gwendolen's story, except for one or two quite important incidents where her relation to Deronda could not be disentangled from his relation to Mordecai, Mirah and the Meyricks – who otherwise vanished, along with Princess Halm-Eberstein. In addition to this basic abridgement, Leavis abandoned the division of the text into separately titled books, removed all the Chapter and book epigraphs (many of which, as he recognized, were written by George Eliot herself), and renumbered the Chapters in arabic rather than roman numerals. Michie proposed that the title page should read:

'GWENDOLEN HARLETH'
by
GEORGE ELIOT
an abridged version of Daniel Deronda
edited and with an introduction by
F. R. Leavis

Leavis's part in the project was now more or less complete. Michie thanked him for his 'successful and speedy work' and informed him that *Gwendolen Harleth* was scheduled for publication in January 1975.

It seemed that publication of *Gwendolen Harleth* could be a relatively 'simple and satisfactory affair' after all. At this point, however, a series of problems arose which in the end made publication impossible. The first setback was a very hostile report on the new text from one of Michie's professional readers (herself a novelist). Assessing the effect of Leavis's cuts on the coherence of the narrative, the reader concluded that 'the adaptation as it stands does not make sense.' She noted in particular an 'enormous excision' (Chapters 36–43) which 'contains an important advance in the relationship of Gwendolen and Deronda, involves an awkward join, and leaves many references after it quite unexplained (to Mirah and Hans and so on).' This reader was in any case wholly unsympathetic to the idea of abridging *Daniel Deronda*: 'The text . . . is sacred; neither you nor Dr Leavis would add a word to what George Eliot wrote. Is it not then sacrilege to subtract a word? – let alone the true heart of the book?' Michie was understandably troubled by the suggestion that the new narrative did not make sense. Forwarding the report to Leavis, he invited him to reconsider his earlier decision not to add any 'interlinking passages' to the excised text:

> In one of my earlier letters I remember saying that I doubted whether it would be possible to make substantial cuts without some interlinking passages provided by yourself to explain time jumps, developments of plot and character, etc., to help the reader bridge the gaps. Do you still think that this is unnecessary and if you do still think so don't you think that your preface needs to be expanded to defend in advance the sort of criticisms which the present report embodies? . . . As a publisher I cannot help wanting 'GWENDOLEN HARLETH' to be as accessible to the average reader as possible and as a result of my report I now have some nagging doubts.

Leavis promised to re-read the abridged novel and consider the 'doubts' raised by the report. But after he had done so his attitude was uncompromising. He was more convinced than ever that the abridged narrative worked without additional passages, and felt that Michie's reader had completely missed the point of the exercise he had undertaken, which was not to shorten *Daniel Deronda* but liberate *Gwendolen Harleth*. To make this clearer, Leavis even suggested that the title-page should be altered to read:

GWENDOLEN HARLETH
George Eliot's superb last novel
liberated from
DANIEL DERONDA

He added an extra final page to the Introduction, but insisted that 'interlinking passages' in the text would only compromise the basic conception of *Gwendolen Harleth* as 'a self-sufficient great novel'.

Michie declined the new sub-title, but otherwise accepted Leavis's position: his only concern was 'that it should be a decision made after the most careful reflection'. A more serious obstacle to publication had now emerged: rapid inflation meant that The Bodley Head could not afford to publish *Gwendolen Harleth* without sharing the costs with another publisher. As Michie explained to Leavis in the same letter, publication now depended on finding a partner:

> I have already had a rough estimate of the book done by our production department. To my alarm the steeply rising printing costs have produced a selling figure, assuming a printing number of 3,000, of somewhere between £6 or £7. This is, of course, a quite unacceptable price to the public. Our only way to lower it will be by getting American co-operation so I am writing to Pantheon in the hope that they will want to join our printing run and so lower the costs of production.

Leavis had been impressed by Pantheon's energetic promotion of his controversial *Two Cultures? The Significance of C. P. Snow* in the 1960s. Michie offered *Gwendolen Harleth* to them in similar terms:

> I am sure that when we publish it this case of sacrilege by a high priest will cause immense discussion: has one the right, even with the authority of Dr Leavis, to tamper with a masterpiece? It could be quite a publishing event.

Pantheon declined on this occasion, however – and so did every other American publisher to whom Leavis's marked-up copy of *Daniel Deronda* was then forwarded. Many were apologetic: 'Our reasons are the usual, I'm afraid. We don't think we could sell it in the general trade at all and our college department tell us that there would be no interest in academia. Indeed, they tell us that Leavis is a fading name on this side of the water. Can this be?' Others clearly regarded the project as eccentric. As one university press put it: 'Our scholars here take a rather dim view of bringing out an edited version of George Eliot's work. In fact, I might say that they were enthusiastically opposed, in spite of the fact that, of course, Dr Leavis's reputation is great.' There was a similar response from Penguin, to whom Michie offered the paperback rights: 'As you know, we do publish the novel as written by George Eliot and in fact sell it rather well, and I'd prefer not to get involved in an abridged edition, even one on the best of authority.'

No other publisher, it seemed, was prepared to back James Michie's vision of *Gwendolen Harleth* as 'a publishing event', and he was forced to re-open the question of the viability of the narrative without 'interlinking passages'. At least one publisher had made this her principal objection to the project:

> I'm extremely sad to say that I don't think *Gwendolen Harleth* works. While there are two stories in *Daniel Deronda*, they are so closely intermingled that in one's attempt to cut one, a lot of the other is lost. There are also a great number of references throughout the book to characters whom Dr Leavis has cut out. Some of this can easily be fixed, but the rest is almost impossible unless one is prepared to re-write and add in some sentences and scenes . . . if Dr Leavis is not willing to do this, it does become very difficult.

Michie passed on these comments to Leavis in December 1974, noting that they were very similar to those made in his reader's report and encouraging Leavis once again to reconsider his position: 'I feel there is much to be said for making these editorial additions if you can see your way to doing it.' But Leavis's response was an even more forceful re-statement of his earlier position. He doubted now whether he should ever have undertaken the project since it was so clear that no one understood his intention. Occasional 'rough edges' in the narrative would be irrelevant to the reader who appreciated what *Gwendolen Harleth* had to offer: 'it was *criticism in practice* that I undertook – which was what, I thought, you were asking for.' Leavis appreciated Michie's situation, nevertheless, and was reluctant to write off the project altogether. He was still unwilling to compose 'interlinking passages', but he offered to provide occasional footnotes explaining the *lacunae* in the text, and did in fact write five of these.[3] He also cut another Chapter (XLV) which included a lot of reference to the Deronda plot. In all his correspondence on this matter Leavis stressed the importance of his Introduction – it would explain to the intelligent reader how to interpret the project and the narrative, and would make further apparatus unnecessary. He was worried that readers might ignore it if it was simply labelled 'Introduction' and urged The Bodley Head to use a more arresting title. Michie was reluctant, but seems to have agreed in the end that the Introduction should carry the sub-title: 'Why Surgery Was Necessary'.

Thus amended, *Gwendolen Harleth* was sent on the rounds again. But the rest of the file consists simply of more rejections – the last one in 1982. One response in particular is worth quoting:

> We have pondered rather carefully the abridgement of *Daniel Deronda* as planned by F. R. Leavis, and concluded that we should not take this on . . . We would have preferred to see Leavis make the statement he wants to make in an article, or even in a published list of the excisions he proposes in the text. We can't wax enthusiastic, though, with what he is doing with the wholeness of the original work, where even the failed parts are interesting. In short, his plan deserves a hearing, but we are not sure it deserves book publication.

What this publisher preferred is what actually happened. Leavis's Introduction was published posthumously in 1982, completing a triptych with his two earlier essays on *Daniel Deronda*.[4] *Gwendolen Harleth* has remained an idea only. It must be recognized, nevertheless, that it came quite close to being realized. The failure of the project was in one sense simply an accident of the economic circumstances prevailing at the time: if the sums had worked out differently, or another publisher had been willing to share the costs, it is clear that The Bodley Head would have proceeded with *Gwendolen Harleth* as planned and it would be on our library shelves today. On the other hand, if Leavis had edited the book differently, as several publishers suggested, it might have been easier for The Bodley Head to find a partner in the project – and so in a sense the failure of the project was determined by Leavis's own conception of it.

Gwendolen Harleth is easily dismissed as a Leavisian 'folly'. When the Introduction was published in the *London Review of Books* the Editors described it as 'an interesting document of a confident time which is now past: such-and-such a Chapter "had to go in", and others had to stay out'. It is a paradox that Leavis's radical interference with a 'sacred' text should seem old-fashioned in an era when literary studies is generally geared towards the *empowerment* of the reader. But in another sense, as the publishers' rejections suggest, the failure of the project does seem to epitomize the end of something – Leavis's authority, perhaps, or a way of thinking about novels in terms of 'pervasive unreality' set against 'vivid livingness and actuality'.[5] From another point of view, Leavis's approach just seems unfair: he does not really explore, in any of his essays on *Daniel Deronda*, the possibility that the two parts of the novel may be symbolically related and complementary – and even if the novel does not finally support this hypothesis, *Gwendolen Harleth* denies the reader the insight that 'even the failed parts are interesting'. On the other hand, Leavis was only doing to *Daniel Deronda* what countless writers have done to literary texts in adapting them for other media: *Daniel Deronda* has actually been produced on BBC Radio as 'Gwendolen Harleth'. Leavis's project only appears perverse because he did not change media but insisted on adapting a novel for publication as a novel. In a sense, though, *Gwendolen Harleth* was never intended by Leavis to be read as a novel – or not as a new novel to be read by new readers in the sense that James Michie envisaged. Rather, it was 'criticism in practice' – a way of *re*-reading *Daniel Deronda*. It was not designed for readers who would be distracted by such narrative 'rough edges' as Deronda's unexplained presence in Genoa, but for the 'educated public' who were assumed to be somehow already collectively familiar with George Eliot's distinction. This sense of a particular readership clearly determined the difficult form in which Leavis presented *Gwendolen Harleth* and led to the prolonged negotiations over 'interlinking passages' that might make it more accessible. It was an article of faith for Leavis that a fragmented 'educated public' that shared his judgments still existed somewhere. But it was rather difficult, as The Bodley Head discovered, to make this concept coincide with an actual book-reading (and book-buying) public.

NOTES ON LEAVIS'S ANNOTATIONS

The heavily thumbed and annotated Torchbook edition of *Daniel Deronda*, which Leavis used to prepare the text of *Gwendolen Harleth*, is in the Bodley Head file – ironically, it has fallen into two halves by itself – and thus provides an interesting opportunity to compare Leavis's 1973–4 annotations with the earlier markings in the Blackwood edition analysed by Professor Baker. The Torchbook edition is not such a good specimen, as Leavis rubbed out many of his annotations before he submitted the text and it was also subsequently marked up by someone else, at Bodley Head, for page-breaks etc. It is still possible to trace many of Leavis's annotations, however. In general, the system of endnotes and hieroglyphics seems to have been abandoned. Leavis still uses initials for other authors, but otherwise scribbles comments longhand around the margins. The annotations clearly relate to Leavis's reading *before* he excised the Deronda chapters from the book – many of these are quite heavily marked, confirming that he was in many ways as interested in 'the failed parts' as the successful.

Some of the same pages and passages are annotated in both editions (the text and page numbers are identical). On page 36, the long sentence in the opening paragraph of Chapter VI is again marked 'GE', and against the next paragraph – particularly the comment that Gwendolen would 'at once have marked herself off from any sort of theoretical or practically reforming women by satirizing them' – Leavis has written 'GH v GE'. The criticism of the Cambridge examination system in Chapter XVI – 'a demand for excessive retention and dexterity without any insight into the principles which form the vital connections of knowledge' – is again underlined. The proposal scene between Gwendolen and Grandcourt in Chapter XXVII (pp. 224–5) is also quite heavily annotated. The words 'lizard', 'boredom (life)', 'will' and 'conflict of will' appear in the margins – also 'Tho' I call them mine', the first part of the statement about his works attributed to Blake which assumes great significance in Leavis's later writings (and which he quoted in his Introduction to *Gwendolen Harleth*): 'Tho' I call them mine I know they are not mine.' On page 225 the sentence 'She thought his behaviour perfect, and gained a sense of freedom which made her almost ready to be mischievous' is underlined and marked 'Shakespeare . . . her blank verse'.

The opening of Chapter 28 (pp. 228–9) carries some interesting new annotations. Around the margins Leavis has written 'GE's wisdom <u>not</u> Gascoigne's', 'GE poses: "What standard?" – <u>not</u> Maggie' and 'The nature of mature valuation: selfhood-identity'. The long analysis of Deronda's 'many-sided sympathy' in Chapter XXXII (pp. 271–2), which was marked 'GE' and 'Prose' in the Blackwood edition, is also heavily marked in the Torchbook. Against the sentence 'But anyone wishing to understand the effect of after-events on Deronda should know a little more of what he was at five-and-twenty than was evident in ordinary intercourse' Leavis has written 'Il n'existe pas.' On both pages there are references to 'DHL': on top of page 272 Leavis has written 'GE's self-reflection – "theoretical"' and underneath 'DHL: Tiger & Holy Ghost'. Further down there is another 'DHL', another reference to 'selfhood and <u>identity</u>' and the words 'Romola and DD'. In Chapter XXXVI (p. 340) Deronda's advice to Gwendolen, 'the refuge you are needing from personal trouble is the higher, the religious life . . .' is again marked, this time also underlined and with an accompanying 'DHL'. On the previous page, another of Deronda's maxims 'some real knowledge would give you an interest in the world beyond the small drama of personal desires' is marked 'WB' for William Blake. One of the pages cross-referenced 'characteristic moral formulation' in the Blackwood edition (p. 468) is marked in the Torchbook edition with a 'GE!' in the margin and a quotation and note at the top of the page: '"the very best of human possibilities" – a female savant's fairy-tale'. Page 561, which is cross-referenced 'images of impartial sympathy' in the Blackwood edition carries the note 'GE. Oh! may I . . .' in the margin in the Torchbook – a reference to George Eliot's poem 'O may I join the choir invisible' which evidently typified, for Leavis, his sense of the 'idealizing' tendency that was responsible for the bad half of *Daniel Deronda*.

PART 2

Education in the University

Rubrics and Reading Lists

Rubric . . . [ad. F. *rubrique* or L. *rubrica*.] A. sb. . . . 2. A heading of a chapter, section, etc. of a book, written or printed in red, or otherwise distinguished in lettering . . .' *Oxford English Dictionary*

Nowadays, 'rubric' ordinarily means the text giving instructions at the head of an examination paper. But etymologically it refers to text printed in red, often with liturgical or church-calendar significance (as in 'red-letter day'); it is said that this was once the red of the advertising placard on a Roman market-stall for reading matter. Pope possibly alludes to this usage in his expostulation, 'What, tho' my Name stood rubric on the walls . . .', which the *OED* cites. It means 'Attention, please!' In this essay I am taking the word in a rather broad sense, to include, certainly, matter relating to university examinations, but also quite a range of the instructions and memoranda ('meet to be remembered', one said at school) that are encountered in the academic life. This material has two seemingly contrary qualities: its disposability and its extreme importance. In the academic world many papers are junked, rightly. None the less, some of these papers have made intimate impress upon their readers. After all, if an academic writes a brilliant essay, his pupil may take, leave or forget it. If he composes a brilliant essay question, the pupil roughly speaking *has to* address it. In spite of the egalitarian diffidences of humanities university teaching practice ('wonder if . . .', 'leave it open', 'up to you . . .'), academics still tell their students what to do, admittedly sometimes almost invisibly. And the instructions are influential, even life-changing. Much student time is spent dealing with essay-questions, with reading-lists, with examinations. These mundane papers, the institutional documents, are especially influential because they are read, but also *obeyed*. They are the papers that make the daily differences. These are the papers which I am gathering under the general head of 'rubric'. In a sense these are the stage-directions of academic life, so have a strong bearing on what actually happens.

In this essay I would like to remark some of Leavis's 'ordinary' papers, examination papers, reading lists and memoranda which reveal what he actually did with his pupils, and what he thought they should be doing. I will begin at college level, and move out to some papers that relate to his ideas for his subject on the wider stage, at English Faculty level. One day-to-day document is not dealt with here, that is, the teaching material distributed by Leavis for his lectures, or his 'dating sheets'. Some of this is given and discussed by Charles Page in Chapter 6 of this book, '"Cunning Passages": Leavis's Lectures on Poetry and Prose'.

I

In June 1931 Downing College acquired F. R. Leavis as a 'supervisor' in English. The post of supervisor was a humble one in the Cambridge hierarchy. The term means what it says: a person to look after the undergraduates' preparation for the Tripos, one who was probably free-lance, and not at all necessarily one who gave lectures or belonged to the Fellowship of a college. Leavis's appointment, however, was of some moment for Downing College. The college was poor: in 1931 it could not even afford its annual ball. Its few undergraduates were mostly reading law or medicine. Anxious to increase its academic reputation, it had elected a young classicist to a fellowship, W. L. Cuttle, not an academic high-flyer, but one who might set up relationships with the schools, care for under-graduates, and encourage them to take subjects new to Downing, like Classics, Modern Languages, Mechanical Sciences, Mathematics, Archi-tecture and the Cambridge boom subject, English. Cuttle thought English would be good for Downing's diminished reputation and it was his inspiration to acquire Leavis. Although Leavis's probationary lectureship in the English Faculty was about to expire, without possibility of further renewal, he was a very popular Cambridge supervisor and lecturer. He had also been, incidentally, an athlete – and college sport could not be neglected. Leavis remarked with amusement that Cuttle treated him 'as though I'd won the mile in the 1908 Olympics'. Six months after being appointed supervisor Leavis became Director of Studies in English at a termly stipend of five guineas and in May 1932 he was elected to membership of the High Table, though he was not elected to a Fellowship until 1936. In 1932 two scholarships were awarded to young men to read English: R. G. Cox and Geoffrey Walton became Leavis's Downing lieutenants. Both went on to research. So Leavis had by 1933 his own freshman scholar and exhibitioner. The college initiative paid off: in 1938 Downing took four out of eight Firsts in Part One of the English Tripos, noted by the London newspaper *The Observer* as 'a triumph for what may be called the Downing School of Literature'. In 1939 in Part Two there were four Downing Firsts out of seven. Part One numbers had dropped, but Downing took one out of the three Firsts.

The 'Downing School of Literature' operated within the overarching system of 'Cambridge English' whose examinations, the English Tripos, were of course taken by the Downing men. But the 'Downing School' was near-autonomous, and carefully devised by Leavis, so carefully (and so successfully) that it probably caused a certain amount of resentment elsewhere in Cambridge. The 'School' had its junior and senior end. At the upper end there were the graduate students (like Cox and Walton), who taught as supervisors for the college, and there was *Scrutiny*: it was not unknown for a third-year undergraduate to have a piece published in the journal. At the junior end the influence of Downing English reached out into the schools and did this by several means, of which a notable one was the Scholarship Examination.

Every year a clutch of examinations was set and admissions made accordingly. The examination papers were published and hungrily purchased by schools and used in English classes. Schoolboys were therefore educated in the Downing way even before they went up to university. The examination papers portrayed vividly the kind of education in which the Downing English undergraduates participated. The parameters were given in a paper issued to schools by Leavis, explaining the four examination papers in English. A General Essay paper also had to be taken. Candidates travelled to Cambridge for several gruelling days of scribbling, a procedure that lasted until the early 1960s. How the scholarship system worked for Leavis and his pupils in the 1930s is of some interest. Schools which liked to be well prepared for the scholarships applied to Downing for information and received the following. It is dated 'July 1934'.

DOWNING COLLEGE, CAMBRIDGE
Entrance Scholarship Examination in English

THE FOLLOWING NOTES are given as some guide to the nature and scope of the examination in ENGLISH:

PAPER 1. SHAKESPEARE

Candidates will be expected to have a general knowledge of Shakespeare's development, and to know well half-a-dozen of the greatest plays. No particular critical works are recommended, but candidates will find some helpful observations on Shakespeare criticism in *Elizabethan Stage Conditions* by M. C. Bradbrook and *How Many Children Had Lady Macbeth?* by L. C. Knights.

PAPER 2. ENGLISH LITERATURE AFTER 1600

Candidates are advised to specialize in some degree, though they ought to know enough about the characteristics of the various periods since 1600 to be able, in taking Paper 3, to place representative passages of verse and prose (see the next paragraph). Thus a candidate might reasonably devote his attention mainly to the Seventeenth Century and the Romantic period, or to the Seventeenth and Eighteenth Centuries, or to some equivalent combination. But in any case he ought to know something about the Seventeenth Century, and is advised to read the following works: H. J. C. Grierson, *Metaphysical Poetry, Donne to Butler;* T. S. Eliot, *Selected Essays* (the relevant parts); M. van Doren, *John Dryden.* Other recommendations: *Scrutinies I* (edited by Edgell Rickword); J. Middleton Murry, *The Problem of Style, Aspects of Literature, Countries of the Mind* (1st series).

PAPER 3. PRACTICAL CRITICISM

This paper will be designed to test the quality of the candidate's reading. Work in preparation for it should be at the same time a large part of the preparation for Papers 1 and 2. Candidates will be asked, for instance, to assign passages representing different periods, authors and kinds. There will be various simple exercises in critical appreciation and discrimination. Cases, for instance, of sentimentality or insincerity or mere versifying might be offered for analysis. The paper will permit a great deal of choice.

Methods, approach and appropriate reading are suggested in *Reading and Discrimination*, by Denys Thompson. But candidates will not be expected to acquire a technical terminology or to cultivate a highly technical procedure. The essential is that they should train themselves in their reading to perceive and to describe differences of quality and kind.

PAPER 4. PARAPHRASE AND COMMENT

This paper will differ from Practical Criticism in not being so closely correlated with Papers 1 and 2. Besides containing passages for paraphrase, and for criticism with regard to style and cogency, it will test general intelligence, taste and cultivation in ways suggested in *Culture and Environment*, by F. R. Leavis and Denys Thompson.

MASTERS directing preparation in English will do well to have read *The Principles of Literary Criticism* and *Practical Criticism*, by I. A. Richards; *Seven Types of Ambiguity*, by W. Empson; *Selected Essays*, by T. S. Eliot; and *Determinations*, edited by F. R. Leavis.

2

The scholarship examination papers themselves have numerous interesting features. It is not surprising that the number of answers required is higher than in 'English' three-hour examinations sixty years later. What is surprising is that a standard number of answers is not required. For the 'subject' papers the requirement is 'not less than three, not more than four'. But the 'method' papers are open-ended, this being the characteristic rubric: 'Candidates should attempt the first question, and as many others as they may find time for. Credit will be given for quality rather than quantity.' There is another disparity between these examination papers and those of the late twentieth century: they are invariably unattributed to an author, and sometimes in the 'Shakespeare' papers the play from which a passage is taken is not given.

Shakespeare

The question-papers were usually in three parts. Section A required detailed textual commentary, including commentary on metaphor. Section B had passages inviting broader treatment, involving critical comparison or discrimination of the ersatz-Shakespeare from Shakespeare. Section C consisted of ordinary essay questions. Section A was always compulsory and often based on an editorial issue. We have this, for example, in 1936:

When, in *King John*, the King is giving his orders to murder Arthur, he says that his message is too terrible for daylight, and that it demands an atmosphere of horror and secrecy:

If the mid-night bell
Did with his yron tongue and brazen mouth

> Sound on into the drowzie race of night:
> If this same were a Church-yard where we stand
> And thou possessed with a thousand wrongs . . .
> I would into thy bosome poure my thoughts.
>
> Folio, 1623

In the third line Theobald read [sic]:

> Sound one unto the drowsy race of night;

Dyce, Staunton and the Temple Shakespeare have;

> Sound on into the drowsy ear of night.

Say which of these versions you prefer, briefly giving your reasons. (Candidates are not expected to give very much time or space to this question.)

In 1936 a Section A question was on modernization of the text of Sonnet 129, with 'If you can, add a note on Elizabethan punctuation.'

In Section B the passages for analysis are substantial. More than once commentary is solicited on 'Shakespearean' qualities, for example in 1938:

> The first of the following pairs of passages is from *Pericles*, the second from *The Two Noble Kinsmen*: in each pair one passage is probably by Shakespeare, and the other not. Make a short critical comparison of each pair and give reasons for assigning one passage to Shakespeare rather than the other.

Or (also in 1938), with non-Shakespeare selections:

> The following passages have all been described, by various critics, as 'Shakespearean'. Say how far you consider the description justified in each case, and in what precise sense.

In Section C there are simple (i.e. difficult!) questions ('Consider Shakespeare's aims and achievement in any one of his tragedies'), but also provocative ones. In a question (1936) on 'Shakespeare's comic genius', with reference to the *Henry IV* plays, the following are among the statements for consideration:

> The comic appeals to the intelligence pure and simple; laughter is incompatible with emotion. (Bergson)

> for only when we are gay over a thing, and can play with it, do we

show ourselves masters of it, and have minds clear enough for strength . . .
(W. B. Yeats)

On individual plays or groups of plays, the following occur:

'Both workmanship and thought are in an unstable condition.' Discuss
this judgment of *Hamlet*. (1936)

'It is in the total situation rather than in the wrigglings of individual
emotion that the tragedy lies.' Consider this statement in relation to
one of the great tragedies. (1937)

'*Lear* is not, according to the standards set by *Macbeth*, in every respect
a balanced and finished work of art. The ending, great as it is, seems
to nullify the triumph of poetic harmony which preceded it in the
reconciliation scenes, and we are reminded at times of the wholly
destructive intensity of *Timon*.' How far do you agree? (1939)

At this time Leavis was considering writing an essay on *Timon of Athens*,
never to be completed.

English literature after 1600

This paper had about a dozen questions on subjects from Milton to the
end of the Victorian era, with occasional, incidental forays beyond. They
tended to be comparative, like 'Bring out the distinctive characteristics of
Pride and Prejudice or *Wuthering Heights* or *To the Lighthouse* by making
comparisons and contrasts between the chosen novel and other novels
you know' (1939). They could be frankly opinionated:

'Yet the influence of Dryden and Pope over the middle of the eighteenth
century is by no means so great, or so noxious, as has been supposed.
A good part of the dreariest verse of the time is written under the
shadow of Milton.' How just and truly critical do you find these
suggestions as they regard the three poets named? (1938)

They could be 'open', expecting rather a lot of reading:

If you were invited to fill twenty or so pages of print with illustrations
from a discussion of 'poetry of the Victorian age', which poems would
you choose? Give your reasons. (1939)

Among the dozen questions there was almost always a whole poem, like
Shelley's 'England in 1819' ('An old, mad, blind, despised, and dying

king . . .') of which this question was asked: 'How far do you find this sonnet representative, or otherwise, of Shelley's poetry?' (1934).

Practical Criticism

The question-papers are similar to those set in Britain sixty years later where the practice of 'dating' has survived. The Downing papers have a compulsory dating section, with six passages of verse and prose set, all ('or as many of them as you can') to be attributed 'to their periods', or 'approximate dates'. In the rest of the paper, analysis or analytical comparison is required, and straightforward questions asked:

> How would you have known that the following stanzas were of the seventeenth century? (1938)

> The following passages are by the same poet. Some people would point to them as exhibiting, in the comparison, a remarkable unevenness in the command of the technique of verse. What are your views? (1939)

> How can you tell the following is not really by Shakespeare? (1937)

> Establish a preference for one over the other of the following poems. (1934)

> To what period does the following poem make a show of belonging? To what period does it really belong? What criticism would you make of it? (1934)

The following question gives the 'feel' of the Downing scholarship papers in Practical Criticism.

> The following passages are by the same novelist. Critics have remarked that it is surprising that the writer who was capable of the distinguished prose of one of the passages should also have been capable of such inferior writing as that of the other. Discuss this attitude, giving your own views of the passages.

> (a) There was a long silence, during which the tide returned into Poole Harbour. 'One would lose something,' murmured Helen, apparently to herself. The water crept over the mud-flats towards the gorse and blackened heather. Branksea Island lost its immense foreshores, and became a sombre episode of trees. Frome was forced inward towards Dorchester, Stour against Wimborne, Avon towards Salisbury, and over the immense displacement the sun presided, leading it to triumph ere

he sank to rest. England was alive, throbbing through all her estuaries, crying for joy through the mouths of all her gulls, and the north wind, with contrary motion, blew stronger against her rising seas. What did it mean? For what end are her fair complexities, her changes of soil, her sinuous coast? Does she belong to those who have moulded her and made her feared by other lands, or to those who have added nothing to her power, but have somehow seen her, seen the whole island at once, lying as a jewel in a silver sea, sailing as a ship of souls, with all the brave world's fleet accompanying her towards eternity?

(b) The other smiled, and looked at his watch. They both regretted the death, but they were middle-aged men, who had invested their emotions elsewhere, and outbursts of grief could not be expected from them over a slight acquaintance. It's only one's own dead who matter. If for a moment the sense of communion in sorrow came to them, it passed. How indeed is it possible for one human being to be sorry for all the sadness that meets him on the face of the earth, for all the pain that is endured not only by men, but by animals and plants, and perhaps by the stones? The soul is tired in a moment, and in fear of losing the little she does understand, she retreats to the permanent lines which habit or chance have dictated, and suffers there.

Paraphrase and Comment

'Comment' was principally required in this paper, though there was one compulsory 'paraphrase' question asking for candidates to re-state the sense of a given passage either of 'high' art (*The Ambassadors*) or low, like advertising copy. Candidates answered as many questions as they liked, except for the mandatory first one. There was an occasional straight question, as in 'Explain briefly the meaning of (a) dilettantism, (b) cliché, (c) fine writing, (d) belles lettres' (1937). But generally passages for comment were given, nearly all prose, some embodying attitudes to literature, but mostly passages relating to 'mass civilization'. A candidate would have done well who came from a sixth form which had worked through Leavis's primer, written with Denys Thompson (and containing much material culled by Q. D. Leavis), *Culture and Environment: The Training of Critical Awareness* (1933). Its sections were well represented in the choice of material for the examination, with questions on 'The Place of Advertising in a Mass Economy', 'Levelling-Down' and 'The Supply of Reading Matter'. Some of the material was of the J. B. Priestleyian, let-the-plain-man-have-what-he-likes-and-good-luck-to-him variety, but there were examples of left-wing rhetoric. The following question is a typical one, and illustrates attitudes that Leavis handled in the 1930s:

> Assuming, for the sake of argument, that the statement of the situation is well-founded, does the writer's attitude seem to you justifiable and intelligent or otherwise?

> If art survived censoring by the whims of princelings in the feudal ages, and censoring by the profit motives of publishers, the illiterate Comstockians and Catholic Church in American today, why should it not survive censoring by highly educated officials of the Commissariat of Education, who judge from the standpoint of its usefulness to socialist culture?

> To the author in the U.S.S.R. the 'censor' is not unlike the publisher's reader in America – a person who attempts to forecast the judgment of one's future public . . . Important plays are increasingly censored by previews attended by leading critics, and even by workers and children – the future audience. Sometimes as many as fifty persons make comments during these previews. Only an artist who produces for his own solitary enjoyment finds in such collective comment a bar to creative work.

> As the forms of the socialist society become more established, the tension between artists and censors tends to lessen, since both are increasingly attuned to the same social environment.

The Scholarship Examination papers of 'the Downing School of Literature' (in *The Observer*'s phrase) show what Leavis wanted; they do not prove that he got it. But we can say, at the very least, that as a result of Leavis's work his conception of English became a presence in the schools. The booklets of examination papers, annually purchased, became primers, and it is fairly clear that their use brought potential Downing undergraduates up to a point of knowledgeability and confidence that other undergraduates might envy. They were well into the English Tripos before the others started – one reason why many switched to a different Tripos after Part One, with Leavis's blessing, given that he saw English both as a core subject, and also as a bridging one. The knowledgeability and confidence of the Downing men, who scored so impressively in the Tripos, exasperated other members of 'Cambridge English'. For this one has only refer to E. M. W. Tillyard's *The Muse Unchained* (1958), and subtitled an 'intimate account', in which it is claimed that an 'incipient corruption' penetrated the garden of 'English'. In the early 1930s the undergraduates appeared to know what's what all too well: they had been trained, he believed, not educated. One rather doubts it could have been otherwise in a period of intellectual urgency – or that the undergraduates were so wrong. It is their voice, however, which has not been heard in this paper, though the post-scholarship (that is, published) work can in some cases be found. We do not have, unfortunately, the scholarship answers of the 1930s. But still there is room for research elsewhere. When Leavis was writing *D. H. Lawrence: Novelist* (1955) he thriftily used the back of old scholarship examination scripts as manuscript paper. These college papers were not required to be kept so secure as university ones. The sheets survive in the Harry Ransom Humanities Research Center at the University of Austin, Texas. They show that if we cannot be sure of the level of examination answers of eighteen-year-olds in the 1930s, there is no doubt of the sophistication of pre-university students in the early 1950s. But that is another story.

3

We have seen above what Leavis wanted sixth-formers to read. What did he ask his undergraduates to read and write about? D. F. Rowe, a Downing pupil who went up in 1938, kept the letters in which Leavis made his recommendations. On 14 September 1938 he listed 'the books to be specified as indispensable at this stage: *Oxford Book of English Verse*, [Grierson's] *Metaphysical Poetry, Donne to Butler*, a Donne (I recommend the Nonesuch edition), a Milton (ditto, Oxford edition); a Chaucer; a Dryden . . .' and the Shakespeare set-plays. He suggested that Rowe contact the Gordon Fraser shop in Portugal Place, where he had noticed some second-hand copies. 'If you sent him a card he would no doubt reserve them for you till you made your call (otherwise, even with the postage, there would be a saving in sending for them).'

For Part One of the Tripos in 1940 he suggested that Rowe should sketch, and leave at his room at the beginning of term, a scheme of the main questions '(not answers – unless you like)', of any kind relevant to a Tripos paper, that seemed to him raised by each of the set Shakespeare plays. He also suggested writing a review of D. A. Traversi's *Approach to Shakespeare*, comparing it to other approaches, like Bradley's, Wilson Knight's and J. Middleton Murry's.

For the Nineteenth Century his instructions were to read '(but don't make this a long job) for an essay – write it if you like – on "The Victorian Critics of the Victorian Age": Carlyle, Ruskin, M. Arnold, Morris, Samuel Butler (and note where Newman comes). This doesn't mean reading a great deal of Carlyle and Ruskin: look them up in Elton and/or other works of reference. Also, Wilenski's *Ruskin*, L. Trilling's *M. Arnold*, Clutton Brock's *William Morris* (Home University Library) . . . Other books on the age: G. K. Chesterton's *Victorian Age in Literature* (H.U.L.), H[arold]. Nicolson's *Tennyson*, G. M. Trevelyan's *British History in the 19th Century*. Read *Don Juan* (our second English epic), asking how far it's covered by the note on the Vision of Judgment in *Revaluation* (end of Chapter.IV).' Then there were novels: 'Jane Austen (noting differences); two or three of Peacock; *Wuthering Heights* (see Ford's essay in *Scrutiny* for March, 1939); critical and placing notes on Dickens and Thackeray (Elton; also Gissing's *Dickens* and Santayana's essay in *Soliloquies in England*); George Eliot's *Middlemarch*; Meredith's *Egoist*; James's *Portrait of a Lady*; Bennett's *Old Wives' Tale*; Conrad's *Nostromo*; Virginia Woolf's *To The Lighthouse*; E. M. Forster's *A Passage to India*; Stendhal, *Le Chartreuse de Parme* (can be got in translation); Flaubert, *Madame Bovary*.'

Leavis suggested some topics and reading for Wordsworth and some general reading:

Consider these questions:

> (1) 'But Wordsworth's eyes avert their ken
>   From half of human fate.'
> (2) 'The poetry is the reality, the philosophy illusion.'
> (3) Wordsworth's brief creative life.

(Arnold's essay, and Bradley's in *Oxford Lectures*, Elton's chapter, James Smith's essay in *Scrutiny*, June 1938; Chapter in *Revaluation*; C. H. Herford's *Wordsworth*. General Reading: R. H. Tawney, *Religion and the Rise of Capitalism* (Pelican, 6d.): L. C. Knights, *Drama and Society in the Age of Jonson*; Brailsford, *Shelley, Godwin and their Circle* (Home University Library).

He concluded that it 'would be a good thing to make yourself write a certain number of essays (show them up, by all means). In any case, write critical and summing-up notes.'

Ten years later there was more *Scrutiny* to refer to. On 12 January 1950

Leavis wrote to R. T. Jones, who had just got his place at Downing, about how he should prepare for Cambridge. (Later Jones became an English lecturer at the University of York.) He recommended improving his general reading, especially in the novel: 'The great thing is to improve your general reading. I have, of course, to guess what you've read already. If you haven't looked through *Fiction and the Reading Public* by Q. D. Leavis, do so.' On Chaucer he recommended John Speirs and Livingston Lowes's *Chaucer*. For the eighteenth century, 'do you know Leslie Stephen: *English Literature and Society in the 18th Century*? If you have not been through Boswell's Johnson, do so. Also read Joseph Krutch's Johnson. Nineteenth Century: L. Trilling's Matthew Arnold, Clutton Brock's William Morris.'

Leavis also talked his pupils through plans for reading. Charles Winder, whose notes on Leavis classes are to be found elsewhere in this book, recorded the advice given by Leavis for second-year reading in 1958.

For Coleridge he recommended 'The Ancient Mariner' as the greatest poem and 'Kubla Khan' as interesting fragment, with Harding and Bewley on him as well as J. Livingston Lowes's *The Road to Xanadu*. Coleridge was recommended as an 'impulsive force': 'see J. S. Mill's tribute' and 'read Henry James's "The Coxon Fund"'. On Byron, he recommended Eliot in *On Poetry and Poets*. For Shelley: Brailsford's *Shelley, Godwin and their Circle*, and Aylwyn Ward-Campbell's, *Shelley and the Unromantics*. He thought the influence of Dante in the Romantic period important: Shelley, 'The Triumph of Life' (his utterly different *terza rima*) and Keats's 'Hyperion'. Students should be able to trace 'the line': early Tennyson-Pre-Raphaelites-the Nineties, and Wordsworth-Arnold-Georgians, garden-suburb culture. Wordsworth was seen not just as a fact of literary history, but a part of English religious history: 'Mill was saved in a spiritual crisis by Wordsworth.' This line could be discerned in Lord Acton and Leslie Stephen, with his agnostic flavour. For the Victorians, Leavis evoked 'the eternal Sunday afternoon, desolate, spellbound; the mirror symbol in "The Lady of Shallott"' and Ruskin's *Praeterita*: 'his father wanted him to be a great poet like Byron, but pious.'

For 'transatlantic literature' Leavis recommended Hawthorne, 'a marvellous genius (see Q. D. Leavis's essay in *The Sewanee Review*)', especially 'My Kinsman Major Molineux', 'Young Goodman Brown', then on to *The Scarlet Letter*. 'Behind Hawthorne's allegory, Bunyan. Hawthorne is behind James, who is supremely interested in manners. See the influence of Jane Austen on *The Europeans*'. Santayana's essay on Dickens in *Soliloquies in England* is highly recommended, against 'the not very profound' essays by Edmund Wilson and George Orwell.

4

At about the same time that Leavis was telling Winder and his fellows what to read for their Nineteenth Century studies, Leavis was engaged in debate about some aspects of the whole English curriculum at Cambridge. He began what he called – see below – 'stickling over the issue of a criticism paper' to be taken in Part One of the English Tripos. He sent a number of memoranda to the Faculty for Board discussion, another of the ordinary papers of significance of which not many survive. One of Leavis's memoranda, called 'A Further Note re Criticism', follows. One point of interest might be noted in advance. Clearly, behind the document there had been a debate about the relative claims of 'theory' and 'practice' in undergraduate studies in literary criticism. It should be remembered that at this historical moment the term 'theory' had a very different sense from its later usage. As is evident below, 'theory' meant two things, either 'history of ideas' or 'aesthetic theory'. The two meanings ran together in that the relevant 'history of ideas' (sometimes called an 'independent branch of intellectual history') was invariably of 'aesthetic theory'. Leavis resisted these claims, believing that a literary criticism course should be a course in critical usage: that the critics and criticism set for undergraduate study should actually assist them in the evolution of their own powers as literary critics. Only in this respect did he stand against 'theory', which in his mind, where the English Tripos was concerned, was connected with what was out-of-date, or 'history'. The relevant tripos examination paper for Part Two was 'The History and Theory of Literary Criticism'.

Leavis's memorandum about 'Criticism' is dated 'February 1958.'

Since the issue is recognized to be important and a good deal of time has been spent in discussing it, I think I ought, even at the risk of appearing over-insistent, to add a clarifying note (I am thinking of the measure of responsibility I have for the discussion's having taken place).

Our school has its distinctive discipline; our business is to promote the intelligent study of literature and the discipline will be manifested in the power to 'be intelligently articulate about it' – it will be manifested in sensitive and cogently relevant thinking (which entails perceptive judgment) expressed in sensitive, lively and scrupulous prose: there is a consensus among us (I hope I may say) to this effect. The lack of unanimity regarding the kind of attention to criticism that this consensus committed us to was associated, it seemed to me, with the fact that the term 'criticism' can portend something very different from what I myself have in mind – as it certainly did, for instance, when Dr Daiches commented that he had rather our undergraduates turned their attention on creative literature. In cultivating the kind of interest in criticism that in my notes (and elsewhere) I have tried to define, they would be – that would be the point and essence of it – turning their attention on creative literature: I myself should never wish to encourage any other kind of interest – or any other kind of criticism than that which derives from, requires and commands such an interest.

Dr Daiches observed that the history of criticism could be studied as a branch of the history of ideas. This phrase is certainly applied by Wellek to his own *History of Criticism*, which has now superseded Saintsbury's. Such 'histories' (Wellek's exemplifies this truth) can be written by authorities who give us no reason at all for supposing that they are in the least intelligent about literature in the concrete – that they are capable of intelligent first-hand judgment when faced with creative works. That is, they give us no reason for supposing that they are capable of being intelligent about criticism as *criticism*. The lack of enthusiasm I confessed to for what is commonly portended by the 'History and Theory of Criticism' is perhaps sufficiently explained: good marks may very well be won on Tripos papers set under that title, and very often are, by candidates who are quite unable to deal intelligently with actual works of literature. For going with the conception of 'History' there is a conception of 'Theory'. It was pointed to by Dr Daiches when, distinguishing between theoretical criticism and practice of criticism, he represented the theorizing he had in mind by a pre-occupation with the possibilities of formulating an aesthetic theory. But such 'theorizing' as (if my view prevailed) we should be encouraging in work for Part I of the English Tripos would be inseparable – as indeed I think *all* profitable concern with critical theory is likely to be – from critical practice, and would be a matter of close consideration of works of creative literature.

It will perhaps be remembered that when I began my stickling over the issue of a criticism paper it took the form of a protest against our merely agreeing to retain the paper while leaving 'texts' to be prescribed 'from time to time': the actual texts prescribed, I said, would define 'criticism' and determine what the fostered concern with it would amount to. Subsequent discussion has perhaps done something to explain my attitude. And perhaps, by way of answering the suggestion that the attention to criticism I advocate our promoting would be at the expense of literature, in the sense of taking the overtasked undergraduate away from it, I may be permitted to make one or two obvious points about my own proposed list of critics.

They are all themselves distinguished writers, and their criticism is itself literature. Three of them, as creative writers, have, in literary history, a decisively major significance in relation to their respective arts. The other two, while also having their distinguished places in creative literature, are recognized to be peculiarly central and classical in critical tradition — to be major figures in English literary history *as critics*. That is, they are all in a different class from I. A. Richards or W. P. Ker or Harold Osborne or Frederick A. Pottle — compared with any of these they are seen to be in another and fuller sense critics and to offer a different order of study. The undergraduate studying in them the art and discipline of criticism hardly needs to be reminded that an intelligent interest in criticism cannot be merely theoretical; it starts and ends in engagement — in actual perceptions and judgments, from which it can never be far away (and that judgment entails discrimination). Nor will he need much reminding that engagement has its most significant manifestations here and now, in clear and direct relation to our own time, and that this is a truth that has the closest relevance to a real and vital, and *intelligent* interest in the literature of the past. (The undergraduate's characteristic engagement will of course be that which is represented by the problem of dealing with his reading and writing his essays.)

It is in the course of a study of the art and discipline of criticism focussed, in this spirit, on such critics that the general or theoretical questions are profitably grappled with — the question that everyone *must* grapple with and be intelligent about (a different matter, I repeat, from aspiring to formulate or master an 'aesthetic theory'): the nature of judgment, of criteria and of standards; the necessary assumptions involved in the belief (to which we are all committed) that intelligent and profitable critical discussion is possible; the nature of the existence of a poem and a literature; art and morality . . . The questions are 'raised' in peculiarly challenging and illuminating ways in the criticism of these writers by reason of the fulness and inwardness of its relation to the concrete (and the 'concrete' here is not merely the actual work of art and the creative activity, but the conditions of society and civilisation in which, in their time, the creative writer writes and to which the critic has to address himself). As creative writers of fine critical intelligence they show in their approach to the matters they handle the most responsive awareness of these conditions. Taken together, as I have said, they give us essential history. It is with an understanding so informed by history – by the concrete in this sense – that the undergraduate (and anyone else) needs to tackle the 'theoretical' issues.

I was surprised that there should seem to be some support for Professor Lewis's suggestion that the issue lay between what I have been proposing and an obvious (and obviously desirable) alternative: 'freedom'. When I asked whether 'freedom' was to include freedom to be unintelligent about literature my intention, I suppose, was plain. Undergraduates, of course, will always be free to be unintelligent; but we, surely, shall always feel ourselves free to correct unintelligence and, in examining, to penalize it. This habit, or conviction, brings up the question of 'criteria' – brings it up implicitly, at any rate. And, committed as we thus are to applying what we take to be the criteria, we all of us implicitly believe that there is, or ought to be, a critical discipline – a discipline of intelligence – proper to our field. What surprises me is that some of us should find it possible to contend that there is no need to give it full and serious recognition as such, and nothing to be gained by turning our thoughts and our pupils' thoughts on it in a disciplined way as something repaying a conscious and cultivated attention. I should have thought the untenableness of this view had been incidentally demonstrated in the course of our discussion. Where the kind of full, serious and active recognition I have been contending for is not given, even we ourselves, the teachers, are at a disadvantage; we may easily slip into unawareness of the necessary principles underlying our work, and so deny them casually, or, by inconsistency, stultify or compromise them. It is in the commerce, collaboration and interplay of active intellectual life that principles and key-concepts are defined, re-defined (a constantly necessary process) and kept present. The issue, I feel bound to say again, is a momentous and urgent one:

1. If there is to be any chance at all of saving the idea (and the reality) of humane education – and at the same time the idea of a university – we have not only to face the rapidly and insidiously developing threat with something better than the kind of journalistic 'literary mind' we

might reasonably be charged with offering as our representative product, but to *make plain* that we are producing something better – and that we know, and can state convincingly, how and what.

2. On the vindication of its claim to stand for a real and central discipline of intelligence depends, as I have pointed out, the English School's status and reality as a *liaison* centre – *the* indispensable centre, if we have any hope for liberal education.

3. An English School has its own essential 'engagement' in relation to the contemporary world, but there will be no adequate recognition of this truth where there is not a full and practical consciousness of principle and function – and no survival for long as anything that matters.

Leavis's Downing Seminars:
A Student's Notes

The material which follows is taken from notes which were made between 1957 and 1960, while I was an undergraduate at Downing College, Cambridge. Morris Shapira, who shared the teaching of English at Downing with Leavis, remarked that I arrived at Downing as 'a hard-working schoolboy'. In that role I made it my business to record what I could of what Leavis said. There are many gaps, but much has been preserved. Misunderstandings and obscurities show that I made no effort to turn what I wrote into what I thought it ought to mean, so my notes have some integrity as a record. They exist because the seminars inclined to monologue and they continue to exist because I have always resisted the urge to clear them out along with other old papers.

Compared with Directors of Studies in other colleges, Leavis seemed very generous with his time and energy. He held the strong conviction that the university English Faculty, with its system of formal lectures, fell far short of what Downing could offer its students. Whilst making it plain that we should decide for ourselves whether to attend the lectures he made equally plain what he thought the decision ought to be. I for one was easily persuaded that the seminars, rich in humour, allusion and content and running several times a week, were the better choice though it was still possible to attend lectures as well. Like the English Tripos, these were wide in range and reference and I later regretted some opportunities. Expectations at Downing were always high and the initial pressure towards independence of judgment was too much for an undergraduate with little knowledge. Despite what I have said, Dr Leavis prompted continual informal discussion amongst his students and beyond his seminars. It was his energy and seriousness that were pervasive rather than his opinions and, even though his seminars ran to repetition, they never seemed dull to me. To an undergraduate his absorbed continuing interest, his vivid relationship with figures of the past, his belief in the importance of what we were doing – these were the things that struck me, as these notes partly testify, and they have stayed with me.

Editors' Note: The notes below are copied directly from Charles Winder's typescript of his handwritten notes. We have not made any attempt to correct, rewrite or reorder them – except in one instance: two substantial sections of the notes were headed 'Shakespeare' and 'Tragedy' and these have been moved next to each other. Otherwise the material appears here in the order it appears in the typescript. Our only other editorial interference has been to select – with Mr Winder's approval – the passages below from the complete set of notes, which was several times longer than this and too large to reproduce here. The ellipses (. . .) indicate where material has been omitted.

. . .

Dissociation of Sensibility. Eliot recorded a fact of first importance about the seventeenth century, but there is no satisfactory account or interpretation of it. There was a radical change. Compare 'All for Love' and 'Antony and Cleopatra'.

. . .

Donne 'The Good Morrow' – a representative poem. How does it show Donne's originality? The colloquial voice which need not be a metaphysical 'symptom' – like Shakespeare 'the play of the verse-movement against the speech structure'. (See particularly 'Satyre')

This is dramatic in two ways as in Shakespeare. There is a situation. You feel that the intellectual expression is eminently part of the mode of feeling. The poem has an arguing, introspective, analytic manner, which allows Donne to point the 'metaphysicalities'.

Cowley in the metaphysical decline; he marked a disintegration.

. . .

The Emblem, a European convention from C17 – Quarles. But Marvell's work is not emblematic; it is original. But it owes much to Donne, although it is totally unlike Donne.

Dean Inge said 'Donne was not a gentleman,' but he was in the sense of being cultured, erudite, a man of the world. But in his poetry we see no manners. He is concerned primarily with the individual and his relation to other individuals. There is no social context. Here a comparison can be made with Marvell, who was, however, not a great poet.

. . .

Both Jonson's prose and verse are in touch with colloquial speech. The vernacular is in the background, it is inseparable from the personal assertiveness and idiosyncracy. The erudite and vernacular are integrally associated, unified. This didn't happen after C17. It has a basis in actuality – behind is the Caroline court. Jonson is an arbiter of taste. In the tavern he met the courtly poets and *dilettanti*. His influence was remarkable. Jonson tried to secure the unity of the classic and the contemporary. The Latin dignity and ease along with the vernacular force, the consciously achieved Latin dignity.

Much of Jonson is too erudite, clumsy, surly, heavyweight.

Unlike Marvell he was a full time poet and he is a great poet. There is a great complexity in his work, but a different complexity from Marvell's. In C17 a great transition occurred; English was mediaeval in 1603 and modern in 1700. Economic, political revolution. The economic reality deployed by Jonson in his satires is anti-capitalist. It is the imminence of the change which produces the awareness in Jonson and the general nostalgia.

About Dryden's modernity there is a great deal of complacency e.g. 'Mr Waller reformed our numbers and civilisation began.' A metropolitan smart set with the new empirical rationalism in the background. Jonson had a greater heterogeneity of background, being at the beginning of the century.

. . .

Background of thought. Read Russell, 'History of Western Philosophy'.

. . .

Is Dryden a great poet? (the paradox). He is a large fact; he is English Literature virtually in that crucial period. But this is misleading; the great works of the time were outside the period – Milton and Bunyan. But

Dryden dominated the change taking place. He was the arbiter of taste, the first literary critic, although there were Elizabethans before e.g. Sir Philip Sidney. The most important name in prose, verse, satire, theatre, for which he had no real vocation. Unequivocally a journalist; the great executive power. A journalist. Johnson uses the word 'occasional'. He was a man of letters; that's why Eliot overrated him. The paradox; great and yet not great. He is not a great creative spirit – dull, uninteresting.

Milton – a titanic figure; not pusillanimous, he had trouble with his wife, so revise the laws of the universe. His paper on divorce.

.   .   .

Pope's wit refers to Marvell or the element of the seventeenth century which he represented. Just local patches: the cumulative effect is Pope. He is the great poet of Queen Anne Augustanism, but he is more than that. Eliot; no one today could write satire in the line of Pope – right. Pope had order and light. First paragraph of Dunciad IV; Miltonic, magnificent. Also 'conscious neatness and precision of statement tending towards epigram'.

.   .   .

1660 onwards saw a new reading public, nurtured on the vast output of pamphlets etc. No newsheets except L'Estrange's. The great bulk were practical works, improving religion and morals. In a sense Bunyan is part of this, though obviously he is a man of genius and important in the development of the novel. The theatre couldn't serve everyone. What was needed was the novel though no one knew; it was realized though when the novel developed.

.   .   .

In 'The Tatler' and 'The Spectator' the gentleman is the norm; nothing is worth exploring, science, religion, morals etc., except in that it administers to the civilisation. They define the gentleman, give his outfit. 'The Tatler' is much more lively – journalistic, even Dickensian, the matter of the novel. 'The Tatler' and 'The Spectator' play an important part in the novel's history. What people wanted was the novel; note the reception of 'Pilgrim's Progress'. 'The Tatler' and 'The Spectator' filled the gap. The novel was slow to start and starts in journalism. In 'The Tatler' and

'The Spectator' the drama turns into the novel by way of the periodical. The De Coverley Papers are relevant but they are not the most important instance; unanthologised instances recur throughout 'The Tatler' and 'The Spectator'. Letters are important in this context. Richardson's letters, Defoe's matter of fact verisimilitude. Richardson provokes Fielding; after Fielding the novel is there; an army sprang up. The extension of the Reading Public, the growth of the trade of writing; Johnson had a great deal to do with that. There was, of course, a trade of writing before, but nothing like the Grub Street Pope recreates in Dunciad IV.

. . .

Pope: Lytton Strachey – 'Pope's poetic criticism of life was simply and solely the heroic couplet', a starting point. Strachey thinks only in terms of technique. 'No one could ever write satire in the line of Pope' – Eliot; 'the line', not technique, a social gesture. Pope brings to bear the values of a contemporary civilisation. The grandeur and significance in Pope – key concepts, order and light, sense of profound moral truths. If Dryden swells his victim, as Eliot says, so does Pope – and he's a much greater poet; the intensity and engagement are there. Dunciad IV, riotously fantastic play of satiric irony. At the same time as the presentation of decorum and manners we have the wild surrealistic play of imagination, against the background of order and reason.

. . .

Cowley, the Aldous Huxley of the seventeenth century; Huxley's contemporaneity of the wrong kind; it turns out to be unreal – see 'Point Counter Point' – Cowley is the same. Ability but not creative – all kinds of modes. The shifting of civilisation can be seen in Cowley. See his 'Elegy to Mr Harvey', a charming poem. All the charm of Gray, Collins, without their stiltedness. Compare 'Lycidas', which is classic right enough. Cowley, a decency of feeling. A few poems like this, but Cowley usually for illustrative purposes, bad conceits. See the dissociation of sensibility in his 'Ode on Wit'. Tennyson also dazzling genius, but the wrong kind of contemporaneity. Browning, crude; 'The Grammarian's Funeral' is characteristic but good. A gross brute, such a rotarian in the grain. Though the rhythm is there it's not the kind which could have influence on life and language. No rehabilitating influence. But he did influence Pound.

Eliot credits Pound with two achievements; he established poetry as song, poetry as speech. See 'Mauberley'.

.   .   .

Augustan poetry, a social gesture, the polite smirk; feel it in the first stanza of the Elegy. Mildly absurd – the gentle incongruity between the manner and the subject matter. The prize poem manner, see Matthew Arnold. The rot starts with Gray. Something slightly absurd in Gray's coy, modest stance and the polite smirk. Read 'The Scholar Gipsy', the relation of language to thought; his thoughts are prose thoughts. What makes it poetry? Prize poem phraseology, 'soul'. You would never guess from his poetry that Arnold was one of the supreme ironic pamphleteers of the language.

After Gray and Collins. Cowper can be parodied; Johnson can't – he is too strongly poised. See Cowper's 'The Castaway'.

.   .   .

Blake; he was as far from Johnson as Eliot. See Eliot's essay on Blake. 'Spring'; Hebraic parallelism played off against the decasyllabic verse: 'the hills tell each other . . .'. 'Autumn'. Look at the prose pieces in 'Poetical Sketches'. Behind them and his decasyllabics is Ossian. (See Lawrence's 'Princess' – the father, straight from the Ossianic north.) Ossian everywhere in the Prophetic Books. 'Elenor'; read Young's 'Night Thoughts', the murder in 'Macbeth'. Blake is not a Shakespearian poet, but learning from Shakespeare he vindicated the poetical use of language. Song, 'My silks and fine array' – remarkable; complete escape from the eighteenth century. Elizabethan song; lovely lapsing movement. Read Middleton Murry on Collins; Swinburne – Kipling – Masefield. For this song, see 'Hamlet'. Cumulative evidence of the radical association of Blake and Shakespeare. An unconscious reminiscence; when writing these lines he lives in part with Shakespeare. 'Memory, hither come', see 'As You Like It'; the response to Shakespeare, the lapsing, living movement. 'Mad Song' – 'Lear', a response conceived. How could Blake read Shakespeare like this? That's genius. 'I love the jocund dawn'; folk culture, children's games; characteristic poetic rhythms which are inseparable from bodily movement.

Complete antithesis to any other C18 poet. No public; he was committed to making a public thing of his most inner intuitions and perceptions. Blake's blow-offs, compare Lawrence. Obviously not meant to be poetry. But there is a great deal in Blake which is in a between-world; not one thing or another. Read Krutch on Johnson.

Dryden laid all the stress on the social; this continued through the Augustan age. Blake shifted the emphasis to the individual, but more is needed or no art. Blake is lacking in this more; a full, creative impulsion but no means to satisfy it. Contrast Lawrence, Mark Twain, backed by a cultural heritage; see Twain's 'Puddn'head Wilson'. Finally Hemingway in America – the language but nothing else. On the other hand, Dreiser – seems as though he learned English from a newspaper. He gives the feeling that he doesn't have any native language – Hemingway doesn't do this. In Dreiser life is absolutely emptied of significance. You don't get this feeling in Mark Twain; his novels developed from story-telling, a European cultural heritage; see 'Huckleberry Finn'. Lawrence, the whole heritage of European culture; he'd read everything. Blake hadn't Lawrence's triumphant creativity. He didn't take enough trouble. How could he when he thought no one else was going to read him. The Prophetic Books a creative disaster; nothing in them. Blake, no C18 politeness, the popular culture at a higher level than children's games. See 'Broadsides'. Ability to be educated by popular art. This precedes the more powerful manifestation, the power to do Shakespeare.

C18 vignettes – Austin Dobson. Edmund Gosse and Courthope on the eighteenth century.

Blake, research fatuous – vast output, only two need be read.

. . .

Revision topics:

– 'Marvell's status as a poet is unique.' Try and define his status as a poet by comparing and contrasting him with other poets. He has to be 'placed'.

– 'Eliot's formulation may have passed out of fashion and he lays too much responsibility on Milton and Dryden but a change answering to his phrase "dissociation of sensibility" did occur.'

– 'Gray with the mind and soul of a true poet was isolated in his century; he never spoke out.'

– '"Pilgrim's Progress" and "Robinson Crusoe" – the authors' lives overlapped and both have been called Puritans, but one of the great changes in civilisation lies between them.'

– 'Milton, a mature Marlowe turned Puritan'

. . .

Shakespeare

Dover Wilson on 'Henry IV'; not original but not bad; the morality tradition; see Quiller Couch, 'Shakespeare's Workmanship'.

Currie, 'Shakespeare's Philosophical Patterns' – the orthodox side of Shakespeare, the background of theologico-moral knowledge.

Kitto, 'Form and Meaning in Drama'; the essay on 'Hamlet', a very good corrective to Eliot and Bradley. Eliot concentrated on Hamlet's disgust about his mother. Compare 'Tradition and the Individual Talent', the absolution of poetry, the greater the art, the greater the separation. In fact there is the closest relation between the man who suffers and the mind which creates. See 'The Family Reunion'; Eliot identified with the aristocratic protagonist, no 'objective correlative'.

Read Kitto on 'Hamlet' and try the same on 'Macbeth'. Can 'Macbeth' be made noble hero of the Aristotelian kind? Not a sympathetic hero like Hamlet.

. . .

'Lear'. Impossible to say anything; much more complex than any other. Traversi says the daughters are all implicitly in the old man himself. Close relation between 'Lear' and 'Measure for Measure' – 'man proud man'.

How does 'Measure for Measure' relate to the idea of tragedy? The ending isn't formally tragic, but it is really a tragedy. The question of the problem play. Is it valid to include it amongst the problem plays? They begin with 'Troilus and Cressida', nasty and its meaning is difficult to probe. 'Measure for Measure' forced into the problem category because of sex and convention. Traversi on 'Lear' and 'Antony and Cleopatra' in 'Scrutiny'.

'Measure for Measure'. Angelo, a representative figure; he is you and me. Barnadine – the comment on the duke's admonition of Claudio. Claudio can't conceivably take the attitude; Barnadine can. Read Raleigh's chapter on 'Measure for Measure'. His theme, Shakespeare's moral neutrality; 'Measure for Measure' is his example.

. . .

'Antony and Cleopatra', for all its memorable poetry, is curiously empty from the human point of view. Where is the love in it? Compare 'Lear', its range of human experience. We feel the hollowness and emptiness of 'Antony and Cleopatra'. See Eliot 'The Use of Poetry and the Use of Criticism', the satiric aspect.

Satire, illustration of a fallacious approach, Humbert Wolfe's book, ed. Rylands. Distinguished satire in our time? Eliot's 'Coriolan' sequence, the nearest thing. Also Pound's Mauberley.

Eliot couldn't have done a good critique of 'Antony and Cleopatra'; he hadn't enough poise on the theme of sex.

. . .

What is the radical fallacy of Santayana's 'Tragic Philosophy'?

Consider Eliot's 'Tradition and the Individual Talent', full of ambiguities, pseudo-precisions, non-sequiturs. Compare with Lawrence's conception of art, its relation to life. Eliot's idea: the separation of the man who suffers from the mind which creates. There is no gap: 'Women in Love', 'Anna Karenina'. Why is Eliot so intent on the separation?

. . .

Something happened to Wyndham Lewis in the fourth form; a product of the public school mishap.

Relate Eliot's 'Hamlet' to his 'Family Reunion'.

. . .

Eliot's 'Tradition and the Individual Talent', a masterly piece of equivocation. It has all the weaknesses of 'The Sacred Wood', which, however, is the work of a fine talent, essays on Blake, Ben Jonson, which isn't about Ben Jonson. Eliot, no concept of tradition, you can't expect that kind of thing in an American. The great preoccupation in this essay is in absolving the poet from his responsibility towards life. No conception of a living tradition; this explains his attitude towards Lawrence, who springs

from a rich and vital culture, 'A Study of Thomas Hardy'. The real Eliot
in 'After Strange Gods'. See what he says about Lawrence's relationship
with his mother and the chapel. In 'Tradition and the Individual Talent'
Eliot eliminates the most important thing which is to have lived.

. . .

The Last Forty Years of Shakespeare Criticism. Since Bradley the concept
of poetic drama has been explored. Bradley had no idea of it; he looked
at the plays as one would look at a psychological novel. Eliot is in the
Lamb, Swinburne, F. L. Lucas line. Compare Lawrence's 'The Study of
Thomas Hardy'. Eliot some good suggestions on blank verse and dramatic
convention, not consistently developed, though. Wilson Knight; his weak
side derives from Middleton Murry, the creative self-exegesis. See Murry's
'Keats and Shakespeare', slimy blurry-Murry exegesis. He refuses to submit
to discipline and intelligence, a kind of afflatus, intimacy with the poet's
soul: Keats, Shakespeare, Chekov, Katherine Mansfield. The curious conversion of criticism into pseudo-prophecy, symptomatic of a civilisation,
which needed religion, stability. The strong side of Wilson Knight; imagery, symbolism, the poetry works through them. He wasn't the first
but he had the inspiration, pseudo-creative, pseudo-messianic conceit. He
hadn't the discipline, strength of relevance. A man though he's aberrant.
No timidity, he's respectable. Caroline Spurgeon: tabulation, but you can't
take the image from its context, it's a node in the organisation. Wilson
Knight, a titanic figure; Middleton Murry, a low worm. Middleton Murry's
'D. H. Lawrence, Son of Woman' one of the most disgusting episodes
in literary history. The line: Murry, Wilson Knight, Traversi a truly
admirable outcome. Granville Barker, nothing to say, just the ordinary
sort of useless thing.

See Preface to 'The Tempest', New Cambridge Shakespeare, the reasons
for further textual criticism. The medieval continuity behind Shakespeare,
Curry.

Folk Lore, the anthropological context. Read Gilbert Murray, 'Hamlet
and Orestes', Kathleen Philpotts, 'The Elder Edda'. Shakespeare nearer to
the Greek by way of the native tradition than by way of Seneca.

Why is Shakespeare so different from Racine? Racine hasn't got the
massive continuity. Why do England and France become so unlike? Were

they so unlike in C14th, the same background, racial composition. Utterly different in language, thought and literature.

. . .

Tragedy

No such thing as 'tragic philosophy', but there is an aura of associations with a dark centre portended by that word 'tragic' or we wouldn't use it. A conceptual nebula with a composite nucleus.

. . .

The irrelevance of Aristotle in one's approach to tragedy. There's a change in temper between the Greece of Aeschylus and that of Aristotle, equivalent to the change from fifteenth (?) century England to the England of Johnson.

. . .

Except for Shakespeare the Elizabethans don't matter. You've got to say two things at once; Shakespeare was an Elizabethan dramatist; oh, dammit he wasn't. See Fluchère's book, 'Shakespeare and the Elizabethans'. What in fact is the nature and status of Elizabethan Drama?

. . .

What do you make of phrases like Tragic Philosophy, Tragic Effect, Tragic Attitude? Can't you discuss Greek Tragedy without invoking them? Note the variety of Greek Tragedy. Compare 'Oedipus Rex' and 'Oedipus Coloneus'; the superficial organisation is the same but the fundamental organisation . . . 'Philoctetes', a happy ending – and it's not the only Greek Tragedy with a happy ending.

. . .

Serious drama an impossibility in the twentieth century. You can't have a serious drama without a theatre and you can't have a theatre without a community.

. . .

Racine, he's eloquent, he's moving, he's French. The operatic conception of love in Racine, sexual passion. Has he any sense of 'male' and 'female'? So much more about love in Shakespeare. 'Antony and Cleopatra' much more impressive than 'Phèdre'. 'Othello' deals with sexual passion; that's where Bradley goes wrong, thinks Othello should be a gentleman in love, but somehow that doesn't fit.

. . .

'Othello' turned into an Italian opera. It deserves it. It can be done without any radical excision. Everything is appreciable at that level.

. . .

Relate 'la passion' as in 'Antony and Cleopatra' to what we have in 'Phèdre'. There's quite obviously a relation but there's a difference. Something alcoholic about 'Antony and Cleopatra'; after all alcohol is there and a great force in the world. How far can one go in taking the play seriously? It's certainly not bogus – but alcohol. 'Glory' an interesting note. Compare glory for Burns. Does Burns in the background, 'o'er all the ills of life victorious', provide an approach? The French, 'Cherchez la Femme'. Sex in one sense plays the same part in 'Phèdre'. It's 'la passion'. But there's no 'sin' in 'Antony and Cleopatra', that's odd, even though one knows that Racine had Port-Royal and the Jansenist background. Othello a most effective man of action. But how did he get away if he smote the Turk in Aleppo? Can't help thinking it was a part that Othello acted once. Compare on the one hand with 'Antony and Cleopatra' and on the other with 'Macbeth'.

. . .

'King Lear', certainly there the disturbing radical attitude to life. The desperate Shakespeare is certainly there. The last turn of the screw, really disturbing. Not prepared to talk glibly about it. No one is. Not prepared to say anything about it.

. . .

Greek plays that tell: the 'Antigone', mainly because of Hegel. 'The Eumenides'. It brings us face to face with the recognition that we can never be fully critical about or inward with Greek Tragedy. In spite of archaeology and anthropology it's still very difficult; that civilization is so remote and alien. We can never discuss Greek Tragedy properly as achieved, created art; we see it's impressive but we're too far away. Translation is impossible; there are no parallel concepts or ideas to place up against the Greek. We can't even see what the Greek ideas are. Writing on the 'Oresteia' is a matter of delicately amplifying one's agnosticism about it; we don't really know what it means.

· · ·

The Greeks didn't have a 'tragic'. We have a 'tragic' idea because of the Renaissance? The Greeks had Tragedy, but no 'tragic'.

· · ·

Nineteenth- and Twentieth-Century Literature

You can learn more about the essential changes in civilization from the novel than in any other way; literature in general and the novel in particular. The Americans, utterly alien; see Trilling on Jane Austen. Never will a line of intelligent comment emerge from America on Lawrence; they're too alien.

· · ·

The nature of Arnold's interest in politics, he could put the case admirably. He was obviously a serious person. See 'Friendship's Garland', 'Culture and Anarchy'. The dichotomy; we have on the other hand 'the Scholar Gipsy' which is Victorian poetry. What it really is – that Arnold wants a holiday. A symbol, the need to be free. 'He had ONE aim.' His poetry, some of the virtues of the eighteenth century, 'le mot juste' without the wit. The repetitiveness; compare the repetitiveness of his prose, part of his tactics, making his argument carefully foolproof, insultingly foolproof. The difference between his prose and poetry, one of intellectual achievement.

The use of 'soul' in criticism from Coleridge to Bridges; an interesting essay to be written on this word.

Two factors in Arnold's poetry, prize-poem phraseology and uniformity of emotion, the phial of poetic essence. Arnold's afflatus, all impossible.

Like Victor Hugo, the sublime old windbag, but he did it with genius. Anyway, English isn't French.

.   .   .

The nineteenth century. Life was in the novel. The energy and creativeness of Shakespeare were caught up in the novel. The poetry of the age was completely cut off from that sort of life and organisation. See Arnold on 'Anna Karenina'; he says, life yes – but not art. 'Anna Karenina' is on the contrary a miracle of organisation, every phrase having bearing on the theme of characters played off against each other. A marvellous richness about it. Read Lawrence on the novel in 'Phoenix'. However great Shakespeare's achievement it certainly doesn't outweigh the achievement of the English novel on both sides of the Atlantic from Jane Austen to Mark Twain.

Arnold's criticism of great value because we have the relevance of literary-critical thinking to other modes of thought. Trilling on Arnold; the best part is when he deals with Thomas Arnold, Arnold's father.

.   .   .

In 'The Palace of Art' we have Tennyson's case.' Discuss. Essay. 'The Palace of Art' sets out to have a moral but Tennyson never gets to grips with it, gets lost in his words. The French influence, 'l'art pour l'art', Gautier. Differences between French and English poetry in the nineteenth century; see Eliot in 'On Poetry and Poets'. The French are superior, yes, but in his appraisal of French superiority Eliot forgets the novel; he's not interested in it at all.

'The Grecian Urn', Bridges says the superiority of art to nature. What we have in fact is a desire to have it both ways, characteristic of Keats. But Keats wasn't interested in 'art'. In Keats fine sensations are cultivated with quasi-religious unction; it becomes 'art' later. Along with this goes transience. See 'La Belle Dame', a poem for which Keats had no use. What did the Victorians do with it? Separated from life, 'The Lady of Shalott', the mirror symbol. The Victorians were interested in the eternal Sunday afternoon, 'a land where it was always afternoon' – 'The Lotos Eaters'. William Morris, the essential bent that is in the poetic; that's what he gives us, the Sunday afternoon and a certain amount of archaism. We feel the poverty of 'The Palace of Art' in comparing certain tracts with their sources in Keats.

The 'intellectual' facets of 'The Palace of Art': 'And there was Milton like a seraph strong / With Shakespeare bland and mild.' Shakespeare 'bland and mild', the Victorian sense of Shakespeare. An absurd schoolboy solemnity and the poetic, take them together.

.   .   .

Eliot's introduction to Baudelaire's 'Journaux Intimes', how disgusting and unforgiveably so he can get. He criticised Lawrence – but this is what he was doing. Only Dante saves 'The Waste Land' – and that's not life. Sex is Eliot's only interest. The curious thing about Eliot, so correct and so spinsterly.

.   .   .

William Morris, Clutton Brock. Ought to know where Morris comes and roughly what his significance is.

.   .   .

Browning, 'The Grammarian's Funeral', a good starting point; it shows Browning to advantage. Note the movement apart from the rhyme, strikingly original in poetic. That's genius to be free from the prevailing atmosphere. But then comes the vulgarity, Browning's always earnest and unctuous. Note the rhyme and compare Hopkins' audacities. Hopkins' greatness that the feat of bringing off the rhyme recedes from our notice, is absorbed into the context. In Browning the point of the acrobatic rhyming is to draw our attention. This is a neat back-somersault, you know; incurable vulgarity. Chesterton calls Browning's tricks 'the grotesque habit', justifies it as well as comparing him with Tennyson. See how Browning's rhyme comes out in the most inappropriate places in, for example, 'Christmas Eve and Easter Day'. Like a modern American evangelist. Billy Graham, the preacher who will do a back-somersault in the middle of a sermon to keep the crowd on his side. Billy Sunday did it in terms of baseball. Browning's Anglo-Saxon spirit; like Mormonism, the pioneering habit for immediate ends. Browning's insistence on the quantitative achievement. Eupeptic, eternal youth.

Tillyard, a bumpkin Machiavelli.

Santayana on Browning, 'Poetry and Religion', the poet as barbarian.

Essay, 'Browning is the exception that proves the rule,' the rule referring to Victorian poetry. What's odd about Browning: the combination of provincial nonconformity and metropolitan confidence. He's a fact in English poetry, the contemporary of Tennyson. There's a talent, though he'll never be read again. He's gone out as completely as Thackeray.

Browning's characteristic form, the monologue, derived from the Jacobean soliloquy. His drama, for example 'Strafford', what's wrong with it? He's not interested in the interplay of life and consciousness; he moves all the time towards the monologue.

'Meeting at Night', say why not Tennysonian or pre-Raphaelite. The trouble with Browning, too healthy-minded. 'The Ring and The Book', supreme application of the monologue method, but unreadable. Browning's energy, undoubtedly a prodigious talent, but . . .

.   .   .

Swinburne. Tennysonian, subordination of sound to sense, lapsing away from the sense. Use of words; what could happen after Swinburne? Gilbert Murry's Euripides happened.

.   .   .

Between Tennyson and Eliot note the attempts to do something original, Hardy and Hopkins. Hardy's novels, he's an innocent old bird. His prose, the very absence of distinction is a distinction; cliché, but never mere cliché, always Hardy.

.   .   .

The Pre-Raphaelites, a large fact in the Victorian age. Rossetti not like Swinburne; no nonsense about liberty etc. Hothouse atmosphere. Pre-Raphaelitism is primarily a phenomenon of painting, visual art. Rossetti and Morris painters as well as poets.

Christina Rossetti; why draw her into it? She was Gabriel's sister. But note her relation to Herbert; devotional, she has the speech movement (relation to well-bred speech) but not the wit. Religion; Dante Gabriel transmuted it for his own aesthetic ends. Her relation to Hopkins. Note how Hopkins associates with Herbert, though so ostensibly unlike, the same basic questioning; the undoubted success is in the analytic and exploring side. Hopkins has no religious doubt; he has his accepted dogma. Like Herbert. They're both gentlemen as well, but Hopkins had to be eccentric to be himself fully. Herbert could engage a code of manners.

Christina, always a lady. That well-bred quality; it's Herbert. There is a side that is more closely related to the essential Pre-Raphaelite movement, her children's poetry, for example 'Goblin Market'. It's a line from Poe to De La Mare. Something unpleasant, sadistic about De La Mare. Something queer in 'Goblin Market', the thwarted spinster. She needed some sort of therapy, not necessarily Freudian.

D. G. Rossetti, in a sense a genius; he is the source of the Pre-Raphaelite influences. The outstanding Pre-Raphaelite poem is Dante Gabriel's 'Blessed Damozel', remarkable that it was written by a boy of eighteen or nineteen. See the sonnet 'Soul's Beauty', profoundly metaphysical and symbolic and full of unction. Beauty, you know there'll be a kind of corrupt Platonism. Note all the large phrases and romantic gestures, he cashes in on them. Nothing particular. Life, Death, Terror, Beauty. Vague suggestions of the central Christian tradition. What does it do? Nothing. It's not even unpleasant. In other poems Rossetti starts getting erotic.

.   .   .

'Hugh Selwyn Mauberley'; that that astonishingly delicate work should have come from that brute.

.   .   .

Jane Austen. Read Harding, 'Regulated Hatred', the viewpoint of a social psychologist with the limitations that implies. Jane Austen belonged to a social civilisation where the social values centred on the family. But note her sense of herself as an individual; on the other hand she couldn't do without society. She learned from the stage; 'Mansfield Park' represents an evangelical period; see the attitude that is expressed towards the theatre. Her family were avid amateurs of the theatre. Jane Austen's acquaintance with eighteenth-century comedy and farce, which plays a large part in her writing. Not to mention her reading of Shakespeare.

.   .   .

Dickens potentially a greater artist than actually he became. Note 'Edwin Drood' (forget the mystery, of course). What is Dickens's status as an

artist? There's some very good entertainment in him and it's all life-en-
hancing, so to speak. But something more. Trouble is that Dickens was
essentially uneducated; note how Lawrence with the same class-status was
so much more educated, he's in possession of the whole European heritage,
much more than T. S. Eliot; he read everything. What Eliot said about
Shakespeare finding out more of the civilisation of Ancient Rome from
North's 'Plutarch' than a scholar could find during a life spent in the
British Museum can be applied to Lawrence. Lawrence had an intense
interest in life, see his excitement about Greek Tragedy; this marks him
off from Dickens.

· · ·

When you say Dickens is potentially greater than actually he is you're
making a point about Dickens. A lack of intellectual culture, ignorant,
provincial. Education needn't necessarily have had an ill effect on his
prodigious creative force. Note 'Dombey and Son'; greatness, yes, but
note the indulgence in lushness etc. (serious Victorian melodrama). Dickens
was a great histrio, loved to stand on the platform and sway the multitude.
But the vilest Victorian art (Dickens's slush) is done with absolute genius.
Dickens a best-seller. Dickens mobilised the mob. But don't think Dickens
is like Horatio Bottomley – a calculating blackguard of the lowest order.
Reading his serials in 'John Bull' one didn't want to come home. We
have the chapter 'Nightmare' in 'Kangaroo' which gives us Bottomley's
England. Read R. C. Churchill in 'Scrutiny', 'Dickens, Drama and Tradition'. Dickens's language, that vitality is absolute genius. He belongs to
a different culture from ours, before the Education Act of 1870; they
talked. And there were no pools, no television. The life of the Working
Class; they might die from typhus tomorrow, but they lived.

· · ·

'Mill on the Floss'. Much more interesting than Leslie Stephen suggests.
The first part too much written by Maggie Tulliver. We see this particularly
if we compare it with 'The Rainbow'. George Eliot tends to confuse one
adolescent emotion with another. Just compare the first part of 'Mill on
the Floss' with the corresponding second part of 'The Rainbow'. Lawrence's piety, traditional; a greater genius than George Eliot. See 'Fanny
and Annie', George Eliot's world done by Lawrence. Stephen's book a

very good example of the fallacious approach to George Eliot; you know, the intuitive woman whose intellect gets in the way. James on the other hand does pay tribute to George Eliot's intellect, but his attitude isn't a consistent one. The weakness of 'Mill on the Floss' not any excessive intellectuality, but the excessive intrusion of femininity, a certain immaturity. Three terms to use for George Eliot: the feminine imagination and sensibility; Intellect, the capacity for higher navvying; Intelligence. Betrayals in the novel, the ugly duckling theme; Maggie becomes a swan, betraying personal significance as far as George Eliot's concerned. The river trip with Stephen Guest, superbly clairvoyant psychologically and utterly convincing. Bring out its strength by comparing the death by water at the end.

'Silas Marner', superbly concentrated and done, no waste there, Leavis has never done justice to it. After she's written as far as 'Silas Marner' she's exhausted her material of reminiscence. She has now to be the wholly inventive novelist. 'Romola', there's a lot of day dream in it besides the research.

'Felix Holt', again she has to manufacture it, a Victorian three-decker. Felix Holt, radical; some sort of education at Glasgow University, but faithful to his class, he remains 'shaggy'. Tht best thing is the Transome drama, the nearest thing to Greek Tragedy outside Greek Tragedy. Some of the finest things in the English novel are lost and buried in George Eliot, 'Gwendolen Harleth', for example, the most Tolstoyan thing in English. 'Felix Holt', a wonderful piece of work; that is, the Transome drama, the hubris-nemesis theme.

George Eliot couldn't do elections; Mary Anne Evans couldn't go into pubs. There Disraeli (the only one who could compare with her prodigious knowledge) had one over her.

.   .   .

Meredith: Middleton Murry said, 'the ear of an organ-grinder and the eye of a chorus-fancier'.

.   .   .

Conrad. Heyst in 'Victory', an intellectual déraciné with aristocratic, intellectual Swedish father. The point about Heyst, how the inner dialectic is worked. Testimony to the need for collaboration even in the most

individual human beings. Decoud in 'Nostromo'; what they've done to
the working classes. Still as urgent today, the way Trade Unions have in
fact betrayed the working classes. Higher Wages, Standard of Living; that
on the one side, Marxism on the other. Scenes in 'Nostromo' done with
Flaubertian care. Something aesthetic, the other extreme from the characteristic perfect work of Lawrence. Conrad without that irresistible creative drive.

.   .   .

James, 'The Tragic Muse', the part politics can play in a life. The theatre,
the artist. James on the outside of the country house culture; he saw a
glamour which George Eliot, being an insider, knew wasn't there. The
country house is functional; 'The Tragic Muse' not one of the world's
great books.

'What Maisie Knew'. The idea came to James from Dickens, the
situation of young David in the Micawber household.

.   .   .

The eighteenth century no soul, as Arnold said, but Arnold writes in
terms of the nineteenth century. The implication of the eighteenth-century
habit is that everything a man might have to express is already provided
for in the common currency. The eighteenth century closed the springs
of originality, would soon cause the death of poetry. Shakespeare, the 'if
it were done' speech, you have it there analogically, 'surcease' turns into
'success' We need the actor who is concerned with the meaning of
Shakespeare; for narcissistic habits Shelley is as good as Shakespeare, we
need to get the noise out of the way. Not saying Shakespeare shouldn't
be acted, saying he should be; he's highly dramatic. This means one has
to pay the most sensitive attention to the specificities of the content.

.   .   .

Every age has its assumptions and habits; those of the nineteenth century
soul prevailed till the Eliotic revolution. As a critic Eliot is most sure and
strong in the area closest to his problems as a poet.

.   .   .

Swinburne, Tennyson; alcohol an important analogy when considering magniloquence, relaxation of the higher centres, not able to handle and articulate complex thought.

. . .

Yeats trying to find something more real than Browning's world. The curious loosening of Victorian rationalism in Yeats's syntax. 'Wind among the Reeds' might have been the end had there not been an Irish Movement, involving the theatre, bringing Yeats into contact with men and politics. Then the later sardonic Yeats.

. . .

What could happen after Swinburne? – Mr Lucas.

Frank Harris. Why did Shaw and Wells retain a tender feeling for him? It's the period.

Shaw; some distinguished journalistic dramatic criticism. Arrested development, emotional unrest. Taken to see Shaw's 'Pygmalion' in 1917 when on leave; the indignation, the rage, the disgust at being exposed to this. Insufferable except at the pamphleteering level. In his plays when he tries to be serious you can't stand it. Comedy very amusing. A journalist and pamphleteer but not a creative artist. A gross flatterer of the lower middle-brow in a very obvious way.

Ford Madox Hueffer, a very good editor, he found and backed the talent. Not a poet or novelist though – but still a novelist in the U.S.A.

Wells, the triumphant figure, no doubt Stalin's favourite reading; again the pamphleteer. After Wells visited Russia in the thirties, Stalin said, 'My God, what a bourgeois.' Wells's line; improve the drains, exploit the methods of applied science and everything will be all right. Education Act of 1870 beginning to tell in the nineties.

. . .

American universities, they have an impossible task.

'Cunning Passages': Leavis's Lectures on Poetry and Prose

Many of Leavis's lectures are known quantities. Of those delivered and published in the later part of his career, there is the notorious 'Richmond Lecture' on C. P. Snow and the Two Cultures. The title-piece of *'Anna Karenina' and Other Essays* was delivered originally as a lecture to the Cambridge University Slavonic Society. His attacks on the 'new orthodoxy' of the 1960s in Leavis's phase of 'higher pamphleteering' (so he called it) appeared in *Nor Shall My Sword*. Early in his career there is evidence that he read out his lectures, rather than improvizing or speaking from notes. His scripts clearly contributed to the material of *New Bearings in English Poetry* and *Revaluation*. But there is one strain of lecturing in Leavis's career which has gone unrecorded, and oddly these are the lectures that are most remembered by the people who went to them. From 1937 to his retirement in 1962 Leavis gave a general lecture course in Cambridge on the criticism of verse and prose, unconfined to any particular period. It was called 'Appreciation and Analysis'. These were, of course, for the English Faculty, not college lectures, delivered in one of the large Mill Lane lecture theatres. They were an indispensable port of call for students of English, many of whom lasted through the whole course of eight or sixteen occasions (the length of the Cambridge 'Full', or teaching, term). These lectures never really found their way into print. Parts of them were published in *Scrutiny* in the form of three essays with the general title 'Notes in the Analysis of Poetry' between 1945 and 1952. These essays were reprinted, and slightly supplemented, in *The Living Principle* in 1975 as 'Judgment and Analysis'. Some of the material for the lectures was used in *Education and the University*. But there is no record of the whole series, and certainly no transcription. And this is a pity, for these were hardly bread-and-butter lectures. They were considered by those who heard them to epitomize Leavis, and Leavis himself valued them highly: his uncertainty about how to publish was a sign of his high valuation of them rather than the reverse.

Today, the nearest we can get to these lectures is the set of passages which Leavis had printed to accompany them, supplemented by such reminiscences as survive, and, of course, the commentaries mentioned above. By themselves the passages give off the appearance of being a set of 'dating passages', pieces designed to show period characteristics of prose and verse. But it was clear to those who heard the lectures that this was the material on which Leavis based arguments and meditations about the nature of prose and verse – and of criticism. The lectures were not exactly demonstration exercises in how-to-do-it. They were reflections on the processes of reading. The collocation of passages was Leavis 'doing criticism'. In a sense, it is the spaces between the passages which gave them their meaning. The sheets as we have them are, as it were, *scores* for the lectures.

These 'Appreciation and Analysis' lectures evidently varied a little over the years, and there were occasional changes in the passages selected. But on the whole the material remained stable, with the result that after the war Leavis could be heard on extracts of writing which no longer had a timely presence in Cambridge English. But the charge that he was simply using his old material is not quite appropriate. His reflections on reading prose and poetry were meant to be geared to the modes of reading that had emerged under certain conditions and of certain authors *in Cambridge*: He was deliberately reflecting upon 'old Cambridge pieces'. Indeed, some of 'his' passages had never been 'new': quite deliberately he went back to passages handled in Richards's *Practical Criticism* and Read's *English Prose Style*.

In this essay I reproduce the four sets of passages that were used over the years, adding some commentary, partly reliant on my own memories and notes about the lectures in the late 1950s. I am also indebted to some notes made by Robert Jefford, who heard the lectures a little earlier, for some identifications and commentary. Some of the sheets survive with Leavis's jottings on them, which obviously I have used. I have identified the passages, or as many as I could. I am not altogether disappointed that the provenance of some remains elusive. As a result the reader has an opportunity to recreate the anxiety which once invested not knowing in such a situation, one in which what one did not know was something about English literature, but was more than likely, also, to be something about oneself as well. We have here, therefore, the offer of an experience which previously many of today's readers will have refused – and from which more will have been unknowingly protected.

So that the reader can do a straight reading if desired the passages are simply given without introduction. The passages were originally in four sets with no general title, except Roman numbers. Thinking interpretively about them I came up with possible explanatory titles, which I give in a final note below. Attributions and commentary by myself follow, and my final note, a brief 'user's guide' – or *mode d'emploi*, the phrase translated in the title of Georges Perec's *Life: A User's Guide*, another work of cunning corridors: for so may Leavis's passages be accounted.

One not-quite-trivial point should be noted on embarkation: each set of passages was given out *as a whole* at the beginning of the lecture courses so they were in the students' hands for the duration. And they were in printed (not 'cyclostyled') form, done by the Cambridge University Press printing works. Leavis's texts are reproduced below exactly as they were distributed. In the 'Commentary' alternative sources are given – for finding purposes – in modern editions.

I

1.   All our service
In every point twice done, and then done double,
Were poor and single business to contend
Against those honours deep and broad, wherewith
Your majesty loads our house.

2.   There's no art
To find the mind's construction in the face:
He was a gentleman on whom I built
An absolute trust.

3.   Call country ants to harvest offices.

4.   Does the silkworm expend her yellow labours
For thee? For thee does she undo herself?
Are lordships sold to maintain ladyships
For the poor benefit of a bewildering minute?
Why does yon fellow falsify highways
And lays his life between the judge's lips
To refine such a one? Keeps horse and men
To beat their valours for her?

5.   On a huge hill,
Cragged and steep, Truth stands, and hee that will
Reach her, about must, and about must goe;
And what the hills suddennes resists, winne so . . .

6.   The pale road winds faintly upward into the dark skies,
And beside it on the rough grass that the wind invisibly stirs,
Sheltered by sharp-speared gorse and the berried junipers,
Shining steadily with a green light, the glow-worm lies.

We regard it; and this hill and all the other hills
That fall in folds to the river, very smooth and steep,
And the hangers and brakes that the darkness thickly fills
Fade like phantoms round the light and night is deep, so deep

That all the world is emptiness about the still flame
And we are small shadows standing lost in the huge night.
We gather up the glow-worm, stooping with dazzled sight,
And carry it to the little enclosed garden whence we came,

And place it on the short grass. Then the shadowy flowers fade,
The walls waver and melt and the houses disappear
And the solid town trembles into insubstantial shade
Round the light of the burning glow-worm, steady and clear.

7.   I am that creature and creator who
        Loosens and reins the waters of the sea,
        Forming the rocky marge anon anew.
        I stir the cold breasts of antiquity,
        And in the soft stone of the pyramid
        Move wormlike; and I flutter all those sands
        Whereunder lost and soundless time is hid.
        I shape the hills and valleys with these hands
        And darken forests on their naked sides,
        And call the rivers from the vexing springs,
        And lead the blind winds into deserts strange.
        And in firm human bones the ill that hides
        Is mine, the fear that cries, the hope that sings.
        I am that creature and creator, Change.

8.   Come out and walk. The last few drops of light
        Drain silently out of the cloudy blue;
        The trees are full of the dark-stooping night,
                The fields are wet with dew.

        All's quiet in the wood but, far away,
        Down the hillside and out across the plain,
        Moves, with long trail of white that marks its way,
                The softly panting train.

        Come through the clearing. Hardly now we see
        The flowers, save dark or light against the grass,
        Or glimmering silver on a scented tree
                That trembles as we pass.

        Hark now! So far, so far . . . that distant song . . .

Move not the rustling grasses with your feet.
The dusk is full of sounds, that all along
      The muttering boughs repeat.

So far, so faint, we lift our heads in doubt.
Wind, or the blood that beats within our ears,
Has feigned a dubious and delusive note,
      Such as a dreamer hears.

Again . . . again! The faint sounds rise and fail.
So far the enchanted tree, the song so low . . .
A drowsy thrush? A waking nightingale?
      Silence. We do not know.

9.   When you to Acheron's ugly water come
Where darkness is and formless mourners brood
And down the shelves of that distasteful flood
Survey the human rank in order dumb.
When the pale dead go forward, tortured more
By nothingness and longing than by fire,
Which bear their hands in suppliance with desire,
With stretched desire for the ulterior shore.
Then go before them like a royal ghost
And tread like Egypt or like Carthage crowned;
Because in your Mortality the most
Of all we may inherit has been found –
      Children for memory: the Faith for pride.
        Good land to leave: and young Love satisfied.

10.   You were a brute and more than half a knave,
Your mind was seamed with labyrinthine tracks
Wherein walked crazy moods bending their backs
      Under the grim loads. You were an open grave
For gold and love. Always you were the slave
      Of crooked thoughts (tortured upon the racks
Of mean mistrust). I made myself as wax
To your fierce seal. I clutched an ebbing wave.

Fool that I was, I loved you; your harsh soul
Was sweet to me: I gave you with both hands
Love, service, honour, loyalty and praise;

I would have died for you. And like a mole
You grubbed and burrowed till the shifting sands
Opened and swallowed up the dream-forged days.

11.   What's this of death, from you who never will die?
       Think you the wrist that fashioned you in clay,
       The thumb that set the hollow just that way
       In your full throat and lidded the long eye
       So roundly from the forehead, will let lie
       Broken, forgotten, under foot some day
       Your unimpeachable body, and so slay
       The work he most had been remembered by?
       I tell you this: whatever of dust to dust
       Goes down, whatever of ashes may return
       To its essential self in its own season,
       Loveliness such as yours will not be lost,
       But, cast in bronze upon his very urn,
       Make known him Master, and for what good reason.

12.   That time is dead for ever, child!
       Drowned, frozen, dead for ever!
                   We look on the past
                   And stare aghast
       At the spectres wailing, pale and ghast,
       Of hopes which thou and I beguiled
       To death on life's dark river.

       The stream we gazed on then rolled by;
       Its waves are unreturning;
                   But we yet stand
                   In a lone land,
       Like tombs to mark the memory
       Of hopes and fears, which fade and flee
       In the light of life's dim morning.

13.   Whence that low voice? — A whisper from the heart,
       That told of days long past, when here I roved
       With friends and kindred tenderly beloved;
       Some who had early mandates to depart,

Yet are allowed to steal my path athwart
By Duddon's side; once more do we unite,
Once more beneath the kind Earth's tranquil light;
And smothered joys into new being start.
From her unworthy seat, the cloudy stall
Of Time, breaks forth triumphant Memory;
Her glistening tresses bound, yet light and free
As golden locks of birch, that rise and fall
On gales that breathe too gently to recall
Aught of the fading year's inclemency!

14.   The One remains, the many change and pass;
Heaven's light for ever shines, Earth's shadows fly;
Life, like a dome of many-coloured glass,
Stains the white radiance of Eternity,
Until Death tramples it to fragments. – Die,
If thou wouldst be with that which thou dost seek!
Follow where all is fled! – Rome's azure sky,
Flowers, ruins, statues, music, words, are weak
The glory they transfuse with fitting truth to speak.

II

1.   The darkness crumbles away –
It is the same old druid Time as ever.
Only a live thing leaps my hand –
A queer sardonic rat –
As I pull the parapet's poppy
To stick behind my ear.
Droll rat, they would shoot you if they knew
Your cosmopolitan sympathies
(And God knows what antipathies).
Now you have touched this English hand
You will do the same to a German –
Soon, no doubt, if it be your pleasure
To cross the sleeping green between.
It seems you inwardly grin as you pass
Strong eyes, fine limbs, haughty athletes
Less chanced than you for life,
Bonds to the whims of murder,
Sprawled in the bowels of the earth,
The torn fields of France.
What do you see in our eyes
At the shrieking iron and flame
Hurled through still heavens?
What quaver – what hearts aghast?
Poppies, whose roots are in man's veins
Drop, and are ever dropping;
But mine in my ear is safe,
Just a little white with the dust.

2.   She lives to tell thee, thou art more inconstant
Than all ill women ever were together.
Thy faith is firm as raging overflows,
That no bank can command; as lasting
As boys' gay bubbles, blown i' th air and broken.
The wind is fix'd to thee; and sooner shall
The beaten mariner, with his shrill whistle,
Calm the loud murmur of the troubled main,
And strike it smooth again, than thy soul fall
To have peace in love with any: Thou art all

That all good men must hate; and if thy story
Shall tell succeeding ages what thou wert,
Oh! let it spare me in it . . .

3.   Softly, in the dusk, a woman is singing to me;
Taking me back down the vista of years, till I see
A child sitting under the piano, in the boom of the tingling strings
And pressing the small, poised feet of a mother who smiles as
   she sings.

In spite of myself the insidious mastery of song
Betrays me back, till the heart of me weeps to belong
To the old Sunday evenings at home, with winter outside
And hymns in the cosy parlour, the tinkling piano our guide.

So now it is vain for the singer to burst into clamour
With the great black piano appassionato. The glamour
Of childish days is upon me, my manhood is cast
Down in the flood of remembrance, I weep like a child for the past.

4.   You always had good luck; it has not failed you
Even in this, your brightest escapade,
But extricates you now
From the most cruel cunning trap of all,
Sets you at large and leaves no trace behind,
Except this dummy.
                O senseless hurricanes,
That waste yourselves upon the unvexed rock,
Find some employment proper to your powers,
Press on the neck of Man your murdering thumbs
And earn real gratitude! Astrologers,
Can you not scold the fated loitering star
To run to its collision and our end?
The Church and Chapel can agree in this,
The vagrant and the widow mumble for it
And those with millions belch their heavy prayers
To take away this luggage. Let the ape buy it
Or the insipid hen. Is Death so busy
That we must fidget in a draughty world
That's stale and useless; must we still kick our heels

And wait for his obsequious secretaries
To page Mankind at last and lead him
To the distinguished Presence?

5.   The night is freezing fast,
             Tomorrow comes December;
                And winterfalls of old
          Are with me from the past;
             And chiefly I remember
                How Dick would hate the cold.

          Fall, winter, fall; for he,
             Prompt hand and headpiece clever,
                Has woven a winter robe,
          And made of earth and sea
             His overcoat for ever,
                And wears the turning globe.

6.   Tears, idle tears, I know not what they mean,
          Tears from the depth of some divine despair
          Rise in the heart and gather to the eyes,
          In looking on the happy Autumn-fields
          And thinking of the days that are no more.

          Fresh as the first beam glittering on a sail,
          That brings our friends up from the underworld,
          Sad as the last which reddens over one
          That sinks with all we love below the verge;
          So sad, so fresh, the days that are no more.

          Ah, sad and strange as in dark summer dawns
          The earliest pipe of half-awaken'd birds
          To dying ears, when unto dying eyes
          The casement slowly grows a glimmering square;
          So sad, so strange, the days that are no more.

          Dear as remember'd kisses after death,
          And sweet as those by hopeless fancy feign'd
          On lips that are for others; deep as love,
          Deep as first love, and wild with all regret;
          O Death in Life, the days that are no more.

7.   If so, the shaft
Of mercy-winged lightning would not fall
On stones and trees. My wife and children sleep:
They are now living in unmeaning dreams:
But I must wake, still doubting if that deed
Be just which is most necessary. O,
Thou unreplenished lamp! whose narrow fire.
Is shaken by the wind, and on whose edge
Devouring darkness hovers! Thou small flame,
Which, as a dying pulse rises and falls,
Still flickerest up and down, how very soon,
Did I not feed thee, wouldst thou fail and be
As thou hadst never been! So wastes and sinks
Even now, perhaps, the life that kindled mine:
But that no power can fill with vital oil
That broken lamp of flesh. Ha! 'tis the blood
Which fed those veins that ebbs till all is cold:
It is the soul by which mine was arrayed
In God's immortal likeness which now stands
Naked before Heaven's judgment seat.

8.   Wake; the silver dusk returning
         Up the beach of darkness brims,
      And the ship of sunrise burning
         Strands upon the eastern rims

      Wake: the vaulted shadow shatters,
         Trampled to the floor it spanned,
      And the tent of night in tatters
         Straws the sky-pavilioned land.

9.   Out of the wood of thought that grows by night
      To be cut down by the sharp axe of light, –
      Out of the night, two cocks together crow,
      Cleaving the darkness with a silver blow.
      And bright before my eyes twin trumpeters stand,
      Heralds of splendour, one at either hand,
      Each facing each as in a coat-of-arms:
      The milkers lace their boots up at the farms.

10.   Oh
         My God! Can it be possible I have
         To die so suddenly? So young to go
         Under the obscure, cold, rotting, wormy ground:
         To be nailed down into a narrow place;
         To see no more sweet sunshine; hear no more
         Blithe voice of living thing; muse not again
         Upon familiar thoughts, sad, yet thus lost –
         How fearful! to be nothing! Or to be . . .
         What? Oh, where am I? Let me not go mad!
         Sweet Heaven, forgive weak thoughts! If there should be
         No God, no Heaven, no Earth in the void world;
         The wide, gray, lampless, deep, unpeopled world!

11.   Ay, but to die, and go we know not where,
         To lie in cold obstruction and to rot;
         This sensible warm motion to become
         A kneaded clod; and the delighted spirit
         To bathe in fiery floods, or to reside
         In thrilling region of thick-ribbed ice;
         To be imprison'd in the viewless winds,
         And blown with restless violence round about
         The pendent world; or to be worse than worst
         Of those that lawless and incertain thoughts
         Imagine howling: 'tis too horrible!
         The weariest and most loathed earthly life
         That age, ache, penury and imprisonment
         Can lay on nature is a paradise
         To what we fear of death.

I

1. Such are *their* ideas: such *their* religion, and such *their* law. But as
to *our* country and *our* race, as long as the well-compacted structure
of our church and state, the sanctuary, the holy of holies of that
ancient law, defended by reverence, defended by power, a fortress
at once and a temple, shall stand inviolate on the brow of the
British Sion – as long as the British monarchy, not more limited
than fenced by the orders of the state, shall, like the proud Keep
of Windsor, rising in the majesty of proportion, and girt with the
double belt of its kindred and coeval towers, as long as this awful
structure shall oversee and guard the subjected land – so long the
mounds and dykes of the low, fat, Bedford level will have nothing
to fear from all the pickaxes of all the levellers of France.

2. When two days previously, the news of the approaching end had
been made public, astonished grief had swept over the country.
It appeared as if some monstrous reversal of the course of nature
was about to take place. The vast majority of her subjects had
never known a time when Queen Victoria had not been reigning
over them. She had become an indissoluble part of their whole
scheme of things, and that they were about to lose her appeared
a scarcely possible thought. She herself, as she lay blind and silent,
seemed to those who watched her to be divested of all thinking
– to have glided already, unawares, into oblivion. Yet, perhaps,
in the secret chambers of consciousness, she had her thoughts,
too. Perhaps her fading mind called up once more the shadows
of the past to float before it, and retraced, for the last time, the
vanished visions of that long history – passing back and back,
through the cloud of years, to older and ever older memories –
to the spring woods at Osborne, so full of primroses for Lord
Beaconsfield – to Lord Palmerston's queer clothes and high de-
meanour, and Albert's face under the green lamp, and Albert's
first stag at Balmoral, and Albert in his blue and silver uniform,
and the Baron coming in through a doorway, and Lord M.
dreaming at Windsor with the rooks cawing in the elm-trees, and
the Archbishop of Canterbury on his knees in the dawn, and the
old King's turkey-cock ejaculations, and Uncle Leopold's soft
voice at Claremont, and Lehzen with the globes, and her mother's

feathers sweeping down towards her, and a great old repeater-watch of her father's in its tortoise-shell case, and a yellow rug, and some friendly flounces of sprigged muslin, and the trees and grass at Kensington.

3. If Newman had died at the age of sixty, today he would have been already forgotten, save by a few ecclesiastical historians; but he lived to write his *Apologia* and to reach immortality, neither as a thinker nor as a theologian, but as an artist who has embalmed the poignant history of an intensely human spirit in the magical spices of words.

4. The grainy sand had gone from under his feet. His boots trod again a damp crackling mast, razor-shells, squeaking pebbles, that on the unnumbered pebbles beat, woods sieved by the shipworm, lost Armada. Unwholesome sandflats waited to suck his treading soles, breathing upward sewage breath. He coasted them, walking warily. A porter-bottle stood up, stogged to its waist, in the cakey sand dough. A sentinel: isle of dreadful thirst. Broken hoops on the shore; at the land a maze of dark cunning nets; further away chalk-scrawled back-doors and on the higher beach a dryingline with two crucified shirts.

5. Through the large opening so suddenly made the life of the street came in like a puff of smoke. The voices under the window were much more numerous now. They were all fused together into a level nondescript buzz like that of a full ball-room or banquet-hall. This made a kind of ground colour of sound, with a vague neutral texture or tone of its own, nothing more; it was just a low wash of audible life. But now and again some separate and salient sound would plant itself on this indefinite background and show up against it. A snatch of song or chorus would break out into clearness. Or some lull would come; the background would fall down, as it were, to a fainter shade of itself, and a single voice would stand out for a little while, undulating in oratorical rises and falls, and so maintain a precarious distinctness till at some burst of laughter or cheers it was re-immersed in the general multitudinous hum.

6. They became silent to listen. The only near sound was the fussing

of some small bird late to bed and nervous about it. As foreground daisies stand out against a distant Mont Blanc, this clear little rustle was planted upon a vast and vague background of sound – an immense murmur that dinned and dinned on. You might have fancied you saw the huge hum rise from the city like a thin column of smoke and roll up to tarnish the stars with its fumes.

7.   Quiet descended upon her, calm, content, as her needle, drawing the silk smoothly to its gentle pause, collected the green folds together and attached them, very lightly, to the belt. So on a summer's day waves collect, overbalance and fall; collect and fall; and the whole world seems to be saying 'that is all' more and more ponderously, until even the heart in the body which lies in the sun on the beach says too, that is all. Fear no more, says the heart. Fear no more, says the heart, committing its burden to some sea, which signs collectively for all its sorrows, and renews, begins, collects, lets fall. And the body alone listens to the passing bee; the wave breaking; the dog barking, far away barking and barking.

8.   A cloud over the sun woke him to consciousness of his own thoughts; and he found with perplexity, that they were continually recurring to two periods of his life, the days after the death of his mother, and the time of his first deep estrangement from one he loved. After a bit he understood this. Now, as then, his mind had been completely divided into two parts: the upper running about aimlessly from one half-relevant thought to another, the lower unconscious half labouring with some profound and un-knowable change. This feeling of ignorant helplessness linked him with those past crises. His consciousness was like the light scurry of waves at full tide, when the deeper waters are pausing and gathering and turning home. Something was growing in his heart and he couldn't tell what.

9.   The realities and passions, the rumours of the greater world without, steal in upon us, each by its own special little passage-way, through the wall of custom about us: and never quite detach themselves from this or that accident, or trick, in the mode of their first entrance to us. Our susceptibilities, the discovery of our

powers, manifold experiences – our various experiences of the coming and going of bodily pain, for instance – belong to this or the other well-remembered place in the material habitation – that little white room with the window across which the heavy blossoms could beat so peevishly in the wind, with just that particular catch or throb, such a sense of teasing in it, on gusty mornings; and the early habitation thus gradually becomes a sort of material shrine or sanctuary of sentiment; a system of visible symbolism interweaves itself through all our thoughts and passions; and irresistibly, little shapes, voices, accidents – the angle at which the sun in the morning fell on the pillow – become parts of the great chain wherewith we are bound.

10.   The love of security, of an habitually undisputed standing-ground or sleeping-place, came to count for much in the generation and correcting of his thoughts, and afterwards as a salutary principle of restraint in all his wanderings of spirit. The wistful yearning towards home, in absence from it, as the shadows of evening deepened, and he followed in thought what he was doing there from hour to hour, interpreted to him much of a yearning and regret he experienced afterwards, towards he knew not what, out of strange ways of feeling and thought in which, from time to time, his spirit found itself alone; and in the tears shed in such absences there seemed always to be some soul-subduing foretaste of what his last tears might be.

And the sense of security would hardly have been deeper, the quiet of the child's soul being one with the quiet of its home, a place 'inclosed' and 'sealed'.

11.   Also Florian could trace home to this point a pervading preference in himself for a kind of comeliness and dignity, and *urbanity* literally, in modes of life, which he connected with the pale people of towns, and which made him susceptible to a kind of exquisite satisfaction in the trimness and well-considered grace of certain things and persons he met with, here and there, in his way through the world.

12.   Our friend had by this time so got into the vision that he almost gasped. 'After all she has done for him.' Miss Gostrey gave him

a look which broke the next moment into a wonderful smile. 'He is not so good as you think.' They remained with him, these words, promising him, in their character of warning, considerable help: but the support he tried to draw from them found itself, on each renewal of contact with Chad, defeated by something else. What could it be, this disconcerting force, he asked himself, but the sense, continually renewed, that Chad was – quite in fact insisted on being – as good as he thought? It seemed somehow as if he couldn't *but* be as good from the moment he wasn't as bad. There was a succession of days, at all events, when contact with him – and in its immediate effect as if it could produce no other – elbowed out of Strether's consciousness everything but itself. Little Bilham once more pervaded the scene, but little Bilham became, even in a higher degree than he had originally been, one of the numerous forms of the inclusive relation, a consequence promoted, to our friend's sense, by two or three incidents with which we have yet to make acquaintance. Waymarsh himself, for the occasion, was drawn into the eddy; it absolutely, though but temporarily, swallowed him down; and there were days when Strether seemed to bump against him as a sinking swimmer might brush against a submarine object. The fathomless medium held them – Chad's manner was the fathomless medium; and our friends felt as if they passed each other, in their deep immersion, with the round, impersonal eye of silent fish.

13. But heaven and earth was teeming around them, and how should this cease? They felt the rush of the sap in the spring, they knew the wave which cannot halt, but every year throws the seed forward to begetting, and, falling back, leaves the young-born on the earth. They knew the intercourse between heaven and earth, sunshine drawn into the breast and bowels, the rain sucked up in the day-time, nakedness that comes under the wind in autumn, showing the birds' nests no longer worth hiding. Their life and interrelation were such; feeling the pulse and body of the soil, that opened to their furrow for the grain, and became smooth and supple after their ploughing, and clung to their feet with a weight that pulled like desire, lying hard and unresponsive when the crops were to be shorn away. The young corn waved and was silken,

and the lustre slid along the limbs of the men who saw it. They took the udder of the cows, the cows yielded milk and pulse against the hands of the men, the pulse of the blood of the teats of the cows beat into the pulse of the hands of the men. They mounted their horses, and held life between the grips of their knees, they harnessed their horses at the wagon, and, with hand on the bridle-rings, drew the heaving of the horses after their will.

14. There was a long silence, during which the tide returned into Poole Harbour. 'One would lose something,' murmured Helen, apparently to herself. The water crept over the mud-flats towards the gorse and the blackened heather. Branksea Island lost its immense foreshores, and became a sombre episode of trees. Frome was forced inward towards Dorchester, Stour against Wimborne, Avon towards Salisbury, and over the immense displacement the sun presided, leaving it to triumph ere he sank to rest. England was alive, throbbing through all her estuaries, crying for joy through the mouths of all her gulls, and the north wind, with contrary motion, blew stronger against her rising seas. What did it mean? For what end are her fair complexities, her changes of soil, her sinuous coast? Does she belong to those who have moulded her and made her feared by other lands, or to those who have added nothing to her power, but have somehow seen her, seen the whole island at once, lying as a jewel in a silver sea, sailing as a ship of souls, with all the brave world's fleet accompanying her towards eternity?

15. The other smiled, and looked at his watch. They both regretted the death, but they were middle-aged men, who had invested their emotions elsewhere, and outbursts of grief could not be expected from them over a slight acquaintance. It's only one's own dead who matter. If for a moment the sense of communion in sorrow came to them, it passed. How indeed is it possible for one human being to be sorry for all the sadness that meets him on the face of the earth, for all the pain that is endured not only by men, but by animals and plants, and perhaps by the stones? The soul is tired in a moment, and in fear of losing the little she does understand, she retreats to the permanent lines which habit or chance have dictated, and suffers there.

II

I.   (a) We sat down by the side of the road to continue the argument begun half a mile or so before. I am certain it was an argument because I remember perfectly how my tutor argued and how without the power of reply I listened with my eyes fixed obstinately on the ground. A stir on the road made me look up – and then I saw my unforgettable Englishman. There are acquaintances of later years, familiars, shipmates, whom I remember less clearly. He marched rapidly towards the east (attended by a hang-dog Swiss guide) with the mien of an ardent and fearless traveller. He was clad in a knicker-bocker suit, but as at the same time he wore short socks under his laced boots, for reasons which, whether hygienic or conscientious, were surely imaginative, his calves exposed to the public gaze and to the tonic air of high altitudes, dazzled the beholder by the splendour of their marble-like condition and their rich tone of young ivory. He was the leader of a small caravan. The light of a headlong, exalted satisfaction with the world of men and the scenery of mountains illumined his clean-cut, very red face, his short, silver-white whiskers, his innocently eager and triumphant eyes. In passing he cast a glance of kindly curiosity and a friendly gleam of big, sound, shiny teeth towards the man and the boy sitting like dusty tramps by the roadside, with a modest knapsack lying at their feet. His white calves twinkled sturdily, the uncouth Swiss guide with a surly mouth stalked like an unwilling bear at his elbow; a small train of three mules followed in single file the lead of this inspiring enthusiast. Two ladies rode past one behind the other, but from the way they sat I only saw their calm, uniform backs, and the long ends of blue veils hanging behind far down over their identical hat-brims. His two daughters, surely. An industrious luggage mule, with unstarched ears and guarded by a slouching, sallow driver, brought up the rear. My tutor, after pausing for a look and a faint smile, resumed his earnest argument.

(b) There's a certain sort of man whose doom in the world is disappointment – who excels in it – and whose luckless triumphs in his meek career of life, I have often thought, must be regarded by the kind eyes above with as much favour as the splendid successes and achievements of coarser and more prosperous men. As I sat with the lieutenant upon deck, his telescope laid over his lean legs and he looking at the sunset with a pleased, withered old face, he gave me a little account of his history. I take it he is in nowise disinclined to talk about it, simple as it is: he has been seven-and-thirty years in the navy, being somewhat more mature in the service than Lieutenant Peel, Rear-Admiral Prince de Joinville, and other commanders who need not be mentioned. He is a very well-educated man, and reads prodigiously – travels, histories, lives of eminent worthies and heroes, in his simple way. He is not in the least angry at his want of luck in the profession. 'Were I a boy tomorrow,' he said, 'I would begin it again; and when I see my school-fellows, and how they have got on in life, if some are better off than I am, I find many are worse, and have no call to be discontented.' So he carries her Majesty's mails meekly through this world, waits upon port-admirals and captains in his old glazed hat, and is as proud of the pennon at the bow of his little boat, as if it were flying from the mainmast of a thundering man-of-war. He gets two hundred a year for his services, and has an old mother and a sister living in England somewhere, who I will wager (though he never, I swear, said a word about it) have a good portion of this princely income.

2.   Meantime it is my earnest request that so useful an undertaking may be entered upon (if their Majesties please) with all convenient speed, because I have a strong inclination before I leave the world to taste a blessing which we mysterious writers can seldom reach till we have got into our graves, whether it is that fame, being a fruit grafted on the body, can hardly grow and much less ripen till the stock is in the earth, or whether she conceives her trumpet sounds best and farthest when she stands on a tomb, by the advantage of a rising ground and the echo of a hollow vault.

3.   It is as dangerous to generalize about the poetry of the eighteenth century as about that of any other age; for it was, like any other age, an age of transition. We are accustomed to make a rough tripartite division between the poetry of the age of Pope, the poetry of sentimental philosophizing – Thomson, Young, Cowper

– and the early Romantic movement. What really happened is
that after Pope there was no one who thought and felt nearly
enough like Pope to be able to use his language quite successfully;
but a good many second-rate writers tried to write something
like it, unaware of the fact that the change of sensibility demanded
a change of idiom. Sensibility alters from generation to generation
in everybody, whether we will or no; but expression is only
altered by a man of genius. A great many second-rate poets, in
fact, are second-rate just for this reason, that they have not the
sensitiveness and consciousness to perceive that they feel differently
from the preceding generation, and therefore must use words
differently. In the eighteenth century there are a good many
second-rate poets, and mostly they are second rate because they
were incompetent to find a style of writing for themselves, suited
to the matter they wanted to talk about and the way in which
they apprehended this matter.

In such a period the poets who are still worth reading may be
of two kinds: those who, however imperfectly, attempted innovations in idiom, and those who were just conservative enough
in sensibility to be able to devise an interesting variation on the
old idiom. The originality of Gray and Collins consists in their
adaptation of an Augustan style to an eighteenth-century sensibility. The originality of Goldsmith consists in his having the old
and the new in such just proportion that there is no conflict; he
is Augustan and also sentimental and rural without discordance.
Of all the eighteenth-century poets, Johnson is the nearest to a
die-hard. And of all the eighteenth-century poets, Goldsmith and
Johnson deserve fame because they used the form of Pope beautifully, without ever being mere imitators. And from the point of
view of the artisan of verse, their kind of originality is as remarkable
as any other: indeed, to be original with the *minimum* of alteration,
is sometimes more distinguished than to be original with the
maximum of alteration.

4. My dear Wells, I am bound to tell you that I don't think your
letter makes out any sort of case for the bad manners of 'Boon',
as far as your indulgence in them at the expense of your poor
old H. J. is concerned – I say 'your' simply because he has *been*

yours, in the most liberal, continual, sacrificial, the most admiring and abounding critical way, ever since he began to know your writings: as to which you have had copious testimony. Your comparison of the book to a waste-basket strikes me as the reverse of felicitous, for what one throws into that receptacle is exactly what one doesn't commit to publicity and make the affirmation of one's estimate of one's contemporaries by. I should liken it much rather to the preservative portfolio or drawer in which what is withheld from the basket is savingly laid away. Nor do I feel it anywhere evident that my view of 'life and literature' or what you impute to me as such, is carrying everything before it and becoming a public menace – so unaware do I seem, on the contrary, that my products constitute an example in any measurable degree followed or a cause in any degree successfully pleaded: I can't but think if this were the case I should find it somewhat attested in their circulation – which, alas, I have reached a very advanced age in the entirely defeated hope of. But I *have* no view of life and literature, I maintain, other than that our form of the latter in especial is admirable exactly by its range and variety, its plasticity and liberality, its fairly living on the sincere and shifting experience of the individual practitioner.

5. The greatest poetry then, the poetry which most faithfully mirrors creative perfection, is of a temper that has reconciled the spontaneous and the enduring and attained wisdom in strength. For poetry both tests life and is tested by it. What authority attaches in the end to tumultuous aspiration, however musically expressed, and to all that passionate legislation which is the pitfall of inexperience? It holds us by the infection of a symbolical enthusiasm, for where there is so much ardour there must also be some vision, however nebulous and untried. It holds, it cannot convince us. But in the poet whom wisdom has ripened, aspiration has survived discernment. He confirms what we surmise with him of the possibilities of life by sharing with us his knowledge of its foundations. He sees the present and foresees the future. He has lived the good life and paid its price. His poetry is life itself, and flows from him with a sure promise.

6. The effect, if not the prime office, of criticism is to make our

absorption and our enjoyment of the things that feed the mind as aware of itself as possible, since that awareness quickens the mental demand, which thus in turn wanders further and further for pasture. This action on the part of the mind practically amounts to a reaching out for the reasons of its interests, as only by its so ascertaining them can the interest grow more various. This is the very education of our imaginative life; and thanks to it the general question of how to refine, and of why certain things refine more and most, on that happy consciousness becomes for us of the last importance. Then we cease to be only instinctive and at the mercy of chance, feeling that we can ourselves take a hand in our satisfaction and provide for it, making ourselves safe against dearth, and through the door opened by that perception criticism enters, if we but give it time, as a flood, the great flood of awareness; so maintaining its high tide unless through some lapse of our sense for it, some flat reversion to instinct alone, we block up the ingress and sit in stale and shrinking waters.

7. As things are, and as fundamentally they must always be, poetry is not a career, but a mug's game. No honest poet can ever feel sure of the permanent value of what he has written: he may have wasted his time and messed up his life for nothing. All the better, then, if he could have at least the satisfaction of having a part to play in society as worthy as that of the music-hall comedian.

8. Mr Housman has given us an account of his own experience in writing poetry which is important evidence. Observation leads me to believe that different poets may compose in very different ways; my experience (for what it is worth) leads me to believe that Mr Housman is recounting the authentic process of a real poet. 'I have seldom,' he says, 'written poetry unless I was rather out of health.' I believe that I understand that sentence. If I do, it is a guarantee – if any guarantee of that nature is wanted – of the quality of Mr Housman's poetry.

9. 'Again I laughed aloud and heartily; and thinking it was now my part of the game, I held out both my arms and protruded my whole body toward the stranger. He would not receive me from my father's neck, but he asked me with benignity and solicitude

if I was hungry; at which I laughed again, and more than ever: for it was early morning, soon after the first meal, and my father had nourished me most carefully and plentifully in all the days of famine. But Xanthus, waiting for no answer, took out of a sack, which one of his slaves carried at his side, a cake of wheaten bread and a piece of honey-comb, and gave them to me. I held out the honey-comb to my father's mouth, thinking it the most of a dainty. He dashed it to the ground; but seizing the bread, he began to devour it ferociously. This also I thought was in play; and I clapped my hands at his distortions . . . The more violent my cries, the more rapidly they hurried me away; and many were soon between us. Little was I suspicious that he had suffered the pangs of famine long before: alas! and he had suffered them for me. Do I weep while I am telling you they ended? I could not have closed his eyes; I was too young; but I might have received his last breath; the only comfort of an orphan's bosom. Do you now think him blameable, O Aesop?'

10.   (a) The Oxford Movement may be a spent wave, but, before it broke on the shore, it reared, as it successor is now rearing, a brave and beautiful crest of liturgical and devotional life, the force of which certainly shifted the Anglican sands, though it failed to uncover any rock-bottom underlying them. It is enough if now and then a lone swimmer be borne by the tide, now at its full, to be dashed, more or less urgently, upon the Rock of Peter, to cling there in safety, while the impotent wave recedes and is lost in the restless sea.

(b) The Oxford Movement may belong to the past, but before its end it produced, like its successor of to-day, a fine sense of liturgical devotional life, the force of which certainly had some effect on the looser elements of the Anglican Church, though it failed to reach any fundamental body of opinion. It is enough that the Movement, when at its height, led a few desperate individuals to become converted to the Church of Rome, and there these remained in security of mind when the Movement, losing its force, became a merely historical phenomenon.

COMMENTARY

Verse Passages I

1. *Macbeth* I, vi, lines 14–19. Discussed by Leavis in *How To Teach Reading* (1932) to show the inadequacy of Ezra Pound's conception of imagery, this passage reappears in *Education and the University* (1943) with the comment that 'it is in the incomplete realization of the metaphors that the realizing gift of the poet and the "realized" quality of the passage are manifest.' (pp. 77–78).

2. *Macbeth* I, iv, lines 12–13.

3. John Donne, 'The Sunne Rising', line 8. A discussion of this line opens 'Imagery and Movement', in *Scrutiny* XIII (1945), pp. 9–21. It is transferred verbatim to the similarly titled section of *The Living Principle* (1975), pp. 107–108. In the essay the opening stanza is printed in full; comment stops short of any reference to 'offices'.

4. Cyril Tourneur (or Thomas Middleton), *The Revenger's Tragedy* III, v, lines 71–79. An analysis of these lines follows the passage about (3) in the essay cited above, famous, it is observed, because of the use made of them by T. S. Eliot in 'Tradition and the Individual Talent' and 'Philip Massinger', *The Sacred Wood* (edition of 1928), pp. 56–57, 128: see *Selected Essays* (edition of 1951) pp. 20, 209.

5. John Donne, 'Satyre III', lines 79–82. Discussion of this piece follows that of (4) in the essay cited above but is preceded by paragraphs on 'realization' which refer to the 'globed peonies' of Keats's 'Ode on Melancholy' and the old Arden Shakespeare note on Lady Macbeth's 'Screw your courage to the sticking place . . .'

6. Edward Shanks, 'The Glow-worm', *The Queen of China* (1919), reprinted in *Georgian Poetry 1918–19* (1920), p. 143. Our copy of this handout bears the annotation 'Respect[able] Georgian verse – unobtrusive.'

7. John Freeman, 'Change', *Music* (1921), reprinted in *Georgian Poetry 1920–22* (1922), p. 72. Annotation on the handout: 'Cf. 9, both literary, general feebleness + an assured manner'. In *Penguin New Writing 35* (1948) Alan Pryce-Jones describes the neglect into which Freeman has fallen as 'inexplicable' in view of a few poems, including this one which he quotes

as 'the best of the sonnets'. See T. Rogers, ed., *Georgian Poetry 1911–1922: The Critical Heritage* (1977), p. 357. For Leavis on Pryce-Jones's role in the literary politics of the 1940s, see his 'Comment: Mr Pryce-Jones, The British Council and British Culture', *Scrutiny* XVIII (1951–52), pp. 224–28.

8. Edward Shanks, 'A Night Piece', *The Queen of China* (1919), reprinted in *Georgian Poetry 1918–1919* (1920), p. 141. Annotation: 'Unconscious reminiscence' [arrow pointing to lines 9–10]; 'Reminiscence of cadence' [against second stanza]; 'Keats' [against line 23]. During the 1920s Shanks was assistant editor of the anti-highbrow *London Mercury* and later chief leader writer of the *Evening Standard*.

9. Hilaire Belloc, *Complete Verse* (1954; revised edition of 1970), p. 17. Annotations imply a commentary on the allusions to Virgil and Dante.

10. Lord Alfred Douglas, 'The Unspeakable Englishman', *Complete Poems* (1928), p. 103. Annotations: 'Calling names − "strength"' [against lines 4–5]; 'No connection among images'. In 1933 Douglas published *The True History of Shakespeare's Sonnets*.

11. Edna St. Vincent Millay, *The Harp Weaver* (1923); *Collected Poems* (1956), p. 595. Annotation: 'Practical Criticism'; 'Eliz. B. B. mode', alluding to currency in USA of *Sonnets from the Portugese* [against line 3]; 'Literary quality' [against lines 4–5]; 'Confidence trick'; 'Brooke' [against line 7]; 'Unimpeachable' [underlined]; 'E. B. B. [Elizabeth Barrett Browning: against line 9]; 'Just words-poetical' [against line 11]; 'Feelings in the lead: what we ought to [be] feeling.' In the introduction to *English Literature in Our Time and the University* (p. 16) one of the 'protocols' concerning this poem in *Practical Criticism* (1929) is quoted and attributed to Mansfield Forbes, as exemplifying his 'essential vivacity'. Leavis would read these lines plangently.

12. P. B. Shelley, *Posthumous Poems* (1824): *Poetical Works*, ed. Hutchinson (1961 edition), p. 546. Excited and rather illegible annotations include: 'Wallowing; what danger attends upon this kind of undertaking; Shelley − not usually as bad as this. But he is *liable* to this.' At the head of the sheet there is the annotation 'Break, Break, Break and 519/542; 759', references presumably to the *Oxford Book of English Verse* (1935 edition). This poem is cited in *Revaluation*, p. 215, as representing the 'basest Regency album taste'. In 'Thought and Emotional Quality' reference to

it supports an assertion about Shelley's 'gross sentimentality'. In *The Living Principle*, p. 80, the whole poem is printed in a note to a similar passage.

13. William Wordsworth, *The River Duddon: A Series of Sonnets* (1821) XXI; *Poetical Works*, ed. Hutchinson and de Selincourt, p. 300. Annotations indicate that this was offered for comparison with the previous poem on the 'Practical Criticism' examination paper in Part Two of the 1929 English Tripos, a paper set by Mansfield Forbes. 'Wrong emphasis [against line 5, with 'athwart' ringed]; 'Spontaneity' [against lines 10–12]; 'Movement' [against lines 12–14]. In *Reading and Discrimination* (1934), p. 68, Denys Thompson offers this poem for comparison with Passage 12, which he has apparently failed to identify.

14. P. B. Shelley, *Adonais* (1821), lines 460–68. Commenting on the 'declamatory' quality of *Adonais* in *Revaluation*, p. 232, Leavis wrote of these lines 'the famous imagery is happily conscious of being impressive, but the impressiveness is for the spell-bound, for those sharing the simple happiness of intoxication.' In his seminars he would say that in the early 1920s he had learned the poem by heart in an effort to suppress obsessive thoughts and images resulting from his war experiences.

Verse Passages II

1. Isaac Rosenberg, 'Break of Day in the Trenches', *Complete Works* (1979), pp, 103–104. D. W. Harding quoted this poem to support his claim that 'it was Rosenberg's exposure of his whole personality that gave his work its quality of impersonality', *Scrutiny* III (1935), p. 364; see *Experience into Words* (1963), p. 98. Harding's terms are suggestive of those in which Leavis was developing his critique of Eliot's 'Tradition and the Individual Talent'.

2. Unidentified. If confidence that this is a piece of seventeenth-century dramatic blank verse (from a Caroline tragi-comedy?) needs some support, it is available in the jottings Leavis made on another handout which includes the passage. He does not identify the author, but the names 'Purcell' and 'Dryden' establish that this is not a pastiche, but a piece of verse which could provide the starting point for an account of seventeenth-century cultural development, such as is implicit in his comparison of *Antony and Cleopatra* and *All for Love*: see *Scrutiny* V (1936), pp. 158–69;

The Living Principle, pp. 144–55. The significant feature is the succession of separate and only loosely related similes to which the scribble 'Il-lust[rative?]' may refer.

3. D. H. Lawrence, 'Piano', (1918); *Complete Poems* ed. de Sola Pinto and Roberts (1964 and 1977), p. 148. This is 'Poem VIII' in Richards's *Practical Criticism* - about which Leavis himself supplied a 'protocol' printed by Richards. It is compared with Tennyson's 'Tears, Idle Tears' in 'Thought and Emotional Quality', *Scrutiny* XIII (1945), pp. 53–71. This section of the essay appears without revision in *The Living Principle*. The argument involves reference to the comparison of 'Piano' with Shanks's 'The Grey Land' made by D. W. Harding in 'A Note on Nostalgia', the opening essay in the first issue of *Scrutiny* in 1932.

4. Unidentified. Despite what could be taken for Audenesque mannerism at the beginning, it seems likely that this piece dates from the early 1920s. The attempt at sophisticated pastiche suggests Aldous Huxley's way with the stanzaic poems from Eliot's 1920 volume, and the understanding of Eliot's play with Shakespearean quotation and allusion is very much at his level. Here is more testimony to the popularity of the Eternal Footman passage from 'Prufrock'. While there is no way of telling whether Leavis talked about this passage immediately after 'Piano', the sequence makes it quite likely that some reference was made to Huxley's representative significance.

5. A. E. Housman, *Last Poems* (1922); *Collected Poems* (1939), p. 121. A Cambridge graduate of around 1950 recalls Leavis breaking off a reading of the poem to ask, 'Who is Dick?' The point would have been clearest to those who knew that G. H. W. Rylands had written: 'The Tom, Dick and Harry of *A Shropshire Lad* – Dick who hates the cold is the child of Dick the shepherd blowing his nail in *Love's Labours Lost* – correspond (despite their criminal tendencies) to Thestylis and Corydon in the artificial world.' (*Words and Poetry* [1928], p. 83) The choice of this poem was influenced, surely, by the apparent derivation of the second stanza from Wordsworth's 'A slumber did my spirit seal'.

6. Alfred, Lord Tennyson, 'Tears, Idle Tears', *The Princess: A Medley* (1847), *Poems*, ed. Ricks (1969), p. 748. See note to Passage 3.

7. P. B. Shelley, *The Cenci* (1819), III, ii, lines 1–24. The significance of

the Shakespearean reminiscences in this passage is discussed in *Revaluation*, pp. 224, 235–38.

8. A. E. Housman, 'Reveille', *A Shropshire Lad* (1896); *Collected Poems* (1939), p. 14. The comparison of these stanzas with Edward Thomas's 'Cock-Crow' was familiar to users of *Reading and Discrimination*: it represents an early stage of Leavis's unfinished 'Judgment and Analysis' project, in which he planned to write a book which would be more concerned with authority and method in analysis of poetry than Richards's book, which had essentially been concerned with the psychology of mostly rather incompetent readers. The comparison of the poems in 'Imagery and Movement' reappears in *The Living Principle*, pp. 122–24.

10. P. B. Shelley, *The Cenci*, V, iv, lines 48–60. The 'comparison' of this passage with Passage 11 appears in *Reading and Discrimination* where Thompson acknowledges (p. 25), that it is 'taken from a broadcast talk by Mr Eliot', before figuring in Leavis's Shelley chapter in *Revaluation*, pp. 225–27.

11. *Measure for Measure*, III, i, lines 117–27. See commentary on Passage 10. This speech is discussed in context in 'Measure for Measure', *The Common Pursuit*, pp. 164–65.

Prose Passages I

1. Edmund Burke, *A Letter to a Noble Lord* (1786); *Works*, World's Classics, VI pp. 65–66. The passage is discussed by Vernon Lee in *The Handling of Words* (1923) which was mentioned in the lecture. Jefford's notes suggest that Leavis drew attention to Lee's discussion of de Quincey's comment on it in *Rhetoric* in *Works* X, ed. Masson (1897). De Quincey chose it because Burke himself had chosen it to exemplify his dictum that every 'key' passage 'ought to involve a thought, an image, a sentiment' (evidently quoted by Leavis). A shift away from Lee's emphasis is indicated by Jefford's notes: 'Attention on audience. Shoddy appeal to mass prejudice.'

2. Lytton Strachey, *Queen Victoria* (1921), pp. 309–10, the final paragraph. Jefford's lecture-notes quote Leavis: 'Items in second part of passage an endeavour to replace what is missing in the first half. Mere contrivance (any item could be replaced by any other). Stylised dance of puppets. *A pue de procédé*.' The French exclamation is also inscribed on our copy of the handout. Leavis sometimes compared this passage unfavourably with

D. H. Lawrence's letter about the death of Rupert Brooke (to Lady Ottoline Morrell on 30 April 1915), on which he wrote at the end of 'Lawrence "Scholarship" and Lawrence' in 1963, reprinted in *'Anna Karenina' and Other Essays* (1967).

3. Lytton Strachey, 'Cardinal Manning', *Eminent Victorians* (1919; Phoenix Library, 1928), p. 14.

4. James Joyce, *Ulysses* (Bodley Head, 1960). Jefford's notes record that this passage was praised for 'specific realization', and contrasted with Passage 2. In *Reading and Discrimination* this is paired with another description of a man walking by the sea, ascribed to 'Anon'. Leavis had made it familiar to a Cambridge audience before I. A. Richards used it in *Coleridge on Imagination* (1935) to illustrate a change of perception that (Richards claimed) occurred between Defoe's *Robinson Crusoe* and Joyce's *Ulysses*. In the eighteenth century a walk on a beach mattered for what was happening; in the twentieth the very pulsations of the mind mattered: a person *merely* experiencing, 'for the sake of the appearances themselves or the reverberations of their *sensory* qualities in the percipient's mind'. This view of 'dissociation of sensibility' is criticised by Leavis in his review of Coleridge on Imagination, 'Dr Richards, Bentham and Coleridge', *Scrutiny* III (1935); reprinted in *Valuation in Criticism* (1986), pp. 151–166.

5. Unidentified. Jefford notes Leavis saying: 'Imagery accomplished – elaborated. Auditory-pictorial: static suggestion bad. "Plant" discordant.' The last phrase suggests that Leavis ignored prompting from the context to recognize that what was 'planted' would be the feet of a model in a life-class.

6. Unidentified. Jefford's notes record an ascription to C. E. Montague that may refer to this piece (as I would wish to believe) or to Passage 5. It is possible that remarks (noted by Jefford) about Dorothy L. Sayers indicate that she is the author. In 'The Case of Miss Dorothy Sayers', *Scrutiny* VI (1937), pp. 334–40, Q. D. Leavis lists Montague among writers with whom Sayers takes her place and whom 'she admires herself'. The choice of the passage is probably accounted for by the careless and unimaginative 'improvement' of the '"plant" metaphor' from Passage 5.

7. Virginia Woolf, *Mrs Dalloway* (1925), Penguin Modern Classics, pp. 44–45. It is difficult to guess where Leavis would have placed his emphasis

in discussing this passage. The best clues are the proximity on the sheet to Pater and the offer of Passage 8 for comparison.

8. Unidentified. It is particularly embarrassing that this piece should remain so since it seems to be offered as something against which the hypnotic routine of 'collect, overbalance and fall' in the Woolf can be judged. In this passage close attention to external fact is simultaneously disinterested comprehension of an inner condition. An impulse to look for it in D. H. Lawrence's *Kangaroo* should be checked by 'estrangement' and 'heart'.

9. Walter Pater, 'The Child in the House', *Macmillan's Magazine* (1878); *Miscellaneous Studies* (Library Edition, 1910), pp. 177–78.

10. Pater, *Miscellaneous Studies*, p. 180.

11. Pater, *Miscellaneous Studies*, p. 176. Jefford's notes: 'Aestheticism and immaturity. Difficult to attend, Pater not negligible – rep[resentative] – went on through Swinburne to Wilde. Yeats's early prose (1890s) more respectable. Pater's prose always "enclosed" or "sealed"'. The last observation suggests how these passages may have been linked with Passage 7. Jefford's 'Rossetti" confirms that Passage 11 was chosen for its reminiscence of *Hand and Soul*, a text that Leavis could quote, disconcertingly, from memory.

12. Henry James, *The Ambassadors* (1903), Book IV, Chapter 2; New York edition (1909), XXI, pp. 171–72. This passage gets extensive treatment in Vernon Lee, *The Handling of Words*, pp. 241–45. It seems from Jefford's notes that Leavis accepted her argument, subject to some qualifications about her use of 'abstract' that James achieves a 'concrete abstraction'. He did not use the passage to support the judgment of the novel which appears most memorably in 'Henry James and the Function of Criticism', *The Common Pursuit*, p. 225.

13. D. H. Lawrence, *The Rainbow* (1915); Penguin English Library edition, ed. Worthen (1981), p. 41. In *D. H. Lawrence: Novelist* (1955) Leavis writes of the passage from which this is an extract: 'Lawrence is not indulging in descriptive "lyricism" or writing poetically to generate atmosphere . . . words here establish as an actual presence . . . something that is essential to Lawrence's theme', p. 99. In cutting a sentence about the Brangwens'

habits of thrift from the beginning, Leavis appears to have been signalling his readiness to meet the audience's prejudices and preconceptions head on.

14. E. M. Forster, *Howards End* (1910); Abinger Edition (1973), p. 172. This is quoted in Leavis's essay on Forster (*The Common Pursuit*, p. 271) with a comment about its 'poeticality (which had there been a real grasp behind his intention, Mr Forster would have seen to be Wilcox rather than Schlegel) . . .'

15. E. M. Forster, *A Passage to India* (1924); Abinger Edition (1978), p. 235. There is a detailed discussion of this in the essay cited immediately above (pp. 274–75), in the course of which Leavis reflects 'how extraordinary it is that so fine a writer should be able, in such a place, to be so little certain just how serious he is.'

Prose Passages II

1. (a) Joseph Conrad, *A Personal Record* (1912); *Collected Edition* (1946), pp. 4041. An idea of how this and the following passages were handled can be gained from the section on 'Prose' in *The Living Principle*, pp. 140–43, where the source of the 'comparison', in an unspecified English Tripos examination paper, is acknowledged. (b) Ascribed by Leavis (*The Living Principle*, p. 142), to Frederick Marryat (Captain Marryat). During the twenty-odd years in which Leavis used this piece he did not verify his 'guess', but neither, it seems, did he meet with contradiction.

2. Jonathan Swift, *The Tale of a Tub* (1705), Section X; *Prose Works*, ed. Davis (1934), I, p. 118. Discussed in *The Living Principle*, p. 137.

3. T. S. Eliot, 'Introductory Essay', *London: a Poem . . . by Samuel Johnson* (1930); *The New Pelican Guide to English Literature* (1991), IV, p. 282. When Leavis reprinted *How To Teach Reading* as an Appendix to *Education and the University* (1943), he added a 'Note' to the 'Critical Method' section in which he quotes this paragraph, introducing it with his often-to-be-repeated remark, 'You can't write like that, but it can do you nothing but good to try!' In it he also regretted that this Eliot essay was not in *Selected Essays*, but advertised its presence in the World's Classics volume, *English Critical Essays: Twentieth Century (Second Series)*.

4. Henry James, letter to H. G. Wells, 10 July 1915: *Henry James and H.*

G. *Wells* . . ., ed. Edel and Ray (1958), pp. 265–66; *Letters*, ed. Edel (1984), IV, pp. 768–69. The chapter about James which Wells inserted in *Boon* shortly before publication had had as its immediate pretext the essay represented by Passage 6.

5. Unidentified. The metaphors ('mirrors', 'tumultuous', 'foundations', 'flows from') insist that there is nothing to be said, that the last thing we want is that the writer should really try to say something about poetry. Vague, flattering allusions to texts about which it is quite proper to be vague ('passionate legislation') are much more the thing. It looks like literary journalism of the 1920s. Would Sir John Squire have been capable of the clichéd vulgarity ('the good life . . . paid the price')?

6. Henry James, 'The New Novel', *Notes on Novelists* (1914), pp. 249–50. Apropos of another passage from this essay, Leavis wrote 'And again the student should note the way in which the criticism is conveyed. James has his idiosyncrasy of expression, but his essential method, his approach and movement in criticism, can hardly be imitated. The learning that can be done by the reader is only of the right kind.' 'James as Critic', *Henry James: Selected Literary Criticism* (1963), ed. Shapira, p. xxii.

7. T. S. Eliot, 'Conclusion', *The Use of Poetry and the Use of Criticism* (1933), p. 154. The inclusion of this and the following passage is explained by 'T. S. Eliot's Stature as a Critic: A Revaluation', *Commentary* (November, 1958), pp. 399–410; *'Anna Karenina' and Other Essays*, pp. 177–196.

8. T. S. Eliot, review of A. E. Housman, *The Name and Nature of Poetry* (1933) in the *Criterion* (October 1933) XIII, p. 133.

9. Walter Savage Landor, 'Aesop and Rhodope'; *Imaginary Conversations of the Greeks and Romans* (1853); *Complete Works*, ed. Welby, I (1927), p. 22. From Jefford's notes it appears that when Leavis referred to Vernon Lee on Burke, he recommended also her pages on Landor. 'One might imagine that Landor sometimes thinks his sentences first as grammar and syntax . . . and then fits in the items irrespective of their values as meaning.' 'Landor . . . appeared to me in the semblance of a boy provided, by heartless teachers, with a theme, and obliged to produce a given number of lines thereon.' *The Handling of Words*, Weekend Library edition (1927), pp. 165, 170.

10 (a) Herbert Read's identification, in *English Prose Style* (1928), p. 29, is 'M. A. Chapman, in *Blackfriars*, April 1921. (Quoted by Stephen J. Brown, *The World of Imagery*, p. 308).' (b) Read's 'translation' of Passage 10a in *English Prose Style*. A discussion of these passages opens the 'Prose' section of the 'Judgment and Analysis' chapter of *The Living Principle*, pp. 135–36: 'In eliminating [the metaphors] Read has eliminated the writer's insistent intention – his essential thought, it can fairly be said.'

MODE D'EMPLOI

These notes are offered in the belief that interpretive effort need not be, should not be, deferred. One way to start is by suggesting a title for each sheet.

Verse: I – A Discipline and its History. The discipline is made visible first as a narrowing of focus so pronounced as to provoke questions and objections (e.g. is Leavis that interested in *The Revenger's Tragedy*?). The Tourneur passage invokes Eliot (a myth of origin?), but the scene of the history is definitely Cambridge. The series of poems opened by Edward Shanks's 'The Glow-worm' ends with the Millay used by Richards in *Practical Criticism*. In *English Literature in Our Time and the University* Leavis attributed to Mansfield Forbes a comment on this poem reproduced by Richards in *Practical Criticism*:

> This is a studied orgasm from a 'Shakespeare – R. Brooke' complex, as piece 7 from a 'Marvell – Wordsworth – Drinkwater, etc., stark-simplicity complex'. Hollow at first reading; resoundingly hollow at second. A sort of thermos vacuum; 'the very thing' for a dignified picnic in this sort of Two-Seater Sonnet. The 'Heroic' Hectoring of line 1, the hearty quasi-stoical buttonholing of the unimpeachably equipped beloved, the magisterial finger-wagging of 'I tell you this'! Via such conduits magnanimity may soon be laid on as an indispensable, if not obligatory, modern convenience.

The passage on the sheet is an allusion to Forbes (formative for Cambridge English – and Leavis), amongst other things. The passage had resonance far away from Cambridge, England. Edmund Wilson recorded (in *The Shores of Light*) that 'In 1920 . . . I read in the March issue of the new literary magazine, *The Dial*, a sonnet called "To Love Impuissant", which I immediately got by heart and found myself declaiming in the shower.'

The practice of reading which the lecture demonstrated is oppositional in character. This character was preserved in the paper which Forbes set when 'Practical Criticism' was first examined in Part Two of the newly divided English Tripos in 1929. From that paper Leavis took the comparison passages which set 'That time is dead for ever, child!' ('the basest Regency album taste') against 'Whence that low voice?' which meets it 'athwart' (Forbes's cunning places the poem so that its most obvious flaw acquires an unexpected significance.) In an audience who scanned this handout over a period of three or four weeks the placing together of the Millay poem and Lord Alfred Douglas's 'The Unspeakable Englishman' would have aroused a good deal of speculation, some of it quite uneasy. The situation was constructed so as to produce a felt need for 'a delicately exacting discipline for relevance'.

Verse: II – Reading, Interpretation, Performance. The second sheet begins with two passages which do not stand in any obvious relation. The point about the unidentified second passage is that it goes by itself, or it does if the reader has acquired the real, specialized, very limited accomplishment it demands. If one asks oneself why 'Piano' and 'Tears, Idle tears', such familiar companions, have been separated here, the answer may be that it is the best way to bring out the different kinds of performance they demand. (The final line of 'Piano' reminds the reader that it is a text for, as well as about, performance.)

Prose: I – The Problem of Prose, in Cambridge. The coherence of the first prose sheet seems clear enough and possibly undiscussable, except in terms borrowed from Leavis himself. Comment is not superfluous, however, because what might be missed is the position being taken in relation to the tradition, very much part of Cambridge English, that is represented by F. L. Lucas's *Style* (1955). Certainly Lucas had his reservations about Lytton Strachey as a model for undergraduate essay writers, but as far as he was conerned *procédés* were there to be learned and practised. Against the unassailable confidence Lucas had inherited, Leavis sets the witness of Vernon Lee, who when she published *The Handling of Words* (1923) had not only outlived the Paterine persona of *Euphorian* (1884), but offered telling reflections on the process. She was more intelligent than Herbert Read in *English Prose Style*, Jefford notes Leavis as observing. She had indeed a curiosity about the psychology of reading more lively and profitable than I. A. Richards's. Evidence of that comes from her discussion of the place of Burke which heads this sheet, a piece which in this position seems to inaugurate several historical narratives, besides that in which she figures. The Pater passages appear to have been chosen to create similar opportunities. The lectures did not allow any of these narratives a dominant role, but scanning the handout, the audience, noting (for instance) a relation between Burke's 'poetry' and that of the extract from *Howards End*, could enjoy a sense of being wealthy in such possibilities. They found themselves in circumstances that allowed them to recognize the poverty revealed by I. A. Richards's improvization with the passage from *Ulysses* (here No. 4) which he may or may not have borrowed from Leavis.

Prose: II – Learning to Write Criticism: Desire, Impersonation, Identity. The second prose sheet does not, as it might appear, offer the basis for an early, rather diffuse version of the 'Prose' section of 'Judgment and Analysis' in *The Living Principle*. The passages dropped, as it were, from discussion in the essay introduce the topics of parody (the Henry James letter), attempted mimicry in the biological sense (Nos. 7 and 8), mere going through the motions, and variously inimitable models of critical discourse (Eliot on eighteenth-century poetry, James on the nature of literary criticism). It is the placing of the Conrad passage at the beginning which establishes the coherence of this material. Not that Leavis should be suspected of pointing this out; the commentary in *The Living Principle* corresponds closely to my own fragmentary recollection of a lecture. To make the function of the passage explicit would involve a difficult excursion into gender theory. Conrad's first Englishman does not tempt the narrator to expose his calves, nor to go in for some expensive dentistry, let alone to aspire to the possession of female dependants by whom his independence could be defined. Certainly, the Englishman is an object of desire but he is deeply memorable, however, because he brings to consciousness the narrator's desire for his own gendered identity, that which, if only because he will continue to represent it to himself, he will never simply be. This is not, of course, what Leavis says Conrad says. He would have rejected the interpretation because he rejects interpretation. It would have been enough that the suggestive power of the Conrad would have become apparent, to those capable of responding to it, as the lectures proceeded. It is the arrangement of the handout which elicits the meaning.

Education and the University: Structure and Sources

Education and the University: A Sketch for an 'English School' (1943) is a relatively short book, but it contains a disorientating variety of different subjects and styles, exemplifying in extreme form Leavis's habit of quoting from and re-using his own previously published work. Leavis published four articles under the heading 'Education and the University' in *Scrutiny* between 1940 and 1943, but there is no exact correspondence between these articles and the book of the same title, which contains material dating back to 1932. The first chapter, 'The Idea of a University', incorporates material from both a 1934 and a 1943 article. It deals in general issues, relating the case for a modern liberal education to the nature of humanism as concrete rather than theoretical. This is offered as groundwork for the second chapter, 'A Sketch for an "English School"', which is really the core of *Education and the University* and its most distinctive element. This chapter draws again on the 1934 article for some more general observations on teaching and examination methods, but chiefly consists of Leavis's proposal for an English course that could form the final part of an Honours degree at Cambridge. In marked contrast to the first chapter, the 'Sketch' is absorbingly detailed and specific: Leavis even goes so far as to present in tabular form a list of possible topics for special study and 'a summary of the scheme, rather like that which might appear in a *Student's Handbook*' (I have reproduced the summary, and the corresponding details from the actual *Student's Handbook*, at the end of this chapter). After this the third chapter, 'Literary Studies', seems in many ways more like the first of the Appendices than a conclusion to the main argument. It consists mainly of 'detailed illustration' of the kind of literary study that the student taking Leavis's proposed Part II course should already have been well trained in at school and in Part I. The sense of an Appendix is heightened by the fact that most of this material is presented as a long quotation from another book by Leavis, not yet (and in fact never) published. This chapter is followed by two genuine Appendices. The first, Leavis's review of 'T.S. Eliot's Later Poetry', which originally appeared in *Scrutiny* in Summer 1942, seems at first to continue the kind of 'detailed illustration' of attentive critical reading offered in the last Chapter. But the kind of analysis demonstrated is in fact much less rigorously detailed: its avowed purpose is to substantiate Leavis's point, made in the first Chapter and exemplified (as he saw it) in Eliot's later poetry, about the concrete and creative nature of 'humanism'. The second Appendix is an edited version of *How To Teach Reading: A Primer for Ezra Pound*, Leavis's pamphlet originally published by the Minority Press in 1932. With its numerous sub-headings and occasional 'pamphleteering emphasis' (p. 107) it provides yet another strong contrast within the book. Yet it contains in embryonic form many of the points developed in the later essays that make up the main part of *Education and the University*. In such a short book the importance of these two quite bulky additions to the main text should not be discounted. When *Education and the University* was reprinted in 1948 a third Appendix was added, the complete text of Leavis's 1930 pamphlet, *Mass Civilization and Minority Culture*, which meant that almost exactly half the book consisted of Appendices. The complete book had become in itself a kind of 'sketch' of Leavis's writing career up to 1943.

It is not possible here to explore the full significance of Leavis's argument in *Education and the University*. But we can at least note some details of the various stages it went through, from the source documents to the final text and on to later restatements. In his 1943 Preface Leavis claimed that *Education and the University* addressed 'problems' which had formed his 'main preoccupation for twenty years' – a period corresponding roughly to his career as a university teacher, which began in 1924. As a teacher his initial preoccupation had been with speaking rather than writing: 'finding out how to talk to the point about poems, novels and plays, and how to promote intelligent and profitable discussion of them.'[1] The developing argument of *Education and the University* can be traced from the moment when these interests combined with those of the 'aspiring critic' – once Leavis had established himself as an author and editor, in other words – and particularly from two works, a pamphlet and a short review, published near the end of 1932.

How To Teach Reading, which took the form of a response to Ezra Pound's *How To Read*, seems to have been written after the first two numbers of *Scrutiny* were published.[2] Leavis praised Pound's general account of the function of literature in society, but criticized his rather eccentric proposals for a 'minimum basis for a sound and liberal education in letters'. He then turned this into an opportunity to set out his own 'Positive Suggestions', many of which eventually found their way, modified or developed, into the second and third chapters of *Education and the University*. He even included a detailed 'scheme of work' which focused on the seventeenth century and was clearly the germ of the more detailed course later set out in the 'Sketch'. The other important stimulus to the formulation of imaginary schemes came from an American book, Alexander Meiklejohn's *The Experimental College*, which Leavis reviewed in *Scrutiny* in December 1932 in a short article entitled 'An American Lead'.[3] *The Experimental College* was adapted from a detailed report, submitted to the University of Wisconsin, Madison, on the educational experiment at Madison over which Meiklejohn had presided from 1927 to 1932. With the support of the new President at Madison (Glenn Frank, to whom Pound's *How To Read* had been ironically dedicated), Meiklejohn and his team of 'Advisers' had been allowed to devise and run an alternative 'lower college' course, which attempted to overcome the problems of fragmentation and 'disarticulation' which the elective system seemed to have produced. The attempt at reform was typical of many American colleges, as Meiklejohn himself noted: what was distinctive about his experiment was his 'single enterprise' principle, whereby all the different subjects studied were related to a comparative study of fifth-century Athens and modern America. The aim was to devise a form of liberal education which was not just an accumulation of unrelated specialisms but a general training of the intelligence. Leavis admired the scope of Meiklejohn's approach, but the emphasis on 'intelligence' gave him an obvious 'Yes, but . . .' cue, since he had already argued in several key articles that the right kind of critical 'intelligence' was inseparable from a complementary critical 'sensibility'.[4] The Experimental College syllabus, for example, required students to compare Greek Tragedy in translation with *Mourning Becomes Electra* by Eugene O'Neill – for Leavis this was a telling example of intelligence applied without any sense of relative value:

It is not merely that without an ability to read literature (that is, to see

that Eugene O'Neill doesn't exist), and without a sense of the human
tradition such as cannot be acquired apart from an education in literature,
one cannot acquire the sense of 'human values' desiderated. It is that,
if one cannot see that it is impossible to read Aeschylus (in English or
Greek) as one reads Shakespeare, then one cannot read Shakespeare in
any serious sense; and if one cannot read Shakespeare, then one cannot
think (with the kind of 'thinking', at least, that I am sure Dr Meiklejohn,
if it were put to him, would agree to be implied in his undertaking).
(p. 299)

Leavis returned to this particular example of the Experimental College
programme in the final text of *Education and the University,* and he even
adapted one or two phrases from the above paragraph. He did not repeat
the statement 'Eugene O'Neill doesn't exist', however; and the statement
'if one cannot read Shakespeare, then one cannot think . . .' modulated
into 'if you cannot read Shakespeare, then your intelligence has missed
an essential training – however rigorous the linguistic, logical and philosophical trainings you may have had.'[5]

Leavis ended 'An American Lead' with the promise of a more detailed
response, and it seems clear that what he already had in mind was the
kind of alternative proposal that eventually materialized in his 'Sketch for
an English School':

> The true tribute to Dr Meiklejohn and his colleagues would be to
> suggest how the spirit, and, to a great extent, the technique, of the
> Experimental College, might be applied in a real training of intelligence,
> a real education, which should start from, and be always closely associated
> with, the training of sensibility in the literature of the student's own
> language (where alone it is possible). But this must wait until the next
> number of *Scrutiny.* (pp. 299–300)

In fact it had to wait much longer than that, as Leavis wryly acknowledged
when he quoted this paragraph at the beginning of his 1934 article 'Why
Universities?'. Leavis immediately announced, moreover, that he was still
not ready to present 'plans for a rival Experimental College'. There were
'prior considerations':

> If, with an eye on the actual conditions in front of us, we ask what it
> is worth hoping to see attempted in this country, there are certain
> generalities to handle first; and a truly practical spirit inhibits a blithe
> advance into detailed schemes.[6]

For tactical reasons, Leavis opted at this stage for theory rather than practice, and posed the general question: 'What, then, is the function of the university?' (p. 117) Meiklejohn had been concerned to develop a form of modern liberal education that would counter the 'drift of American life'. Leavis shared this concern, and devoted several paragraphs in 'Why Universities?' to his own diagnosis of 'general technocratic drift' in modern civilization.[7] But he felt it was a mistake to conceptualize a solution to this problem solely in terms of education – of *producing* a new kind of citizen:

> How to produce the 'educated man' – the man of humane culture who is equipped to be intelligent and responsible about the problems of contemporary civilization – is an urgent study, but a study that apart from an adequate 'Idea of a University' is likely to end in despair.[8]

It was not enough to fashion individual minds via a scheme of liberal education: there had to be a collective central mind – a 'centre of co-ordination and of consciousness'[9] – and materializing this centre was the true function or determining 'Idea' of a University.

The problem then became how to relate the two different functions represented by 'education' and 'university'. Here Leavis quoted from another American essay, Brooks Otis's 'Thoughts After Flexner', which seemed to acknowledge the need for a centre but formulated it in terms of 'a genuine philosophical and historical unification, which will exhibit the actual interplay of ideas, influences, and forces . . . It might not be too much to say that we need for our own age what the *Summa* of Thomas Aquinas was for his.'[10] Leavis described this as an 'admirable theoretical statement of the problem' – but to have to wait for a modern *Summa,* he suggested, was a 'paralysing' prospect. A readier way to achieve 'actual interplay of ideas', if not a final unification, was for university specialists to engage in a project like the Experimental College. Here Leavis drew on one of the passages from Meiklejohn's report that he most admired, and which seems fundamental to the whole argument of *Education and the University*:

> It must be possible, it must be arranged, that all members of the teaching force shall have genuine and intimate intellectual acquaintance with one another. This is another way of saying that the teachers, as they attempt to educate their pupils, must themselves be gaining education from one

another, and from their common enterprise. They must be trying to create the wisdom which they wish to impart.[11]

Meiklejohn had been describing a college within a university but, Leavis added, 'a university should be an inclusive and more complex "common enterprise"'.

Leavis had made clear, then, that if he did go on to develop his own 'plans for a rival Experimental College', this would be the fundamental organizing principle: it would not be designed simply to produce a new kind of 'educated man' but to activate (Leavis's rather odd choice of word was actually 'innervate'[12]) the 'Idea of a University'. By functioning as a site of 'interplay', 'informal intercourse' and 'common enterprise' the university would become the humanizing centre of an otherwise de-humanizing modern society:

> The universities make it possible to hope something of education because their function, fully performed, comprises so much more than any talk of education can suggest. It is pre-eminently their responsibility, in our time, to make the 'autonomy' spoken of real; to represent it and assert it in every way. They are its appointed organs; and now as never before would it be disastrous, for the world and for them, to lend any colour to the contemptuous use of the word 'academic'. If they stand for a measure of withdrawal from the common grind and pressure of the world they make possible, not merely a cloistral vegetation, but also a free play of spirit and a concentration of humane forces impossible anywhere else.[13]

The core of 'Why Universities?' was reproduced with hardly any changes in 'The Idea of a University', Chapter One of *Education and the University*. Leavis replaced the paragraph quoted above, however, with a long quotation from his recent editorial 'After Ten Years', in which *Scrutiny* was seen as embodying the function he had outlined in more general terms before: 'The promoters of *Scrutiny* . . . were consciously appealing to the idea that it was more than ever the *raison d'etre* of a university to be, amid the material pressures and dehumanizing complications of the modern world, a focus of humane consciousness, a centre . . .'[14] Several more paragraphs from 'Why Universities?', in which Leavis briefly compared Meiklejohn's examination system with the Cambridge English Tripos, were reproduced in Chapter Two as part of his 'Sketch'.[15] But in 1934, having briefly raised the question 'whether, at Cambridge, something might not be made of the English Tripos' (p. 125) he was reluctant to go much further with a 'detailed scheme of reform and experiment' (p. 126). He made one or two interesting suggestions in passing, however, such as that 'there would have been some point in setting Newman's *Idea of a University* for special study if Dr Meiklejohn's book (and, one now adds, Mr Otis's essay) had been set at the same time' (pp. 129–30). The idea that students should study and discuss 'the general problem of humane education (*The Experimental College* and any other suitable texts being used)' was retained in Leavis's later proposals.[16] But the specific (and only) reference to Newman was dropped – a deliberate break with the figure classically associated with 'the Idea of a University'.

Between 1934 and 1940 several more articles appeared in *Scrutiny* on the universities and liberal education. Leavis's main contribution to the debate was to edit 'The Spens Report: A Symposium-Review' in 1939. This article, which collated the views of eight different contributors, was unsigned. But Leavis quoted the epigraph and introductory paragraphs at the beginning of his final 'Education and the University' article in 1943 and attributed them to 'the present writer', so it seems reasonable to assume that he edited the whole article.[17] The Spens Report was mainly concerned with secondary education rather than the universities: Leavis seems to have used the 'Symposium-Review' to air a particularly hostile view of the process of reform which it represented. 'Symposium' is somewhat misleading, because three quarters of the article was given over to the views of one contributor, a 'radically adverse critic' of the Report who argued that the idea of liberal education was being undermined by widening access since it was originally intended – in a pre-industrial 'stable society' – for 'no more than a small number of persons, those who, among other things, might be called upon to guide society through unforeseen contingencies' (pp. 255–6). These were not necessarily Leavis's views, but they had an oblique bearing on his argument in *Education and the University*. When he published his 'Sketch' in 1940 he emphasized that the course he proposed would be 'taken by a comparatively small number of students': 'For the reformed Part II – this would be a condition of its influence and importance – would be essentially designed for an *elite*.'[18]

'Sketch for an English School', published in September 1940, represented a crucial stage in the development and presentation of Leavis's argument: 'challenged, then, to say how one's generalities could be brought into any relation with practice, how one's principles could be put into effect, here is the reply.'[19] Leavis's sense of such a challenge dated back to the embattled early years of *Scrutiny*. He suggested that the wartime context ('by common consent an occasion for radical searchings and stocktakings') provided a 'licence' to respond at last (p. 101). But his decision to publish his Cambridge-based proposals at this moment may have had more to do with the recent renewal of his Lectureship to the retiring age. Relatively secure at last (he had not had a Faculty post at all in 1934) he could afford to be less scrupulous about 'seeming to usurp the office of an authorized committee on reform' (p. 101). Tripos reform had also become more topical: in the immediate pre-war years there had been an undergraduate movement for reform of the Cambridge English Tripos, and Leavis had contributed to a programme of alternative lectures and seminars organized by the dissatisfied English Club in 1938–9.[20]

'Reform' and 'Licence' are the two poles between which Leavis's 'sketch' oscillates. On the one hand it appears to be offered as a serious and practical proposal for reform of the existing second part of the Cambridge English Tripos:

> The aim is to suggest nothing more than, once embodied in the report of an authorized committee would, it can be imagined, have a good chance of being implemented by authority.[21]

On the other hand, as 'suggest' and 'imagined' imply even here, the 'sketch' is also a kind of indulgence. Leavis several times anticipates that it will attract the label 'Utopian', and in the 1943 version he admitted that he was sketching his 'ideal university' (p. 39). His reference to a 'reformed Part II' is ironic, since the course outlined in the 'Sketch' retained hardly any recognizable elements of the existing Part II. For all the repeated gestures towards practicality, it is hard to imagine that his proposals could have been accommodated within the brief of any authorized 'reform' committee. For what was envisaged was much more than a course amendment: it entailed a radical critique and reconstruction of established teaching and assessment methods, replacing the traditional regime of lecture, supervision and formal examination, with an emphasis on group discussion and assessment of prepared 'pieces of work'. The precedent for this comprehensive approach came from Meiklejohn, whose sweeping brief for the Experimental College had covered all 'the determining conditions of undergraduate liberal instruction'.[22]

The other aspect of the Experimental College that Leavis particularly admired was the integrating function of Meiklejohn's Athens-America scheme. This clearly provided a model for the major *curricular* innovation of Leavis's 'sketch' – his proposal that most of the course work should focus on one historical period, 'the Seventeenth Century, not merely in literature, but as a whole; the Seventeenth Century as a key phase, or passage, in the history of civilization'.[23] Leavis introduced this idea by pointing out that the existing Tripos provided for an optional paper called 'Special Period of English Literature'. But again the apparent similarity was misleading, since his proposal was for much more than one paper, and the period focus he envisaged was not optional but integral to the course (there were, in fact, no optional components in his scheme). Moreover, the original Special Period had varied from year to year, whereas the Seventeenth Century was uniquely significant in Leavis's interpretation of English history:

> It is at one end in direct and substantial continuity with the world of Dante, and it shows us at the other a world that has broken irretrievably with the mediaeval order and committed itself completely to the process leading directly and rapidly to what we live in now.[24]

This reading of history was clearly derived from Eliot's early essays (cited later as useful reading). What Leavis was proposing was in effect a broad study of the 'dissociation of sensibility' – one that would inevitably involve the student in a comparative diagnosis of the condition of the modern world. Indeed one of the required 'pieces of work' was to write a historical narrative – a kind of 'chart' – showing how the modern world had developed from this 'key phase . . . in the history of civilization'.

Almost all of Leavis's 'Sketch' (apart from some necessary introductory material reviewing the argument of 'Why Universities?') was reproduced with minimal changes in Chapter Two of *Education and the University*. There Leavis supplemented it with a passage from 'Why Universities?', as already mentioned, and several more paragraphs noting the shortcomings of the Experimental College curriculum and dismissing the rival claims of Classics and Philosophy as subjects traditionally associated with liberal education: 'there is an essential discipline which must be found elsewhere' (p. 39). The 'elsewhere' Leavis had in mind, of course, was an English School based on literary criticism (as he believed the Cambridge English Faculty originally was) because 'the non-specialist intelligence in which the various studies are to have their centre is to be one that gets its own special training in literature'.[25] Leavis insisted that 'it is of the essence of the scheme that the work of all kinds would be done by the "literary mind" . . . by, that is, an intelligence with the sensitiveness, the flexibility and the disciplined and mature preoccupation with value that should be the product of a literary training. It is an intelligence so trained that is best fitted to develop into the central kind of mind, the co-ordinating consciousness, capable of performing the function assigned to the class of the educated.'[26]

The 'Sketch' was followed in the next number of *Scrutiny* by a 'Criticism and Comment' symposium, in which Leavis reviewed some of the correspondence he had received on his proposals. Hardly any of this article was reprinted in *Education and the University*, but it is extremely useful as a gloss on two important aspects of the 'Sketch' – its relation to society and its relation to literature. The first correspondent Leavis engaged with questioned the social value of his proposals, and challenged particularly his notion of 'the co-ordinating consciousness, capable of performing the function assigned to the class of the educated':

> But what is this function, and when was it so clearly assigned that it may be referred to without definition? . . . Your course of study seems too much to presuppose people who are going to live a life of comparative leisure . . . it is a course of study implying a society which exists on the fringe of things and can only take a minor place in the affairs of the world. On what are your 'central minds' going to work, except the production of further central minds, in an endless involution?[27]

The charges of 'comparative leisure' and detachment from 'the affairs of the world' were rendered particularly acute by the wartime context. But, as Leavis noted in his reply, the criticism was really directed against the whole idea of liberal education, 'of education as opposed to special training' (p. 266). To admit a critique of this tradition on the basis of particular circumstances or immediate needs would be to emulate the Nazis, 'who, one hears, have replaced the outmoded types of liberal education by training in leadership and accountancy' (p. 264). Leavis tentatively explored some possible exercises of 'the function assigned to the class of the educated' but he was reluctant to admit any formal link between liberal education and 'the affairs of the world' that would identify 'the class of the educated' with an existing social formation. He rather awkwardly distinguished between the 'elite' for whom he had designed his course and 'THE ELITE' in a social or political sense (p. 261). He also referred back to his argument in 'Why Universities?' that the function of a scheme of liberal education was not just to produce a particular kind of graduate but in the process to make the university an effective 'centre' for the 'interplay of ideas'.

What puzzled another correspondent in 'Criticism and Comment' was that the proposed English School seemed hardly concerned with the study of English Literature at all. The list of topics which Leavis provided, for example, ranged widely over economic, social, political and intellectual history, but contained almost no conventionally literary projects:

> One doesn't, I think, see clearly demonstrated the incidence of the courses you have sketched on the specific exercise of judgment on pieces of 'literature', the training and testing of which is, I take it, the ultimate end in view . . . As it stands, a superficial censor might say that the article seems to show more concern for history. (p. 266)

Leavis conceded that he had not made sufficiently clear what he meant by the literary-critical discipline and how he would provide for training in it. He denied, however, that the 'ultimate end' of the course he had proposed was to produce competent literary critics: on the contrary, literary competence was its starting-point. The test of a student on the course would be 'his handling of a historical or sociological work as much as his handling of a novel or a book of poems' (p. 267). In this sense it was true that the 'Sketch' was more concerned with history than literature: the idea of liberal education dictated that Leavis's proposals were not for a course in English Literature but for a study by the 'literary mind' of the transformation of modern civilization in England. The aim was to produce humane historians, endowed by their literary-critical training with 'a maturity of outlook such as the study of history ought to produce but even the general historian by profession doesn't always exhibit'.[28]

This correspondent also suggested that Leavis should complement his 'Sketch' with a demonstration of 'the specific exercise of judgment on pieces of "literature" and thus complete a triptich with the more general *Why Universities?*' (p. 266). This was in fact the basic chapter-structure which Leavis adopted for *Education and the University*. 'Why Universities?' and the 'Sketch' formed the first two parts; a further article entitled 'Literary Studies' (quoting at length – as already noted – from 'a book on analysis and appreciation not yet published'[29]) supplied the suggested third chapter;

and book publication provided an opportunity to reprint *How To Teach Reading*, an earlier treatment of the same theme, as an Appendix. The 'triptich' thus seemed to be complete by March 1941. But between 1941 and 1943 Leavis added two further sections, framing the original structure within a new first section of Chapter I and a new Appendix on 'T.S.Eliot's Later Poetry'. The stimulus for this development was 'criticism and comment' from a more distinguished source – Eliot himself had mentioned the 'Sketch' in his speech on 'The Christian Conception of Education' at the Archbishop of York's Conference at Malvern in January 1941. The context for his fairly brief notice of Leavis's article was a more detailed analysis of educational developments in America, particularly Irving Babbitt's Humanism and the various experiments in higher education (of which, although Eliot did not mention it, the Experimental College had been one) designed to counter the centrifugal effects of the elective system. All were examples, for Eliot, of 'humanism', and subject to the same test: 'if a secular or non-religious humanism can provide an adequate foundation for general education . . . we could afford to leave to the disciples of Irving Babbitt in America and such groups as Dr Leavis and his friends in this country, the elaboration and implementing of policies'. Humanism could not provide such a foundation, however:

> I have read an admirable article by Dr. Leavis, which appeared some months ago in *Scrutiny*, in which he makes very sensible suggestions for the improvement of the English Tripos . . . he quotes a sentence by a Mr. Brooks Otis, an American writer: 'it is an urgently necessary work . . . to explore the means of bringing the various kinds of specialist knowledge and training into effective relation with informed general intelligence, humane culture, social conscience and political will.' One agrees. But to such questions as: 'Why should we want humane culture? Why is one conception of humane culture better than another? What is the sanction for your conception of social conscience or political will as against that, for instance, now dominant in Germany?' I do not think that the humanist can give a satisfactory answer.[30]

Only 'Christian doctrine', Eliot asserted, could provide a satisfactory basis for an educational policy.

Leavis was peculiarly sensitive to recognition – or lack of it – from Eliot, so it is perhaps not surprising that this passing notice had a disproportionate effect on the final shape of *Education and the University*. His response to Eliot, in the new first part of Chapter One, was respectful but combative. He strongly rejected the assimilation of his approach to Babbitt's Humanism. His approach *was* 'humanist' inasmuch as it was concerned with a particular 'living tradition' – a human achievement. But in this sense literary criticism must always be humanist: 'whatever it may end in it must be humanist in approach, in so far as it is literary criticism and not something else. It seems to me obvious that the approach needed in education must be in the same way humanist.'[31] Developing his defence of 'humanism' Leavis pointedly invoked Eliot the poet *against* Eliot the Christian social theorist. Eliot's later poetry provided an analogy for the way in which liberal education would bring the 'living tradition' of which it was a part into focus. He was, as Leavis had implied in his recent *Scrutiny* article on the poetry, supremely a poet of human reality rather than religious doctrine:

> Eliot is known as professing Anglo-Catholicism and classicism; but his poetry is remarkable for the extraordinary resource, penetration and stamina with which it makes its explorations into the concrete actualities of experience below the conceptual currency . . . endlessly insistent in its care not to confuse the frame with the living reality, and heroic in its refusal to accept.[32]

The point was 'of such radical importance' that the whole of the article, elaborating this reading, was reprinted as an Appendix. Eliot thus emerged, rather bizarrely, as the hero of Leavis's argument rather than its critic: the exploration of 'living reality' in his poetry typified the true function of the university and offered 'an education intellectual, emotional and moral'.[33]

Leavis submitted the complete text of *Education and the University* (a combination of typescript, pencilled notes and old *Scrutiny* galleys) to Chatto & Windus in June 1943. Despite wartime exigencies – or perhaps because of them – the book was turned round very rapidly and was published in November 1943. Leavis's editor reported almost immediately that 'the book has made an excellent start and we have already sold within a few hundred of the first impression of two thousand'. Another thousand were printed on some extra paper stocks that had become available. At this stage, though he had had several articles published in American journals, none of Leavis's books had been published in the USA. After the war, however, Leavis found an enthusiastic publisher in George W.

Stewart, whose New York firm published *Revaluation* in 1947 and *The Importance of 'Scrutiny'*, a selection of *Scrutiny* articles edited by Eric Bentley, in 1948. Leavis was particularly anxious that what he regarded as his educational campaign should also benefit from this new exposure, and he urged Stewart to publish *Education and the University* as well. Stewart arranged to import 500 copies of a new Chatto & Windus edition with his imprint on the title page (this became the method for all the Leavis titles he subsequently published). At Eric Bentley's suggestion, 'Mass Civilization and Minority Culture' was reprinted as a third appendix to this edition. But no formal attempt was made to assimilate this extra text to the argument of *Education and the University*: Bentley's idea was simply to maximize the impact of Leavis in America by making available some of his earliest pre-*Scrutiny* 'classic statements'.[34]

Leavis wrote two articles for American journals around this time which are particularly interesting for their extension of the general argument of *Education and the University* to more specific comment on the British educational system.[35] *Education and the University* also provided the sub-text for his contribution to the 'Critic and Leviathan' debate in *Politics and Letters*, the short-lived journal edited by (among others) Raymond Williams. Since this has become one of his more inaccessible uncollected essays, it is worth quoting Leavis's restatement of his position at length. The context was a debate started in the first issue of *Politics and Letters*, between R. O. C. Winkler (a former *Scrutiny* contributor) and the Marxist historian Christopher Hill, on (Winkler's phrase) 'the bearing of the values implied by literature on political practice'. Leavis sided strongly with Winkler against Hill, though he acknowledged that it was always easier to demand a crude political definition of 'values':

> Nevertheless, we have to insist that a literary critic justifies his activity as politically valuable if he makes it more difficult for public-spirited intellectuals to be complacent in exhibiting such unawareness and confusion and poverty of thought as Mr Hill does when he talks about 'values'. That is, the critic's business is to be as good a critic as he can, to promote critical intelligence, to do what he can to make good criticism influential. He is performing then his political function as a literary critic, and it is an essential one.

One way to promote this function, Leavis suggested, was to run an 'intelligent review' – like *Scrutiny*, and possibly like *Politics and Letters*. But *Education and the University* significantly extended this argument:

> In my own mind this way is intimately associated with another way, so that I could offer a much stronger account of the literary critic's function. To make what seems to me an essential point I must be personal, and I hope I shall be forgiven for bringing in here my own standing preoccupations. I speak as a literary critic whose job is the study and discussion of literature in a university school of 'English'. On the one hand I have made it my business to insist that the study of literature should be a discipline – a specific discipline of intelligence (and in consequence I have been charged with a narrow concern with the 'words on the page'). On the other hand I have insisted that an English School should exploit to the utmost the ways in which serious literary studies lead into 'extra-literary' fields (and in consequence I have been charged with being more concerned with history and sociology than with literature). In short, I think that 'English' should be a liaison 'subject'. There would be no point in attempting even the briefest summary here, but some who read this will know I think, that I can, on demand, produce a detailed account of what I mean. I permit myself this reference because it seems to me in the strictest sense relevant.
>
> 'It is to be expected,' says Mr. Winkler, 'that, in a society where specialisation and division of function are characteristic symptoms of disintegration, some kind of assimilation of competences will be necessary before the disintegral tendencies can be reversed . . .' I should make my attack on that problem from a university school of 'English'. Make literary criticism a real discipline of intelligence and the distinctive discipline of literary studies, and promote the entry of minds trained in this discipline, and fully aware of the disastrous wrongness of the 'historical attitude' advocated by Mr. Hill, into other than literary fields. Then we could hope to produce literary critics who had also some acquaintance with other disciplines and special studies, and to produce also some specialists – historians, psychologists, sociologists, anthropologists, students of politics, economists . . . who were also literary critics. Further, the serious and sustained attempt to establish and develop such an English School would tend to make the university less a mere collocation of specialisms – to make it truly (what it ought to be) a higher centre of co-ordination, a focus of knowledge, conscience, human awareness and political will, capable of real influence in the community at large.

If there were such an English School actually working – if universities were really universities – the editors of *Politics and Letters* would be finding it easier to recruit an adequate team of contributors. Perhaps this truism will be taken as clinching the relevance of my commentary. There can be no answer that is both simple and satisfactory to the question: What are the political bearings of a serious interest in literature? *Politics and Letters* will justify itself in so far as it promotes the process I have assigned to my English School and to my university. The more intelligent reviews there are to favour the formation of an educated public, and to combat the disintegrating effects of specialization, the better.[36]

Politics and Letters did not remain long in the lists of 'intelligent reviews': its next issue, which included a 'Critic and Leviathan' article by George Orwell, was its last. Five years later *Scrutiny* followed it. Leavis's often-quoted letter to Storm Jameson, in 1953, shows how closely he identified the journal with the argument of *Education and the University*: 'How could *Scrutiny* be made a permanency except from a continuing centre of intellectual life at an ancient university? . . . The fact intimately associated with the death of *Scrutiny* is that my *Education and the University* has never been recognized to exist, even to disagree with, at Cambridge.'[37] The two publications had seemed to validate each other, and the death of the journal provided a melancholy epilogue to the book. But the basic argument of *Education and the University* – if not the 'Sketch' in any detail – was given a new lease of life after Leavis's retirement from Cambridge and reconstructed in more polemical form in the lectures that formed *English Literature in Our Time and the University* and *Nor Shall My Sword*. In the Richmond Lecture, which inaugurated this new phase in his career, *Education and the University* was put forward as the ultimate sign of Leavis's difference from Snow: 'Like Snow I look to the university. Unlike Snow, I am concerned to make it really a university, something (that is) more than a collocation of specialist departments – to make it a centre of human consciousness; perception, knowledge, judgment and responsibility. And perhaps I have sufficiently indicated on what lines I would justify my seeing the centre of a university in a vital English School.'[38]

NOTE: CAMBRIDGE ENGLISH, PART II

Existing course (1940)

Candidates were required to take (1), (2) and (3), plus three others.

1.   Essay

2.   Criticism and Composition: 'Passages of English prose and verse for critical comment. Exercises in English composition, or in translation from other languages into English Prose or Verse, may be set provided that translations shall not be compulsory.'
[Candidates were required to answer 'three or four' questions out of six. (1) was a dating exercise; (2) a stylistic and grammatical critique of a series of very short passages; (3) analysis of descriptive prose; (4) analysis of discursive prose; (5) critique of a single sonnet (Wordsworth's 'Mutability'); (6) a comparison of two poems. No questions were compulsory.]

3.   Tragedy: 'Tragedy ancient and modern in connexion and comparison with English Tragedy'.

4.   French and Italian Set Books: These included Ronsard, Montaigne, Racine, Corneille; Petrarch, Bocaccio, Machiavelli, and Dante (*Inferno* 1–5, 26, 32 [l.124–739], 33, *Purgatorio* 6–8, *Paradiso* 32). OR

5.   Anglo-Saxon and Early Norse

6.   English Life, Literature and Thought 1066–1350

7.   Special Period of English Literature: 1785–1824
[The period had been 1557–1596 and reverted to this again in 1945].

8.   Special Subject: The English Moralists and their relation to the history of philosophical thought

9.   Special Subject: Chaucer
[Between 1941 and 1944 the special subject was Milton; in 1945 it became 'George Eliot and her setting'.]

10.   The History and Theory of Literary Criticism 'with special

reference to English Literature': Author prescribed for special study: Arnold.

11.   The History of the English Language, including historical grammar

Papers 4 or 5 were compulsory for students who had taken English Part I (and therefore not done any other language study).

(Based on *The Student's Handbook to the University and Colleges of Cambridge* [1939] and the 1940 Tripos Papers.)

Leavis's proposals (1940)

1.   Practical Criticism: a number of papers, to be taken at the end of the course. These are to provide the test of literary education and critical competence.

2.   The Seventeenth Century in England: four or five 'pieces of work', on subjects chosen according to the principles explained, to be done during the course.

3.   An essay, to be written during the course, on the process of change by which England of the Seventeenth Century turned into the England of to-day.

4.   Dante, a general study: a paper, or papers, to be taken at the end of the course.

5.   A subject from French literature or literary history: a substantial essay, to be written during the course.

6.   Reviews, to be written during the course, of a number of books which are to be chosen in consultation with authority.

7.   A *viva voce* examination to be held at the end of the course.

N.B. – Participation required in organized discussion- and seminar-work.

(Reprinted from *Scrutiny* IX.2 [September 1940], pp. 118–9; *Education and the University*, pp. 63–4)

PART 3

Analytical

The Impersonal Objective:
Leavis, the Literary Subject and
Cambridge Thought

Leavis throughout his career was given to warning about the effects of a break in continuity that English culture generally, and literary culture in particular, had undergone in the modern period. One way to interpret this has been to link it with his writings about a breach in the 'organic community', a phrase redolent of rustic nostalgia and historical yearnings, an indicator, it has been claimed, of Leavis's conservatism and general out-of-touchness.[1] In this way the thrust of Leavis's claim has been deflected and the credibility of his warning dismissed. Yet a very instance of this breach of continuity has occurred in the treatment, by recent theorists and critics, of Leavis's own criticism, and that of his Cambridge contemporaries. I. A. Richards and William Empson have suffered as much as Leavis has from a blanket of historical ignorance that descended upon British criticism from about the mid-1970s onwards. Driven by the Saussurean *zeitgeist* to re-start all critical clocks from *Writing Degree Zero* (so to speak), critics in this country have virtually ignored an extensive heritage of native twentieth-century literary critical argument and debate about topics such as meaning, sense and reference, signs and signification, and society and the literary subject. The questionable grounds for this neglect are, presumably, that literary theory did not begin until language theory was put upon a 'scientific' i.e. Saussurean footing. All previous enquiries into the role of language in literature were deemed too antediluvian to be of interest to the contemporary – i.e. post-Saussurean – critic. The fact that I. A. Richards not only knew about Saussure's linguistics but declined to accept such a theory of meaning on the grounds that it was too rarefied, too remote from our experience of the way linguistic signification works in practice, may not of itself be a reason for doubting Saussure's contribution, but it should at least be a factor in current literary debate that the first significant theoretician of English in modern times saw Saussurean semantics as leading only to a dead end.[2]

In the rich critical matrix created by the English Cambridge critics of the first two or three decades of this century can be found an extensive engagement with matters fundamental to any theory of literature and theory of criticism: the nature and role of language; the relationship between thought, sign and referent; the question of the nature of value in critical judgment; and, especially, the extent to which expressions of subjectivity in literature can acquire objective status: in short the impersonality question. Such topics formed a distinctive Cambridge tradition of critical debate in England in the twenties and thirties; topics that, for convenience in discussion, might be brought together under the heading of 'thought in literature' ('thought in' rather than 'theory of' because at this time the 'theory/anti-theory' argument is a sub-debate within the larger field of discussion about the nature of literary criticism in itself). Throughout his career F. R. Leavis had a particularly strong interest as a critic in the idea of literature as a distinctive mode of thought, partly because of his inherently intellectual temperament but also because he was educated as a critic in the philosophically-conscious world of Cambridge of the immediately post-war years.

Like his contemporary, William Empson, Leavis absorbed an ideology of intellect that emanated from the young English school there and which originated in the background and interests of the two leading literary thinkers of the day: I. A. Richards and T. S. Eliot.[3] Both lectured at Cambridge in the 1920s and both had professional philosophy credentials. Richards was a graduate of Cambridge philosophy who went on to establish a powerful methodological basis for the new English teaching in his *Principles of Literary Criticism* (1924) and *Practical Criticism* (1929); T. S. Eliot completed a Ph.D thesis on 'Knowledge and Experience in the Philosophy of F. H. Bradley' (1915), and, on arrival in England at the outbreak of the First World War, renewed his Harvard contact with Bertrand Russell with the intention, at one point, of becoming a philosophy don.[4] He subsequently established himself at Richards's instigation as a frequent visitor to Cambridge in the role of literary critical consultant. This role was institutionally recognized when Eliot gave the Clark lectures at

Cambridge in 1926/27 on 'The Varieties of Metaphysical Poetry'.[5] There was, in other words, a discernible Richards-Eliot axis in Cambridge when F. R. Leavis was a student and young teacher there. It was one that, dismissive of the late Victorian aestheticism that still clung fast in cloisters such as King's, placed particular emphasis upon professionalizing English Studies as an intellectual discipline, one capable of ground-breaking innovation similar to that which their colleagues, Moore, Russell and Wittgenstein, had achieved in the Cambridge philosophy school.[6] This emphasis ensured that methodological awareness about the nature of English, and its teaching, was particularly highly developed in its ablest practitioners, Leavis and Empson.

For the young Leavis especially, literary criticism was at one and the same time a demonstration of, and engagement with, intelligence. This was a quality held to be always in short supply and felt by him at the time to be (de)pressingly so in the post-Arnoldian world that Eliot and Richards had variously delineated in the diagnostic *The Waste Land* (1922) or the prognostic *Science and Poetry* (1926). Contemporary England appeared there as debilitated by cultural deficits across a broad band of intellectual modes, deficits thought to be compounding in the 1920s at an alarming rate. Thus literary criticism was to be (for Richards and Leavis) an attempt at cultural anti-Keynesianism, an attempt to restore the credibility of literary transactions by guaranteeing them with what were felt to be the devaluation-proof assets of enlightened intelligence. Like their philosophical colleagues, who were understood to have cleared away the metaphysical clutter of the Victorians so that knowledge could be re-defined in the epistemologically more secure terms of linguistic logic, these Cambridge critics saw their task as one of de-aestheticizing literature so that it could take its place as a key component of cultural science. Specifically English literature was to be a vehicle for education, education in the higher understanding of the humane self and of the social conditions which enabled, or failed to enable, a newly-modernized notion of this self to emerge. In this sense Cambridge criticism had a philosophical dimension from the outset. Under the particular inflection given to it by Richards, supported (as it was believed) by T. S. Eliot's *The Waste Land*, and adopted as programmatic by Leavis, Cambridge criticism pressed modern poetry forward as manifesting contemporary humane consciousness in its most developed (i.e. philosophically informed) form. Eliot's poem, Richards claimed, had effected a severance between poetry and 'all beliefs'; it had shown how poetry could develop a post-metaphysical stance by absorbing the anti-metaphysical climate of the new realists within the very rhythms and movement, as well as the content, of the new free verse. By de-mythologizing itself, it was felt, *The Waste Land* had demonstrated that the contemporary mind could be purified of its anachronistic need to seek solace in escapist metaphysics or pseudo-religious pieties in literary reading.[7]

In this guise criticism at Cambridge acquired the character of a vocation, a crusade for a higher level of expertise in literary thinking than that evident in the journals of metropolitan *belles lettres*, Oxford classicism or Gower street philology. Without wholly endorsing Richards's own force-fully anti-metaphysical ambitions, Leavis had no difficulty in accepting this larger critical claim, a claim the concomitant of which was the launching and sustaining of a programme of socio-cultural reform as manifest in *Scrutiny*. He also had no difficulty with the postulate that Cambridge criticism and contemporary philosophy were moving along separate but related lines, a distinctive element in Ricardian poetics, but one the justice of which was not immediately evident to contemporaries, especially con-temporary philosophers.[8] Some such doubt in the critic's philosophical credentials may well have been behind Wittgenstein's celebrated remark to Leavis: 'Give up literary criticism.' In glossing this comment, Leavis makes clear that: 'it was evident that . . . [Wittgenstein] couldn't in any case imagine that literary criticism might matter intellectually.' He also makes clear how much he opposed and resisted such a dismissal:

> Even at that time I had an opposing conviction: it was, as it is, that the fullest use of language is to be found in creative literature, and that a great creative work is a work of original exploratory thought. With that conviction went the tendency towards the view I expressed recently, writing on Blake: 'philosophers are always weak on language.' So, while I had great respect for Wittgenstein, and he, I suppose, had some for me . . . there was on both sides certainly some reserve in our sense of the other's intellect. For Wittgenstein my kind of addiction was hardly, if at all, more than pseudo-intellectual, and I, on my part, found myself at times thinking of his unmistakable genius as hardly more relevant to my own intellectual concerns than a genius for chess . . .[9]

'A genius for chess' – the orientation of Leavis's attitude to Wittgenstein's distinction is expressed in terms of its relevance to what Leavis himself was concerned with, and which he could not see as at all resembling a game: that of demonstrating how the state of culture was intimately at one with an intelligent interest in, and understanding of, language. In particular, 'creative literature' is here being presented as a way of using language so as to bring out its unique epistemological character. That Wittgenstein, and most other philosophers, were incapable of seeing this *qua* philosophers, is, of course, the kind of claim that Leavis became notorious for, and not just among those who were his traditional antagonists.[10]

But the position, notwithstanding its provocative thrust, is consistent with the view that literature is more than a linguistic epiphenomenon; that literature, as such, cannot properly be understood as a mere rhetorical category. In Leavisian poetics it is a descriptive term for a particular kind of cognitive process, or, if that sounds too philosophically provocative, for a way of relating to the world. Literature, as Leavis sees it, is a way of using language such that it enforces the subjective origin of the objective character of our experience; it adumbrates and reinforces the role of the individual as the locus of all significant understanding or insight ('mind,' Leavis insists, 'is "there" only in individual minds'[11]). This understanding or insight is contingent in the sense that without language it could not find expression, but in another sense it is the reason why language is as it is and not something else: it is the soul of language, its shaping characteristic. When, at the turn of the century, Russell and Moore looked for a way of guaranteeing the objectivity of judgment in the face of Idealist scepticism, they took for granted that logic was the standard by which truth was to be measured. And in doing so they simultaneously accepted that language was not logical; that it was, in logical terms, highly irregular and therefore unsuitable for use as an epistemological tool. They gave much thought to the problem of finding a way to purge it of its illogicalities. Wittgenstein may have been still brooding over the way he had addressed this particular problem in the *Tractatus-Logicus-Philosophicus* (1922) around the time that Leavis describes meeting him.

We are talking, of course, about meaning, about meaning understood as normative in language, and as carrying a subjective component intrinsic to it. When Leavis talks about literary language he sees it as language used in a way that brings out this normative characteristic; it is a way of using language so as to highlight and enforce recognition of its subjective, but not subjectivist, origins. 'Subjective' in most contexts is a notoriously difficult term to be clear about. In discussing Leavis this is particularly so, because the idea of the subjective origin of meaning that he developed into such a powerful generator of critical enterprise was one that only gradually emerged as his career as a critic progressed; it was not always present or available to him at all stages of his development. This is to say that it was not always immediately available as Leavisian theory, as an acknowledged set of principles. Anyone vaguely familiar with Leavis's career will know of his exchange with Wellek in the 1930s when he repudiated the idea that a critic needed a theory or needed to be a theorist; in later years this translated itself into an even more provocative stance, in that he declared his intention of being known as an 'anti-philosopher'.[12]

But although there is a programmatic component in this utterance, in the sense that Leavis very much intended to insist on such occasions that literary criticism is an intellectual activity independent of philosophical method, there is also a pragmatic element that dictated that his ability actually to provide a comprehensive theoretical statement of his idea of literary meaning may not have been wholly within his control. This is because the circumstances of Leavis's introduction to critical thought were such that they required him to find his critical coordinates in the midst of a very fast moving, and inherently unstable, phase of intellectual development in English life. In particular in the intellectual circles Leavis frequented in 1920s Cambridge, the effects of the discrediting of Victorian absolutes had been felt as the fracturing and dispersal of positives over a wide spectrum; a search for common values could no longer be conducted with any confidence that they could be found or, if found, sustained and defended. In these disorientating circumstances, which could in significant part be traced back, as far as the English school was concerned, via Richards, to the epistemological upheavals of Cambridge philosophy, it should not seem surprising if Leavis, as a tyro critic, were to delegate to those more professionally qualified responsibility for philosophical navigation in the new ideological climate. Specifically, that he felt the philosophical training of I. A. Richards and T. S. Eliot qualified them to negotiate the ground of the modern critic's new territory more effectively than he himself or other non-philosophical critics were capable of doing.

To the extent that Richards and Eliot were sophisticated thinkers, sensitively responsive to the new intellectual climate, he was right to do so; but in recognizing this we also have to recognize that by adopting a critical agenda set by Richards and Eliot, Leavis found himself initially committed to a poetics that was in important respects incomplete. It was incomplete to the extent that in seeking to address the cognitive pressures arising out of the new emphasis upon objectivity, it had lost a firm hold on the literary subject. Because the new philosophical realism had undermined the Victorian metaphysics of the subject, Richards and Eliot, in their varied responses, tried to re-locate poetics within a 'subject-free' zone, one that did not require validation through an appeal to expressive values. This resulted in a new emphasis upon 'impersonality,' an impersonality that to Leavis came increasingly to resemble depersonalization, a notion at odds with his commitment to pursue a modern meaning for the humane self.

In 1934 Wyndham Lewis published an essay (that Leavis does not appear to have read) called 'T. S. Eliot, The Pseudo-Believer'.[13] Lewis's argument there was that T. S. Eliot and I. A. Richards were at one in abdicating from a defence, or a view, of poetry as an expression of authorial experience in favour of a poetics of spurious objectivity:

> Of course I know that such a statement as 'the poet has, not a "personality" to express, but a particular medium, which is only a medium and not a personality' fits in very well, for instance, with Bertrand Russell's account of the psyche – a rendezvous as it were for a bundle of sticks, not the sticks but just the rendezvous – or with the functional picture of the Behaviorist . . . (p. 62)

The problem, as Lewis saw it, was that subjectivity in literature was a matter of personal integrity and this was inescapably an ethical issue ('sincerity can only mean identity with truth'). It was clear to him that in the public debate which Richards and Eliot had conducted throughout most of the 1920s, they had found sincerity, and the related topic of belief, problematic because they had largely removed personality, the authorial presence, from the literary centre, substituting for it a quasi-idealist 'point-of-view' (Eliot) or a Benthamite-materialist notion of a 'system of interests' (Richards). This, claimed Lewis, created an aesthetic as well as a moral vacuum, in that it evacuated poetry of what makes it poetic, namely its integrity, its expression of human interiority:

That 'the being oneself' [in *Practical Criticism*] should be the fundamental difficulty hit upon by Mr Richards is instructive. For manifestly the pseudo technique must tend to undermine the vigour of this all-important selfhood to a peculiar degree. And Mr Eliot's insistence upon the suppression of the personality and the creation of a privileged play-boy alter ego is not going to help matters – not going to promote 'sincerity' – either . . . (p. 72)

Poetry for Lewis had to be grounded upon a self, a human subject:

Those who succumbed to the theory of Mr Pound or Mr Eliot should scarcely expect not to lose coherence – they must expect to 'sacrifice' more and more of that 'self' or 'personality,' which is merely a living adequately at any given moment . . . [by personality] I mean only a constancy and consistency in being, as concretely as possible, *one thing* – at peace with itself, if not with the outer world, although that is likely to follow after an interval of struggle . . . (p. 62)

Unsophisticated as this might seem as a moral theory of the soul, it provided Lewis with a fulcrum from which to exert some leverage upon what he saw as the artificiality and eccentricity of the Eliot-Richards position:

Am I here accusing Mr Eliot of being a 'humbug' then? To that I can only answer – No: rather he is *pseudo* everything, and he has found his theorist to explain and justify him, namely Mr I. A. Richards . . . (p. 64)

It is not so much the injustice, or the justice, of Lewis's commentary that is important here. Rather it is his attracting attention to the conjunction of Eliot and Richards as moving on a common axis of literary theory hostile to the idea of subjectivity as the ground of meaning in literature. Poetry, in Lewis's eyes, cannot dispense with the notion of a soul, with the idea of human integrity, both emotional and ethical, as an originating source of literary expression that takes 'truth' as its objective. And, as his forcefully satirical and polemical account makes clear, he felt that Eliot and Richards had recklessly done just that.

What Lewis is drawing attention to is the extremism of the new poetics. In their determination to escape from the subjectivism of the Victorian literary humanism of which Lewis's might be said to be a belated ex-pression, the two critics had acquired some notoriety for two views in particular: Eliot's claim (in 'Tradition and the Individual Talent') that 'the poet has, not a "personality" to express, but a particular medium,' and Richards's argument (in *Principles of Literary Criticism*) that poetry is a form of 'pseudo-statement', an utterance incapable of positive content. In the eyes of a hostile commentator, such as Lewis, both claims could seem preposterous. But to the young Leavis, conscious of a different cultural perspective, they were ideas that had to be considered seriously because, in circumstances then felt to be current, they might offer radical, redeeming insights.

Because of his Cambridge connection, Leavis understood that both ideas were indicative of more philosophically complex positions. As a young Cambridge intellectual he must have been aware – and in this his acquaintance with Wittgenstein may have played a part – that in problematizing the role of language in the cognitive process, the new realism had simultaneously problematized the metaphysics of the subject, and the question of cognition in literature. He knew that in attempting to meet this development Richards and Eliot had produced radical, if different, solutions to the problem of poetic truth and the objective status of literary meaning. Richards, for instance, took an extreme form of empiricism (derived via C. K. Ogden from Bentham) as the basis upon which to erect a behavioural model of language. Because it was empirical it was still dependent upon the new realism for its epistemology, and thus its theory of truth. Hence the need for a division between 'symbolic' (i.e. logical, truly referential) language and 'emotive' (i.e. expressive, non-referential) language. But Richards was only interested in philosophy of language as a means to an end; his true objective was that of cultural renewal through what he saw as a redrafting of humanism upon a wholly secular, and scientific, basis. Literature could become, he believed, the theology of this new humanism once it had a coherent poetics and once it was suitably purged of its anachronistic elements, specifically its metaphysical associations. From this followed his anti-aestheticism and his promotion of modern (i.e. 'non-metaphysical') poetry.

Richards, in other words, wanted to define literature as language that was fully charged with psychological (as opposed to logical) truth, language that declared itself free of all metaphysical trappings. To do this he had to reduce all that traditionally came under the heading of the subjective so that it would fit within a much-reduced category of academic psychology, an abridgement which he readily made but which most of his readers (including Leavis) found too disconcertingly drastic to accept. The contemporary condition was felt to be dire, but not so dire that only that which could be registered electro-chemically could be regarded as subjective.

As a graduate of the Harvard philosophy school, T. S. Eliot had a more sophisticated – but less generally accessible – solution to the challenges of the new realism. This was to subject the premises upon which the thought of Russell and other realists was based to a philosophical critique. The argument of Eliot's thesis on F. H. Bradley was that Bradley's epistemological argument was unanswerable except in terms which were not relevant to it. In that sense, for Eliot, the recent revolution in philosophy had not happened; the intellectual bases of the metaphysics of Absolute Idealism were still intact, and emphasis upon the new logic as the criterion of truth could not be taken with the seriousness that the new realists wanted it to have. Nonetheless Eliot did not oppose the swing towards objectivity that they had initiated; he did not see that as a move in the wrong direction. This is because Bradley's Absolute Idealism was a philosophy of anti-subjectivity even more extreme than that of the realists themselves. Bradley demonstrated, with logical virtuosity, that discursive thought was a continuing source of error and that the very basis of realist thinking, its dependence upon a relational duality of subject and object with attendant categories of space, time and causality, was typically befogged with errors of logic and metaphysical confusion. In particular the empirical self, the observing mind, was not a primary reality because it too was, metaphysically speaking, a construction, a product of the discursive process. This then became a key concept in Eliot's poetics, where it is turned round, so to speak, to become a central tenet of impersonality:

> The point of view which I am struggling to attack is perhaps related to the metaphysical theory of the substantial unity of the soul: for my meaning is, that the poet has, not a 'personality' to express, but a particular medium and not a personality, in which impressions and experiences combine in peculiar and unexpected ways.[14]

Language, as Eliot presents it here and in related essays in *The Sacred Wood* (1920), is an extrusion from the discursive process in which numerous 'selves' declare or express themselves in cognition but which, from a metaphysical point of view, are fictions or constructions: elements of illusory substance that have no final claim to reality. It is only in art, in literary art of the great masters that the illusory and insubstantial nature of these cognitively-derived 'personalities' emerges clearly into view. Art for Eliot is so far from being mimetic or representational that it creates its own world:

> We cannot call a man's work superficial when it is the creation of a world; a man cannot be accused of dealing superficially with the world which he has himself created; the superficies is the world. Jonson's characters conform to the logic of the emotions of their world. It is a world like Lobachevsky's; the worlds created by artists like Jonson are like systems of non-Euclidean geometry. They are not fancy because they have a logic of their own; and this logic illuminates the actual world, because it gives us a new point of view from which to inspect it.[15]

The extremism of this position began to be modified in the 1920s as Eliot came under the influence of Anglicanism and the historicist politics of Maurras and Hulme. But his idea of subjectivity as a pathological condition that poetry was contaminated by and had to be distanced from, an idea which was then extended historically in the notion of tradition as the erasure of personality from the progress of art over time, became one of the key tenets of a literary modernism which was immensely influential in this country until very recent times.[16]

Leavis's career as a critic could be described as a continuing emancipation from the methodological field surrounding these two powerfully influential figures in the Cambridge of his time. Initially however, Leavis had to discover that he needed to escape from them; he had to become aware of the shortcomings that impersonality, as variously adumbrated by Richards and Eliot and integrated and assimilated by his early self, imposed upon the critic. He had also to become aware of how far the notion was inescapable: of the extent to which impersonality had to be a primary concept in any account of the significance of literature for the modern world. In this respect two major phases of Leavis's preoccupation with impersonality can be identified: an early phase when, from his own amalgamation of the accounts of Richards and Eliot, he attempted to fashion a poetics that would identify a canon of central literary works for his larger pedagogic and cultural purposes; and a later phase when this canon is more or less abandoned and a body of work from a differently-derived understanding takes its place. *New Bearings in English Poetry* (1932)

and *Revaluation* (1936) represent the first phase; most of the writing after
D. H. Lawrence: Novelist (1955) is typical of the second.

The first instance of Leavis's application of impersonality as a working
principle of critical judgment comes in *New Bearings in English Poetry*
(1932), together with two essays that lead up to it, 'T. S. Eliot – A Reply
to the Condescending' (1929), and 'English Poetry and the Modern World'
(1930).[17] The theme of the three writings is to promote Eliot as the
foremost literary intelligence of the day, especially as this is manifest in
the critically informed character of his poetry.[18] The stress falls unequivocally upon the poet-critic who has changed the consciousness of the age,
both in his criticism ('[this] is so entirely controlled by the will to "see
the object as in itself it really is". . . [that it] makes some of us feel that
we never read criticism before') and in his poetry ('Mr Eliot is a poet of
profound originality . . . His poetry is more conscious of the past than
any other that is being written in English today.')[19] But, as the Arnoldian
allusion makes clear, the stress on a new level of consciousness and the
critic's capacity to impersonalize poetry is diagnostic: it is part of a larger
case that interprets Eliot's criticism and poetry as part of an argument
about culture and 'mass civilization' and parallels the Ricardian-inspired
pamphlet in which Leavis declared his critico-cultural manifesto, 'Mass
Civilization and Minority Culture' (1930).

Because, notwithstanding the prominence given to the poet as an
ultra-modern consciousness in *New Bearings*, Eliot does not appear in that
book as a modernist poet. The concerns with poetic enactment, with
impersonality, with the innovative technique of Eliot, Pound and Hopkins,
are not presented as aspects of a modernist analysis. Their significance is
to be understood in other terms: as elements in a budding programme of
cultural renewal, one which, thanks to the ground-breaking originality of
T. S. Eliot, can continue to advance in the work of younger poets on
the basis of a new poetics and new models of achievement. Leavis's
argument in the book conflates two central ideas: T. S. Eliot's idea of
tradition, and I. A. Richards's postulate of poetry as an expression of the
post-metaphysical mind. Both concepts are anti-subjective, and both
powerfully influence the way the thesis develops. The thesis is that
contemporary poetry has a unique responsibility to discharge because the
cultural dislocations attendant upon the paradigmatic shift into modern
consciousness are so great that poetry has necessarily acquired a critical

rather than a normative function in respect of the poetry-reading habits of its readers: modern poetry is structured so as to disable conventional readings and to create ideological voids that reflect, rather than merely state, the anomie of the modern condition. Thus poetry of the Romantics and Victorians, a poetry of the expressive subject, is held to be quite helpless to confront the new conditions because the new poetry has to be a reflector of fractured consciousness, not a vessel of elevated sentiment. Equally a new idea of historical continuity is needed, one that, as 'tradition', re-assembles literary history as a continuity of particular levels of consciousness, not a series of established personal valuations.

Impersonality emerges in this account as a form of mentality, as the possession of an intellectual capacity to confront, to identify and to formulate in words the extreme alienation of the modern condition. Leavis appeared to believe, following Richards, that Eliot had not only independently identified and diagnosed a malaise of contemporary culture in terms essentially identical with his own, but that he had simultaneously begun to address and redress this in the innovations of his own poetry and criticism. Richards had argued that Eliot's *The Waste Land* was a great poem not simply because it took cultural dislocation and sterility as its subject, but, as remarked above, because this was a poem that had effected 'a complete severance between his poetry and all beliefs'.[20] Leavis phrases it less provocatively, and with a different emphasis:

> All that we can fairly ask of the poet is that he shall show himself to have been fully alive in our time. The evidence will be in the tone and the rhythm, in the very texture of his poetry . . .*The Waste Land*, more than any other work, brings the general malaise of the human spirit into the centre of full consciousness.[21]

Eliot's poem is here being appraised in ways that owe everything to Ricardian cultural theory and analytical technique. 'Tone and rhythm', 'texture' and 'full consciousness' are evaluative indicators of poetic competence, psychological complexity and intellectual awareness that trace their lineage back to *Principles of Literary Criticism* and *Practical Criticism*. The phrase 'fully alive' explicitly evokes Richards's vitalist Benthamism as presented in *Science and Poetry*.

Such terms point to psycho-linguistic elements that Ricardian poetics predicated as culturally significant. They functioned as verbal or psychological markers in that the 'general malaise of the human spirit' becomes a function of the expressive dynamics of the verse, not an observation emerging from it. Richards's preoccupation with aesthetic order as a cultural register is the governing principle of this analysis.

In fact the weight of paradox is evident in the phrase 'fully alive'. Eliot's poem, we understand, is a manifestation of malaise, of the age's deracination, not by virtue of what it 'says' — it is not designed to 'say' anything — but by virtue of its texture, its expressive disposition. The form of the poem, its fractured and fragmented structure, its limp movement and depressed rhythms, enact, it is claimed, a larger human sterility, an emotional vacuity at the heart of society. It does not state but formulates a lack of life and virility. In a sense then we are being invited to see its vigour in its fidelity to inertia, its force in its very feebleness. The creative energy behind the poem, the subjective dynamic, has been so effectively displaced, disguised or defaced, as to be invisible as an irrelevance. To this extent *The Waste Land* is here presented as a poem without a poet, without a creator, without personal origin. Wyndham Lewis had made clear that such an idea was an abomination in his eyes. But, following Richards, Leavis stresses this as an unmitigated positive: that it is high art because it is an expression of an informed intellect and a high degree of consciousness; a manifestation of a sophisticated awareness of contemporary conditions. The very renunciation of personality is held to be culturally indicative of poetic penetration and percipience, its 'objectivity'. This in fact strikes the key-note for this phase of Leavis's appreciation of literary culture in general and T. S. Eliot's work in particular. Poetry as the enactment of a degree of contemporary awareness, a particular level of consciousness, is linked to an idea of the non-subjective as a criterion of authenticity.

As long as impersonality was linked to a poetics of crisis, this position was a consistent and coherent one. Because Richards had shown that modern culture was uniquely situated, epistemologically, in a phase characterized by its loss of human centrality, it followed for Leavis that the crisis of modern poetic form exemplified in poetry such as *The Waste Land* and 'Hugh Selwyn Mauberley' must be similarly acute, similarly insoluble. With no hope of re-instating the human subject as the criterion of poetic significance, the implication was that all subsequent poetry would have to be like *The Waste Land*, and all interpretation confined to exegesis and technical appraisal. But an important divergent strand of enquiry in

New Bearings follows a different path to this one: one that shows Leavis displaying the first of the many critical initiatives that were to identify him as capable of independence of his mentors and having the capacity to emerge as a major critic of our day.

In the first of the essays on Eliot, 'A Reply to the Condescending' (1929), Leavis had drawn a fairly sharp distinction between Eliot the poet-critic and Eliot the cultural savant. As the first, Eliot was to be seen as a figure of remarkable originality and innovative thinking; as the latter, although Leavis does not presume to pass judgment on Eliot's recent conversion to Anglicanism, it is evident that he thinks Eliot's decision to become a Christian is odd, puzzling certainly.

Three years later, when *New Bearings* was published, a quite different attitude to Eliot's religious interests is evident in the book. This is because Eliot himself had changed the poetic landscape significantly by adding to his creative *oeuvre* a number of religious poems. Leavis, in the earlier essay, was able to disregard Eliot's Anglicanism because it was confined just to the occasional essays that made up *For Lancelot Andrewes* (1927). By 1932 Eliot had published the 'Ariel' poems and 'Ash Wednesday' (1930), adding a new kind of poetry, modern religious poetry, to the contemporary literary scene and thus creating a new interpretive task for the critic.

In *New Bearings* it is clear that a shift of critical emphasis had taken place in Leavis's position, even over the short period that existed between his writing on Eliot in 1929 and 1930, and the publication of the book in 1932. *The Waste Land*, as it appears in the two essays, is the epitome of modern creative verse; it is the definitive model for how the modern sensibility was to confront and contain the modern crisis of consciousness. In the book the poem is still a central component of Eliot's achievement, still a model of its kind, but it is no longer the *non plus ultra*; there are now reservations to be expressed about it that found no place in the earlier writing:

> It [*The Waste Land*] has, that is, certain limitations in any case; limitations inherent in the conditions that produced it. Comprehensiveness, in the very nature of the undertaking, must be in some sense at the cost of structure; absence of direction, of organizing principle, in life could hardly be made to subserve the highest kind of organization in art.[22]

Here we note that the absence of subjective order is being construed as the basis of a failure in the structure of the poem. This would not have been said, because it would not have been thought, in the earlier essays. More radically, in drawing a comparison between Ezra Pound's technical virtuosity and Hopkins's technical skills and innovations, Leavis questions whether Eliot was right to see Pound as a master of technique. As far as Leavis is concerned the American is a virtuoso, deploying elaborate and complex expressive techniques to no very good purpose; by contrast Hopkins's technical complexities justify themselves because they are part of a larger meaning:

> But remarkable as 'The Wreck of the Deutschland' is, it does not put his technical skill to the utmost stretch. This skill is most unmistakably that of a great poet when it is at the service of a more immediate personal urgency, when it expresses not religious exaltation, but inner debate . . . Hopkins's genius was as much a matter of rare character, intelligence, and sincerity as of technical skill: indeed, in his great poetry the distinction disappears; the technical triumph is a triumph of spirit (pp. 180–181)

Hopkins, though a Victorian, is in effect a more modern poet, one closer to Eliot, than Pound, on Leavis's reading. 'Inner debate' and 'personal urgency' are qualities that are here invoked to vindicate a modern poet's technical virtuosity; they are the ingredients of an inner condition that expresses itself only through complex elisions, allusions, discords or other dislocating devices. Thus a spiritual condition now begins to emerge as a validating factor in the matter of challengingly difficult verse. Hopkins is more sincere than Pound because the tensions inherent in his verse are deemed to be fully expressive of inner tensions that are not only not part of some superior game of form, such as Pound is thought to be playing, but are resolvable into a 'triumph of spirit'.

And the same spiritual qualities are found, unsurprisingly, to be central in Eliot's verse. This poetry is now celebrated not only because in it Eliot 'compels a poetic triumph out of the peculiar difficulties facing a poet in the [modern] age', but also because:

> . . . in essentials Mr Pound's poetry is very different from Mr Eliot's. There are in it none of Mr Eliot's complex intensities of concern about soul and body: the moral, religious, and anthropological preoccupations are absent (p. 140)

For this reason the area of Eliot's work that Leavis finds of most interest in *New Bearings* is not the cultural diagnoses of *The Waste Land*, but the deep seriousness prompting Eliot's excursions into areas of religious belief in the 'Ariel' poems and 'Ash Wednesday'. As Leavis had tactfully pointed out in 'A Reply', these were areas within which 'we may not always follow him, in either sense of the word.' Nonetheless it is this new poetry which, in *New Bearings*, is felt to be leading criticism into new areas and confronting it with new challenges. Hopkins's poetry had been commended for its complexity of expression because that reflected a commensurate conflict of spiritual experience:

> the association of inner, spiritual emotional stress with physical reverberations, nervous and muscular tensions, that characterizes his best verse is here [in 'The Wreck of the Deutschland'] explicitly elaborated in an account of the storm which is at the same time an account of an inner drama (pp. 175–6)

Similarly, this new poetry of Eliot's represents a poetry of profound depth, a poetry of anguish as in the 'Ariel' poems ('If the extreme agony of consciousness has passed, so has the extraordinary vitality that went with it'), or a poetry of painful probing and seeking as in 'Ash Wednesday':

> For the poet 'technique' was the problem of sincerity. He had to achieve a paradoxical precision-in-vagueness; to persuade the elusive intuition to define itself, without any forcing, among the equivocations of 'the dreamcrossed twilight.' The warning against crude interpretation, against trying to elicit anything in the nature of prose statement, is there in the unexpected absence of punctuation . . . The poetry itself is an effort at resolving diverse impulses, recognitions, and needs (p. 119)

Unlike Hopkins, however, Eliot is writing poetry of a new kind, or new level, of spiritual disaffection:

> The poetry of the last phase may lack the charged richness and the range of 'Gerontion' and *The Waste Land*. But it is, perhaps, still more remarkable by reason of the strange and difficult regions of experience that it explores . . . this poetry is more disconcertingly modern than *The Waste Land*: the preoccupation with traditional Christianity, the use of the Prayer Book, and the devotion to spiritual discipline should not hinder the reader from seeing that the modes of feeling, apprehension, and expression are such as we can find nowhere earlier (pp. 131–2)

What interests Leavis is that this poetry explores 'strange and difficult regions of experience'. This is not Christian belief, in the usual sense, but the inner processes by which a person arrives at a belief, the interrogation and exploration of the inner self, so that what is believed in is something felt, something experienced at a spiritual level. For Leavis this takes the problem of sincerity in poetry to a new level of difficulty, one which called for quite different modes of analysis than those associated solely with cultural diagnosis. For him Eliot had up to this point been the ultra-modern consciousness, the mind that had appeared, in *The Waste Land*, to see no grounds for belief and no possibility of redemption from meaninglessness and nullity. If, as Eliot's new poetry seemed to show, technical development in verse was possible beyond that point this may have been, he came to realize, because the Ricardian diagnosis of the cultural plight had been too simplistically reductive, too unaware of the resilience of the religious spirit to survive even in the cryogenic regions of modern scepticism. It also called for a fuller reappraisal of the place of subjectivity in poetry.

Between 1929–30 and 1932 Leavis had begun to shed some of his Ricardian-based notions of the literary subject (he had never adopted, or perhaps even understood, Eliot's subjective theory). No longer did it seem adequate to envisage impersonality as a purely intellectual or psychological quality, as a condition of high consciousness. High consciousness, in the sense of a bleak view of the survival of culture, was still held to be essential to the modern poet, but the appearance of a new kind of personally sensitive poetry, one associated with religious belief and spiritual explor- ation, made a larger, more comprehensive idea of the impersonal subject necessary. This could not be found in either Richards or Eliot. What Leavis needed was an idea of impersonality that began from quite different premises than theirs: that did not renounce the old humanist idea of the subject but transformed it in a way that released it from its links with impressionism, dilettantism and the 'adventures of the soul among the masterpieces'. What was needed, in fact, was a way of looking at the humanist subject that would permit Leavis to escape from the realist dualism of Richards and the speculative metaphysics of Eliot into a new conception of how subjectivity can be impersonal in literature.

This was what D. H. Lawrence helped him to do. Lawrence showed him how a philosophy of human meaning could be developed out of literary art conceived of as an exploration of the impersonal aspect of personality. Michael Bell has described how modernism embraced two opposed conceptions of impersonality. One, associated with Joyce and Flaubert, was the impersonality of authorial detachment, an attempted erasing of all affective elements from the literary work. The other, polarized against it in the work of Lawrence, Dickens and Dostoievsky, was an impersonality of deep subjectivity:

> [this impersonality] . . . is frankly personal to the point of being pro-phetic. Yet the prophet's voice, like the novelist's, is necessarily in some sense impersonal. The difference is that for [Lawrence *et al.*] the im-personal is a quality of their explicit involvement in the subject and is, therefore, a quality achieved within and through the personality. Im-personality, in this conception, is not the minimum but the maximum degree of personality.[23]

Bell goes on to argue that in the case of T. S. Eliot, who identified himself firmly with the first of these positions, Leavis eventually detected that:

> There is a revealing disjuncture between the critical principle and its rhetorical formulation . . . Neither the techniques of impersonality, nor the conscious aesthetic commitment to it can guarantee the achievement of it and may indeed constitute precisely the symptom of a fundamental anxiety, or failure, in that area. The celebration of impersonality can be a mystification; the technique an unwitting alibi.[24]

This gives a perspective on *The Waste Land* which was beyond Leavis when he was writing *New Bearings*. He was at that point conscious of technique as a manifestation of impersonality, but not of impersonality as itself a condition of sincerity, an index or expression of inner worth. It was only when he had come to see that 'Lawrence's very vulnerability, even his manifest errors, [were] part of an exemplary self-exploration that achieved its representative, or impersonal, value through its very open-handedness'[25] that Leavis changed to a standpoint that could release him to find and express his full critical potential. And which was to permit him then to look at Eliot's verse with a truly critical eye and Richards's poetics with dismissive impatience.

This was a process, of course, that took many years. But it was protracted because a great deal more than a change of critical stance, or emphasis, was required to bring it about. In effect, Leavis had to re-educate himself in a range of assumptions about the nature of language, truth and reality that were foreign to him both as heir to I. A. Richards and to the tradition of Cambridge academic worthies that his wife celebrates in her essays on the 'Cambridge tradition' in *Scrutiny*.[26] Although he began his criticism in the positivistic tradition of Cambridge social science that Richards had adopted and adapted for the young English school, Leavis's sense of literary worth was to become much broader than this and to lead him to a conception of literary truth, of knowledge, that broke new ground and took him into unfamiliar territory. (Bell puts it: 'we need to see [Leavis] not just as the inheritor of the Arnoldian critical endeavour but also as the English equivalent of the continental phenomenological tradition.'[27]) In effect, under the pressure of his expanding knowledge of, and reflection upon, literary experience, Leavis had to become not just his own literary critic but his own literary philosopher as well. Unlike Richards, who, in attempting to fit literary judgment into the narrow confines of logical realism, drastically reduced its possible range; or Eliot, who abandoned it as a species of temptation in the path of discovering the true light (he cast D. H. Lawrence as one of the four tempters – devils – in early drafts of *Murder in the Cathedral*), Leavis developed a poetics that accepted and refurbished the traditional understanding of literature as possessing cognitive power and a capacity for making normative judgments.[28] In the climate of post-metaphysical philosophy, this was a challenging position to adopt.

Specifically, he devised a notion of literature as a particularly salient instance of the 'third realm', the realm of the distinctively human. This, to the extent that it is a philosophy of meaning – 'you cannot point to the poem; it is "there" only in the re-creative response of individual minds to the black marks on the page'[29] – one that ran counter to the philosophical orthodoxy then current – committed him to a philosophical account of sorts; it had to be negotiated with considerable intellectual care, given the complexity of the epistemological issues involved. Leavis met this challenge by making a rhetorical virtue out of his refusal to enter the philosophical arena, emphasizing that he was acting not in a spirit of evasion but choosing to make a deliberate methodological statement. He contested, as a matter of intellectual principle, the right of modern departments of philosophy (he was thinking, I imagine, primarily of Cambridge) to establish the credentials upon which literary criticism and literary understanding could be validated. He refused to accept that critical enquiry and literary creation should be seen, methodologically, as philosophical activities:

He [Michael Tanner] has a strong tendency to assume . . . that an argument of the kind I offer [in *The Living Principle*] is inevitably philosophical and challenges the criteria natural to a reader of philosophical training and habit. But what I offer Tanner is not consistently even an equivalent in my 'anti-philosophical' mode of thought. My distinctive preoccupation with the nature of thought and language isn't separable from my preoccupation with the problem of creating a new educated public; hence the part played in my argument by the university and the English School.[30]

The link indicated here, in an essay of 1976, between his methodological concerns and the objective of creating a 'new educated public' is one that brings to mind the historico-cultural critical path mapped out for Leavis in the early thirties by I. A. Richards and T. S. Eliot. The difference is that then the coordinates for the journey ahead had been partly established, via Richards, by current philosophical (i.e. positivist-realist) thinking; in 1976 the same philosophical forces, now consolidated as professional interests and endorsed in the massive prestige of Wittgenstein, had come to seem to him forbidding aspects of the cultural problem. Modern philosophy, Leavis believed, frequently lent intellectual force to those habits of mind obstructive to an understanding of how and why a correct understanding of the nature of literary thought is vital to the continuation, or rehabilitation, of a living culture. In response to Michael Tanner's request for him to provide an account of how literary taste is justified, Leavis replied:

> Tanner's assumption that value-judgements in literary criticism are to be justified by philosophical analysis is explicit. Tanner, I think, never escapes from that assumption (in common, I suspect, with most philosophers . . .) . . . 'Verifiable' . . . must have, if used of literary-critical judgement, an utterly different meaning ('value') from that which it has in natural science − and at the mathematico-logical end of discourse from which the thinking of philosophers seems in general to begin, and continues to treat as the inevitable basic mode (pp. 189−90)

The problem, as Tanner sees it, is one of criteria: how does Leavis justify his judgments *logically*?

> [Leavis] may have fallen into the very common mistake of the British Empiricist Tradition . . . of substituting biographical-psychological descriptions [of critical judgements] for philosophical analyses (p. 189)

But, Leavis replies, logic does not, and cannot, come into it, given the nature of literary judgment and how it operates:

> I point out that the word 'value' changes its value as we move along the spectrum from the coercively verifiable to the 'values' I deal in when I discuss, say, Hardy's 'After A Journey' . . . Most, if not all, philosophers seem, having started from the mathematico-logical end of the spectrum, to be powerless to escape from limitations implicit in such a start. The discipline itself entails the limitation. They can't get beyond the shift in the force of 'value' that leaves behind the ideas both of the quantitative and the provable (p. 197)

For Leavis there are other, larger criteria than that of logic:

> . . . the creative writer in his creativity isn't confined to one part of the spectrum; he has the freedom of his native language, freedom along the whole range of the spectrum to use the resources of English, and you can't tell beforehand what liberties will justfiy themselves (p. 192)

These are not Derridean 'liberties', of course: Leavis is not interested in the extent to which creativity is an exercise in *jouissance*. For Leavis, '. . . the surest insight into human nature, human potentiality and human situation is that accessible in the great creative writers. They establish what human centrality is.' With its emphasis upon creativity as the mark of the distinctively human, a formative constituent of the human world, such a pronouncement indicates how far Leavis has travelled since he made his early, quasi-philosophical repudiation of philosophy in his exchange with Wellek. His view of criticism, preserving an essential continuity with that early debate, extends the idea of the critic as a 'realizer' of the text before him, to that of a recognizer of its truth, its grasp and perception of human reality:

> The rare real critic too has a more than average capacity for experience, and a passion at once for sincerity and complete conviction. He knows that, in the nature of things, he can't attain to the completeness that is finality, and that some of his certitudes may be insufficiently grounded. But though words used in ordinary ways are felt as merely words, and can't give the quality *an sich* that makes the immediate experience irresistably real, the nearest the perceptively thinking individual gets to the certainty that he is grasping in direct possession significance itself, unmediated, is in the certitude that he has taken possession of the basic major perceptions, intuitions and realizations communicated with

consummate delicacy to the reader in the mastering of the creative
work of a great writer (p. 192)

The kind of certainty that Tanner associates with logical proof is presented
here as overridden by a different kind of certainty: the certainty of
conviction. This certainty is a certainty of intellectual intuition. It begins
in 'sincerity and complete conviction', but its force is extra-subjective in
that it consists in a 'grasping in direct possession significance itself'. Literary
criticism for Leavis is an addressing of the whole psyche – the judgments
here express a full emotional as well as mental engagement – to making
the right kind of recognition; a recognition that postulates a reality external
to itself to be recognized, but one that has no reality that can be known
independent of such a recognition. What is being grasped is a meaning,
a significance, that arises in and out of language, the primary component
of that reality which Leavis characterizes as the 'third realm', the human
world.

It is in the nature of philosophical enquiry that statements of this kind
are inevitably going to provoke further discussion and questioning. But
from Leavis's position, such enquiry has no force because it is not governed
by an acceptable view of an outcome; it has no culturally constructive
objective in mind to direct and channel the direction of its speculation.
By contrast, Leavis argues, criticism is always directed to an end, that of
elucidating the nature of literature which is, in itself, directed by purpose
and meaning:

> The principle of organization, and the principle of development, in
> [Jane Austen's] work is an intense moral interest of her own in life
> that is in the first place a preoccupation with certain problems that life
> compels on her as personal ones. She is intelligent and serious enough
> to be able to impersonalize her moral tensions as she strives, in her art,
> to become more fully conscious of them, and to learn what, in the
> interests of life, she ought to do with them. Without her intense moral
> preoccupation she wouldn't have been a great novelist.[31]

Jane Austen's purpose is to understand her own humanity, an effort that
forges art-as-thought, as human meaning, out of the dark recesses of her
personality, her psyche, so that it can come into the light of language as
an objectively knowable reality.

Leavis was, we can see, faced with a powerful exhortation when
Wittgenstein said to him: 'give up literary criticism.' Even in those early

days it must have been apparent to him that if literature was not to be vindicated as a form of knowledge with its own kind of objectivity then, in the contemporary world, it would cease to matter; it would become one of the amenities of life, like scuba-diving or bell-ringing. It would be no more than what Eliot had said it was, 'a form of superior amusement'.[32] If however it was to be defended as a form of knowledge – and Leavis was not prepared to see it as anything less – then by what methodology was it to be so justified? Where was the philosophical weaponry that could be deployed in its favour or on its behalf? Now, as we know, arguments can be deployed to show that there are philosophical equivalents to the kind of critical claims that Leavis made on behalf of literature; Michael Bell in his book on Leavis has developed an analogy between Heidegger and Leavis that enhances the latter's critical efforts in a way which might not have earned him gratitude from Leavis himself but which certainly does the rest of us a valuable service. Yet such an approach, assuming he approved of it, was not available to Leavis. He relied entirely on his knowledge of literature and the support, as he saw it, of great writers such as Blake, Dickens, and Lawrence. The salient fact is that Leavis was at one with his origins as a Cambridge critic of the early modern era in seeing that literature in the modern era could not function as it should, as a force for cultural and social renewal, if it lacked intellectual authority. Yet he was very much his own man in further understanding that any attempt to justify literature in terms that would satisfy the philosophic guardians of the new 'Benthamite-utilitarian' world that we live in, would falsify and misrepresent its nature. Thus he became the only modern critic to do what Samuel Johnson had done two hundred years before him: to make his practice the principal expression of the principles of that practice.

Leavis is a literary philosopher – not a philosopher of literature – because he understood that the nature of literary enquiry is determined by the nature of literature, and the nature of literature is determined by the recognitions that it enables. These recognitions are elusive in that they frequently depend upon a view of meaning that is not only not in itself self-evident but which in much current advanced thinking is almost unrecognizably out of sight. Which is why the critic, in Leavis's eyes, has still an important task to perform.[33] But this task cannot be done unless the critic is wholly inward with such meaning. His or her practice as a critic must be a demonstration of this inwardness, a demonstration that can only take the form of displaying the appropriate recognitions. This was what Leavis himself spent a lifetime trying to do, and what, a hundred years on from his birth, continues to indicate to us why the study and criticism of literature are important. It is for us to show whether, faced with this truth, we can effectively recognize it by putting it into critical practice.

Leavis and Post-Structuralism

In a lucid account of the rise of British post-structuralism, Antony Easthope says that it 'engages critically with English national culture . . . in an attempt to transform it'. At the heart of this national culture is English Literature and at the heart of that is Leavis. His notion of 'seriousness', for example, is the literary equivalent of 'the particular British national tradition of moral seriousness and obsession with "the real"'.[1] Following the logic of Easthope's argument it would be reasonable to assume that he would give some account of how British post-structuralism 'engages' with Leavis, but this he fails to do. He has six references to Leavis, all of them fleeting. He does, however, refer the reader to Catherine Belsey's elegant introduction to post-structuralist theory, *Critical Practice*. Belsey argues that Leavis's criticism rests on the presupposition of what she calls 'expressive realism'. This is 'the theory that literature reflects the reality of experience as it is perceived by one (especially gifted) individual, who expresses it in a discourse which enables other individuals to recognize it as true'.[2]

Now, if this represents a post-structuralist 'engagement' with Leavis it is a very disappointing one. First, Leavis does not talk about literature 'reflecting' reality. This, in fact, was the crude Marxist view with which he took issue in the 1930s. Second, the phrase 'reality of experience' – which is not, to my knowledge, to be found in Leavis – suggests it is prior to literature whose job is to 'reflect' it. But even the most cursory reading of Leavis reveals that reality is not prior to language but created by it, and this is not totally inconsistent with the post-structuralist claim that the 'real' is not named but constructed by language. Language, writes Belsey, 'is not a nomenclature, a way of naming things which already exist, but a system of differences with no positive terms . . . [it] precedes the existence of independent entities, making the world intelligible by differentiating between concepts' (p. 38). Further, Belsey's claim that 'only a social group can generate signs' (p. 41) finds an echo in Leavis's discussion of the 'third realm' where critics, through the institutions of criticism and the apparatus of education, create the poem they discuss:

> What we call analysis is a creative . . . process . . . One is engaged in discussion; discussion of? – the poem, which is there for discussion only in so far as the discussers have each for him [her] self created it. The discussion, in fact, is an effort to establish the poem.[3]

A third objection to Belsey's characterization of Leavis's criticism concerns the idea of expression. Belsey links expression to 'the author's ideas, psychological state or social background' – in short, to the author's intention.[4] But Leavis is extremely circumspect about such a notion:

> The critic will be especially wary how [s]he uses extraneous knowledge about the writer's intentions. Intentions are nothing in art except as realised [and] the deep animating intention (if that is the right word) is something very different from the intention the author would declare.[5]

Moreover, Leavis rarely, if ever, uses the word 'expression' in relation to literary language. For him, literary language is consistently a mode of exploration or enactment:

> language [is] not a medium in which to put 'previously definite' ideas, but [a medium] for exploratory creation. Poetry as creating what it presents, and as presenting something that stands there to speak for itself, or rather, that isn't a matter of saying, but of being and enacting he [Johnson] couldn't properly understand.[6]

Its probing quality unsettles conviction: 'significant art challenges in the most disturbing and inescapable way to a radical pondering, a new profound realisation of the grounds of our most important determinations and choices'.[7] Literature, for Leavis, does not reassure. It provides no answers:

> 'What for – what ultimately for?' is implicitly asked in all the greatest art, from which we get, not what we are likely to call an 'answer' but the communication of a felt significance; something that 'confirms our sense of life as more than a mere linear succession of days, a matter of time as measured by the clock'.[8]

Enactment is a more complex phenomenon, and needs to be seen in the context of the divisive nature of modernity. Essentially, it is a sensuous attempt to reunify the subject whose various faculties have been severed from one another by the rigid classifications of 'mass civilization'.

It is important to stress the subversive quality of Leavis's work since Belsey is intent on presenting 'expressive realism' as a conservative force. In the first place, she argues, it is tautological:

> The claim that a literary form reflects the world is simply tautological. If by 'the world' we understand the world we experience, the world differentiated by language, then the claim that realism reflects the world means that realism reflects the world constructed in language. This is a tautology.[9]

In the second place, expressive realism is conservative because it aims to promote single rather than plural meanings. It achieves this by guaranteeing meaning either by reference to 'the author's mind', to 'the world we all know', or to a combination of the two.[10] It has already been argued that Leavis's criticism does not view literature as a 'reflection' of reality. This is one example of Belsey's misreading or even non-reading of his work. Another is her emphasis on meaning. The key term in Leavis's vocabulary is not meaning but 'significance'. What the critic asks of a work is '[h]ow, as we come to appreciate it and realise its significance, does it affect our sense of things that have determining significance for us?'[11] Obviously one cannot exist without the other. It would not be to the purpose to be drawn into a discussion of what is understood by each term.[12] What is relevant is that while meaning can be neutral, significance never can. Theoretically at least, it is possible for meaning to be 'value free', but not significance. Questions of significance are inseparable from those of valuation. The difference between Belsey and Leavis is that while she appears to abdicate responsibility over the matter of significance, though of course her advocacy of the plurality of meaning is itself a value choice, Leavis does not. He does, however, avoid the issue of interpretation. For him the meaning of a work is self-evident, a view underscored by his frequent use of the term 'obvious'.

Belsey's aim to generate a multiplicity of meaning is strangely at odds with the single meaning with which she invests 'expressive realism'. In other words she is guilty of the very crime with which she charges Leavis. What is apparent from this is that Leavis functions as a foil in her argument, a straw figure against which her own 'critical practice' can appear more progressive. The Leavis that Belsey presents is one who bears little relation to the one who emerges after a close 'engagement' with his work. That she can misread Leavis in this way is sanctioned by her 'critical practice'. Throughout, her aim is to show that, because meaning is socially constructed, it can always be changed. This gives Belsey a licence to construct the Leavis she needs for her argument. Of course every argument requires a selective presentation of an opponent's views, but what is worrying here is her attribution of a viewpoint and a terminology to Leavis for which there is little or no evidence at all. 'Construction' of a meaning, as Belsey constructs the meaning of Leavis, needs to be based on something more than the exigencies of one's own particular case; otherwise there is no possibility of critical dialogue, only monologue.

The fact that meaning is constructed means that it is plural. Belsey gives an example of how the sentence 'democracy will ensure that we extend the boundaries of civilization' will be given different meanings by 'a Conservative M.P., a committed socialist, or the Vice President of Pepsi-Cola'. She goes on to argue that though '[t]he context of such a sentence might be expected to narrow the range of possible meanings, [that] context [itself] is also subject to interpretation'.[13] The problem with this is how to reach an agreement about meaning. One solution is social groups who 'generate signs', but these must always already have come to an agreement about meaning since such an agreement is the condition of their existence rather than their goal. Even if this objection could be surmounted, there is the more serious one that Belsey's emphasis on the ceaseless proliferation of meaning militates against any notion of cohesion, without which not just a social group but the idea of society itself is impossible.

Belsey's goal of pluralizing meaning is premised on the assumption that traditional criticism, particularly 'expressive realism' imposes limits on a text and 'refuse[s] . . . to liberate its plurality'.[14] Again, the promotion of plurality depends on a single meaning imposed on a rich and diverse body of work. Yet it is simply not true that traditional criticism was a consensus about the meaning of works which composed the 'great tradition'. The most cursory glance at 'traditional' criticism reveals more disagreement than agreement, but it is precisely through such differences of opinion that criticism evolves. Leavis at least allows for a divergence of views with 'Yes, but,' his anticipated response to the question 'This is so, isn't it?' It is the case that Leavis rarely modified his position in dispute with other critics and the manner of some of his exchanges is one of the less pleasant aspects of his work. This does not, however, invalidate his observation. The value of the writing is not cancelled by the behaviour of the person who writes, unless one wants to resurrect the biographical form of criticism. No, Leavis's insight is sound. There needs to be a measure of agreement about a work in order to make differences of opinion about it fruitful. As Empson noted, 'some degree of imaginative sympathy is necessary if criticism is to be profitable.'[15]

It has been suggested that Leavis was more concerned with significance than meaning. Read in one way, Leavis's concern that the study of literature would not be enhanced by studying 'the time patterns in Iris Murdoch's novels or the philosophy of Angus Wilson' does seem good evidence for the view that he wanted to curtail the meanings that could be attributed to a work.[16] Read in another way, however, this can be understood as a response to the uncertainties and anxieties of modernity. Samuel Hynes notes that the economic crisis of 1931 was seen by many people in England 'as more than a temporary economic reverse [as in fact] the collapse of an inherited system of values and the end of a secure life'.[17] Writing in 1930, Leavis put the problem this way: 'the modern is exposed to a concourse of signals so bewildering in their variety that . . . he can hardly begin to discriminate. Here we have the plight of culture in general. The landmarks have shifted, multiplied and crowded upon one another, the distractions and dividing lines have blurred away, the boundaries are gone . . .'[18]

Leavis's construction of a poetic tradition and a tradition of the novel is an attempt to organize this 'concourse of signals', to assert distinctions and dividing lines, and to draw boundaries. It is an attempt 'to be vigilant and scrupulous about the relation between words and the concrete',[19] a relation which 'civilization' has atrophied, replacing it with a consciousness of what is abstract and general. In such a climate words become imprecise, 'the same words are used with different meanings'[20] and it is the task of the literary critic to curb and, if possible, reverse this process. In this Leavis is following Pater, who wrote that it was the job of the literary scholar 'to resist a constant tendency . . . to efface the distinctions of language'.[21] Leavis develops this when he writes that 'literary criticism provides the test for life and concreteness; where it degenenerates the instruments of thought degenerate too.'[22]

The attempt to limit the meaning of words should not be seen as oppressive. On the contrary, where words have no fixed meaning they are more easily appropriated by the apparatus of power. Democracy, to use Belsey's example, may mean different things to different people but those people are not equally placed to persuade others to accept their meaning. It is therefore imperative that there is some measure of agreement about what democracy 'means' so that those who try to limit its extension can be confronted, at least rhetorically, with an ideal definition.

There are, of course, numerous problems with the above argument. One is that it seems to suggest that words have a trans-historical meaning which does not alter with either the different sentences or the different contexts in which they appear.[23] Another is the enormous, perhaps insurmountable problem of stabilizing the meaning of words given that, as Leavis recognized, there is no ultimate grounding for them in reality since 'reality', even at its most 'objective', 'is a product of human creativity'. The only mechanism capable of achieving a widespread agreement about meaning is the mass media, but at the cost of simplifying it with the result that language and therefore 'the world' are 'impoverished'.[24] Both these objections invite a deeper consideration of the problem than can be given here.

Although a more thoroughgoing analysis of the problem is needed before either Belsey's or Leavis's position can be more fully appreciated, the fundamental argument remains: without some control over the meaning of words they are apt to be exploited. Literary criticism is one – very small – defence measure. It develops awareness of the relation between words and the concrete and so promotes the value of the particular against the general.

It seems then, that Leavis has been misread. The question then arises as to what motivates this misreading. The reason has already been given: that by presenting Leavis as conservative, post-structuralism can appear more progressive. What this disguises is post-structuralism's complicity with the existing order. This is too large a subject to be entered into in any detail here, but the following observations are in order. First, post-structuralism has flourished during a period of conservative government. Second, the post-structuralist stress on the primacy of the signifier over the signified means that the latter 'is only a moment in a never ending process of signification where meaning is produced . . . only within the infinite, intertextual play of signifiers'.[25] The signifier, in short, continually exceeds the signified, rather as the credit expansion of the 1980s exceeded the amount of available money in the economy. A third point suggests itself in the form of a question. How far has post-structuralism's attack on the notion of a unified, autonomous subject facilitated the gradual erosion of civil liberties in this country over the last decade? It is not suggested that post-structuralists deliberately align themselves with the existing order – indeed, since 'the individual . . . can no longer be seen as the origin of meaning, knowledge and action' this would not be possible.[26] Rather it is the case that post-structuralist thought is caught up in a network of determinations even more complex than those it describes. If 'language . . . speaks us'[27] then it is reasonable to suggest that the interests of capital can speak post-structuralism.

One indication of the symmetry between post-structuralism and con-sumer capitalism lies in the very style of Belsey's prose. Clear, polished and beautifully balanced, it suggests a control of her material – which ought not to be possible on the basis of her argument. She shows a divided subject too caught up in the determinations of language ever to be able to stand apart from and summarize its general and institutional organizations and effects. Yet this is precisely what she does. Her prose gives no sense of struggle but has a transparent quality illustrating the "'tyranny of lucidity", the impression that what is being said must be true because it is obvious, clear and familiar'.[28]

The complicity of post-structuralism with consumer capitalism weakens its charge of conservatism against Leavis, whose writings can be considered radical. As Eagleton noted of the *Scrutiny* enterprise, 'no subsequent movement within English studies has come near to recapturing the courage and radicalism of their stand.'[29] Even Easthope has to acknowledge that 'the work of Leavis was potentially . . . radical.'[30] Recognitions of Leavis as radical do not, however, prevent him from being constructed as conservative. It is strange that, faced with a radicalism within the English tradition, post-structuralists should use French theory to repress it.

It would need a separate paper to bring out in what ways Leavis's work could be described as radical, but the following observations are important. First, Leavis has a published record of opposition not only to the institutions of mass culture but also the organs of government. In particular, he consistently opposed government attempts to make education the servant of industry.[31] He strove to maintain its critical and reflexive capacities in an age which increasingly marginalized them; there is no parallel effort to be found in the work of post-structuralists, whose fire is directed not at what is happening to education but at the limitations of tradition. Although, as Leavis recognized, it is doubtful whether voices raised within education can ever have a direct influence on policy, they nevertheless help to create a climate of opinion which might inhibit the implementation of policy.[32] That there have been numerous changes in higher education over the last few years, many to its detriment, argue the absence of such a climate.[33]

The second point to make about Leavis's 'radicalism' concerns his prose style. It will be remembered that Belsey uses the phrase the 'tyranny of lucidity' because she believes that clarity conveys the impression that 'what is being said must be true because it is obvious, clear and familiar.' It will also be remembered that Belsey's prose is itself a model of clarity. By contrast, Leavis's prose has been described as 'extraordinarily difficult', a characteristic which arose due to 'the stress of needing to say radically new things'.[34] Thus on Belsey's criteria alone Leavis emerges as a more oppositional figure than she herself.

Third, although Leavis's prose is difficult it is, on the whole, free of the convolutions and cumbersome terminology of some varieties of post-structuralism.[35] This is not to say that there is no place for such writing, only that its difficulty should be proportionate to the novelty of its insights. The inaccessibility of some post-structuralist theory gives it an élitist character which is absent from Leavis's prose. His writing is more accessible and therefore more democratic than that of post-structuralists. It simultaneously connects with literature and 'ordinary' language, refining the perceptions and having its own perceptions refined by its contact with both. It is therefore a charged and vital language in contrast to that of post-structuralism. As such it is a source of resistance and protest in a way that post-structuralism is not. This is because post-structuralism emphasizes that words mean because they differ from one another, not because they correspond to the world. Its focus is therefore on language rather than on language and the world. Leavis, however, insists that there is no final separation between the two – though he speaks in terms of literary criticism and 'life' rather than of language and the world.[36] It may be objected that since both Leavis and post-structuralism share the belief that reality is the product of language then it is impossible to use this as a basis for distinguishing between them. This can be countered by noting that it is a question of emphasis. For post-structuralists reality is determined by language, for Leavis it is created by it and this means that his writing has therefore a more positive quality than that of post-structuralism.

Leavis still awaits, then, a post-structuralist reading. What form might such a reading take? A useful text to start with would be *Mass Civilization and Minority Culture*. This is an example of Leavis's early cultural criticism, which as Stefan Collini has pointed out had been too readily identified with nineteenth-century criticism instead of being seen in its own, proper context.[37] Part of that context is Freud's *Civilization and its Discontents*, which appeared in its English translation in 1930, the same year that *Mass Civilization and Minority Culture* was published.[38] Straightaway this establishes Leavis's work as part of a wider pre-occupation with the state of civilization. It was not merely an isolated grumbling against the garishness of the modern world.

Admittedly, Freud is writing as a psychoanalyst, Leavis as a literary critic. Furthermore, Freud is concerned with the nature of civilization as a whole whereas Leavis is concerned with the relation between civilization and culture in England in the late 1920s. In addition, Freud and Leavis posit different reasons for the present state of civilization. For Leavis the 'unprecedented' nature of 'the modern phase of human history' is due to 'the machine' whereas for Freud 'the inclination to aggression . . . constitutes the greatest impediment to civilization' (p. 59). Finally, whereas Leavis is concerned with evaluating the present condition of civilization 'it is very far from [Freud's] intention to express an opinion upon the value of human civilization' (p. 81).

There are, then, obvious differences between *Mass Civilization and Minority Culture* and *Civilization and its Discontents*, and it would be easy to add to the above list. But alongside these differences there are also some similarities which have to do with the structure of their respective arguments, in particular their attitude to and use of metaphor.

The chief metaphor that each employs is an economic one. Leavis writes that '[t]he accepted valuations are a kind of paper currency based upon a very small proportion of gold. To the state of such a currency the possibilities of fine living at any time bear a close relation' (p. 144). For Freud, '[h]appiness . . . is a problem of the economics of the individual's libido' (p. 20). Both writers, then, approach their respective problems in terms of economics; this speaks a concern for balance, equilibrium, order and proportion. As Freud notes, '[i]f the loss [of instinctual satisfaction] is not compensated for economically, one can be certain that serious disorders will ensue' (p. 34). Leavis makes the relevant point in his own case when he observes that 'the catastrophe' of civilization is due to 'the currency [being] debased and inflated' (p. 152).

It is not surprising that both *Mass Civilization and Minority Culture* and *Civilization and its Discontents* should be dominated by an economic metaphor when it is remembered that the years between 1929 and 1931 were marked by severe financial crisis. There was the Wall Street Crash of 1929 and in 1930, in Vienna, where Freud lived and practised, the Credit Anstalt bank failed through the depreciation of its holdings. Despite support from the Bank of England it collapsed, precipitating a crisis in German banks which led to a flight from the Mark. In July 1931 the Bank of England was losing gold at the rate of £2 million a day, which led to the August crisis, necessitating the recall of the Labour Cabinet. Ramsay Macdonald, the prime minister, proposed serious economies such as reducing unemployment payments and coming off the gold standard. The latter happened in September, but Macdonald's proposals to cut the dole along with other measures were opposed by eleven members of his cabinet as 'ask[ing] too much of the poorest poor'.[39] This split in the cabinet led to the downfall of the Labour government and the formation of a National one.

The economic crisis does not appear in Leavis or Freud as the cause of the problems of civilization, though in fact that is precisely what it was. However, it does register its presence through the metaphors of libidinal economy in Freud and the gold standard in Leavis. In both cases metaphor is treated with suspicion. Leavis, having just given the metaphor of the gold standard, writes 'there is no need to elaborate the metaphor' (p. 144) and yet this is precisely what he does by quoting a passage from I. A. Richards which illustrates his point that 'to the state of such a currency the possibilities of fine living at any time bear a close relation' (p. 144). Moreover, Richards's quotation 'gives the hint for another metaphor' (p. 144). Thus, despite saying that there is no need to elaborate his metaphor Leavis not only does so through the use of quotation but that quotation itself leads to another metaphor. Metaphor proliferates. Freud too is wary of metaphor. He uses the history of the building of Rome as a metaphor for psychic development, but abandons it because it leads to

things 'that are unimaginable and even absurd' (p. 7). And though his
argument remains heavily dependent on 'the similarity between the process
of civilization and the libidinal development of the individual' (p. 34) he
continually cautions that we should not 'pursue analogies to an obsessional
extreme' (p. 77) for 'we are only dealing with analogies' (p. 81). Both
Leavis and Freud depend upon metaphor but are alert to the way that it
conveys meanings beyond those they intend. It is as though each fears
that meaning will share the same fate of inflation and debasement suffered
by the currency of Austria and England.[40] In addition to the anxiety that
metaphor multiplies meaning there is also a sense of redundancy in both
texts. In Leavis this occurs principally in relation to his notion of the
'obvious'. What is obvious should, of course, be plain to everyone, but
Leavis finds that, as regards the state of civilization, it is 'not unnecessary
to restate the obvious' (p. 145). He continues to make similar comments
throughout *Mass Civilization and Minority Culture* (pp. 146, 149, 152, 153,
for example) which suggest a worry about being able to articulate the
obvious. Freud too is aware that his enquiry may result in nothing 'that
is not already common knowledge' (p. 23) and like Leavis he is troubled
by the fact he cannot illustrate what lies at the heart of his argument.
'[T]he meaning of the evolution of civilisation [is] the struggle between
Eros and Death' (p. 59), he writes, but it is 'not easy . . . to demonstrate
the activities of this . . . death instinct' (pp. 56–58).

The 'redundancy' of *Mass Civilization and Minority Culture* and *Civilization and its Discontents* resides in their repeating what seems to be common
knowledge but which at the same time eludes expression. Metaphor would
seem to aid expression but at the risk of introducing other considerations
not to the purpose. For this reason attempts are made to control metaphor,
but it successfully eludes them. In Freud, metaphor approaches a pathological state, so that far from illuminating a psychoanalytical insight it
becomes a condition which itself requires psychoanalytic investigation. In
Leavis, metaphor at first seems to be a rhetorical device for presenting an
abstract point in concrete form, but then it migrates inwards becoming
synonymous with consciousness itself. Finally, Leavis equates metaphor
with language itself, '[i]n their [the minority's] keeping, to use a metaphor
that is metonymy also . . . is the language . . . By "culture" I mean the
use of such a language' (p. 145). No longer a part of language, metaphor
is all of language and thus lies at the base of consciousness and the world.[41]

Since metaphor is the very condition of thought and reality, it under-
mines the distinction implicit in the economic metaphor of both texts
between, in Leavis's case, true and false value and, in Freud's, between
scientific and literary truth. Freud, in fact, has to resort to the metaphor
of the killing of the primal father, in order to establish the origin of human
guilt (p. 68). Scientific truth is thus rooted in metaphor. The case of Leavis
is more complex. In the first place, *Mass Civilization and Minority Culture*
begins with the observation that, in contrast to the Victorian period, 'one
must face problems of definition and formulation where Arnold could
pass lightly on' (p. 143). It is in this context that metaphor first makes its
appearance and hence can be understood as a supplement, an addition to
the inadequacies of definition and formulation. The metaphor of the gold
standard implies that valuation should have a precise worth and, in this
respect, it seems to contradict the idea that the modern age is characterized
by the inability to produce such specific articulations. This, indeed, may
be one of the reasons why Leavis shies away from elaborating the metaphor.
Another is that it almost dissolves into a literal statement, since there can
be no doubt that 'the possibilities of fine living' are closely related to 'the
state of [the] currency' (p. 143). But if metaphor does so dissolve then it
cannot function in the supplementary way that Leavis requires it should.
The problem is that metaphor is both a supplement and the expression
of the need for a precise value.

But although Leavis seems to argue, through his choice of metaphor,
for a precise value he also opposes that very notion. This is clear in his
disagreement with Richard Paget, who views language as 'a method of
symbolising human thought'.[42] Leavis clearly implies that language is
something more than this, though what he does not say. The reader may
therefore conclude that since metaphor, through its place in the argument,
functions as a supplement, it can be regarded as that 'something more'.
It is, however, a 'something more' which Leavis refuses to elaborate and,
moreover, it is identified with precision and exactitude, the very things
it is supposed to exceed. On top of all this metaphor is, of course, not a
supplement but the basis of language itself and therefore escapes any
attempt to grasp or define it.

The failure of Leavis and Freud to recognize the extent to which their
respective texts are dependent on metaphor calls into question their ability
to 'read' civilization. Indeed, a close reading of each text reveals that,

despite their declarations, they offer not a single cause for the parlous state of civilization but several.[43] This, though, is not acknowledged by either writer, nor are these causes either synthesized or brought into relation with one another. As a result it is not ultimately clear why civilization is in the state it is. The problem is that both Leavis and Freud are working within the paradigm of an economic metaphor that presumes a distinction between true and false which is not borne out by the textual operations of either *Mass Civilization and Minority Culture* or *Civilization and its Discontents*. The result is that the logic of both texts is skewed and the consequence, particularly for Leavis, is that his reading of civilization becomes an instance of the 'inflation' that he is trying to combat. Reading, for Leavis, is a matter of observing limits; 'the plight of culture in general', he notes, is due to the fact that 'distinctions and dividing lines have blurred away' (p. 158). However, the troublesome nature of metaphor in *Mass Civilization and Minority Culture*, on which his reading of civilization depends, can only contribute further to the dissolution of boundary lines, since it continually transports the text beyond what Leavis intends to say.

The consequences of the economic metaphor in both texts make themselves felt as a concern with how things are related to one another. This has already been seen in Leavis in his anxiety about 'distinctions and dividing lines', but it is also present in his claim that there is no public to endorse the 'first hand judgement[s]' (p. 143) of critics. Precisely what is absent here is relation, and it is noteworthy that this lack of relation is juxtaposed to the metaphor of the gold standard. Metaphor is thus implicated in the absence of relation. Freud too finds that metaphor presents problems in terms of relation. His analogy of Rome for the development of the psyche has to confront the problem that 'to represent historical sequence in spatial terms [can only be done] by juxtaposition in space: the same space cannot have two different contents' (pp. 7–8).

To explain why metaphor is implicated in the disorganization of relations in each text would take more space than is available here, but two points are in order. The first is a linguistic one. According to Roman Jakobson there are two poles of language, metaphor and metonymy.[44] Metaphor is the substitution of one term for another, whereas metonymy is the relation between them. In normal usage there is a balance between the two, but this is disturbed in aphasia. Jakobson concludes his analysis by noting that metaphor tends to be dominant in poetry, metonymy in prose fiction. In

Leavis and Freud metaphor is dominant. On Jakobson's scheme, this makes their analysis akin to poetry. It would be possible to proceed from this to claim both essays for post-modernism, which regards writing in terms of poetics. More interesting is to try and account for why metaphor is the dominant trope in each text, which brings in the second point. As noted, according to Jakobson the dominance in a discourse of either metaphor or metonymy indicates the presence of aphasia. Obviously it would be incorrect to apply Jakobson's description of a type of speech disturbance to discursive writing. Nevertheless, the parallel is a fruitful one. The claim is that the relative incoherence of the metonymic relations in both texts, manifested in the problem of relating one event to another, is due to a lack of confidence in the historical sense. Leavis notes that the period of history in which he is writing is 'unprecedented' (p. 145), while Freud struggles to reconcile his theory of the origin of guilt with history (p. 75) though, in fact, his history is nothing more than myth, specifically the killing of the primal father. History, for Leavis and Freud, threatens to escape representation altogether and in this it approaches the condition of the sublime.[45]

The challenge that *Mass Civilization and Minority Culture* and *Civilization and its Discontents* face is that of establishing divisions and dividing lines. It is the challenge, in other words, of being articulate, since without distinctions articulation or, in post-structuralist terminology, signification is impossible. For Freud this is broadly a matter of drawing 'the boundary lines between the ego and the external word' (p. 3) and for Leavis it is to make the 'bewildering' array of signals more coherent. This challenge has to be seen in the context of the emergent mass culture of the 1930s, which saw the transition from a society based on class to one based on consumerism.[46] This necessitated a realignment of persons and objects as competition within the mass market confronted the former with an array of goods vying for their attention. Which was the best way to present these goods? How could they be organized in relation to others? It was not only Leavis and Freud who faced problems of articulation and organization.

The coming of the mass market can be seen as an attack on the old order of society. It represents a challenge to its authority, the democracy of consumerism against the patriarchy of class. In short, the development of the mass market invites an Oedipal reading. It is perhaps no coincidence that Freud's text is so much pre-occupied with guilt at either killing the primal father or the wish to kill the real one (p. 69). But there is a paradox here. Although there is an attack on authority there is also a need for it, and this is apparent in the 1930s obsession with strong men.[47] The paradox is evident in Freud's notion of guilt: there is a desire to kill the father and to cling to him for protection (p. 9). Civilization for Freud revolves around this paradox. It is inseparable from a recognition of the father's authority and a wish to defy it. Leavis's understanding of culture is not the same as Freud's of civilization, but there is one similarity. Culture, like civilization, is dependent on the recognition of a paternal lineage, for it is with the 'minority capable . . . of appreciating Dante, Shakespeare, Donne, Baudelaire [and] Conrad [and] of recognising their latest successors' (p. 144) that the survival of culture rests. Leavis's tradition asserts the paternal line as mass culture begins its assault on the authority of that line, though at the same time it expresses a need for heroes. Freud's text captures this ambiguity more precisely.

This is not to denigrate Leavis's text. Rather it is to suggest that it is best read by being attentive to the time in which it was written. Part of this attentiveness consists in connecting it with other texts written in the same period. In paralleling *Mass Civilization and Minority Culture* with *Civilization and its Discontents* a psychoanalytic reading of the former becomes available. This is facilitated by the basic structure of Leavis's text, which assumes a 'critically adult public' (p. 159) to have the powers of 'rationalised second thought' compared to the majority in thrall to mass culture, which promotes 'more primitive feelings and impulses'.[48] Despite Leavis's dismissive attitude to psychoanalysis, Freud's basic scheme of consciousness – trying to control but often being controlled by the unruly unconscious – is unmistakably apparent here.

It is difficult to speculate on the value of a psychoanalytic reading of Leavis, but one possible outcome might be a view of his work which renders terms like 'seriousness', 'maturity' and 'tradition' more complex, thus preventing his work from being too easily or dismissively characterized along these lines. A psychoanalytic reading would also highlight the struggle, certainly in *Mass Civilization and Minority Culture*, between ordering meaning and any such attempt being undermined by the proliferation of meaning. This shows that what Belsey sees as the distinction between traditional criticism and post-structuralism, the battle between singular and plural meaning, is actually constitutive of 'traditional' criticism as conceived by Leavis. This problem is the impulse behind his work. In not recognizing this, Belsey merely repeats the past, she does not come to terms with it and this is profoundly ironic given how she promotes psychoanalysis as part of the post-structuralist enterprise. Psychoanalysis aims to redeem the past, not to repeat it, and a psychoanalytic reading of Leavis would certainly aim to recover tensions in his work which would make it a force in the present.

This has to be balanced against the need to contextualize his work in the past. The parallels between *Mass Civilization and Minority Culture* and *Civilization and its Discontents* suggest different responses to a common problem. This raises the question of conceiving society as a whole. Post-structuralism is unsympathetic to this notion. But it is necessary to enable a perception of society's contradictions, which are a necessary condition for change. To contextualize Leavis is thus to locate his work in a dynamic historical moment, a moment which the parallels with psychoanalysis reveal is still with us. This latter possibility would then make Leavis's texts directly relevant to the present, inviting the kind of 'engagement' with them which, despite Easthope's protestations, they have not yet had.

Leavis on Lawrence

First, the stir of apprehension, and then the prolonged repetitious wrestle
to persuade it into words.

I

Lawrence died in 1930. After 65 years we think we understand him. More
exactly, we have reached understandings of him which vary from reader
to reader, depending on the number of his books we have read and the
amount we have thought or read about him. Some people think he is an
influence which was once strong and has now passed; others that he is
the greatest writer of the century. Both groups, perhaps, think that he is
at any rate a known quantity: the novels and short stories and poems are
familiar, and don't seem, now, to be 'difficult', because unlike some other
classics of modernism, they are in normal syntax and seem to be plotted
in classical ways. This is an illusion. Lawrence is a difficult writer whom
we have gone a fair way towards understanding, but who has become
over-familiar, though the work now going on on his texts should produce
new understandings, by causing us to look at them afresh. The position
we have currently reached is, though not many readers now recognize it,
largely due to the criticism of F. R. Leavis. He wrote more about Lawrence
than about any other author: understanding Lawrence was for him an
enterprise of nearly fifty years, from the first pamphlet in 1930 to the last
book in 1976. For historical, personal and critical reasons the whole process
was deeply bound up with his thought and writing about the other great
writer of his time, T. S. Eliot: thinking about the one, he would find
himself bringing in the other as a contrasting figure. Since Leavis himself
is the third important writer of the time, in the sense that Eliot is the
great poet, Lawrence the great prose-fiction writer, and Leavis the great
critic, there is an obvious fittingness here.

By way of announcing my theme, I quote some prophetic words
published in 1932 by Catherine Carswell, Lawrence's friend and first

biographer, in *The Savage Pilgrimage*. She made, over sixty years ago, the point in my first paragraph; and it still has intrinsic truth, in spite of all that has been written since, and most notably by Leavis.

> Lawrence as a whole remains to be read and to be re-read. He has to create the taste for his work, and this takes time. But it is a taste that grows . . . his books are easy to read but hard to understand. Therein lies part of their potency . . . Therein also lies their vital difference from the books of such writers as Joyce or Proust, which are hard at first to read, but comparatively easy to understand once the initial difficulty is overcome. They have evolved a new technique, but they belong themselves to an outworn way of life. What they do – and it is much – is to interpret and express the old in a fresh language. Lawrence, on the contrary . . . has elected to speak in a familiar language. But his story-shapes, his incidents, his objects and his characters are chosen primarily as symbols in his endeavour to proffer a new way of life . . . Most, however, even of those who have vocally admired him, will make any admission except just this . . . so they prefer to continue with simplifications that are away from the point. . .

2

Lawrence's death in 1930 provoked the first attempts to come to terms with the whole completed *oeuvre*. The critic who was then in possession of the field was John Middleton Murry, who seemed to be in a strong position because he had known Lawrence well, indeed had been painfully involved with him, had reviewed most of Lawrence's books as they appeared, and as Editor of the *Adelphi* carried considerable weight. He once went so far as to say to Lawrence that he had only started the *Adelphi* in order to hand it over to him if he wanted to come back to England from the USA: meanwhile he accepted contributions from Lawrence, went on reviewing his books, and also printed some of his own reminiscences of Lawrence. To the regular reader, therefore, the *Adelphi* might have seemed almost a Lawrence house-magazine, and certainly the place where an evolving critical attitude was being fostered.

In Cambridge in 1930, Leavis's friend and pupil Gordon Fraser, founder and editor of the Minority Press, wanting in his new series of Minority Pamphlets to record a sense of Lawrence's importance in the year of his death, published as Numbers 4 and 6 in that series: *D. H. Lawrence (Two Essays)* by Murry, and *D. H. Lawrence* by F. R. Leavis (K1).[1] The pamphlet by Murry was in fact a reprint of two reviews from the *Adelphi*, – a natural way of doing something quick but authoritative: Murry was the man to turn to as the critic who had written most about Lawrence.

One needs to spend some time on Murry's writing because it stated an influential position which was opportunistically used by Eliot, and so became the orthodoxy which Leavis had, over years, to break down. Murry's first essay was a reprinted review of the *Collected Poems*. The line he takes is that Lawrence, the early 'genius', has become a 'prophet', and in doing so has gone beyond the reach of the ordinary reader, becoming 'a creature of another kind than ours, some lovely unknown animal with the gift of speech'. The word 'genius' implies something beyond the ordinary, while 'prophet' may suggest access to the divine. This turns the reader's failure to understand into the writer's transcendence of humanity. Murry goes on to say that Lawrence's poems are not, like Keats's, 'a wording of our own highest thoughts . . . almost a remembrance . . . In order to comprehend them we need to achieve nothing in ourselves . . .' This is wrong in itself, indeed unintelligent about all important writing, but again the tactic turns Lawrence from someone who is ahead of us into someone who is beyond us. 'He cannot reduce himself to our measure' but 'has no right to turn on us because we are not as he'. How often, emerging from the novels, have we said to ourselves, Murry goes on, 'But then men and women are not like that . . . There we see ourselves as trees walking . . . We are not trees.' This might have been a profound remark. The man whom Jesus restored to sight saw people as if they were trees walking; his moment of recovered sight yielded a metaphor; accept the newness of vision and explore the figure, and its initial strangeness disappears as a problem and becomes the basis of insight. This is exactly what we have to do with Lawrence: in particular to abandon old ideas about 'character' in fiction. And indeed, the related general critical point which Murry makes is about the 'element by which we hold – call it personality or the intellectual consciousness . . . [this] exasperates Mr Lawrence . . . that is well enough for him. . . but for the rest . . . it is suicide.' Another good insight made in reverse: just as Lawrence's sense of 'character' in fiction transcends the old models and calls for a deeper vision, so does his profound mistrust of social consciousness and the personality – and behind them Cartesian rationality and its attributes, ego, will and idea. Murry is ahead of his time in rendering as puzzled opposition what needed to be converted into understanding; so in his equivocal way he identified important issues.

His second essay is a review of *Lady Chatterley's Lover*. He uses his key-word again: Lawrence is the 'prophet' of a half-truth, about tenderness in sexuality. But he has not the courage of it, and prefers to hate; if he had the courage, he would become a leader, which he is not. But Murry sees in the book the nucleus of a new kind of consciousness, which 'we believe must some day come'. The thought about being a prophet, a failed leader rather than an artist, became important for Murry, and for the whole debate.

Leavis's own pamphlet is actually immensely ambitious, since it takes the form of a general review of the whole of Lawrence's work, focusing mainly on the novels, but pointing out at the end that the short stories are brilliant, and present fewer problems: 'St Mawr' is singled out as a masterpiece. Looking back on it later, he ruefully concluded that he had been in no way critically qualified to write it, but then sensibly took himself up by asking who was. In fact the essay has the expected merits: it is honest about the difficulties, confesses bafflement in places, and begins to stake out points at which progress could be made.

There is a certain affinity with Murry, which may denote influence: for where else was there to look? Here too the word 'genius' calls up the other word 'prophet' – which in Murry's use turned out quite soon to be a way of saying that it didn't matter that Lawrence was no artist, since being a prophet was the more important thing. But in Leavis's mind the word was associated with Blake: Lawrence was as obviously a genius, a prophet if you like, but as obviously an artist, and presented the same problem for the critic, of discrimination. And here, though silently, Eliot is already an influence, having his words about Blake closely paraphrased and then quoted without attribution: 'He had the same gift of knowing what he was interested in, the same power of distinguishing his own feelings and emotions from conventional sentiment, the same "terrifying honesty".' Murry's point about consciousness and mind is importantly qualified, but still confirmed; Leavis recognizes Lawrence's vindication of impulse and spontaneity against reason and convention, but the point is not pressed: indeed at this time Leavis was troubled by it: 'If we accepted this, and all that it implies, without reserves, what should we be surrendering?' In the *Cambridge Review* article, he had used *A Passage to India* as his answering touchstone; in the pamphlet he adds 'all that Jane Austen stands for'.

This foreshadows a later difficulty. If in 1948 Leavis could define the Great Tradition in the English Novel as running through Austen, George Eliot, James and Conrad, how was Lawrence to be related to that specifically social-ethical tradition, so obviously based on the residual puritan tradition of self-analysis by the vigilant conscience, and, in principle, the habit of saying no to one's instincts and impulses, to one's self? In 1930 this was a baffling element. Leavis, having established the crucial point about Lawrence's 'vindication of impulse and spontaneity', found himself in a consequential difficulty; his commitment to the ethical tradition in the novel seeemed to require him also to say that 'a complete wisdom . . . involves greater concern for intelligence and the finer products of civilisation'; and that Lawrence's 'concessions to ideas and mind are little more than lip-service'. In his extensions of this position, Leavis showed himself in 1930 the product of the Cambridge which had bred him. What must have particularly embarrassed him later, on looking back at this first essay, was an element of intellectual snobbery of the enlightened rational sort: it is 'amusing', he writes, to watch Lawrence going round the world discovering 'strange, strange wisdom in remote or primitive people'; his devotion to the Dark God is 'not so much an evangel of salvation as a symptom: a refuge from the general malady rather than a cure'. This sounds too much like King's and Bloomsbury.

In the main body of the pamphlet – the survey of the works, mainly the novels – the recurrent note is that they are, with the exception of *The Lost Girl*, 'difficult to get through'. Logic seemed to dictate that *The Lost Girl* was therefore Lawrence's 'best' novel, Dickensian without Dickens's weakness. This must later have seemed paradoxical, in relation to both authors. *Sons and Lovers* is warmly praised as beautiful and poignant, showing sincerity in the record of emotional life. It was clear to Leavis that in the novels Lawrence was exploring his problems, living them through, and that from *The Rainbow* on, there were 'certain conclusions'; but the difficulty of the books at this time was daunting: *Women in Love*, 'in which the mature conclusions are embodied' (already a major perception) was so hard to read that 'to get through it calls for great determination and a keen diagnostic interest.' If Lawrence is like Blake a prophet, he imposes on critics the same kind of task: 'We are to approach, that is, as

literary critics.' Indeed, it was Lawrence who had said that art-speech is
the only speech. The difficulty was understanding that speech itself: at
this point Leavis found that 'what can only be conveyed by poetic means'
seemed rather to be a sort of jargon: 'a specialised vocabulary of terms
that [Lawrence] tries to invest with a new potency by endless reiteration',
and this became mechanical. Here was a parallel with the 'turgid cyclonic
disasters of Blake's prophetic works'.

A rapid survey of the later novels produced a dismissal of *Aaron's Rod*
and *Kangaroo* as hurried work produced to make a living, and of *The
Plumed Serpent* as a day-dream, a wish-fulfilment. 'One cannot but grieve
over the dissipation of genius.' But *Lady Chatterley's Lover* is exempt from
this criticism, except that one has to ask how much general validity it can
claim.

Indeed it states a problem rather than a solution. Here Leavis moves
to his own general social-historical-moral concerns, where Lawrence could
be treated as heroic predecessor, and indeed used – not unscrupulously
or in a denaturing way, but nonetheless as a major force in a campaign
which was increasingly identifiable as Leavis's own. The end of the essay
is a grim look round the horizon: Spengler is adduced as offering self-
indulgent fatalism, and behaviourism as crude and defective psychology
offered as social engineering. In the world we inhabit the old rhythms of
life have disappeared, with the old adjustments of man to the environment
and the conditions of living. The rate of change has far exceeded the
powers of adjustment. Industrialism is only a subheading of the problem.
'*Lady Chatterley's Lover* states magnificently in the concrete the major, the
inclusive problem of our time.' It was a judgement he was to regret, to
repudiate, later.

3

Leavis's first essay on Eliot had also been an article in *The Cambridge
Review*, in 1929; like the one on Lawrence it had probably been read and
reacted to, perhaps angrily by some, in the immediate constituency, the
university, but is unlikely to have been noticed outside. There Murry
held sway, and he increased the potency of his point of view with a flurry
of publications. He published his book on Lawrence, *Son of Woman*, in
1931. Eliot reviewed it in *The Criterion* in July of that year. Partly in
reaction to *Son of Woman*, Catherine Carswell published her life of

Lawrence, *The Savage Pilgrimage*, in 1932. The concluding pages were so critical of Murry's account that he reacted angrily, the book was for a time withdrawn, and came out in a revised form next year – the year in which Murry published his self-justifying *Reminiscences of D. H. Lawrence*, which by way of defending his case reprinted all his own reviews and articles. In 1935 he published his autobiographical *Between Two Worlds*, which has substantial sections on his relationship with Lawrence.

The case Murry built up departed from the point which is bound to unite all writing on Lawrence: that there is a relationship between the life and the works, which plainly have elements of what looks like autobiography, or at any rate the use of direct experience. This links Lawrence with other major writers of the century: most obviously Proust, but also Joyce, Conrad, and of course – as we now know – Eliot. But there has been a critical tradition, deriving from Flaubert, that the great artist is 'impersonal' or indeed invisible like the creator-God. That tradition had been given a specific modern twist by Eliot's influential doctrine, in the essay 'Tradition and the Individual Talent', which had imposed the notion of the distance between the man who suffers and the artist who creates.

Murry was convinced that Lawrence was a genius, starting the tradition of the 'genius-but . . .' in which it is proposed that the owner of this difficult property does not have the advantages of the rest of us, like common sense and moderation, and so can be condescended to, or written off as a bit mad. Further, Murry believed that Lawrence was born to be a religious leader, so it does not matter that his writings are not art; there are more important things. Born to lead, he was also born to love, but his love was tragically deflected by his mothering. He became a sort of Christ, and his cross was formed by the intersection of his mission, which, as Murry saw it, was to love all mankind, and his own understanding of that mission, which was to introduce a new understanding of the sexual relationship. But this was a doomed enterprise, since Lawrence was a 'case'. His self-revelation, in *Sons and Lovers* and elsewhere, is of a man whose mothering had made him incapable of loving a woman sexually. This deflected him into the search for a virility which he could find only in a succession of male alter egos with whom he could imagine a quasi-homosexual relationship; and the progression of his case in the later writings led him into horrible imaginings in which the virile male brothers become adepts of human sacrifice and the loved women are required to be so abjectly submissive that they finally abjure their own sexuality.

Murry's analysis rested on personal knowledge of the man and, for the time, wide reading in the writings, and is never less than interesting, with a good deal of truth mixed with the caricatural simplification. It played into the hand of Eliot who, without having read much of Lawrence, did not like what he had read and was predisposed to disapprove. In his review of *Son of Woman* in the *Criterion*, and in *After Strange Gods* in 1934 Eliot felt entitled to be dismissive: by the Flaubertian standard, or Eliot's own standard, of impersonality, Lawrence was no artist; if he was a prophet, he was a false prophet; he was provincial, nonconformist, snobbish, ill-educated and incapable of what is normally called thinking.

The only substantial counter-arguments in the period were Carswell's, Aldous Huxley's long and sympathetic introduction to the volume of Lawrence's collected letters which he edited in 1932, and Jessie Chambers's classic volume of reminiscences of the shared childhood and young love, published in 1935. One should not entirely forget early books by Stephen Potter, Rebecca West and others, which hinted that there was a public of loyal or at any rate open-minded readers of Lawrence which would support some positive criticism, but it is reasonable to say that overall the influence of Eliot, exploiting Murry's equivocal testimony, was producing an anti-Lawrence orthodoxy, was rendering him safe.

Meanwhile Leavis himself had published *New Bearings in English Poetry* in 1932, which had made his name – especially as an expositor of Eliot – and he had become the principal editor of *Scrutiny*, founded in 1932, which gave him his own increasingly influential platform. Surprisingly quickly, he became a force to be reckoned with.

His first writing on Lawrence in *Scrutiny*, 'Reminiscences of D. H. Lawrence', appeared in the second issue, of September 1932 (K3), and was an oblique comment on the Murry-Carswell imbroglio. It appropriates the Murry-Eliot line, but makes it positive: 'the fact of the personal existence of which the works assure us is the most cheering and enlivening fact the modern world provides.' 'His art bears a peculiarly close relationship to the man – "the man who suffered" – and that is its importance.' 'The man appears saner than his art.' '. . . He was not able to maintain steady possession of wholeness in spontaneity; a human naturalness, inevitable and more than humanly sanctioned; a sense, religious in potency, of life in continuity of communication with the deepest springs. . . . But it is equally plain that he didn't merely seek.' Leavis also commends the philosophical writings as essentially sane '– those lyric–expository prophetic extravaganzas'.

In the same year he reviewed Huxley's edited volume of Lawrence's Letters in *The Listener* (K4).[2] He made the same basic point about the relationship of the work and the personal experience, but this did not make Lawrence a case of romantic individualism and egotism: 'his inner search was not a preoccupation with self . . . All geniuses are more than themselves.' He could not, as Dante did (and this reference is an implicit reply to Eliot) 'realise in himself a whole culture – the culture was not there to realise; that is our plight.' That plight is recorded in *The Waste Land*, but Leavis implies it is Lawrence rather than Eliot who has done most to compel recognition of this; moreover his constant preoccupation is fairly to be called religious: 'what he sought was a more-than-human sanction for human life, a sense of the life of the universe flowing in from below the personal consciousness . . . he aimed at "planting" man again in the universe.' The Letters are 'one of the most important books of our time'.

In 'D. H. Lawrence and Professor Irving Babbitt', the next issue of *Scrutiny* (K5), Leavis again reviewed the Letters, but began by surveying the Eliot-Murry position. He adhered to the view that Lawrence was greater than his writings; and attempted to subvert Eliot's position by using his own kind of argument. So Lawrence offers 'classicism' a severe test; and his 'courage to live' offers a positive where Eliot's mentor Irving Babbitt's 'inner check' is a degeneration of Eliot's own moral criteria. Eliot himself never exposed humanism more effectively than Lawrence, who helps us to define also our attitude towards Eliot's religious utterances. In particular Eliot's attitude towards sexuality, as disclosed in his recent critical writings, was morbid, while Lawrence's was religious.

There were two articles in the next issue of *Scrutiny*, 'More Lawrence', a note on the posthumously published *Etruscan Places*, and a crucial editorial, 'Restatements for Critics' (K6 and 7, 1933). The first noted that Lawrence's migrations were 'a technique for inner exploration'. The second is placed at the end of the issue which had opened with the editorial 'Under Which King, Bezonian?', which is the most intelligent response I know to the challenge of 1930s Marxism. 'Restatements' responded to a published criticism that *Scrutiny*, which had seemed once to be committed to Eliot, now refused to be committed or had indeed 'transferred its allegiance' to Lawrence. Those were the days in which 'commitment' was usually followed by the words 'to the class struggle' – or to the alternatives offered by the right wing. The whole editorial is important because it deals simultaneously with the relative valuation of the two major writers and reveals the inescapable relation between a view of contemporary social life, the function of literature, and the role of criticism, and separates these from the crudities inherent in the political polemics of the time, most notably in the idea of 'commitment' and its disabling effect on independent judgment. One's response to an important writer is not the all-or-nothing of 'commitment'; what one is committed to is the more difficult task of relative valuation. Minds which enter into this process find themselves in an exchange with others: in that process 'a centre of real consensus' may emerge, 'such a centre as is presupposed in the possibility of literary criticism', and criticism when it performs its function not merely expresses and defines the 'contemporary sensibility'; it helps to form it. 'There is hardly any need to illustrate the ways in which judgements of literary value involve extra-literary choices and decisions.' The article opens out into a further discussion of the Marxian analysis, where Eliot and Lawrence are indistinguishable elements of 'bourgeois' culture, and there is no ground for preferring one to the other. Not much is specifically said about Lawrence, except that if Eliot's view of sexuality is taken to be 'orthodox', then Lawrence's 'preoccupation . . . seems to us much less fairly to be called "obsession" . . . and very much preferable.' What Lawrence offers is an experience: 'In him the human spirit explored, with unsurpassed courage, resource and endurance, the representative, the radical and central problems of our time.'

Three things are implied here. First, the centrality of the opposition Eliot-Lawrence as the two crucial writers of the age: both of them fundamental explorers of the central problems of belief and life-orientation, presenting the problem of being conscious in this century at a level far deeper than the crudities of politics. Second, the reader evolving a valuation of them is as if re-enacting their quest, turning it into a possession which is in some way public, or at any rate shared; and third, discussing it with other readers in the attempt to reach a shared evaluation is actually helping to create a cultural value. We are on the way to the concepts which

Leavis later called 'The Third Realm' or 'The Human World' – and the importance of these is that they operate in the same spiritual- intellectual dimension as religious belief: that is, they offer a kind of transcendence in that they aim to be more than personal. But for Leavis they do not transcend the world we live in, the world we make.

There is a paradox forming here; Leavis is now urging the claim that Lawrence is a major cultural figure, and the necessary opposite to Eliot; but he has still in the mid-1930s said very little about the specific works. Lawrence is in some danger of remaining a 'prophet', a monitory figure to point to rather than a writer like others.

This continues to be the case in the next writings in the sequence, and it is so because the agenda is dictated by others, notably Eliot himself. In 1934, in the third volume of *Scrutiny*, there is an article called 'Mr Eliot, Mr Wyndham Lewis and Lawrence' (K8) which is a review of Eliot's lectures in the USA, published as *After Strange Gods*. These are Eliot's thoughts on orthodoxy and tradition, and it was here that classically he committed himself to the view that Lawrence had no sense of humour, was a snob, lacked the critical faculties which education should give, and had an incapacity for what we ordinarily call thinking; moreover the brilliant exposure of him in Wyndham Lewis's *Paleface* was conclusive criticism. Leavis's response is pained rather than angry, largely because at this stage he conceded so much to Eliot's point of view. Eliot's own attitudes to sex 'have been . . . almost uniformly negative' revealing 'distaste, disgust and rejection'; but then Lawrence's preoccupation 'is, no doubt, excessive by any standard of health'. Yet who could question his aim, to make the sex-relation valid and precious, not shameful? There is a plain inconsistency here; but it is of a piece with the judgement that *Mornings in Mexico* is 'one of the very inferior books', revealing Lawrence's 'primitivistic illusion', and 'for attributing to him "spiritual sickness" Mr Eliot can make out a strong case. But health cannot anywhere be found whole.' Nonetheless the case against Eliot is that 'it is only by being a literary critic that Mr Eliot can apply his recovered standards to literature. It is only by demonstrating convincingly that his application of moral principles leads to a more adequate criticism that he can effect the kind of persuasion that is his aim. In these lectures, if he demonstrates anything, it is the opposite.'

Between 1934 and 1949 Leavis wrote more about Eliot than about

Lawrence. It was partly that he was pursuing his 'creative quarrel' about the nature of criticism; and partly that he was following the important late stage of the poetic career that, more and more, he saw as a single quest, between *Ash-Wednesday* and the *Four Quartets*, such that in retrospect the apparently separate works seem like one long attempt to formulate the desired utterance.

The publication of *Phoenix*, the substantial volume of uncollected and unpublished material by Lawrence first made available in 1936, provoked the review 'The Wild Untutored Phoenix' in *Scrutiny* in 1937 (K9). Leavis noted that Lawrence was currently out of favour, and was bound to reflect that this was largely Eliot's doing, as the major critical force in the 1930s. He was now able to use Jessie Chambers's memoir as one way of countering Eliot: she showed that Lawrence was in fact very well educated, that the provincial setting he came from was a genuine culture, and his religious upbringing no more to be despised than Eliot's New England Unitarianism. The principal text made available for the first time was the *Study of Thomas Hardy*, and Leavis addressed it, finding it 'difficult to read through'. He still made concessions to Eliot's standpoint: 'The case that Mr Eliot argues does, at its most respectable, demand serious attention.'

There was now a long gap during the War years, and the years in which Eliot was publishing the *Quartets*. The next specific discussion of Lawrence appeared in '"Thought" and Emotional Quality: Notes in the Analysis of Poetry' in *Scrutiny* 13, in 1945 (K10). Lawrence's poem 'Piano' was analysed in a sequence of poems 'tackling that most dangerous theme, the irrecoverable past'. Lawrence's poem is found to be 'decidedly complex . . . feeling is not divorced from thinking'. The interesting fate of this article is that it was taken into the much later book *The Living Principle* (1975), which is about Eliot's quest and his place; the last three paragraphs of the original article became the long, testing and profound analysis in that book of the *Four Quartets*. The initial concern with the relationship between thought and feeling, especially in the business of remembering the past, branched out into Leavis's own related concern: with the way thought and feeling become language, become art, are perceived as such, are discussed between minds, become cultural possessions. It is a small but pregnant instance of the way in which his thought about Eliot and about Lawrence became intertwined.

1949 was a crucial year. It was now nearly twenty years since Leavis had written his first pieces on Lawrence. In *Scrutiny* 16, in March, a letter headed 'D. H. Lawrence Placed' was printed: in it H. Coombes pointed out that there had never been 'a full article on Lawrence in your review'. But meanwhile a sort of orthodoxy had built up; the current view of Lawrence was illustrated in quoted remarks from assorted journalists, critics, historians, poets and novelists, some of them giving the sort of defence which looks more like attack, some of them accusing Lawrence of fascism. Leavis printed a brief reply promising 'some critical treatment' (K11). One wonders, had he actually prompted the letter from Coombes, being now ready to respond?

Meanwhile, in September of that year, in the same volume of *Scrutiny*, he wrote a review of J. M. Keynes's *Two Memoirs*, edited by David Garnett, entitled 'Keynes, Lawrence and Cambridge' (K12). Keynes was reflecting on Lawrence's visit to Cambridge in 1915, when he had been introduced by Russell to Keynes and others of the Bloomsbury group, and had come away filled with an almost mad loathing, recorded in the letters. Leavis was here reflecting on the Cambridge of that time and since, and in the light of Lawrence's reaction asking how the university of Sidgwick and Leslie Stephen had become the university of Lytton Strachey (and the university which both produced and rejected F. R. Leavis: it was not an impersonal historical enquiry). Keynes was the real mind of the group, and capable of seeing some of the truth in Lawrence's diagnosis; but his admissions 'have a way of not being able to realise the weight they ought to carry'.

He was to return to this topic later; but in the same month, in an article in *The Listener* which reprinted a Third Programme talk, he gave a kind of prospectus of the critical study which he had promised in his reply to Coombes. It was called 'D. H. Lawrence – the Novelist' (K13), and the title not only foreshadows the book, it is a declaration of a strategic shift.[3] Lawrence was now going to be treated as a literary artist rather than as the 'prophet' that Murry and others had been able half to commend and half to write off. There is an element of rewriting history also, in that Leavis was now saying that he had been right all along, which was not untrue but ignores his own willingness to concede a good deal to the consensus. He was now saying that despite Eliot's objection to his, Leavis's, insistence that Lawrence was an artist, he saw even more reason now, twenty years on, for standing by the proposition. Lawrence's art was not didactic, nor was he an unreflective genius, dimly aware of his intentions.

One of the greatest of technical originators, he was supremely conscious of what he was doing, and of the problems ('the essential problems of civilised man in our time') in relation to which his art had its significance. *Women in Love* is 'as astonishing a work of genius as can be found among novels'. But since 'St Mawr' 'completely and unquestionably successful as art', is a better way in, especially in a short article, he analysed it at some length. Leavis was here saying things for the first time, and being the first person to say them.

There followed the series of substantial articles in *Scrutiny* which were effectively the first criticism of Lawrence, and remain the bedrock of almost everything of quality which has been written since. *Scrutiny* was running a major critical programme under the general rubric 'The Novel as Dramatic Poem'. It had opened with Leavis's piece on *Hard Times,* followed by Klingopoulos on *Wuthering Heights,* and Leavis on *The Europeans.* Now his article on 'St Mawr', in Spring 1950 (K14) not only made the case for the novella itself, but by putting it in that company made a strong critical claim. *Women in Love* followed, a very substantial critique which was published in three instalments as 'The Novel as Dramatic Poem: V' in Autumn 1950, March 1951 and June 1951 (K15, 16, 17).

In 1951 the 'creative quarrel' with Eliot was renewed, necessarily entering a new phase, since Leavis was himself now producing these massive counter-arguments in the discussion of Lawrence. A review in *Scrutiny* 18, in June 1951, of two books about Lawrence, one of which had a foreword by Eliot, was straightforwardly called 'Mr Eliot and Lawrence' (K18). Leavis saw a change in Eliot's position: he had once been 'the essential opposition in person', but was now making more conciliatory remarks about Lawrence's greatness. If 'our time, in literature, may fairly be called the age of Lawrence and T. S. Eliot . . . though Lawrence appears to me so decidedly the greater genius', Eliot was 'still unemancipated from his disabling prejudices, now more insidious because associated with a recommendatory approach'. His attitude 'has a significance in respect of himself that, pondered, entails limited and qualifying criticism of a kind for which the time is now very decidedly due': a remark which may have caused blood to run cold in Russell Square. The arguments in earlier reviews and articles are restated more formally and with more force; all Eliot's dismissive criticisms of Lawrence are now turned against Eliot. Lawrence's supposed disadvantages were advantages;

his birth made him able to see working-class life from the inside as a
writer middle-class born could not; it was a positive experience, bringing
freedom from illusions. Gifted as Lawrence was, there was nothing to
prevent him getting to know life at other social levels – as indeed he did.
As for his religious upbringing, Congregationalism had a real intellectual
tradition. Lawrence's origin in the English midlands at that time put him
in touch both with the old agrarian order and the new industrial one, so
that in Leavis's eyes he was uniquely qualified to perceive the problems
of the changing life of England which were one of Leavis's own overriding
preoccupations. All in all, 'I cannot see on what grounds Mr Eliot assumes
it to be obvious . . . that he himself at 21 was better trained intellectually.'
And turning Eliot's old gibe upside-down, Leavis concluded that Lawrence's 'thinking . . . is so much superior to what is ordinarily called
thinking that it tends not to be recognised as thinking at all.'

Leavis's remarks about *Psychoanalysis and the Unconscious* continue to
display an inconsistency, or perhaps just point to an intrinsic problem in
Lawrence's thought. Of 'the conditions of health and wholeness in the
psyche', he says 'without a proper use of the intelligence there can be no
solution . . . We are committed, he [Lawrence] insists, to consciousness
and self-responsibility. The mind – mental consciousness – has its essential
part in the prosperous functioning of the psyche; but it cannot, with its
will-enforced ideas or ideals, command the sources of life, though it can
thwart them. The power of recognising justly the relation of idea and
will to spontaneous life . . . is intelligence.' The careful reader of Lawrence
will find that not exactly incorrect: more precisely it is Leavis's appropriation and tidying up of Lawrence's convictions, which are basically much
more distrustful of the mind. Just as Leavis takes Lawrence's exploration
of the changes in English life and relates them, not unjustly, to his own
profound preoccupations, so the relationship of mind and will to impulse
in Lawrence is here related to Leavis's own explorations of the self, its
operations in social life and especially the sexual relationship, and the
treatment of this in the novel. *The Great Tradition* had been published in
1948: as I suggested earlier, the essential element which binds together
the writers in this tradition and makes it and them 'great' – though this
is never explicitly stated – is the tradition of the moral conscience, with
its habit of self-analysis which makes the social person aware of the demands
of the self as egoism, is distrustful of them, and inclined to say no to

them; the secular inheritance of the puritan tradition. Leavis's main critical problem, having identified the tradition, was to relate Lawrence to it, since at first sight he seems engaged in blowing it up. Lawrence is the critic who thought Jane Austen a narrow-gutted spinster and Conrad a defeatist, and who left James out of his *Studies in Classical American Literature*.

A brief exchange in *Scrutiny* 18, in Autumn 1951, is interesting as a re-run of the earlier argument in 'Restatement for Critics'. In 'Lawrence and Eliot' (K19) a correspondent repeated the charge that Leavis had now 'accepted' Lawrence where once he had 'accepted' Eliot. The writer demonstrates what one would now call a crude 'history of ideas' approach, and at one point says he is 'not particularly interested in discussing Lawrence's merits as a creative artist'. Like Eliot, he is someone who has 'beliefs' which can be discussed as such. Leavis was able to make the now obvious reply: the whole approach is inconsistent with understanding either author; you can't even receive the 'beliefs' without a sense of the art which creates them. The episode is significant beyond its few pages, since it shows that since the earlier exchange, in 1932, Leavis had seen the need to move on to the new ground, Lawrence's art, if he was effectively to do the other thing – which was to deal with the ideas as created and embodied in the work, not decanted from it and turned into cliché by the process. This is what he was now doing in the major essays.

There followed, in the next three issues of *Scrutiny*, the three parts of an analysis of *The Rainbow* (K20–22), in the series 'The Novel as Dramatic Poem'. It makes a beginning with the problem of the relationship with the Great Tradition by comparing the early chapters of the novel with George Eliot's regional writing, making a distinction between George Eliot's 'ethical' and Lawrence's 'religious' approach, and pointing out how Lawrence's abandonment of familiar kinds of organization of the novel's structure had puzzled readers. In the very last number of *Scrutiny*, in October 1953, Leavis printed his study of 'The Captain's Doll', noting that it was 'part of a study of four of the tales' (K23). A major critical point was made as if in passing: the doll in the story corresponds to the reader's conventional expectations about 'character' in fiction – one of the crucial impediments to understanding. Another glancing reference – to 'the un-Flaubertian prose, with the unpondered inevitability of its rightness' – set up another crucial contrast, to be developed later.

With *Scrutiny* gone, Leavis had to turn elsewhere for periodical publication. In the *Sewanee Review* in 1954 under the title 'Lawrence and Class' he published a study of 'Daughters of the Vicar' (K24). Here, still, the voice to be answered is Eliot's – partly because *The Cocktail Party* was now there to be used as reference-point, in all its unsatisfactoriness in religious and social terms – including its snobbishness. The main critical point is that Lawrence's shrewd analysis of the class-consciousness diagnosed in his tale has also a 'fundamental reverence . . . something that recommends itself no more to sentimentalists than to cynics, and will be found no more in T. S. Eliot's work than in Pound's or Wyndham Lewis's. Nor will it be found in Flaubert.'

In 1955 came the awaited book, *D. H. Lawrence: Novelist* (K25). There are grounds for thinking it might have been longer considered, but that Leavis was aware of other books being prepared, which might make use of his own published work; for instance Graham Hough's *The Dark Sun* appeared in 1956. At any rate, he had available the substantial articles from *Scrutiny*, which can be seen as intended for eventual book-publication anyway. He added to them a new introduction, a long first chapter on the lesser novels, and at the end of the book a chapter on the Tales. A final section on 'Mr Eliot and Lawrence' carried on the old fight.

The book is still in print after forty years, and was for some years probably the first study of Lawrence that many people read. It has suffered the inevitable fate of any classic: of becoming first a received doctrine, and then the obvious thing to attack. What one needs to do now is first to make clear what one owes to it in the way of general ideas and valuations, and then to try to get beyond it; to stand on its shoulders, but to be sure that one is looking forward.

The real substance is contained in the chapters on the individual works; and the thing which has remained unchallengeable is the relative valuation of *Women in Love*, and, related but subordinate, *The Rainbow*. Similarly with the shorter fiction: he ignores some early triumphs, in general slighting the *Prussian Officer* collection. 'St Mawr' and 'The Captain's Doll' and 'Daughters of the Vicar' were, so to speak, Leavis's tips, and his valuation has been confirmed ever since. Among the philosophical works, he tipped the two books on the unconscious, and the *Study of Thomas Hardy*. The unintended effect was that this 'approved' part of Lawrence has become an institutionalized canon, and the rest has been more or less thrown to the Eliotic wolves.

One might point out that Leavis's practice of apparently dividing literary works into sheep and goats has two justifications, one theoretical, one practical. The first stems from a fact that everyone recognizes 'in theory': you can't claim that every work has the same value as every other unless you are theoretically determined to discredit all valuation. The only honest course is to state, and to be able to defend, one's own valuations, and to engage with others who disagree. The practical element was that Leavis faced the fact that his pupils had three years to do their reading in. Since you can't read everything in three years, the teacher has to suggest that you read this work because it is important, and not that one because it is less so. But Leavis's Lawrence canon, justifiable on that practical ground, is restrictive, and has an unintended effect — that it concedes too much to Lawrence's detractors. The early fiction is quickly written off, and so, more hesitantly, are the later novels. Very little is said about *Sons and Lovers*, which is rather dismissed as the book Lawrence had to 'put behind him': having thus got his own emotional account settled, he could go on to write what he had to write. This must seem reductive to the common reader. One can say now that the publication of the Cambridge Edition of 1992 restored the full text, which Leavis never saw, and makes clear that the book is a masterpiece, but most readers have always thought so, even with a mutilated text.[4] It has been for years the one book by Lawrence that 'everybody' reads. Nothing can please many and please long but just representations of general nature, as Johnson said.

The remarks about *Sons and Lovers* are to be found in the long (fifty-five page) opening chapter 'Lawrence and Art: The Lesser Novels'. The first part of that title makes plain that the old argument (Lawrence was a 'prophet' but no artist, and this does or does not matter according to your point of view) is going to be addressed, and perhaps settled. In a way it was; but to an unusual degree, in Leavis, by assertion rather than demonstration. Even his detractors admire his analytic gift in the close reading of poetry, but dealing with novels seems at first sight to preclude using this technique. Leavis touches on the problem in a number of places: the most explicit occurs in the chapter on *Women in Love*, where he says (e.g. on p. 151) that the problem in discussing it is that 'the organization is so rich and close: the dramatic poem unfolds – or builds up – with an astonishing fertility of life; there is not a scene, episode, image or touch but forwards the organized development of the themes. To discuss this development point by point as the dramatic action advances would take a volume.' It was already a good deal to have dropped this hint; but not to have taken it further, even in a sample passage or two, left him no alternative but to do what he does: to summarize, to hint, to point, and when all else fails to assert. This has been the bane of Lawrence-criticism; the unwillingness to analyse means that the critic has no alternative but to offer a pattern of (one hopes) 'key' quotations linked by hasty summary, thus falling into reductive substitutions and never showing how Lawrence achieves his effects, or even what they are. One can of course give some account of what in the large Lawrence is trying to convey; but this is a matter of intentions and bound to be conveyed in terms of 'ideas', and it was one of Lawrence's main endeavours to make us suspicious of those.

Leavis was well aware of this trap but did not entirely avoid it. Indeed this first chapter rather courts it by contrasting the central assertions with those novels which he found imperfect and left at that. So: Lawrence is a 'great artist, a creative writer. . . a great novelist, one of the very greatest . . . one of the major novelists in the English tradition' (p. 17). This is, we now learn, an Anglo-American tradition, consisting of Austen, Hawthorne, Dickens, George Eliot, James, Melville, Twain, Conrad: 'the great compelling instances'. In comparison with this tradition of the novel, that of formal poetry is 'a marginal affair', not redeemed even by Eliot. Lawrence is 'the greatest creative writer of our time . . . as remarkable a technical innovator as there has ever been' (p. 18). *Women in Love* and *The Rainbow* most demand attention; they can hardly have been altogether understood by anyone at first reading; learning to recognize the success and greatness 'was not merely a matter of applying one's mind . . . it was a matter, too, of growing' (p. 21).

Dismissing the first two novels, he sees *Sons and Lovers* as 'an advance to the direct and wholly convention-free treatment of the personal problem' (a dangerous simplification) after which Lawrence was 'now freed for the work of the greatest kind of artist'. Yet in the bulk of the chapter, on the later novels, Lawrence is still 'living his problems in a tentative and immediately personal way'. The distinction implied is that in *Sons and Lovers* 'that work in its final achieved form . . . offers the achieved insight into the "case", and the delicately verified exhibition of it; the author's judgement that the form is now right is the judgement that intelligence has successfully performed its office' (p. 31). The difference in the later novels is apparently that the 'case' is now a different one (Lawrence's problem in living with Frieda) and that Leavis is here conceding 'to adverse criticism of Lawrence as an artist what I think has to be conceded' (p. 14). One might respond that the 'case' is actually the same one in its later manifestation; but conversely there is no need to concede so much so easily. Leavis established the two great central novels as almost beyond criticism, but, abandoning the later novels, caused them to remain an unresolved critical issue. For that matter, the first two are interesting and important, and not to be so easily written off. The first works of 'one of the major novelists of the English tradition', not surprisingly, show him beginning to be 'as remarkable a technical innovator as there has ever been'.

As for the ancient quarrel with Eliot, it is restated in an important new form, with an important corollary. Now he indicated the way in which, he believed, future criticism, starting with his own, should go.

Lawrence had against him the major personal influence of the 1930s – that of Eliot. 'How could he have been so wrong?' The answer now given is that Eliot was a Flaubertian. There is a brief excursus on Flaubert, which turns into an animadversion on Eliot, as revealed in his late plays. Both express 'classically a contradiction', 'all that would-be creative intensity, that intensity of "doing", devoted to expressing attitudes in which distaste, disgust and boredom have so decisive a part; a cult of art which amounts to a religion, and the directing spirit of it a rejection of life.' Or again: 'the slow meticulous labour of calculating judgement that went to the doing; and on the other hand . . . the sick poverty, the triviality and finally the nothingness of the done – the human and spiritual nullity' (p. 26). This is about *The Cocktail Party*, but might have been about *L'Education Sentimentale*. Clearly related are 'the contrivances of Joyce, where insistent will and ingenuity so largely confess the failure of creative life' or 'the technique of the *Cantos*, where by Eliot's own account, he is not interested in what Pound says, but only in the way he says it.'

Leavis quoted Lawrence on Flaubert's and Mann's rejection of 'life'; this stands in clear contrast with Lawrence's own long effort as it were to stand aside as 'personality' and let life speak through him from somewhere deeper. And actually, this was so systematic – even, to fall into paradox, so programmatic – in Lawrence because it derived from the way he worked. In this too he was anti-Flaubertian. The whole notion of the deeply-pondered total work of art in which every calculated touch is related to the whole is repugnant to him; and it was for this reason that he got into trouble with his early admirers, like Ford and Garnett, who wanted Flaubertian 'form', the 'intensity of doing', the 'slow meticulous labour of calculating judgement'. The essential point which Lawrence saw is that if you plan everything from the start, what you end with is what you planned and no more; you have not advanced or grown; you have not allowed the work to tell you where it wants to go, nor the something deeper inside you which knows better than your fixed ideas. What you do is all willed, old before it is born, and profoundly unlife-like in its lack of gratuitousness. Mallarmé longed to eliminate *le hasard* in his work, but life is *le hasard*. For that sort of reason Lawrence's working method was to abandon himself to a spontaneity, and then to revise, often obsessively, yet in a succession of further spontaneities. By the end of this process his greatest works are deeply considered, but have got there by a quite un-Flaubertian process; and there is a further group which began as remarkably spontaneous and were allowed to remain so. These include the later novels; and it is therefore a question whether they are indeed flawed by the standard set by *Women in Love*, or whether Lawrence has gone on from that novel to do something more provocative and dangerous in terms of 'form'.

Leavis began to see something like this at the point where he touches (pp. 27–31) on Lawrence's working method; grasping that this too is un-Flaubertian yet in its paradoxical way 'willed' or systematic; and that it does follow logically from the deep belief that 'life' has to be allowed to work and not be impeded by idea and conscious will. He recognized the process at work in the enormous years'-long writing that to Lawrence's own surprise divided itself into *The Rainbow* (as something left behind) and *Women in Love*, the supreme achievement. But he still saw something equivocal in it: 'The un-Flaubertian spirit of Lawrence's work, while producing its characteristic vital perfections, has of course its own tendencies to imperfection' (p. 27). This is fair enough; Lawrence's strategy is essentially risk-taking, and not even his most dogmatic admirers will claim perfection in every work. But this is a complex issue, and the admission of 'imperfection' in advance leads to the willingness to write off too easily works which seem to have 'no compelling total significance in control'

(p. 31). Those are actually betraying words because they are Flaubertian; just the sort of thing Henry James said about *Sons and Lovers* in 1914: he could not find the 'centre of interest' or 'the sense of the whole', and only in Compton Mackenzie among Lawrence's contemporaries did he recognise 'a controlling idea and a pointed intention'.

A related problem is the feature which Leavis had from the beginning identified as Lawrence's 'jargon'. This too is here dealt with in a way which is unconsciously Flaubertian: 'What Lawrence offers to reinforce by saying and insisting, though saying could in any case be of no avail, his art has sufficiently done.' A passage identified as jargon in the chapter 'Excurse' in *Women in Love* had been identified by Murry, Leavis points out, as supporting his diagnosis of Lawrence's 'case'; I would characterize it myself as one of Lawrence's thematic metaphors where the reader is puzzled because the force of the metaphor resides in Lawrence's private association-system and so is not communicated, or alternatively it has been established in another work which the reader may not know. It is not so much that the art has 'sufficiently done it' and we have redundancy, as that the art has done it somewhere else but not here, or takes it for granted that the reader possesses Lawrence's associations, so that 'suave loins of darkness' actually conveys to us what it meant to him.

4

The core of *D. H. Lawrence: Novelist* is the chapters reprinted from *Scrutiny*, and especially the massive treatments of *Women in Love* and *The Rainbow*, supported by the substantial pieces on 'St Mawr' and 'The Captain's Doll'. Most of the other works are mentioned, some sympathetically; but the effect of the whole structure of the book is, characteristically, to establish a small canon of the 'achieved' art, and implicitly to write off a good deal of the rest. The Lawrence who emerges is Leavis's Lawrence. Given what had been written and accepted about Lawrence until then, it was a positive transformation, indeed an apotheosis; nonetheless it is also an appropriation, as any very distinctive criticism is likely to be. Lawrence is here principally seen as a seeker after 'normative' relationships between men and women, and as concerned with the drive of modern Western civilization – conveyed above all in the sweeping social survey of England in *Women in Love* or the smaller sharp insights of 'St Mawr'. Nobody now could say that these terms are incorrect: indeed they are everywhere accepted, by readers who

have no idea that it was Leavis who established them. But they have
become a stereotype. It should be said, for instance, that the 'social' aspect
has a particular force partly because Leavis was here finding in Lawrence
support for his own views. I have suggested that the book also holds
Leavisian asides about tangential matters which turn out to have anticipated
one's own best efforts to be original, and it is these which should keep
it as standard reading for years to come.

But in any case the book published in 1955 represented only a mid-stage,
if a major one, in Leavis's thought about Lawrence: he went on thinking
to the end, and the later books all demonstrate that continuation, even
when Lawrence is not the immediate focus. *Dickens the Novelist* (to leap
for a moment to 1970) in its title drops a hint of an affinity; it was the
result of many years of reading and thinking, and redeemed a promise (or
corrected a formulation) made in *The Great Tradition*, where a sort of
place had been reserved for Dickens, if only one could see what it should
be. I don't doubt that the work on Lawrence, with its occasional glances
back at Blake, showed what that place was going to be. A complementary
tradition was established by identifying the relationship between Blake,
Dickens and Lawrence: the anti-puritans, the men who said yes to life
and especially to impulse. I don't doubt either that the work on Dickens
in its turn helped with Lawrence. There were implicit difficulties in the
position indicated in the 1955 book; they are suggested in the possible
conflict between the respect for spontaneity and impulse, the need for
self-fulfilment, and the other need for a normative (i.e. stable) relationship
between men and women, especially if they are to bring up children –
and Leavis saw Lawrence's blankness towards that need (except in *The
Rainbow*) as a failure to transcend his own experience.

Blake gave him a crucial contrast, between the self and the identity;
the great novels of Dickens can be shown, as in Leavis's chapters on
Dombey and Son and *Little Dorrit*, to be dramatizations, in 'felt life', of the
conflict. The novelists in the old 'Great Tradition' are, in classical ethical
terms, distrustful of the mere self; but one can see, in Jane Austen's Emma
Woodhouse (perhaps) and in George Eliot's Maggie Tulliver or her
Dorothea Brooke more certainly, the young identity trying to come into
flower, while in *Daniel Deronda* the contrast between Gwendolen, the
thwarted identity, and Grandcourt, the nightmare self, arrested in his
egoism and arresting her through his possessiveness, is a transitional step

towards what one might call Lawrence's ethic of self-fulfilment. But that term itself suggests the difficulty which the old ethic was based on, and spent so much effort insisting on: who is to adjudicate between the demands of my identity and those of your self (as I see it, from within what may only be *my* selfhood)? Some pages in the Dickens book show Leavis to be a profound moralist in his own right; that discussion also reflects back on the relatively easy formulations he had offered in the book on Lawrence, where one can sense a brushing away of difficulties inherent in 'the supreme importance of "fulfilment" in the individual', or how 'it is only by way of the most delicate and complex responsive relations with others that the individual can achieve fulfilment,' or that 'except between "fulfilled" individuals . . . who are really themselves, recognising their separateness or otherness and accepting the responsibility of that – there can be no personal relations that are lasting and satisfactory' (p. 103). If in that sense Lawrence is 'normative', it is by pointing to enormous and permanent difficulties, not to solutions.

This further thinking was going on slowly in the background. The writings specifically about Lawrence in the late 1950s were minor and occasional, and seemed to be fighting the old battles with Murry (K27–9; three letters to the *TLS*) and Eliot, both still alive.[5] The references to Eliot came in a *Spectator* review ('Romantic and Heretic?': K30) of Nehls's four volumes of biographical documents about Lawrence, and begin to move the argument on to new ground.[6] If Nehls's labour was justified, it was because Lawrence was an artist, 'the man created out of the intensity of his living'. There was no separation between the artist who lived and the man who created – a reference to Eliot's doctrine of 'impersonality' in the famous essay which Leavis now saw as a 'feat of trenchant inconsequence'. But Lawrence was not in the easy sense a 'romantic' surrendering to unpremeditated 'inspiration', and without 'form'. Leavis points out how he rewrote and rewrote, not revising in patches and piecemeal: 'the full-grown perfection could be elicited from the seminal apprehension only by the engagement of the whole man.' Here we move from the asides in the 1955 book to the first formulation of the 'nisus-ahnung' dualism which Leavis was to apply both to Lawrence and to Eliot in his last writings on the two writers, seen finally as a paradigmatic complementary pair. 'Seminal apprehension' becomes 'ahnung'; 'nisus' is the long struggle towards the 'full-grown perfection', which is the finally adequate expression of itself. Once again, the criticism of Lawrence is turned upside-down; the apparent artlessness *is* the art, if only it can be seen for what it is.

The movement to the final position was interrupted by the *Lady Chatterley* trial. Leavis refused to testify on behalf of the book. He could neither wish the prosecution to succeed nor support the terms of the defence. He stated his view in a review of the Rolph volume reporting the case published by Penguin in 1961. His title 'The New Orthodoxy' (K31) indicated his stance; and a sentence towards the end of the review conceded 'I couldn't help feeling that I had a heavy responsibility' for having initiated the fashion.[7] He had once thought the novel was good and therapeutic. He now thought it was bad, largely because 'will and idea play too much of a part.' 'The hygienic purpose is a hygienic purpose' and there is an assertive presence of will and idea both in the use of the once-taboo words and in the insistent renderings of sexual experience. He was shocked by the animus in the portrayal of Clifford Chatterley, and found Mellors a questionable figure. Moreover, 'the evoked Midland decor remains merely decor' – quite a shock, this, since the 'Tevershall' passage, where Connie is driven through the grimy village and is horrified at what she sees, had become a sort of talisman in writing about Lawrence. What depressed Leavis most was the herd mentality which had moved, in a unison flip-flop, from being shocked by Lawrence to accepting him as the Messiah of sexual liberation, so that earnest liberals went into the dock and testified that this was an improving book, and, if anything, supported marriage, in some Pickwickian sense. Not that one would have wanted them to say the opposite. But it was evidence that Lawrence was now cast in a 'progressive' role which would have horrified him. In the years since 1961 the discovery that Lawrence actually hated 'progressivism' has led to a necessary disenchantment, and another reason to start again with the business of understanding him.

A little appendix to the Chatterley case was a letter to *The Spectator* in March 1961 (K32) responding to one by Martin Turnell, former colleague, tweaking the master's tail by reminding the world of what he had said about the book in the pamphlet of 1930.[8] Leavis replied by pointing out that if he was to be convicted of having been unintelligent, it would have been better to use *Women in Love* as the supreme case. He was thinking here, surely, of the lecture he had given in Nottingham in June 1960 on

'Lawrence after 30 Years' (not published until 1973, but more appropriately treated as of this time).[9] He had there confessed that he had been 'stupid' – even if he had been less stupid than others – but extenuated his case by saying that 'Lawrence had to be lived with and lived into.' The transformation in Lawrence's standing was precisely that he was now recognized as a great artist; the difficulty in seeing this had been caused by the difference in the conception of art represented by Lawrence and Eliot. Lawrence 'is the great anti-Flaubertian, the complete, profound and wholly conscious representative in and for our time of anti-Flaubertian art'. The Flaubertian conception is defined as intrinsically self-contradictory: 'art is a justifying perfection, the higher reality, paradoxically engendered by the dedicated and martyred artist . . . out of the meanness and insignificance of life.' Lawrence's art undid the paradox; it was in the service of life (and here we are beginning to see the 'necessary word' being deployed). 'With the undisguised directness and freedom of his use of personal experience in creation, he was, to admirers of Eliot, obviously not a classicist.' Heading off, once more, the cliché-alternative, Leavis said that Lawrence was not, either, a 'romantic': the art was what made the use of the experience impersonal, disinterested and responsible. Lawrence had 'no impulse to separate the man who lived and experienced from the mind that created, and he diagnosed it . . . (for example, in Flaubert) as a malady'.

5

Eliot died in 1965. This put an end to the old quarrel, in the sense that while he was still alive Leavis could, so to speak, scold him as one capable of reform – and indeed he had some success, since Eliot publicly recanted his early views on Lawrence, and made some 'proper' remarks about him. Leavis's remorselessness about this was now at an end, and the rest of his writing life was dedicated first to a considered summing-up of Eliot's achievement as the great poet of the age, and then to a complementary summing-up of 'the necessary opposite', Lawrence. There is a reflexive element in this, in that, in thinking about his own forty-year struggle to get these things 'right' he was also thinking about the whole process of literary criticism, the function of university English, and the nature of a national culture, where the literary consciousness crystallizes the development of the language in which values are collaboratively created. Oddly,

and disconcertingly, the writings in which all this is done are not grand
and general and above the day-to-day conflict. They are studded with
modern (or then modern) instances, with handy eminences – the BBC
and the British Council and the Lords Snow and Robbins and Annan –
getting a lot of stick. This may cause these important books to look dated
– perhaps it does already. One needs to point to the contemporary
references in Pope, Johnson, Arnold and Ruskin, or indeed in Yeats and
Eliot, which show that they too had to be willing to engage with the
specific issues of their day, to give immediate relevance to what they were
saying, and to advance their own cause.

The chapter on Eliot in *Lectures in America* was written in 1966 for
delivery in the USA: one year after Eliot's death Leavis was offering this
prospectus for his final books. The lecture ends with a rousing climax:
'. . . the not massive total product we now have gives no effect of
slightness. The constituent things are in their concentration so completely
what they are, the development is so unforeseeable and yet so compelling
in its logic, that the whole body of the poetry . . . affects us as one
astonishing major work.'

The lecture is amplified in *English Literature in Our Time and the
University*, (lectures delivered in 1967, published 1969) which takes Eliot
as the central reference, though there is a chapter on 'The Necessary
Opposite, Lawrence' (K36). One can say that this chapter is included as
Leavis's characteristic way of putting in a stake on ground which is going
to be claimed later; it says little about Lawrence beyond commending
him as critic of *Hamlet,* on which Eliot had rather let himself down. The
drive of the book is towards the recognition of the peculiar quality of
Eliot's poetic achievement. The peroration of the American lecture is now
refined, in the sense that it is the poems after 'The Hollow Men' which
Leavis now sees as like one work. The nature of the whole enterprise is
that it is a 'nisus' – 'a kind of striving, a kind of unwilled set of the whole
being' and this set is towards a 'reality that should compel belief, claim
allegiance and create a centre of significance'. The distinctive mode is
exploratory, testing: 'he hopes that the affirmation will make itself.' A
specifically positive element in the poetry is a memory of love: 'these
memories play an indispensable part in the effort to build up the sure
apprehension of a spiritual reality, a reality which transcends time.' The
chapter on Lawrence yields another premonition of the last two books,

indeed the title of *The Living Principle*: 'what I am concerned with is something more like a definition of principle, the principle being of such a kind that the defining can't be done in mere general statement . . . the method and spirit (some word between the two is wanted) that "principle" here portends can be effectively presented only with the aid of exemplification.'

This movement towards a definition leads in turn to the last two books, which need to be taken together as one, and which in their own way reflect back on the whole writing career, so that it too can be seen as one long enterprise. All the strands are woven together. In *The Living Principle* (1975) the last long section is devoted to a reading of the first three of Eliot's *Four Quartets*, and here the 'nisus' (to borrow Leavis's term) which had been since 1929 his own long effort to receive and understand Eliot's work has its summing-up – or rather is given its ultimate revision. The long and difficult first chapter, 'Thought, Language and Objectivity', is the essential entry into the two books taken as one; that is to say, it looks forward also into the final treatment of Lawrence in *Thought, Words and Creativity* (1976, K39). The basic contention is that any really important writer is offering a necessary kind of thought, but not of the sort understood as 'thought' by philosophers. Here is a last turn in the long road since Murry's time. If Lawrence had been a 'prophet' for Murry, it was surely because Murry had in some sense seen Lawrence as a thinker. Murry made the mistake of saying the 'failures' of the art didn't matter; it was the prophecy we wanted. Leavis's reply, that Lawrence *was* an artist, was the first step towards what he was now saying, that Eliot and Lawrence were great artists *because* they were, in the way that great artists are, also great thinkers. This was not to be shown by decanting 'ideas' from the art, which could be treated as if it were some kind of container. It was received as their use of language, their development of the language of the community of consciousness. They made themselves available, so to speak, for that which they had to say so that it could speak through them: they had to discover how to say it as the only way to discover what it was. Leavis had always been good at demonstrating how poetic language 'does what it says' but at first this was limited to forms of 'enactment'. Now he is talking about a heuristic language of a more fundamental kind, a way of thinking oneself forward which is self-extension through language, especially metaphor and larger poetic structure. It is at the opposite extreme from the logical deployment of conceptual quanta, where speakers are trying *not* to let language run away with them and create new meanings. Here the references to Blake were given a new aspect; Leavis again quoted Blake on his paintings – that though he called them his, he knew they were not his, but had come into being in a response to something beyond him. In the largest sense both Eliot and Lawrence were religious writers, answering to the need of an age that had lost the old religion but could not be content with 'technologico-Benthamism' as the only aim in life: 'the despair, or vacuous unease, characteristic of the civilised world comes of profound human needs and capacities that the civilisation denies and thwarts, seeming – paralysingly – to have eliminated in its triumph all possibility of resurgence' (p. 10). Both great writers of this phase of our civilization were seeking for a deeper reality which would give a sense of 'the nature of that to which we belong' (p. 55). First there was the anticipation, the 'ahnung' as Leavis called it, and this entailed the long 'nisus'.

These were terms that he had found he needed, to designate what he was identifying in the writers to whom he had been giving this long study; but I suggest that, like 'heuristic' which he also found himself using at this time, they were words which applied equally to what he was engaged in himself. I return to this in my conclusion. Of 'nisus' he said, on page 63 of *The Living Principle*: 'I first found that I needed the word "nisus" in discussing *Ash-Wednesday*. The problem there is to define the sense in which the poet of "The Hollow Men" has become religious. He will not affirm because he cannot, not having left sufficiently behind him the complete nihilism of that waste-land poem: affirmation attempted merely because of the desperate intensity of his need would be empty. Will and ego (selfhood) cannot genuinely affirm. But what he discovers or verifies in his major poet's dealings with the English language is that deep within him there is a Christian nisus . . .' He goes on, a paragraph later, '*Ahnung*, the other word, is intimately related . . . "Inkling" can translate "Ahnung" as used in some German contexts, but it can hardly suggest anticipatory apprehension that carries the weight implicit in "foreboding", which is often the right rendering. . .' 'Ahnung' had been combined with 'heuristic' earlier (p. 44): 'a language is more than a means of expression: it is the heuristic conquest won out of representative experience . . . It exemplifies the truth that life is growth and growth change [a Lawrentian formulation] . . . It takes the individual being, the particularizing actuality of life, back to the dawn of human consciousness, and beyond, and does this in fostering the *ahnung* in him of what is not yet – the as yet unrealized, the achieved discovery of which demands creative effort.' In both Eliot's *Quartets* and Lawrence's *Women in Love* the 'nisus' is evident as a form of thought, requiring 'a recognition by the reader that what he is following is a process of heuristic thought . . . Both Eliot and Lawrence must have had a strongly positive *ahnung* of what the upshot in "significance" would be – the conveyed total sense of "the living principle" in control in either case (the problem being the nature of that to which "we belong").'

As for 'the living principle', that is also defined as 'the principle implicit in the interplay between the living language and the creativity of individual genius'. Since it gives Leavis the title for his book, the phrase needs to be taken as more than phrase-making; it is a pointer to the nature and significance of everything Leavis had been doing from the start: it posits a relation of analogy between the original creation and the effort of reception or construction. It distinguishes both from other kinds of intellection, which are different uses of language: a good deal of energy is spent in the opening sections of both books looking round at current forms of thinking about thought, and finding it insufficiently conscious of its own Cartesianism where it is not also abjectly positivist. There is an unconsciousness of its own preconceptions in that kind of thought such that it cannot even conceive its limitation, and this is always diagnosable in its language. It is in the nature of creation that it is not locked in in that way: but the paradox is that until it has got it out, it does not, cannot, know what it is trying to say. That is why 'a talented artist, a genuinely creative writer has to *learn* to be spontaneous; processes of training and education are required before he knows what his spontaneity is and can tell with sureness what it dictates.' The Blake-analogy is as if waiting to be called up: 'Blake was emphasising his spontaneity when, referring to works of his own (at which he laboured, altering and redrafting) he said: "Tho' I call them Mine I know they are not mine".' (p. 15).

The function of the critic is to follow the process, which requires self-extension, growth, of an equivalent kind. This is called 'the living principle' because it is actually the principle of life itself, the way in which it develops new forms; among other things it distinguishes 'selfhood', which is locked round a static ego, insists on its own will and is slave to its own ideas, from the growing 'identity', which is, as Lawrence put it, 'lapsed out'. His favourite image was the nut or seed which falls from the old plant or tree and has to die as itself before it can grow into the new being (the analogy with some Christian ideas about rebirth is obvious). In this way art is not, as in Flaubert, the opposite, still less the enemy, of life, but its paradigm.

These positions, established in the last work on Eliot, underpin the last work on Lawrence. An article in *The Spectator* in July 1975 had the same title as the book, *Thought, Words and Creativity*, and was reprinted in it when it appeared in 1976 (K38 and 39). It was quite possible, then and now, to seize on the fact that the canon of the approved Lawrence seemed to be the same in 1976 as it was in 1955, and to take this as evidence of an unmoving mind. But the whole approach had been changed by the intervening years of thought, so that the question, *how* is Lawrence to be shown to be an artist? has a deeper answer. The actual terms used in discussing Eliot are not now used: 'nisus' and 'ahnung' had not naturalized themselves, and are reformulated in plain English. Lawrence's repeated diving back into the pool of spontaneity is described as 'the emergence, as he experienced it, of original thought out of the ungrasped apprehended – the intuitively, the vaguely but insistently apprehended: first the stir of apprehension, and then the prolonged repetitious wrestle to persuade it into words' (p. 124). This is a felicitous formulation. The generality of its application, not only to great art but to criticism as well, is aptly shown by turning back two pages, where one finds Leavis reflecting on his own enterprise: 'Nothing important can really be said simply – simply *and* safely; and by "safely" I mean so as to ensure that the whole intuited apprehension striving to find itself, to discover what it is in words, is duly served, and not thwarted' (p. 122).

There is an important implication not extricated from the thought that Lawrence's manifold works can be seen as this prolonged, repeated effort. It is said in passing that 'Laurentian thought is a unity, a coherent organic and comprehensive totality' (p. 67); but the use of the word 'thought' here prevents Leavis facing the possibility that if he had said, of Lawrence as of Eliot, that the works, or even a sequence of them, affected him as constituting one astonishing major work – and this is, I believe, the direction in which Lawrence-criticism will move – this might undermine his notion of a comparatively small canon of achieved works of art, identified in 1955. And in fact that canon is reaffirmed, with very minor reassessments. Though it might seem a sound strategy to go back to the old judgements and validate them by the new criteria, I see a certain weariness in it also. I have the feeling that the extraordinary feat of intellection required by *The Living Principle* exhausted him (he was 80 in 1975) and drained the final book of some substance. Nonetheless, it is full of incidental insights, and its part in Leavis's own 'nisus' is to provide the concluding statement of some of his key-concepts, as for instance in the pages on *The Plumed Serpent*. Here he is prepared to look again at a previously formulated judgement: finds himself reasserting it, but on the way discovers new insights. For instance, he identifies Lawrence's term 'manhood' with his own term 'identity'. Yet he is surely right in his reassessment of that novel. His chapter on it makes both his point and mine. I mean that there is obviously a logical jump between seeing that all Lawrence's work comes from the same preoccupations and is all to be seen as part of the 'nisus' – between that and saying that it is all equally good, or does not contain failures, which need to be seen as such. But the implication of 1955, that a good deal was not worth bothering about, could be written off as immature or opportunistic, did in fact fracture the unity. It performed the function, in 1955, of placing the emphasis on what still seem the right places. But there is nothing in Lawrence which can be safely ignored, for the reason which Leavis's long study exemplifies: you may come to see that what you failed to understand was an art which was beyond you at that time. Canons may be needed, but have to be both argued and reassessed.

That too is one of the lessons of Leavis's whole career. He is conventionally seen as puritan shepherd of a very few sheep, early identified, tagged, and ruthlessly separated from the also-ran goats. No appeal was allowed from the first, eternal, judgement. All caricatures have some basis in the features of the person portrayed; but what this study shows is how much the whole process was a continuous struggle to inch forward into an unknown, and how much he did not know until the 1970s the full import of what he was trying to see and say.

I hadn't in the middle 1920s [Leavis says on page 48] had enough literary experience to be even incipiently intelligent about him [Lawrence]. But this way of putting it doesn't suggest the nature of the

challenge he presented: I most certainly wasn't capable in those days
of a critical appreciation of his importance. But how could anyone have
been, except a genius? Who was there in literary criticism that impressed
one as worth intensive pondering but Eliot . . .? His thought at his
best, even if there had been more of it, could hardly help one to adjust
oneself to Lawrence's. Only Lawrence's was qualified to do that, and
he demanded that one should transcend – transcend so impossibly –
the commonsense, the whole cultural ethos, in which one had been
brought up, and in terms of which one did one's thinking.

6

What we have been following here is not some byway: it is an essential
part of recent English literary history. The primary element in any literature
is obviously the creation of new works; but the notion that these are
somehow instantly recognized is obviously wrong. The influential critic
is the one who shows others how to read, creates a public, or at any rate
widens it. I borrow Eric Hobsbawm's useful phrase: these are the key
figures in the 'short twentieth century': Eliot the great poet and Lawrence
the great writer of fiction; and we know they are that because the great
critic has shown it. That century began to dawn when the schoolboy
Frank Leavis read Lawrence's first published pieces in the *English Review*.
The sun rose, so to speak, with *The White Peacock* in 1911, *Sons and Lovers*
in 1913, *The Rainbow* in 1915, *Prufrock and Other Observations* in 1917,
Eliot's *Poems* in 1919, *Women in Love* in 1920, *The Waste Land* in 1922 –
and so on. This short century ended with Eliot's death in 1965 and Leavis's
in 1978. On this time-scale 1930 was a kind of noontime: the literature
of the time was coming to self-consciousness. What was going on here
was seen as new; was it important, and if so, why? It was Leavis's function
to address these questions: inevitably also to relate this century to previous
literary centuries, and to place it in the life of the culture.

The art-historian's term 'floruit' implies that the artist who flourished
was born earlier. In these cases we know the dates. Lawrence was born
in 1885, Eliot in 1888, Leavis exactly 100 years ago as I write, in 1895.
He was of the same generation, but younger: so that when they began
to write he came upon them as a young reader curious about what was
going on. The intellectual-cultural situation he shared with them is significant: as an educated, a thinking person, he was, like them, of the
second post-Darwinian generation. That is to say, like them and the great

fore-runner Yeats (born 1865) he faced the question of belief, in a society which was abandoning the old spiritual tradition along with some of the social values which went with it. The alternatives before them were four: to adhere to the old faith, taken literally; to turn it into something which could once again be believed in (i.e. to metaphorize it); to find some new belief; to opt for the 'modern' position of the educated class generally − that is, an essentially sceptical, rationalist or positivist or humanist substitute (which turned, as the century progressed, into what Leavis later diagnosed as technologico-Benthamism).

None of them did the first or the last. Eliot's 'nisus' was the pursuit of the second, and Lawrence's of the third. It was Leavis's forty-year enterprise to grasp what they had done, to see where they had gone, and in using Lawrence as contrast to Eliot, and finally rejecting Eliot's remark-ably subtle formulations, to confirm his own stance, which is related to Lawrence's but also peculiarly his own.

Lawrence too followed a religious quest: Leavis could see as much in his earliest essays, but was committed to not extrapolating a belief-system on the despised 'history of ideas' plan, and so left a good deal inexplicit. Yet at the end of his life Lawrence stated in plain terms that he believed in God; though we infer that this god was the nameless faceless impersonal creative power which constantly drives forward all the changes in the living universe − call it 'life'. This replants humans in a living whole to which they are related and to which they need to be open. It is, so to speak, a proto-religion, underlying historical faiths which can be seen as intellectualizations and as metaphor-systems. Lawrence kept more than a soft spot for the Bible-Christianity he had been born into, since biblical language puts us back in touch with an earlier, naturally religious world, and the evident figurativeness of the Bible appealed to him. He does therefore explore the profound analogy between his own systems of natural metaphor and religious language − for instance the seed-plant-flower-seed metamorphosis is an analogy with death and resurrection. His work is packed with implicit Christian analogies, and is in that respect essentially akin to Eliot's long attempt to revalidate Christian language. This is something Leavis did not mention, partly because it is only in close analysis that it comes out, and it is one of the ways in which his own work needs to be taken further than he took it.

Leavis also found his own belief in a form of 'life', but it was subtilized into this 'living principle', which he saw at work not so much in external nature as in the mind and its dealings with other minds: in language as the vehicle of thought and the repository of value, the medium in which minds live with each other and become an intellectual community, a culture. He grasped from Lawrence that each mind is the mind of a body, just as each body is that of a mind. And this being is also inhabited by a self. His 'living principle' is not biological but intellectual, if I can put it in that way, or indeed spiritual; he has spiritualized Lawrence's principle in the sense that he saw works of literature as exemplifying that life and sharing it, so that it is a form of life that the reader is invited to enter. It is in the 'mind' that intellectual life must have its focus, but I put the word in inverted commas to suggest that understanding Lawrence's work must have a profound effect on our sense of the mind and its place. Nonetheless the mind mattered more, vitally, to Leavis. This accounts for his most important early reservations about Lawrence: understanding Lawrence's position better led him to reconceptualize his own, not to abandon it.

It is this ambitiousness which gives Eliot and Lawrence their importance. Compared with them, other modern writers, except Yeats, seem trivial or conventional whatever their 'formal' originality, and there is an element in Yeats which is eccentric without being productively eccentric. There have been interesting writers in the rest of our century properly so-called, but none of this rank, none therefore calling for the same effort of critical appraisal. That seems to me the essential historical judgement, which places Leavis on a level comparable with these two, as a great writer.

PART 4

Biographical

In the 1930s:
Cambridge to New Zealand

Eric McCormick is a senior New Zealand man-of-letters whose interest in the culture of his own country was fostered in the atmosphere of the early days of *Scrutiny* in Cambridge. This extract from his paper 'My Association with F. R. and Q. D. Leavis' shows first the excitement generated by the group, and then how its historical concerns helped McCormick lay the foundation for the study of New Zealand cultural history when he returned home and organized the publications that were issued at the Centennial celebrations in 1940, including his ground-breaking *Letters and Art in New Zealand*. The Canadian scholar, Maria Tibbetts, has claimed that McCormick's work provided a blueprint for her examination of the Canadian cultural heritage.

Though I don't want to be too egotistical, there are some facts about my background that may be relevant in considering my association with the Leavises. When I met them late in 1931, I was twenty-five years of age. I was born and received my elementary schooling in the small inland town of Taihape, of which my father, a migrant from Northern Ireland, was a founder and one of two partners in the first general store. My mother was a New Zealander, born in Canterbury Province and brought up in the city of Christchurch. When I won a scholarship at the end of 1919 my parents managed, with a struggle, to send me as a boarder to Wellington College, where I remained until I left the lower sixth form at the end of 1923.

Since I had no special talents and must of necessity support myself, I entered the Wellington Teachers' Training College and enrolled as a part-time student at Victoria University College. At the end of two years I became a certified teacher and for another two years taught in sole-charge country schools in the Nelson district. I also contrived to complete an

M.A. degree with honours in English and Latin. Unfortunately, the honours were only second class, not good enough I discovered, after a series of rebuffs, to win me the position I sought as master in a secondary school.

So in the middle of 1929 I resigned from my teaching job in the country and enrolled at Victoria College for an M.A. course in English as a single subject. There were seven papers but, instead of choosing Icelandic or some other esoteric option, I elected to write a thesis on New Zealand literature, a subject I had become interested in through browsing among the contents of the Alexander Turnbull Library. 'Is there any New Zealand literature?' was the response of sceptical contemporaries.

It was a question I chose to answer briefly in the introductory sections of the thesis. Certainly there was no large body of great or distinctive literature, I acknowledged. New Zealand was a 'young country', established as a British colony less than a century before. There had not been enough time for imported culture and traditions to become naturalized. Moreover, throughout the country's brief history the emphasis had necessarily been placed on practical achievement. Nevertheless, from early colonial days until the present time, literary work of merit – 'literature' in one of its senses – had been written and published.

Succeeding chapters included an account of the major figures, an analysis of the dominant themes of New Zealand verse, and a selective review of significant novels. Among the prose writers Katherine Mansfield was given most space, and among the poets E. L. Palmer, whom I knew at Wellington Training College and who had died of exposure while tramping alone in the hills. No detailed sources were given, but there was a bibliography and a lengthy appendix on the literary associations between England and New Zealand.

In spite of its deficiencies, the thesis impressed the external examiner, who made special mention of the appendix. His report, combined with fairly good marks for the six papers, gained me first-class honours. Even more important, they led to the award of a postgraduate scholarship. Thus I realized an ambition I had cherished for years, to visit England and study at one of the universities. In mid-August 1931 I left Wellington, travelling tourist class by the Suez route for England. As the voyage came to an end, we learned through bulletins of broadcast news that a national government had been formed to save the country, the Empire, the pound.

I had reached England in the depths of a great depression. I was too ill-informed to realize the fact and, besides, was beset with problems of my own. With an improvidence that now seems hardly believable I had made no definite arrangements for my stay in England. Vaguely – and for the wrong reasons – I was attracted by the idea of attending one of the older universities. On the other hand, London had its attractions and had been recommended by academic friends in New Zealand. As for the subject of research, while reading for English honours I had come across an early-Elizabethan compilation, *The Mirrour for Magistrates*, and thought it would repay further study.

My immediate future was decided with the help of the New Zealand university agent in London. He recommended his own university, Cambridge, advised me to visit the place in person, and gave me a letter of introduction to Raymond Priestly, a university official and fellow of Clare College. Thus by processes I need not elaborate, by October 1931 I was a research student of Clare, working on *The Mirrour for Magistrates* under the supervision of Enid Welsford, author of an exhaustive book on the court masque. Owing to my slightly late arrival I had been obliged to take rather expensive lodgings in Bridge Street, at the centre of the town. I usually had breakfast, lunch, and tea there, but dined in college most evenings and could use the Clare Library as well as the vast University Library. Like most newcomers, I bought a second-hand machine and biked everywhere.

Acutely aware of my scholastic shortcomings, I decided to attend lectures in English literature given by people most of whom I had never heard of. Among them were I. A. Richards (whose name I did know), just returned to Cambridge after a period abroad; his friend Mansfield Forbes, a fellow of Clare; and F. R. Leavis, a younger man who in the face of formidable opposition was struggling to establish himself as critic, lecturer, and teacher. Forbes and Leavis were not only gifted lecturers but most friendly in the small gatherings that often followed a lecture. Both invited me to visit them at home – Forbes in his luxurious villa, Finella, near the college, Leavis in a pleasant two-storeyed house some distance from the town. Soon I was one of the regular guests at the tea-party Dr and Mrs Leavis gave every week.

As a result of the Leavises' hospitality, by the middle of the term my circle of acquaintances had widened considerably. I met most of the other research students in English, notably W. A. Edwards, L. C. Knights, Denys

Thompson and Miss M. C. Bradbrook. But I found myself more at ease
with certain younger students: Iqbal Singh, an Indian undergraduate, who
shared my admiration for D. H. Lawrence (a writer I had discovered just
before leaving New Zealand and was now reading avidly); Donald Culver,
a pleasant American with friends among his literary compatriots in Paris;
and the poet C. H. Peacock, who knew Edmund Blunden and discoursed
at length, to my enlightenment, on the work of John Donne.

Taking advantage of my central position and with the aid of my landlady,
I did a little entertaining on my own account. One modest affair is
mentioned in a journal-diary I was keeping irregularly at the time. I had
some people to tea, I wrote on 3 November, mentioning the guests: Iqbal
Singh, 'little' Peacock, and a 'coarse' unnamed Australian. No more social
functions were recorded in November. But there were references to a
scheme conceived by Singh and myself to start a 'magazine', 'The Phoenix',
that would publish stories, poems, and articles in sympathy with the views
of D. H. Lawrence. Seeking other opinions, we arranged for Culver and
Peacock to join us at Bridge Street on 19 November. Views differed; in
fact, I described the gathering as 'the most anarchic, chaotic' I had ever
attended. Nor were Singh and I encouraged the following day by a round
we made of Cambridge printers to discuss business matters. One experienced man said we would need a circulation of 10,000 to get national
advertising and warned us we were bound to lose money.

On 24 November there was another meeting of the small group. It
was again in my rooms and this time we were joined by L. C. Knights,
probably invited by Culver. Soon it was evident that Dr Leavis had been
consulted and that he favoured publishing a critical journal far wider in
scope than a 'magazine' devoted to the works of Lawrence. On the other
hand, ever since our talk with the hard-headed printer, Singh and I realized
that we were in no position to finance a periodical of any kind. So without
formalities we simply went our own uncertain way. In contrast, the rest
of the group, under the nominal leadership of Knights and Culver, with
Dr Leavis actively in support, continued preparations for publishing a
critical journal which became known as *Scrutiny*. The first number appeared
in May 1932 with Knights and Culver listed as editors. Contributors
included Dr and Mrs Leavis, Miss Bradbrook, and Peacock, represented
by a poem. In the third number Dr Leavis and Denys Thompson joined
the founding editors.

The few weeks during which 'The Phoenix' was discussed were also a critical period in my career as a research student. Indeed, one reason for toying with the idea of a periodical may have been my lack of progress in the study of *The Mirrour for Magistrates*. I had soon discovered I was ill-equipped to work in this unfamiliar period of English literature and had been unwise to commit myself to it. Should I then persevere, or choose another subject, or, since I had found the lectures so rewarding, should I switch over to an undergraduate course, if that were permissible? I badly needed advice and turned to Dr Leavis. I had continued to attend the weekly tea-parties, but on this occasion I think I saw him alone. At any rate, once I explained my dilemma, he was most sympathetic and urged me to return to the subject of my honours thesis, New Zealand literature, which we had discussed in previous conversations. It could, he suggested, be treated more fully than before, with greater emphasis now placed on cultural and historical forces. In a word much used by both the Leavises, the approach could be 'anthropological'.

It was an immense relief to have reached a decision. 'I have abandoned my original thesis . . . thank God!' I wrote in my diary on 11 November. The note of elation was decidedly premature. There were courtesies to be shown and formalities to be observed before I could leave the first subject behind and make a fresh start. To begin with, I must call on Miss Welsford to explain my actions as tactfully as possible. We had not seen a great deal of each other during our short association and she accepted its end with equanimity. More than that, she generously expressed her approval. Then I had to prepare for the authorities a request for approval to change the subject of my research, giving some details for the new topic and the method of treatment. Here I mentioned my previous work on New Zealand literature and, following Dr Leavis's advice, stated my intention of treating it more fully, with the emphasis on cultural and historical factors.

The end of term was in sight before the proposals were agreed to. A new supervisor was appointed – not Dr Leavis, as we had both hoped, but Basil Willey, a scholar and lecturer of Dr Leavis's generation. After a brief meeting we agreed to see each other again after the vacation. He was busy with end-of-year concerns, while I was looking for accommodation to return to at the beginning of the new term. I had decided that the rooms in Bridge Street were too expensive, too noisy, and too accessible to casual visitors. Eventually I found two modest rooms at 43 Kimberley Road, well away from the town, and before leaving for London called on the Leavises. I remember only one incident in the visit: Dr Leavis gave me a letter of introduction to a former student of his, D. W. Harding, now employed as an industrial psychologist and living with his wife in London.

I put off presenting the letter for a week or so. I had decided that in the interests of my new thesis I would spend most of the vacation exploring New Zealand books and records in London. So, on my arrival, I made straight for Gowings Private Hotel in Coram Street, Bloomsbury. I had stayed there after the voyage from New Zealand and, despite the slightly pretentious name, found it an excellent boarding-house – comfortable, clean, well-run, cheap. For my present purpose it was ideally situated: within easy walking distance of both the British Museum and the Public Record Office, it was also near several large reference libraries. Having been issued with a reader's ticket for the British Museum, I began work, taking time off only on Christmas Day and when I went to visit the Hardings, to whom I was immediately attracted and whom I continued to see at intervals until I returned to Cambridge.

Thus I established a routine that I followed, with some variations, for the rest of my stay in England. I would spend the term at Cambridge, lodging first at Kimberley Road and then, during the second year, in Clare College itself. I found Basil Willey a conscientious supervisor, not deeply interested in what I was doing but always eager to read and criticize sections of my thesis as it slowly took shape. Dr and Mrs Leavis, however, continued to be my chief friends and unofficial mentors at Cambridge. I often attended their weekly parties and was occasionally asked to a more formal gathering to meet a visiting celebrity such as Edgell Rickword. I became a subscriber to *Scrutiny*, it goes without saying, and got the two authors to sign my copies of *Fiction and the Reading Public* and *New Bearings in English Poetry*.

At the end of each term I made for London, installing myself at Gowing's and beginning work in one of the libraries. As time went on and I reflected that I might never return to Europe, I visited and revisited galleries and theatres, often in the company of the Hardings, who were connoisseurs of the arts and discriminating admirers of ballet and the opera. For the same reason several times I broke my stay in London to undertake expeditions outside England: I biked through Provence with a friend; in 1932 I took advantage of special excursion fares to tour Italy and confirm my detestation of fascism; the following year I biked to my father's birthplace in Ireland and joined other students in a hurried, frustrating motor tour of Scotland.

As a result of these activities and successive errors of judgement, I fell behind with my work. By the end of my second English summer I had accumulated a large quantity of notes but drafted only about half the thesis. My scholarship had expired and, since money was running out, I was given permission to complete the project in New Zealand (mainly, I suspect, through the efforts of Basil Willey). By chance I was able to bid farewell to Dr and Mrs Leavis in person. They were passing through London on the way to Paris and stopped at Gowing's Hotel for tea.

Soon after, in the summer of 1933, I left for New Zealand by way of Panama. There were only two ports of call – Port Royal, Jamaica, and Panama itself – so I had ample time to reflect on the recent past and take thought for the future. In spite of some failures and miscalculations, largely of my own making, the visit had been fairly happy and richly rewarding. The country I had known through books and immature imaginings had become a complex reality. I had met many people, made some friends, and added both to knowledge and self-knowledge. In particular I had learned that I was a New Zealander, not some species of offshore Englishman. The discovery was gradual, prompted in the first place by the mere fact of migration but accentuated and given direction by the research to which I had finally committed myself. As I sifted through notes and drafts in the privacy of my cabin, the immediate objectives seemed clear: to revise my work, emphasizing the 'anthropological' aspect, and bring it to a conclusion. Beyond all that was conjecture.

Mainly for family reasons, on my return I settled in Dunedin. The city was previously unknown to me and, with its air of age and permanence, made an immediate appeal. Established on the wealth won from Otago's goldfields, Dunedin was more solidly built than the northern provincial capitals and more pleasing to the eyes of a returning Anglophile. It might almost have been an English provincial centre or small university town. More important for my immediate purpose, there were two collections of New Zealand books, manuscripts, and pictures. The larger was the Hocken Library, founded by a scholarly doctor and housed in the Otago

Museum. The other was the McNab Collection, bequeathed to the city by a landowner-politician-historian, and now installed in the Public Library. Given access to these sources and to the University Library, I began to revise and reshape the thesis.

In my speculating and planning I had not given much thought to practical matters. However, while reserving most of my time for work on the thesis, I managed to subsist modestly by lecturing to WEA classes, by broadcasting book reviews, and by coaching a few examination candidates. As I became known to members of the university staff, I was occasionally invited to their homes or asked to speak at student clubs. But for at least a couple of years my literary and intellectual interests continued to centre on Cambridge – or that tiny minority of scholars and writers with whom I had been fortunate enough to associate. I went on subscribing to *Scrutiny* and eagerly scanned each issue when it arrived. I also corresponded with Dr and Mrs Leavis for several years and more briefly with Basil Willey. But the closest and most sustained friendship was with D. W. Harding who had contributed to *Scrutiny* from the beginning and became one of the editors in September 1933 (just after I left for New Zealand). He had taken a lively interest in my thesis, so towards the end of 1935 I was relieved to tell him that I had completed the latest revision and sent copies to Cambridge.

'Literature in New Zealand' had become what I subtitled 'An Essay in Cultural Criticism'. More plainly it was a study of two literatures and two cultures, those of the scriptless Maori people in brief terms; then, at greater length, the literature and culture of their European successors. The underlying idea, presented not very lucidly in an appendix, was that just as the Maori migrants had been forced to adapt their customs to the new environment, so European colonists were under a similar compulsion. Sources were not confined to imaginative literature and ranged in date from the eighteenth century to the early-twentieth. While my honours thesis had been deficient in its scholarly apparatus, this one listed a source for each of the innumerable quotations and footnote-asides. The influence of my Cambridge mentors, though not always acknowledged, was evident in a number of ways: in the treatment of popular fiction where I followed Mrs Leavis; in the stress I placed on education where I emulated Dr Leavis; and in one of the appendices reporting the answers to a questionnaire, inspired by I. A. Richards's *Practical Criticism*. I again gave more space to Katherine Mansfield than to any other writer, but now qualified my praise. I had discovered that in the early story 'The-Child-Who-Was-Tired' she had plagiarized Anton Tchekov! Charitable English examiners, possibly at Basil Willey's suggestion, awarded the dissertation the minor degree of M.Litt.

> Back in New Zealand McCormick was offered a post as assistant to the Dominion Archivist and Parliamentary Librarian, G. H. Scholefield, and became the secretary of the National Centennial Historical Committee that was set up in connection with the hundredth anniversary of the country's accession to the British crown in 1840. The committee was the creation of J. W. Heenan, Under-Secretary of Internal Affairs, who charged it with the production of various publications, including a series of 'Historical Surveys' for the Centennial, authoritative and popular, in some cases both. A series of booklets was planned, partly on the inspiration of an American series, 'Building America' published by Columbia University, in format not unlike the British *Picture Post* which was widely read in New Zealand. The series was to be called *Making New Zealand*. There were also to be 'book surveys', and for this series McCormick augmented his Cambridge thesis on New Zealand literature as *Letters and Art in New Zealand*, a contribution originally generated by the encouragement of Leavis, and consistent with the concern of Leavis, Q. D. Leavis and the *Scrutiny* group for historical study and the sociology of literature.

The intention was to issue the publications at intervals throughout the centennial period, now less than two years away. Hence it was imperative that Oliver Duff (Editor) should be able to start work with the least possible delay. He was introduced to members of the standing committee in the middle of March. Soon afterwards I briefed him on the still tentative publishing programme: the popular *Making New Zealand*, to be issued in parts; the dozen or so 'book surveys'; Dr Scholefield's biographical dictionary; and the historical Atlas. With the decisiveness of the veteran editor, he interviewed prospective authors or wrote to them, and during a visit to Christchurch investigated printing costs and possible arrangements for distributing the surveys. His efforts, combined with those of the standing committee before him, opened the way for the second meeting of the National Historical Committee, held on 17 June 1938 (my thirty-second birthday).

Since Mr Thorn was occupied with parliamentary business, the chairman was J. T. Paul; in fact the meeting was dominated by Messrs. Heenan and Duff. The Under-Secretary wanted from the committee a general endorsement of the publishing programme – something in broad terms that could go before the Cabinet and receive legislative authority. He achieved this aim at the end, but only after lengthy discussion. Some committee members living outside Wellington sought more than generalities. They wanted to have particulars of publications and the name of authors – facts that were not always forthcoming. While it was common knowledge that Dr Scholefield had compiled the biographical dictionary, details of the Atlas and most of the pictorial surveys had still to be decided. Fortunately, Oliver Duff had worked hard on the 'book surveys' and was able to give the authors' names and subjects for most of the series. Among them were: Dr Beaglehole for exploration, Leicester Webb for government, Dr W. B. Sutch for social service, myself for a survey of letters, art, and language. Mr Duff then made a plea for advice: should such fundamental subjects as religion and defence be ignored? He would appreciate the committee's views. Members were glad to oblige and, won over by the editor's frankness, passed a motion expressing their unqualified approval.

The National Historical Committee held its next and final meeting less than six months later, on 2 December 1938. Mr Thorn was again in the chair and from information given by the editor and the secretary reported developments since the previous June. The authors of twelve 'book surveys' were now at work, pledged to deliver their scripts by the middle of the centennial year or earlier. Arrangements had recently been completed for the printing by the offset process of *Making New Zealand*, and a trial number would be brought out early in the new year. Dr Scholefield had now finished his biographical dictionary and suitable type and paper were being chosen for two massive volumes. There remained the Atlas, on which several draughtsmen of the Lands and Survey department were working, while research was continuing.

In fact, the National Historical Committee had served the purpose for which it had been set up and had made itself redundant. Everything now depended on the authors, the editors, and the growing number of assistants. After Oliver Duff's appointment I had no direct responsibility for any publications except my own. Nevertheless, in my position as secretary I attended meetings and did what I could to solve problems that arose as work on publications advanced and the staff increased. Some notable recruits joined us in the second half of 1938. One was David Hall, a Cambridge graduate, originally appointed as publicity officer. He proved to be a most versatile writer, lucid, fluent, and well-informed, and, like his friend, John Pascoe, willing to tackle anything. Another was A. H. McLintock, also a man of parts – scholar, historian, artist, yet quite prepared to draw ingenious diagrams for the pictorial surveys.

There were losses as well as gains. Early in the new year – the fateful 1939 – Oliver Duff resigned to become editor of the newly established *New Zealand Listener*. It was largely on his recommendation that I had been commissioned to write a survey. Now he urged that I should succeed him in the editorial post, a course that would in his view involve the least disruption of our plans and the least possible delay. Except for producing student magazines in Wellington and Cambridge, I had no editorial experience, but gave my reluctant consent when Oliver Duff agreed to continue in an advisory role. I was further reassured by a generous offer by Dr Beaglehole. Nominally typographical adviser, but oracle in all matters, he undertook to design Dr Scholefield's dictionary and see it through the press. During the change-over inevitably there were mishaps, misunderstandings, minor crises; but within a matter of weeks authors had finally been briefed, and we were ready to print a trial number of *Making New Zealand*.

Thus I became a fledgling editor, intent upon fulfilling the programme of publications with which my colleagues and I were entrusted. It was, I soon discovered, an exacting commitment. Henceforward the weekdays and many evenings were taken up with editorial and secretarial duties – meeting authors, reading and revising scripts, correcting proofs, drafting letters. The week-ends I tried to reserve for a little mild recreation and the survey of literature and art (I had dropped language without consulting Oliver Duff or the National Historical Committee). Eventually the book became a version of my Cambridge thesis, divested of theories, stripped of superfluous verbiage, and supplemented by brief sections on art and contemporary writing.

Letters and Art in New Zealand, the outcome of Dr Leavis's inspired suggestion, was published on the eve of the Centennial. There have been successors, of which two appeared during the sesquicentennial, edited by Terry Sturm, and Michael Dunn's *Concise History of New Zealand Painting*.

Pre-war Downing

Keith Dobson experienced Leavis's teaching in the early 1930s, at Downing College, but before Leavis had a permanent University Lectureship. He did not have regular use of college rooms at this time; possibly he preferred doing individual tutorials ('supervisions') at home because of the needs of his wife and young son. He took Part One History and Part One English, then a teaching certificate at the Cambridge University Department of Education. After applying for eighty-six jobs with one interview in 1937–39 he took a post at the Zickelsche Hochschule in Berlin. He wrote this memoir (for Ian MacKillop's *F. R. Leavis: A Life in Criticism*) in 1991, revising it in 1995, when he remarked that his main interest was in politics. 'No-one could teach in a Jewish school in Berlin from 1937 to 1939 without acquiring an everlasting interest in politics.'

I went up to Downing in October 1933 from Scarborough Boys' High School to read history. Because I did not do very well in Part I, and because I needed a second subject to get a teaching job, I switched to English Part I in October 1935. For that year, I attended weekly supervisions at Leavis's house in Chesterton Hall Crescent together with L. C. N. Hardy.

I had heard of Leavis before I came to Cambridge. I was taught by Jack Jenkinson; we used *Culture and Environment* in the Sixth Form. While he was at Emmanuel College, Jack had become involved in argument with Leavis and the upshot was 'Under Which King, Bezonian?' in the third number of *Scrutiny*. I could not make much of this controversy at the time (indeed, I remember sitting in St. Nicholas Gardens in July 1933, when I should have been at the swimming sports, struggling to make something out of Leavis's Introduction to *Towards Standards of Criticism*), but now, towards the end of my life, I see this failure to acknowledge the merits of the Marxist argument as very important. The very poor and at times rude line of argument in these two pieces used to irritate me; now I look on them as works of one who was unsure of his ground.

Leavis was never to my knowledge as rude in person as he is in these two pieces. (I mean such things as the 'appeal of the chic' and talk of differences that have not much to do with thinking.) I remember his encounters at the Doughty Society with E. W. Meyerstein, short, dumpy and impervious; with L. H. Myers, slim, silver grey in his Melton overcoat, impervious in a different way; and with Miss Bradbrook buried in an easy chair and so low in volume I had to guess what she said from what Leavis answered from the other side of the fireplace. I cannot recollect what these discussions were about, but they were not marked by a rudeness or point-scoring. I was very sorry to see a letter some years ago in *The Listener* from Lord Annan saying that Leavis's rudeness to his colleagues was insufferable. I have no reason to think this was true. On the contrary, I was told by three or four people from different colleges what *their* supervisors had said about Leavis. When my brother was secretary of the Shirley Society at St. Catherine's (about 1940) he invited Leavis to speak to the society. I don't know how this came about, but somehow Leavis had to dine at high table and this caused Sidney Smith and Tom Henn to tell my brother that Leavis was a *malade imaginaire* who disdainfully sent back the best food the College could put before him. I don't know whether Leavis had dyspepsia, but I never associated him with 'dyspeptic' colonels in cartoons. Neither do I know whether he had asthma, though people who knew him better than I did told me he had been gassed in the Great War and that this lay behind his love of cross-country running and his preference for open-necked shirts – very open, unbuttoned low down the front.

At our first meeting he gave Hardy and me the names of the lecturers we should attend. Far from ordering us to attend certain lecturers and not others, Leavis said we should try Mrs. Bennett. I learned some time later of his quarrel with the Bennetts at Emmanuel. There was no trace of antipathy in his manner. He did this exactly as our history supervisor had done, without any indication of his own opinion of them. When I told him three weeks later that with one exception they were poor, he did not dissent in the cases of Mr Potts, Mr Henn and Mr Downs, but said I ought to persevere with Miss Murray on Chaucer as she was a genuine scholar and 'a daughter of the Dictionary'. He then asked what I. A. Richards had been on about in his once-a-week lectures. I told him that that week it had been Haiku. He said that he believed Richards had once

had a day or two in Japan. He thought perhaps Richards might be a little
uncertain in direction as his wife, who managed his career, was now
thinking of a good job in America rather than in Japan. I took his advice
on Miss Murray; and he said he would get us a bit of extra supervision
from Mr. Cox to make up for the others.

When I had been to a lecture by Sir Arthur Quiller-Couch, I said to
Leavis that he seemed like a figure from a bygone age. He said 'that's
what he is, and a thoroughly decent one, too.' Then he told me that
when he had been working with Denys Thompson on *Reading and
Discrimination*, he had written to 'Q' to ask for permission to use one of
his poems. 'Q' replied giving his permission. Both Leavis and Thompson
were troubled in conscience by 'Q''s generous nature, and felt that they
ought to write back to say that the poem was needed for an unfavourable
comparison. 'Q' replied that this didn't matter at all. 'Tell your friend
Miss Thompson that she can make use of my poems for whatever purpose
she pleases.'

The one exceptional lecturer in the English Faculty was M. D. Forbes.
The impression he made on me has lasted longer than that made by any
other person I met in Cambridge. Leavis always spoke well of Forbes;
the last time I saw him – in 1970 when he gave a lecture on Lawrence
in Nottingham – he particularly mentioned Forbes's enlightened attitude
towards invigilation of exams. Forbes gave fascinating analyses of Wordsworth's sonnet 'Surprised by Joy', of Edward Thomas's 'Melancholy' and
Blake's 'Morning'. I never heard Leavis make an adverse comment on
anything said by Forbes, though they were not at one on Blake. Leavis
praised the shorter poems, had no liking for the Prophetic Books, and
fought shy of the 'mystical' approach of Kathleen Raine on the one hand,
and of the 'political' approach on the other. I always thought that Leavis's
conception of 'precision' in the use of language interfered with his
appreciation of Blake, though I remember enjoying his analysis of 'The
Sunflower' during one supervision. Forbes was more freely enthusiastic,
though not annoyingly so. He praised Charles Gardiner's 'Vision and
Vesture' and made me feel that the sun really was 'freed from fears'. I
felt that Leavis was inhibited by Eliot, though when I tackled him with
some toffee-nosed bit of Eliot (the 'ingenious bit of home-made furniture'
in the Blake essay for example) he claimed no responsibility for 'Tom's'
views.

Whereas Forbes was provocative and unrestrained, Leavis, though en-
lightening, was very guarded. This diffidence marked particularly his
attitude to foreign literature and to the other arts. I asked him if he thought
Lawrence's judgment of Rilke was adequate. He said he did not feel
competent to pronounce. At a Downing concert Wilfrid Mellers played
his own 'Lullaby for Ginger Rogers'. I asked Leavis what he made of it;
he said he did not feel qualified to speak on such matters. (On this occasion
I sympathized.) This caginess merged at times with something like paranoia.
He often referred to himself as 'the most unpopular of critics'. He wrote
on my essays such remarks as 'But for some unnecessary risks in the matter
of tact, a good Tripos essay'. I will quote in full a remark he wrote on
my essay on Milton's development as a poet (I do not think I had
challenged the views expressed in his Milton article; but I did think the
Milton affair was getting a bit overblown, especially after the packed
meeting in the Cosmopolitan Cinema, which was called, I suppose, to
arrange for the removal of Milton's remains from the mausoleum; I think
it was chaired by Muriel Bradbrook's younger brother, Frank, a year after
me at Downing): 'This manner, directed against the more (sic) objection-
able of modern critics, will serve you well in the examination room, but
don't make a habit of it: directed against accepted values, it will annoy
the examiners.' I think he might have seen something of himself in me;
he told Hardy that he did not think I would do as well as I ought to do
in the Tripos because I had a natural gift for putting people's backs up.
Yet all in all I would say that the complaints he made years later at the
beginning of *The Great Tradition* are fully justified. Even in my day it was
being said that he dismissed most of English Literature as not worth reading
and that he had said this, that, and the other about our most revered
writers. There was absolutely none of this – unless you think Humbert
Wolfe was one of our most revered figures. I think that these falsifications
of his views were deliberately put about by poor-spirited people in the
English Faculty in those days who did not want their own views to be
the subject of enquiry.

When Hardy and I turned up at the Chesterton Hall Crescent house
on that bright October morning in 1935 we found a pleasant room, split
level, with modern light-coloured furniture. Leavis, looking just like his
portrait in pencil (or perhaps a touch of crayon) that hung in the room,
was just dashing in with two firelighters, the sun having put the fire out.

This procedure was very common, though we never felt cold. We never once saw Queenie, though later on Leavis had to dash out on several occasions to comfort a crying baby – their first child. We sat in comfortable chairs and Leavis in a business-like way described the difficulty of doing two years' work in eight months. (Part One of the English Tripos was supposed to be taken after two years.) It meant our concentrating on poetry, otherwise we should never get through the reading. We would start with the Metaphysicals, so bring our Griersons.

I always looked forward to the supervisions and enjoyed them. Leavis liked to keep at least one eye on the exam. He always referred to the examiners as 'the enemy'. If I made a remark that echoed something he had written, he would hold his chin and say 'Caution! Beware the enemy!' I soon ran into *the* fundamental problem of literary criticism: how to prove that something is good. Leavis would ask us to look at two or three poems, and get ready to talk about them next week. In an early supervision we read Arnold's 'Others abide our question'. Leavis said that 'planting his steadfast footsteps in the sea', when applied to something as static as a mountain, showed that Arnold's imagination was not functioning. I mentioned the mix-up between the Lincoln and the National in 'The Rocking-Horse Winner'. Leavis, quite properly, I think, said that was quite a different type of error. Once he chose two Wordsworth sonnets: 'It is a beauteous evening . . .' and 'Earth has not anything to show . . .' Hardy and I looked at them and found them slightly repellent. But we thought we had better go carefully as Forbes had been sorting out 'breathing rhythms' and 'sigh cadences' with his coloured chalks; and Leavis had been talking of kinaesthetic imagery ('Not my word, you notice,' as he always said). So I tentatively suggested that the words might re-create the trance in which the nun was breathless with adoration. Leavis said 'I can't get near enough to say whether that is so or not. It's so nauseating.' So there it was, in a medium-sized nutshell! I had a friend in Scarborough, where I lived at the time, who was always asking me to prod Leavis on the concept of 'significant form'. Leavis dismissed the expression as meaningless jargon, but it did seem to have enough meaning to cause some irritation. It led to the airing of one or more of the following themes in supervisions: the decline of Virginia Woolf after *To the Lighthouse*; the decline of Henry James after *Portrait of a Lady*; the 'applied' style of George Meredith; the overrating of Proust in *Aspects of the Novel*; the wrong-headedness of most of Jane Austen's admirers. I was listening recently to an American art critic, Mr Greenberg, saying that no critic had discovered an objective method of evaluating works of art. The interviewer said, 'What about Leavis?' Mr Greenberg said, 'I admire Leavis immensely; but he was just as much an aesthete as the rest of them. I'd love him to be here today [laughing], and I would tell him so.'

13   *Patrick Harrison*

Downing After the War

This section is taken from a book, to date (1995) unpublished, called *Unaffected Devotion to Serious Ends*. It deals vividly with Leavis and Downing College, but also with the experience of growing up after the war, with a specificity to which this extract, though long, can hardly do justice. Many vignettes, like that of Eric Mathieson, spring from the page in the abbreviated version here given. In the full version they emerge with even greater specificity of characterization. Harrison's account of the brilliant and idiosyncratic Marius Bewley is given here almost intact. These pages illustrate, among other things, a typical relationship between Downing College and the 'feeder' schools from which some of Leavis's pupils came, and also the relationship between 'Downing English' and a professional career outside academe and literary studies. Harrison, formerly a civil servant and Secretary of the Royal Institute of British Architects, gives a more worldly view than many accounts of Leavis. In its full form Harrison's book is as reflective as the abbreviated form in which it here presented. There is one passage, about Leavis and Eliot in general which is perhaps worth giving special prominence:

> T. S. Eliot in the 1930s and 1940s can in some respects be seen as a part-time writer and an amateur critic. To say this is in no way to belittle his significance: it gave to his small *oeuvre* a refreshingly succinct impact, in contrast to the more voluminous works of many professional men-of-letters. But to embody his insights and the significance of his poetry systematically into an academic establishment responsible for the teaching of English called for an operation altogether different in kind from anything in which Eliot was interested or of which he was capable. This was the task Leavis set himself, like an energetic colonial administrator following up an inspired but unreliable conqueror. Mapping the provinces, first of poetry, then the novel. Establishing an appropriate ideology. Discrediting the lingering remnants of former rule. Setting up training establishments for district officers to maintain law, order and morale throughout as much new territory as possible

and defending its borders. Ridiculing enemies. Ruthlessly executing without trial those suspected of disloyalty or heresy. Practising an austere personal regime of life and feeling increasingly betrayed by the slipping into self-indulgence and dotage of the once admired leader in the decadence of a distant capital. How dull, serious, secular and pedestrian all this effort must have seemed to Eliot, at ease in a fashionable world which Leavis abhorred and shunned and in which he could never have felt at home anyway. Yet, if Eliot's new bearings were to have permanent influence beyond a tiny élite and not to be swept away by subsequent tides of fashion, an effort of the kind made by Leavis had to be undertaken by someone.

This 'outside' view of Leavis is revealing.

I

In September 1939 I had been hastily packed off from North London to become a boarder at Lord Williams's School, Thame. My brother, then only seven, followed in April. It was at that time a tiny grammar school, still right out in the country away from the town along the Oxford road. In 1940 the roll briefly reached 182, the highest in the school's 365-year history, thereafter sinking back to the more usual 175 or so.

As the war went on the turnover of staff increased, but among the steady flow of transient misfits and elderly eccentrics were just a few interesting people, two of whom were to reveal Downing connections. One, for a couple of terms in 1941, was Peter Greenham, later to become an RA, run the Academy Schools and paint Leavis's portrait. He was a gentle, shy man who might well have been expected to be a target for brutal ragging, but he was well-liked and respected. His feathery sketches of boys, unerring likenesses, were much sought after by possessors of autograph albums. In some ways they were better likenesses, more deft and assured, than his later oils which sometimes seem (like the Leavis portrait) overworked and finicky. The second was an amiable young English master, E. A. Morley, 'Ned', who turned up at about the same time. He was fresh from Cambridge and lived in. He could sometimes be persuaded to play on the school-room piano for boarders in the evenings ('Go on Sir, Deep Purple, Sir'). Occasionally, less popularly, he would play on his violin.

I must have become a considerable bore about music, too. I went about tunelessly whistling from end to end the works I was getting to know.

It was impossible to hear anything in term-time but Mr Morley proved to be interested and knowledgeable. I used to quiz him about possible holiday purchases suggested by incessant reading of the HMV and Columbia record catalogues. Then he left.

And so it came about not long afterwards that I was sitting on the loo at break one day in the spring of 1943 whistling *Eine Kleine Nachtmusik*, one of Ned Morley's recommendations and a Christmas acquisition, when a voice demanded: 'Who's that whistling Mozart?' 'Harrison I'. 'This is Mathieson. Would you have a word with me in the quad when you've finished?'

Mathieson was head of school and a familiar figure not only by reason of his position but for his curly red hair. ('Not ginger like me, bright scarlet' as my brother described it at home). He was, of course, in terms of school society, light years away from a fourth former and doubly distant for being a day boy. He came from Chinnor, a village about five miles away to the south, right under the ridge of the Chilterns, which was marked by the ever-present plume of white smoke from the tall chimney of its cement works. This may still be seen away to the right under the Chiltern scarp as one emerges from the Beacon Hill cutting on the M40.

'I'm thinking of starting a music club in the school – record recitals on games afternoons. Are you interested?' I eagerly assented to this amazing and totally unexpected prospect both of hearing music and gaining remission from the weekly austerities of rugger on a field regularly grazed by cattle between games. Mathieson quickly detected promising material for influence and enlightenment, because we fell at once into meeting at break each day when he would walk me round the cricket field, a privilege restricted to sixth formers. This continued until the end of the following term. Mostly, our conversation was about music but it ranged quite widely. It emerged that Ned Morley had been at Downing, a college of which I had never heard, reading English under somebody called Leavis. He had encouraged Mathieson to sit the Downing scholarship exam, an event that was to take place in August. Mathieson probably judged, correctly enough, that I was not ready to appreciate the message at that stage because he did not attempt to give me much idea of what Leavis and Downing were all about; though I do remember his passing on Ned Morley's account of some meeting at which Leavis had been asked what he thought of Flecker's *Hassan*. 'I think it's a masturbation' Ned had reported the

Master as saying. And with a chuckle that was more about Ned Morley than the event itself Mathieson went on: 'And Ned said "There were ladies present"!' Nevertheless, under the great elms which then fringed one end of the cricket field (no longer), I formed the visual impression of Leavis as a confident, worldly, athletic and open-neck-shirted iconoclast, as distinctive even at this distance in time as the reality I later came to know, but utterly different.

Mathieson's advent introduced me to altogether more stimulating conversation and to a new and completely different kind of friendship from any hitherto experienced. I had long gone by the nickname Skinny which caused me much pain. He must have sensed this and quickly took to calling me Pat. The world suddenly became immensely more interesting. He encouraged a spirit of intellectual and artistic curiosity and an awareness of unexplored hinterlands of experience and sensibility. He also encouraged me to read, which I had scarcely begun to do in any serious sense. Music had by now loosened the grip of aeronautics on my imagination, although I still took *The Aeroplane* and hoped fervently that the war would go on long enough for me to be a fighter pilot. But Mathieson weaned me further on T. S. Eliot's *Collected Poems* and *The Faber Book of Modern Verse*. I had only just read the first and barely investigated the second before both were confiscated by the headmaster when he found me reading them during prep one evening. Perhaps he saw them (with 'E. Mathieson' inscribed on the flyleaf) as worrying evidence of an unsuitable association. Perhaps just as a frivolous diversion from 'trig'. More probably he simply saw them as constituting a potentially undesirable enthusiasm. Dangerous, incomprehensible, subversive. However, he did permit me to go to tea at Chinnor one Sunday afternoon in response to a written request from Mrs. Mathieson.

It was a hot day. I went by bus, traversing for the first time in its extended agricultural detail the foreshortened view between school and the hills at which I had looked out for three and a half years. Eric met me in the village. The Mathiesons lived in a detached inter-war brick house at the straggling eastern end of Chinnor along the Risborough Road. It was of conservative design for its date. Eric played the piano in the front room and read me some of his poems. I remember one about autumn which contained the line, 'November apples, like dead men's promises, unpicked'. After this we listened in the living room at the back to a Sunday afternoon record recital on the Home Service: Stokowski and the Philadelphia Orchestra playing his transcription of the D minor toccata and fugue, *L'Apprenti Sorcier* (both by then well known from Walt Disney's *Fantasia*) and *Firebird*. I never hear the Dance of the Firebird without seeing the sinuous waves blown by the summer wind through the green wheat on the slopes below Bledlow Ridge. It seems more English than Elgar. '*The Sorcerer's Apprentice* is really good, isn't it' I exclaimed at the end. 'Yes, it's fun. But I think it's probably the least important of the works we've heard this afternoon.'

In August Eric got a scholarship. He stayed with us in London for a few days before he was called up. We'd booked seats for three Proms, culminating in Beethoven's Ninth on the penultimate night. The first, a Wednesday Bach night, was conducted by Sir Henry himself. We went to lunchtime concerts at the National Gallery each day and to a matinee of *Ghosts* with Beatrix Lehmann as Mrs Alving.

Hints of Downing seeped out. There had been a party in the Fellows' Garden at which Leavis, who seemed to be nicknamed Frankie, was present in his open-necked shirt, and clever showing-off talk among candidates. I remember the name of Eddie Mason, who had made an impression with his luridly morbid humour. He had put about the story that the fabled wife Queenie (not seen) sported tartan knickers and he also told some very advanced jokes, one or two of which Eric recounted. Although knowing virtually nothing about the recondite areas of experience to which they referred (the boarding house at Thame was a robust but unsophisticated community) and although neither then nor at any later time did Eric himself make the slightest advance, I nevertheless understood intuitively what was implied and about his own nature as well.

Mathieson developed back trouble during his aircrew training in South Africa and after being shunted in and out of hospitals there was invalided home, demobbed just after V.J. Day and accepted for Downing that October. He stayed with us again. More Proms; and it was at this point he suggested that I have a shot at Downing and offered (there had been no English master for some months from Summer 1945) to coach me by correspondence and during our occasional meetings. He set and commented upon essays and exercises in practical criticism and dating based largely on the Downing sheets.

Eric loved Cambridge and Downing with an intensity I was never to match. He was an excellent mimic and conjured up Leavis's classes with such uncanny vividness as we discussed my exercises and essays that I found when I arrived that I had not only heard almost everything already but had experienced the distinctive atmosphere as well. In Eric's time Leavis had occasionally held classes at home while Queenie was in hospital, during which he would sometimes have to get the children off to school: 'And so gentleman, Johnson in this passage – other arm dear' (as he helped Kate on with her coat) ' – can be seen to transcend the limitations of his age'. The gormandizing Maurice Hussey, the sophisticated Godfrey Lienhardt, the austere Doyle, the enthusiastic Wilfred Mellers playing his Prometheus on the piano ('This is the bit where his liver's torn out') acquired mythic proportions in his colourful tales.

By December 1946 I had read all the published books by Leavis, L. C. Knights, Traversi and other associates, much of the Downing reading list and had become a subscriber to *Scrutiny*, purchasing from the publishers Deighton Bell, Cambridge booksellers in Trinity Street, as many of the pre-war pearl-grey back numbers as were still available. I had read the core of OK texts. I had also learned to use the OK words: 'poise', 'immediacy', 'sharply realized' and so forth. I got an exhibition. Call-up had been postponed during the terrible winter of 1947 and in May, aircrew being no longer available to National Servicemen, I went off for two and a bit years in the RAF to become a wireless fitter. During 1947 I did for Bob Cradock (somewhat less effectively) what Mathieson had done for me. He got a place. So the three of us, Mathieson, Harrison, and Cradock were the product of the little cell established at Thame by Ned Morley during the war.

2

In 1946 the Downing Scholarship Examination in English took place in December, after the end of the Michaelmas term. I set out from Thame via London taking in the King's Pictures at the Royal Academy and going on to Cambridge by a slow, crowded and ill-lit train from King's Cross. Presumably by Eric's arrangement I was allocated B1, the room opposite B2 in which he was installed – the two ground-floor front rooms on B staircase beside Hall. B1 has since been swallowed up by the Hall and kitchen improvements and is now permanently shuttered. Throughout the week the weather was still, misty and very cold.

On the first evening Eric played me his recently acquired set of the incomparable but already deleted pre-war LPO/Beecham Haydn 99 about which he had written enthusiastically. I played it again and again and it has become inextricably woven into my recollections of that time. Another evening we went to the Arts Cinema to see Jacques Feyder's *Une Femme Disparut* with Jeanne Françoise Rosay in multiple roles. On the Monday night I did not feel particularly anxious – not as much as on some less important occasions – but it was nevertheless one of the very few times in my life when I have slept not a wink all night. I spent the slow hours utterly awake trying to fit the chimes of the Catholic church to the so-called Cambridge quarters played on the horn in the introduction to the last movement of Brahms' first symphony. They wouldn't go.

Because I spent most of my time with Eric I saw little of my competitors though I remember on B Staircase a cheerful pink-and-white complexioned candidate with dark frizzy hair whom I recognized four years later as Morris Shapira. He got a scholarship.

We were interviewed on the Tuesday morning not by Leavis, whom we did not meet, or by anyone to do with English, but by W. L. Cuttle. He was then Dean and also tutor to those reading English. Was this a deliberate piece of College policy, I wonder, aimed at introducing a little dispassionateness into the distinctly introverted selection process in English? I remember nothing of the interview; but we were seen in alphabetical order and the next in line was already waiting when I arrived, a very tall willowy, charming and assured boy from Downside, Norman Henfrey.

We sat our first paper on the Tuesday afternoon. Wilfrid Mellers was invigilator. I don't think he introduced himself to us but I learned from Eric that it was he. Our desks in the JCR were also arranged alphabetically and there was Norman Henfrey on my right covering sheets and sheets of paper with demoralizing confidence and industry. He also got an exhibition. Although it was difficult to judge how one was doing I had been well prepared and the papers held no surprises. Tuesday afternoon was also the occasion of the Varsity match. Thame, naturally enough being so near, had Oxford orientations and we had been there a week or so before to see the Major Stanley game and witnessed the dazzling half-back partnership of Donnelly and Newton-Thompson. I felt a guilty hope that Oxford would win. They did. 'Donnelly's game' said all the papers on Wednesday morning, only faintly clouding his triumph by reporting his failure to convert from in front of the posts at the end.

Leavis appeared in Hall on a couple of evenings. Birrell, with his drooping moustache was pointed out. Admiral Richmond was in the chair as Master. We were to be informed by telegram if successful. On the Saturday my father collected us from school. There had been no news when he left home. It was a dark, bitterly cold, dead-still day. Drab, empty, car-less West Wycombe looked like the bottom of the sea. No news when we got home. No news at six. The family sat about silent as if I had suffered a bereavement. Then at seven-thirty came a bang on the door and there was the telegram boy standing in the fog. My very undemonstrative brother threw his arms around my neck. Cuttle wrote a few days later: 'If you hadn't made such a mess of a simple piece of French [from *Madame Bovary*, as I was soon to discover, with rather heavy vocabulary] you would have got a scholarship'.

There were still many people about in my first year who had served in the war and quite a few who had been up before it began. Virtually everybody else was expected to have done his National Service before arriving. This gave a distinctive flavour to College life. Those who had been in the war were serious and keen to get on with their lives: they seemed much older than their years, unapproachably adult and separated by a gulf from those of us who had not. In some respects the gulf remains to this day. By the time I went down in 1953 quite a lot of people were coming straight from school and seemed unbelievably juvenile.

Among those who had read English before the war was Noel Moynihan. In 1949 he was reading medicine and, much later, to be knighted as director of Save the Children. He had reputedly formed part of a posse which had set out one evening before the war to cut Dennis Enright's hair, considered over-long by the hearties of the day. Apparently, this intended assault was prevented by the personal intervention of Leavis. Marius Bewley, from whom I learned this, claimed to have witnessed the incident. It could still be confirmed from the principals.

Another veteran was I. Talog Davis, reading law; and Marius himself who returned from the States in 1949 to work on a Ph.D. Godfrey Lienhardt had by this time left for Oxford, following his mentor Evans-Pritchard (E.-P.) who had gone there from Cambridge to take up the chair of social anthropology, but reappeared from time to time to see his brother Peter and surviving friends such as Ian Doyle and Talog.

Early in this first term a mixed bag of us, including, I think, all the

1949 intake, was invited to tea by the Leavises one Saturday afternoon at Chesterton Hall Crescent. We probably received such invitations at the rate of about two a year, but this first occasion was naturally particularly memorable. The excellence of Queenie's tea-time fare has often been commented upon. The garden at Chesterton Hall Crescent contained a fine walnut tree which had borne very freely following the hot summer. Queenie spoke at some length of the diverse and too little appreciated pleasures to be derived from the proper use of walnuts in the domestic economy. (I remember Leavis once mentioning later how he used every year to take home a sack of mulberries from an unregarded tree in the Fellows' garden: 'My wife, you know, she knows what to do with these things.')

This tea party was also notable for marking the first appearance of Marius Bewley. He arrived a little late, smiling, diffident, courteous, in a well-pressed suit of severe East Coast cut made of some lightweight tweedish cloth, almost black with dark purple flecks. He had been visiting London and was greeted by Queenie: 'Ah, Mr Bewley, come in. How did you enjoy *A London Life*?' He hesitated, obviously slightly confused, then laughed nervously and said 'Why, Mrs Leavis, I thought you meant a London life!' He then settled himself into a rocking chair which he declared made him feel very much at home and there followed a lot of talk, led by Queenie, about James and Hawthorne. Marius was at this time writing a series of articles in *Scrutiny* on the subject, later published in *The Complex Fate*. There was also talk of a forthcoming paper by Queenie on Hawthorne's short stories. This was delivered soon afterwards, I think in College, possibly to the Doughty Society.

Leavis, though scrupulously kindly and polite in a rather stiff way on this as on other similar occasions, was not naturally sociable. He sat in a collapsed and ruminative posture, causing the wide shoulders of his tweed jacket to ride up, emphasising the somewhat scrawny character of his bare neck. He said little unless given the cue by Queenie, or possibly a guest, and then came out with some long established comment, generally pejorative, probably about *The New Statesman*, Bloomsbury, the Sunday papers or somebody associated with them, Desmond MacCarthy for instance. This would often by prefaced by a loud 'Well . . .' or 'I mean . . .', uttered with raised eyebrows and blank expression as he drew his head back. At the end, his head would often sink to one side as if in impotent resignation at the world's impossibility. The guests were generally either too much in awe, too keen to impress, or too keen to avoid putting a foot wrong to create any more natural give and take; and for Marius, who possessed greater *savoir faire* and confidence, the situation was on this particular occasion too public for the establishment of any easier or more intimate tone.

It is now possible to place Marius better than I could at Downing. Not completely; and never to diminish his originality; but he doesn't seem quite such an unclassifiable phenomenon as he did then. For example, his odd mixture of right- and left-wing views can be seen to owe something to his temperament but a lot to his American provenance, where such labels have different meanings to those they bear in Britain. He was Catholic, which carried certain social resonances, but also political, Democratic ones. He was gay, which placed him in a part-fashionable, part-beleaguered minority. He also belonged to the East Coast literary intelligentsia, which was largely anti-imperialist, anti-class and strongly left-wing at that time; but in ways that were intellectual only and wholly divorced from the possibility of serious political power or influence. It is still not always easy for us in tiny Britain to understand the extent of alienation felt by intellectuals in such a vast country from the blundering policies and apparatus of Federal agencies or the brash venality of state politics. I can now see these strands in his background. The realities of practical socialism and the painful business of achieving real change in drab post-war Britain must have seemed very unglamorous to him, and the maligned British class system to have attractive enclaves. He was not taken in by Bloomsbury, a very British sort of literary-leftish-upper-middle-classishness about which he accepted Leavis's judgement, if not the manner of its delivery. But, as Enid Bagnold suggests in her autobiography, it is possible to see the English intelligentsia as less intelligent than smart English society, and to this Marius would have been drawn – indeed, was drawn to what he saw of it. Karl Miller has since written of the allure it came to have for him also.

3

I did not find Downing a cosy college. Perhaps Wilkins's architecture, so elegant in the refined austerity of its neo-classicism and great surrounding spaces, conduced in its never-to-be-completed state to a sense of leakage and lack of heart. There was none of the congenial intimacy and enclosure that exists at the centre of most colleges. Or perhaps this is just the post-rationalization of my mood at the time and of the remoteness and lack of personal interest and encouragement one sensed on the part of the dons. I should exempt Harold Mason, though his kindness, which I mention later, was pedagogic rather than personal. Certainly I must exempt Clive Parry, my third year tutor, who was unfailingly helpful then and later and who would, uniquely, bear one off for a drink in his rooms or the buttery if he encountered one at an appropriate time of day as he cycled slowly round College in his relaxed and insouciant way, so different from his cousin at Thame. But the Leavises' hospitality was essentially impersonal. Cuttle was an irascible recluse. I certainly didn't want or expect an intrusive paternalism or the palsy-walsy counselling fashionable today; and in any event the vitality of Cambridge lay first and foremost in the society of one's contemporaries. What I missed is well described by E. M. Forster in *The Longest Journey*:

> The direction of the swim was determined a little by the genius of the place . . . and a good deal by the tutors and resident fellows, who treated with rare dexterity the products that came up yearly from the public schools. They taught the perky boy that he was not everything, and the limp boy that he might be something. They even welcomed those boys who were neither limp nor perky, but odd – those boys who had never been at a public school at all, and such do not find a welcome everywhere. And they did everything with ease – one might almost say with nonchalance, – so that the boys noticed nothing, and received education almost for the first time in their lives.

I was made vividly aware of other conventions when I was President of the Musical Society. I sent copies of our programme to all Fellows of Downing, also to a few outsiders including the Provost of Kings and George Rylands. Not a word from anyone at Downing but I received a brief hand-written letter from Sheppard: 'What a splendid programme! Congratulations. I am usually rather preoccupied here on Sundays so I doubt if I will be able to get to any of your concerts, which I regret, but I wish you every success'. I also received a nice note from Rylands. In my fourth year, at Fitzwilliam Street, I appreciated the egalitarianism across a wide gap in age cultivated by Henry Morris, from whose example I derived greater ease than I had hitherto possessed with those both older

and younger than myself. He was a difficult and capricious landlord (Karl
didn't care for the experience greatly) but at the same time a generous
and stimulating mentor to whom I owe a great enhancement of visual
sensibility and contacts which were of lasting benefit in my career.

'I sometimes feel as though Downing were becoming an outpost of
the Vatican', Leavis once said to Marius; and when I was there one could
not fail to be aware of the Catholic presence. In addition to Marius himself
there were the Lienhardts (both converts, Godfrey probably under the
influence of E.-P., Peter of Godfrey. Talog was another convert. I believe
he went over during the war. There was Doyle; and Maurice Hussey,
Birrell (just gone off to Nijmegen when I arrived), and Reg Jinks. Later
John Farrelly. Downside and Ampleforth sent a trickle of people to read
English at Downing: in my time Norman Henfrey from the former,
Algy-something-or-other in the 1948 intake from the latter. There must
have been others. These are the ones that spring to mind. Then there
were a number of Catholic-minded fellow-travelling Anglicans – David
Matthews, for example, who attended Little St. Mary's, Geoffrey Strick-
land; and Eric Mathieson had also become one.

Such a concentration inevitably led to quite a lot of Catholic chat,
intensified in 1950 because it was the year in which all Catholics were
encouraged to undertake a sort of hadj to Rome to be blessed by 'HH'
as Talog called him. Some of this was esoteric and particular to the clique;
but quite a bit spilled out amongst the rest of us. The fact that some of
them (the Lienhardts, Talog, Doyle, Marius and John Farrelly, who formed
a loose group of friends) were, with the exception of Leavis himself, John
Coleman and then Karl Miller, the most impressive people around, was
a matter of chance. None the less influential for that: one may not have
been personally susceptible but to see such clever and intelligent people
subscribing meant one treated the idea with respect.

Although Leavis spoke and wrote of the importance of reverence for life
in many of the works he most admired – Blake, Lawrence, later on Dickens
– and while his disciplined and dispassionate openness to a text had
something about it of the selflessness of prayer (I felt this strongly when
I once came upon him reading *The Marriage of Heaven and Hell* privately
on his terrace in Bulstrode Gardens) I am nevertheless sure that formal
belief, the act of submission to any church or organized Christian faith,
would have been wholly repugnant to him. So the Catholic connexion

at Downing was not a direct influence on his part. However, despite his affectation of bewilderment, it was no accident either, but arose from a variety of works he recommended and ideas he propounded.

For example, anyone preparing for Downing would have been expected to have read the criticism of T. S. Eliot and so become aware of the high value he set on Dante. Eliot's views on tradition and the individual talent and the dissociation of sensibility in the early seventeenth century underlie a lot of Leavis's own early criticism, notwithstanding late revisionism. These, and Eliot's ideas about culture being something more pervasive than just high-culture, led many sympathetic readers to temper any over-valuation they may have placed upon spontaneity or originality alone.

If we add to this Leavis's belief in the moral nature of criticism and his ideas about language and sensibility and the way in which the interpene-tration of theology, mythology, folklore and everyday imagery in Chaucer, Langland, the Bible, Shakespeare or Bunyan, supplied moral polarities transcending an author's individual position, it can be seen how compati-bility with a Catholic view of things arose. R. H. Tawney's *Religion and the Rise of Capitalism* and L. C. Knights's application of its ideas to Jacobean comedy, both on the Downing reading list, reinforced these tendencies.

The encouragement from Mellers to listen to what is now called early music, particularly mediaeval and renaissance polyphony and especially the church music of the English renaissance, served to push our tastes back beyond the individualism of Teutonic romanticism and beyond the showiness of the classical and baroque towards an appreciation of the dignified and impersonal splendours of an earlier and Catholic tradition. This all fitted together and the attraction for Catholics is understandable.

How many conversions it was responsible for I cannot say, or whether it persisted. Peter Lienhardt once took me to meet Monsignor Gilbey at Fisher House. John Farrelly took Karl Miller twice. After entering into these encounters in the open-minded curiosity he showed towards every-thing, Karl had informed Gilbey at the end of their second private meeting that he did not feel able to allow the matter to proceed further. John had enquired of Karl how things had gone. 'I formed the impression he was slightly put out', John told me, 'when Monsignor Gilbey had given him to understand that Rome would survive without him.'

Towards me neither Peter nor anyone else ever attempted to proselytise although a casual comment made once by Peter did resonate: 'I found it easier to enjoy literature after I became a Catholic because I wasn't expecting from it things it could not give'. However, whether because of these friendships or because of the tenacious nature of the ideas themselves, this eccentric feature of Downing's influence has proved enduring. Though a unbeliever, I have come increasingly to appreciate the Anglican liturgy I got to know at school during the weekly services at Thame church: its catholic shape, the Book of Common Prayer, King James's Bible; and to be saddened by the penetration not only of the Church of England but the English bastions of Rome itself by the vulgarization of thought, word and deed about which Leavis taught us to be on guard.

4

Reflecting on my recollections of Leavis and the Downing English School, I find myself wondering to what extent he, with Queenie, was just one of the many extraordinary people who become legends among those who have known them; a person such as many encounter at an impressionable period of their lives who becomes a powerful influence for a time, perhaps longer. Or was there more? Does he, in himself and in his work, with or without Queenie, represent something of permanent significance?

I find this difficult to answer for two reasons. First, my working life has been spent in worlds far from English studies. My general reading has been haphazard. My knowledge of Leavis's later writing is slight. I have discussed the subject scarcely at all, even with the few Downing friends with whom I have kept up. The many changes that have taken place in the landscape of literature and criticism over the last forty years have only been glimpsed at irregular intervals.

Secondly, coming to know and like the Leavises as I did, in a way which I deliberately kept at arms' length from their work, I was able to evade the question. Probably I wanted to, as one does with friends and relations older than oneself whose concerns one may not share and whose valuation of their life's achievement one fears may not stand up to close examination. But I am very much aware that, over the years, as people have said to me 'Tell me about Leavis, what does he stand for? what's he all about?' I have given a poor account both of myself and of him. Also I think to my shame of what I said to Henry Morris about his village colleges and feel I owe it to the Leavises not to patronize their memory by pigeonholing them as oddities but to take this opportunity, for myself at least, to try and come to some judgement as to where they stand.

As to his teaching then, some things were essentially ephemeral. The lectures, the classes, quite apart from their content (which does survive) were often memorable performances. But the manner, the wit, the spirit of delivery, the command of situation, things which were so vivid to those who heard him, cannot be conveyed to those who have not. He has no Boswell; he is not (as far as I know) on film; his broadcasts were few. (He hated broadcasting, resenting what editors did to his text and the officiousness of studio staff: 'They made me sit as though I were in a vice. I need to gesture, you know, to move about as I speak!') These qualities cannot outlive those who experienced them.

His own teaching – personal teaching, that is, as distinct from the performances and his writing – was not by the time I knew it particularly good. He gave no one-to-one supervisions and was not very interested in his pupils as individuals or in bringing them out or personally encouraging them. He may possibly have noticed more than he let on, as I discovered years later in his remarks about John Coleman, but I really do not think he saw the personal awakening of his students as central to his task and in effect he organized the Downing regime in such a way as to hold intimacy at a distance.

He once said to me of a couple of people in Karl Miller's year whom I found pretty stodgy: 'First class, both of them. Not a piece of work by either of them that wasn't first class. Yet look at the results!' These were less than first class; but I found his words hard to believe of the two in question. How can he possibly have known? He saw scarcely any written work from anybody. At the time I suspected these remarks were as much a very oblique comment on Karl Miller as praise of the favoured two. Leavis tended to see Karl's success in Tripos and in the sinful world of London letters thereafter as evidence of a pushy Scot on the make. His view both of Karl's two contemporaries and of Karl himself seemed equally superficial.

Another point which deserves mention was probably a consequence of the steadily increasing gap in age between Leavis and his pupils. He was himself widely read, in French as well as English. He had been competent in Latin and Greek. He never paraded his reading, but throughout the time I knew him one received occasional glimpses of its considerable extent. The essence of his message may have been about judgment; but judgment, however provisional he held it to be, meant that some things were seen to be better than others. His teaching and writing specified winners. It was all too easy for his pupils, less well read and of a new generation with a whole new range of post-war distractions, to study only the OK texts and the reasons why they were better than the rest: the rest could safely be ignored. The central act of exploration, discovery and discrimination was therefore missing. I don't think Leavis was ever really aware of this at Cambridge. Although our homes were unlikely to have been as uncultivated as those from which he believed his York students to come, he assumed we had more behind us than was generally the case and that our parents had read Palgrave and Dickens and Thackeray and Mark Twain aloud to us as his father had to him. Perhaps it was not until York that the first dawning of the truth came to him.

I have since encountered a similar phenomenon in the history of twentieth-century architecture. The pioneers of the modern movement, both abroad and in Britain, had all received a good old-fashioned education. Mies, Le Corbusier, Gropius, Goldfinger, Lubetkin, Lasdun, Max Fry, to mention just a few. All were well read; all knew a lot about the history of architecture and appreciated the past. They simply felt that for social, political, industrial, technological or aesthetic reasons, something new and different was necessary. The followers of this first generation in a greatly expanded profession did not possess the same cultural and historical perspective. And the followers of the followers were taught that the past was irrelevant and to show hostility to those who felt otherwise. The physical and social consequences have proved unfortunate. The re-birth of a sense of the past and a new integration of more acceptable forms of architecture and planning with the inescapable demands of modern life and the opportunities created by modern technology has been difficult and painful.

There is no easy route to high-quality literacy in these days of increasing and increasingly early specialization. Where it has not happened at home I believe school is probably the best place in which to encourage a habit of reading, to whet appetites, give some sense of the riches of literature and establish familiarity with a common core, particularly of poetry, that can be widely shared (a large part of its value: a sort of liturgy almost). At school it is also possible on a wide front to inculcate an intelligent use of language and an awareness of the malign ways in which it can be exploited to get at people. If there is to be good teaching of English in schools then I accept that a cadre of people has to be taught in universities to undertake it, fewer perhaps than read English now but not so few that the discipline is confined to would-be teachers only. They should acquire familiarity with the territory, with the history and theories of criticism and with the political and social context with which literature has a fluctuating relationship, including other media with which it co-exists. Such courses should have shape, possess the essential procedures for developing understanding and response, but avoid the restrictive orthodoxy pressed upon us at Downing.

More widely, Leavis has been a detectable force in the theatre. The ADC in my time was outstanding and many of its luminaries, particularly the directors, went on to dominate the London scene: Peter Hall, Peter Wood, John Barton, Toby Robertson and later Trevor Nunn. Peter Wood described in an interview with Ronald Hayman in *The Times* some years ago how struck he was at school by the analysis of 'To Autumn' in *Revaluation*:

> And sometimes like a gleaner thou dost keep
> Steady thy laden head across a brook;

where the reader is made to feel the precarious balancing act, across the brook, across the lines. Only Wood and Nunn were pupils of Leavis but all this generation were influenced, I believe, by his encouragement to understand how the language works and to feel and express the vigorous intelligent speech music of Shakespeare especially. Also, the influence of Leavis was to be detected in John Coleman's criticism. Certainly in the editorial sway exercised by Karl Miller for many years over *The Spectator*, *The New Statesman*, *The Listener* and the *London Review of Books*. All these people where they had once been disciples became in some degree defectors; nevertheless, all retained a seriousness they owe to Leavis. There must be others of whom I am not aware who have carried his influence well beyond English studies. Again, however, it is impossible to quantify the extent of these things.

When Leavis was asked to define his theory of criticism or define the logical bases on which his judgments were founded he always refused to do so. One evening in about 1952 he faced in the Music Room of West Lodge in Downing a large audience from all over Cambridge. Perhaps it was a meeting of the English Club. He was pressed very hard by outsiders to clarify his position but kept repeating 'I seek relevance, relevance'. Relevance to what? Of what? With the best will in the world it was not easy to understand. Then he suddenly went on: 'I ask you in addressing a work of literature to refer to that central area of experience and moral awareness we all share, which the writer shares with the reader, and to apply criteria derived from that' – or words to that effect.

I think this is important. He is saying that our relationship with works of literature resembles our relationship with other people in those areas about which the moral sciences or psychology have very little to tell us: about courage, integrity, truthfulness, discretion, deceit, loyalty, trust. About behaving well. Such relationships can be coarse or subtle in different people and have infinite gradations in the same people at different times and in different circumstances. It is an area in which we all have to learn to operate as best we can whatever our upbringing and whatever our politics, race, sex, class or creed. Learning to imply or infer a world of meaning in a glance. Literature, dealing through language with feelings and ideas and characters and circumstances, by means of irony, humour and all the cross-referencing of history, tradition and allusion, is in its various conventions offering models which illuminate the moral complexities of interpersonal relations. Leavis places criticism firmly in this territory and asks us to exercise judgment on the words before us by applying the criteria we use in life. It is this which gives weight to his view of literature and criticism as a discipline.

I have been reminded in considering Leavis's view of the nature of judgment of the jury duty I was called upon to undertake for the first time a few years ago at an inner London Crown Court. I was assigned to four cases over a fortnight. The jury was on each occasion a very mixed bunch. The judges instructed us in the legal parameters of the cases, then defined the matters on which we had to reach a decision. 'On the basis of your experience of life you must decide which of these witnesses you believe to be telling the truth; whether the arguments of prosecution or defence are adequately supported and where you feel the balance of probability lies'. And so on. It worked. Every time, after quite lively arguments, we reached a unanimous verdict. We found ourselves talking about the same things and able to come to firm conclusions. Despite our widely different backgrounds, we were able to draw upon a common pool of human experience. In relation to literature, judgment can be seen in such a view to be detached from the vicissitudes of intellectual or journalistic fashion and to be something timeless. Anybody, whether a professional critic or a casual reader, who has ever exercised judgment about a work of literature at whatever level of insignificance or excellence and found something funnier, more enjoyable, more boring, more moving than something else, has been operating in this way. I believe it is the true originality of Leavis to have seen the process as it is. One finds hints of a description in Johnson, a few more hints scattered in Coleridge, in Arnold, but nothing so clearly, consciously, set out before. This cannot become unfashionable or old hat because it accords with the way the human mind works and is independent of any particular verdicts themselves.

6

On Monday 18th November 1991 I went to a requiem mass for Eric Mathieson at St. George the Martyr in Borough High Street. At some time during the evening of 6th November he had fallen from a ladder in the clergy house of St. Alphege in nearby Pocock Street and was found dead with a fractured skull on the following morning.

At some point in the 1970s Eric became chaplain to the National Theatre. Whether such a post existed before he filled it or whether it was just an ingenious piece of initiative I don't know: the National Theatre wasn't in his parish. He enjoyed it greatly, especially all the backstage chat. He used to take me there for treats from time to time. 'I'm afraid I can only get the best seats'. 'Have you ever been to the Barbican theatre?' 'Good gracious no, that would be like adultery'.

The service at St. George's was the occasion for a powerful Anglo-Catholic presence with the ostentatious and competitive performance of varying niceties of observance by many members of the congregation. The address dealt mainly with his life as a priest, but referred to Cambridge, his love of music and poetry, his gift for friendship and his chaplaincy at the National Theatre. Someone read four of his poems. One was a very good piece about a rehearsal at the National. These seemed to bewilder most of those present. Secular intrusions. The coffin was censed and sprinkled as the Church bade farewell to its servant.

Afterwards people spilled outside, little knots of black-clad priests smoked and chatted earnestly on the pavement, parishioners shared recollections of the dear departed and the officiant, the Bishop of South-wark, descended the steps of the church bearing his crook and carrying his mitre in a plastic carrier bag. I sought out Iris. The girl I'd met walking home from church in Chinnor in 1943 was now a little old lady. She was standing beside the hearse that was to take Eric to be buried in the same grave with Owen in the village by their cottage.

There was no one else I knew and I walked off up Borough High Street, over London Bridge and along to a lunch at the Royal Society of Arts. Trevor Nunn was there and I asked him if he had been approached for his Downing recollections. He said not; perhaps, he felt, because MacKillop was too much a contemporary to believe he would have anything novel to contribute. 'Leavis really was a terrible man', he said and went on to slip spontaneously into reminiscence as people do, each with his own version of the inimitable voice. By the time Nunn was at Downing, Leavis had become famous and at his classes in College the Downing English School, then amounting to about a dozen, used to be joined by several times that number from elsewhere. This made creative pupil-teacher exchanges of the kind theoretically favoured by Leavis (but only ever theoretically) virtually impossible anyway. But Nunn was determined to take him up on some point about Blake and one day launched his carefully prepared interjection. Leavis paused, considered (much as he had done with Eric about Dryden), then said: 'You may be right'. Pause, then: 'But I feel – imaginatively – that you're wrong'. Another time, talking about the novel, Leavis had said: 'So many of the great English novelists were women; and – they couldn't do the young men. Jane Austen, the Brontes. They couldn't do the young men. George Eliot' – pause – 'E. M. Forster'!

I asked Nunn, in my dark suit and black tie, whether he had gone to Downing by accident. 'Oh, no. Someone at school introduced me to Leavis's books when I was in the sixth form. They made a great impression. I don't think anyone ever went to Downing by accident.'

'Leavisite' Cambridge in the 1960s

Neil Roberts went up to Clare College, Cambridge, in 1964, from Latymer Upper School, Hammersmith. In 1962 Leavis's lecture on C. P. Snow and the 'Two Cultures' had given him national celebrity. This was a period of relative prosperity for Leavis's graduate pupils in Cambridge and appeared to be an Indian summer, until Leavis's withdrawal from Cambridge affairs for the University of York in 1966. These reminiscences were written for this volume. Neil Roberts is a university teacher, at the University of Sheffield, and literary critic.

As far as I know, the first reference to F. R. Leavis that I ever heard was by a teacher in the first year of the sixth form. He was discussing with us Longfellow's 'In the Churchyard at Cambridge', which I. A. Richards (though I hadn't of course heard of him then either) praises in *Practical Criticism*. He read the opening lines,

> In the village churchyard she lies,
> Dust is in her beautiful eyes,
> No more she breathes, nor feels, nor stirs,

and told us that, in a lecture at Cambridge, he had heard 'the great Doctor' quote these lines and comment, 'Well of course not, she's dead!'

I remember this incident as typical of my English 'A' level teaching: we were expected either to know who 'the great Doctor' was or find out for ourselves – once when I asked which novel a passage of Joyce was from I was told 'the one that made him famous' – and to decide for ourselves whether this remark was penetrating or crass. This teacher, Jim McCabe, was charismatic and inspiring, and did more than anyone to arouse my enthusiasm for the study of literature. However, though a young Cambridge graduate, he was not a 'Leavisite'. Another young teacher, Brian Binding, was a pupil of Leavis's. He had the power of turning an English class into a kind of shared meditation. He could sit perched on the radiator in silence while we watched him think. The most important thing I learned from him was disrespect for the canon, since if he did not like the set text (in our case *Much Ado About Nothing*) that he was supposed to be teaching he spent the minimum time on it and used the lessons to read Lawrence stories or analyse passages of James.

Several of us used to spend our free periods in a nearby café, where we would continue the discussion that had begun in the lesson. This was technically against the school rules, and I bitterly resented being disciplined for it.

We were inevitably, and unfairly, contemptuous of the Head of English, whom I now remember as a charming and melancholy semi-bohemian, but who had the misfortune to be an admirer of Bradley. We thought it very funny when one of us read aloud from Leavis's essay on *Othello*, substituting this teacher's name for Bradley's. This, though, was the 'third year sixth', a post-'A' level term spent preparing for the Oxbridge scholarship exams, according to the old admissions system.

I can't have imbibed a set of rigid Leavisite opinions at school since, when the time came to choose a Cambridge college, I chose Peterhouse because, briefly, Kingsley Amis was a Fellow there. It was, however, gently suggested that Clare College was a better choice, and it was there that I went in 1964. The reason for this, though I was not told at the time, was that John Newton, a contemporary of Binding's, was a Fellow there. Newton and Mason were both names to conjure with before I went to Cambridge, and copies of *Delta* (then edited by Martin Lightfoot, Ian MacKillop and Geoffrey Strickland) were circulated by Binding. I had read Mason's essay 'Arnold and the Classical Tradition' and a review by Newton of George Watson's *The Literary Critics*. I had also read, in a fugitive pamphlet recommended by the editors of *Delta*, a satire entitled 'The Ogre of Downing Castle', possibly the first publication of an obscure research student called Howard Jacobson.

I began buying Leavis's books between school and university, starting with *New Bearings in English Poetry*. His lasting importance to me is that, both directly and through intermediaries, he persuaded me then, and throughout my years as a student, that the study of literature is a compellingly serious matter. Without his influence I doubt if I would have thought it important enough to make a career of. More particularly, I would say that Leavis's importance as a cultural influence comes less from the specific judgments of texts, or even his critical method, than from the impression he gave, to a student without a received background of literary culture, that English literature, English culture, belonged to you. That was very fortifying when you were an obscure scholar from a lower-middle-class London suburb about to enter Cambridge. It meant that my ideal Cambridge was not the Cambridge of Bloomsbury, of the leisured classes and the public schools, of an élite culture in the class sense. It centred on a man whose culture-heroes were the tinker's son who wrote *The Pilgrim's Progress*, the clerk's son who wrote *Great Expectations*, the steward's daughter who wrote *Middlemarch* and above all the miner's son who wrote *The Rainbow* and said that the other Cambridge made him dream of beetles. This influence was oddly congruent (given Leavis's reactionary attitude to university expansion) with the egalitarian optimism of the 1960s, when there was an influx into Cambridge of students from state schools, which has not been exceeded, and possibly reversed, in the ensuing decades. It was possible, briefly and no doubt self-deludingly, to believe that the socially divisive traditions of Cambridge were irrelevant.

The Director of Studies at Clare College was John Northam, whom I always imagined to have been (along with Theodore Redpath and Leo Salingar) one of the few 'decent men' Leavis conceded to exist in the English Faculty. Northam was, however, to be decidedly (and in retrospect understandably) frosty when, in our final year, two of us asked to be supervised by Mason instead of himself.

There were eight English undergraduates in my year at Clare, but only three of us, Robin Leavis (Leavis's son), Graham Bradshaw and I, identified ourselves as 'Leavisites'. Robin, Graham and a friend of Graham's were the only new friends I made when I was an undergraduate. This now seems to me quite shocking, but it was not as desperate as it appears, because I was one of at least fourteen boys from my school who went to Cambridge that year. At least half of these subsequently became academics. So I was not overwhelmed by the intellectual quality of the undergraduates I met at Cambridge. I was, however, painfully aware of my lack of general culture, since I really only knew anything about literature, and my new friends were self-consciously highbrow in a way that is almost unknown among students today.

Robin Leavis was nearly two years older than me but, I think, did not look or seem it. He was earnest, intense and eccentric in manner, with a habit of leaning forward and fixing his interlocutor with his eyes, which were brown and strikingly beautiful. His face was extremely expressive, and I remember him always either smiling or frowning, never neutral. He was very open and straightforward. He gave an impression of innocence and vulnerability. He was recognizably the son of old parents, and of academic parents. Nevertheless he proved tough enough to survive the gruelling experiences he had to endure (partly at the hands of his friends) in his student years.

In the first term we read for the medieval paper, under A. C. Spearing. My 'official' work was not very interesting, though Spearing's reading aloud of Chaucer in his lectures brought the poetry alive for me. Much more important to me during this term was the fact that I met Leavis. I first met him and Mrs Leavis at a 'wine evening' in Clare. I don't think I spoke to him, but she told me that she didn't approve of Robin reading English because it wouldn't fit him for a job. I suppose she was teasing me. I told her I thought that this was a materialistic attitude (revolting little prig) and she said that 'a mother has to think of these things.' I liked her a lot at this first meeting, and found her much more approachable and easy to talk to than I had expected.

Northam had belatedly arranged weekly 'supervisions' on Saturday mornings with Leavis, and the first of these was the morning after this meeting. These supervisions (he disliked the word 'seminar') took place in the study of his house at Bulstrode Gardens. As students arrived, he stood by the doorway of the study saying 'Do come in', in a gracious manner. The sessions were based on the reading and discussion of passages, usually anonymous, from a large store of duplicated sheets that he kept on his shelves. ('Practical Criticism' was also a term he disliked, ostensibly on the grounds that all criticism should be practical, but no doubt also because of his hostility to Richards.) Considerable attention was paid to characteristics that were distinctive of period, and it is perhaps a tribute to the effectiveness of Leavis's teaching that, having read no more than one short passage in one of his supervisions, I was later able to identify a different extract from Lord Chesterfield's letters. He began by announcing that it was intended as an informal discussion group, 'among friends, as it were'. He tried all the time to throw the discussion open, but we were unresponsive, so it tended to be a monologue. These extempore lectures covered, of course, the whole range, and inculcated in me a belief, later reinforced by Empson but now almost extinct in the academic world, that a true literary critic is not a 'specialist'. Afterwards I attempted to record some passages verbatim:

> You don't see so many butterflies nowadays. They're killing them with insecticide. And birds too. Hundreds of species of birds are dying off, you know, because the insects that they eat are poisoned – some are poisoned directly by the insecticide, some just starve because their prey is extinguished. The golden eagle's eggs aren't fertilized because of the poison. You can see it everywhere – it's a truth, you know, a symbolic truth. All they care about is the Industrial Society – not that I've got anything against industry, but they're just callous brutes, like old what's his name, Lord Corridor of Power. It's a symbolic truth, you know.

> That group – Leonard Woolf, Forster, Strachey – used to gather around Virginia and worship her. They were all centred on King's and Trinity, you know, and they used to worship Virginia Woolf – and there was Great St Mary's Church not a hundred yards away. I remember old Forster reading an obituary address to her in the Senate House – Forster's still alive, you know – or at least he was when I last heard.

> Virginia Woolf was representative of the Feminist movement that began in the late nineteenth century. Meredith started it, but it couldn't last, it's contrary to nature. Women aren't men, they aren't superior to men.

> I don't think Meredith is read now – I disposed of him thirty years ago. He's dead now – he'll never come back – you can thank me for that. But you might read *The Egoist* – it's a useful introduction to Forster. But Forster is so dated. You read his prose, it's not natural. No great novelist could write like that.

> I remember during the First World war I used to carry cocoa along the roofs of French trains to men who would have died without it. The trains had overhead wires, and it was very easy to get your head caught. Don't ever try it – it's an art.

I think the significance of the first of these passages is its date. It sounds very commonplace now, but I had never heard anyone talking like that in 1964. Rachel Carson's *Silent Spring* had been published in Britain a year earlier, but Leavis was not the kind of man to show sudden enthusiasm for a fashionable cause, and I have no doubt that this represented a long-standing preoccupation.

It was at this time that the controversy about the Downing College fellowship came up. The college appointed Brian Vickers as a Fellow to teach English against the wish of Leavis that his former pupil Morris Shapira, who had been Director of Studies, be appointed. This provoked Leavis's resignation of his honorary fellowship and his final break with Cambridge English: the following year he accepted a Chair at York. There was what I called in my diary 'a very vulgar article' (prig again) about this in the *Observer* and Graham, his friend Alex Brilliant and I sent a letter about it, which was not printed, but was sent to Leavis, who thanked us for it. Actually what happened was that I wrote a very naive and gushing letter and showed it to Graham and Alex who scrapped it and produced one which had much more of the tang of controversy.

During this term I was invited three times to Sunday lunch at the Leavises' along with Robin's other friends. These invitations continued, though not I think as frequently, until the end of 1965, when they stopped. I wrote down verbatim from one of these lunches: 'They're not interested in literature at Oxford. I get letters from desperate undergraduates saying that they can't stand it any longer, and is there any way for them of getting into Cambridge? I tell them that I can't get into Cambridge myself, so how can I help them?' I also recollect that one Sunday there was a picture of Raymond Williams in the paper, about which Leavis said, 'That's a masterpiece of creative photography – makes him look like a distinguished intellectual.'

I once took down from a shelf at the Leavises' a volume of the *Composite Biography* of Lawrence by Nehls, and out fluttered a letter from Frieda (actually a copy: it had been sent via someone else who had kept the original). I copied out the following passage, which I later discovered to be omitted from the printed version in Tedlock's *Memoirs and Correspondence*: 'I think you take that poor fish Eliot too seriously. He is all clean, elegant bone – no flesh and blood. He drove his wife mad. The wife of a real man wouldn't go mad.'

About this time I dreamed I was in a large party climbing a high mountain (I had in reality joined the mountaineering club) and somebody asked me if Leavis was in the party. I said, 'No, he's too old for mountains.' Then I turned round and he was behind me. Every time he came to a difficult move he said, 'This is a dramatic irony.'

On Friday, 27 November 1964 Leavis addressed the Clare Modern Languages Society on the topic of 'The Aims of the English Tripos'. The main significance of this event was that Harold Mason, Leavis's old co-editor on *Scrutiny* and assistant at Downing, was present.

It was the first time I saw him and he and Leavis were evidently on cordial terms. It was the only time I was ever to see Leavis and Mason together. The whole event went on for about three hours. After the formal talk most of the people left and what ensued was a kind of public conversation between Mason and Leavis. The first thing Mason said was, 'I couldn't say this in public, of course . . .' (a mannered introduction, since there were of course still strangers such as myself present) . . . 'but think, what does Eliot know about man and woman? Only what he read in Ovid.' Eliot, of course, was still alive, which might partly have accounted for the affectation of secrecy. They talked about such people as Empson, Richards and James Smith. Leavis remembered Empson, I think with affection, as a fresh-faced young man, and thought that Richards had ruined him. Another episode from this evening was the only time I saw Leavis behave in a way that explained the uglier side of his reputation. Mason spoke, it seemed to me with satisfaction, of having once written a review of new poetry in *Scrutiny*, in which one of the books listed for review was a collection by Dylan Thomas, to which he made no reference at all in the body of the essay. Leavis described Thomas as 'a drunken Welsh lout'. An undergraduate expostulated about this, and Leavis replied, 'Then that is a case in which I say "This is so, isn't it?" and you say "No!"' The following day Mason talked on *Hamlet*, I think in Downing, and I learned that the Downing men didn't like him, and called him a 'waffler'.

By the second term I was seeing Leavis three times a week, having got myself invited, with Robin's other friends, to his Downing supervisions too. I went to L. C. Knights's first lecture as King Edward VII Professor, and was for the first time supervised by John Newton, who had been one of Leavis's pupils at Downing and was not long since a graduate student. I was immensely impressed by Newton, and remained so throughout my student years. I thought he was an excellent supervisor, who threw the initiative on to the students and kept us off balance with quietly provocative comments. He was extremely tolerant of silence. I think he would only have been good with good students, though. I wouldn't say that he was a good lecturer, but I went to all his lectures. Throughout this year he was publicly airing views at variance with Leavis on James,

Dickens and Hopkins. He visited my school to lecture on *The Portrait of a Lady*. Perhaps most significantly he gave a lecture on 'The Importance of Eighteenth-Century Criticism' in which he attacked twentieth-century Shakespeare criticism, especially that of Derek Traversi, the main *Scrutiny* writer on Shakespeare, and said explicitly that the most satisfactory Shakespeare critic he had read was Bradley. I found the prospect of vigorous debate within the Leavis camp exciting and inspiring, and the longest essay I wrote as an undergraduate (48 pages) was a defence of *The Portrait of a Lady* against Newton's attack. I was enormously flattered when he mentioned this in a subsequent lecture, even though he added that it had not changed his mind. My admiration for Newton continued to be fostered in the 1970s by his writings on Hughes, and waned only when, in the late 1970s, his volte-face on Hughes struck me as a minor recapitulation of the events of the mid-1960s.

In February 1965 I went to Exeter University to visit a friend, one of the circle of McCabe-Binding pupils who had failed to get into Cambridge and went, through the Binding-Mason connection, to Exeter where Mason was at this time still lecturing. By the time I paid this visit I had learned that Mason had arranged, through John Stevens, a place for my friend at Magdalene College in Cambridge. I don't know whether Mason made a habit of sponsoring this kind of 'transfer'. If he did, I have some sympathy for the hostility with which his head of department, Moelwyn Merchant, apparently regarded him.

On this trip I did not meet Mason, but I did meet John Speirs, whom I had liked when he spoke to the English Club on *Macbeth* the previous term, and liked even more on closer acquaintance. Speirs was the warden of the Hall of Residence my friend lived in, and I was invited to sherry before lunch and sat next to him at 'High Table', the only time I had such an honour in the whole of my student life. Speirs told me that he visited Leavis three times a year. He also told me about a 'conceited young man from King's' who had suggested to him that he should back him as 'Leavis's successor' at Downing, being '*persona grata* with both sides.'

Back in Cambridge, another friend from school, now at Queens', asked me if I could arrange for him to be invited to Leavis's supervisions. When I raised the subject, Leavis said, 'Well, of course, Queens' is a very delicate college. Not only is there Dr Holloway, but also Professor Knights, so it's doubly delicate. Let's say, if he comes I won't notice. We'll say he's from Sidney Sussex.' This was in May 1965.

My reading plan for the Easter vacation of my first year was:

1. Intense reading of *Troilus and Cressida, Measure for Measure, Winter's Tale, Tempest, All's Well, Pericles, Cymbeline, Comedy of Errors.*

2. Dryden's, Pope's and Johnson's criticism, and essay on their attitudes to Shakespeare.

3. *Pearl, Gawain* and Chaucer.

4. Essay on Blake (with reading of Northrop Frye).

5. If time, work on Donne, Herbert, Jonson, Marvell, Wyatt, Dryden, Swift, Burns . . .

6. If time, novels – *Portrait of a Lady, Daniel Deronda, Anna Karenina.*

I actually seem to have read the Dryden, Pope and Johnson criticism (I can remember reading Pope's preface in an eighteenth-century edition in Manchester public library), *Troilus* and *The Winter's Tale, The Scarlet Letter, The Waning of the Middle Ages* and Krutch's life of Johnson.

Two weeks before Preliminary exam I was proposing to write essays on the Problem Comedies and Late Plays with re-reading of *Measure for Measure* and *All's Well That Ends Well, The Winter's Tale, The Tempest* and *Cymbeline*, re-reading of *Sir Gawain and the Green Knight*, 'rush-work' on Swift and Blake, revision on Donne, Bunyan, Milton, Dryden, Chaucer, Wyatt, Skelton, Surrey, Langland, Pope, Johnson, Dryden and Eliot. God knows what I actually did, though I appear to have written the two Shakespeare essays, and they were good enough for Northam to recommend that I enter for the Charles Oldham Shakespeare Scholarship. (I didn't, probably through arrogance.)

What I wrote on in Prelims was: Shakespeare paper: *The Winter's Tale, Troilus and Cressida*, and 'a modern critical controversy' (thematic and character-based criticism). Medieval paper: *Canterbury Tales, Gawain,* Wyatt. Seventeenth and eighteenth century paper: Donne, Bunyan, Pope, Swift. Criticism: Gobbets from set-texts, essay on impersonality, dating, practical criticism. And there was the translation paper.

Surveying this (and what I wrote on for Part Two – see below) from the distance of thirty years, I seem to have read a lot, and although it obviously bears the marks of Leavis's influence it doesn't strike me as a narrowly 'Leavisite' syllabus. Admittedly, some of them were set-texts. My marks were First for the seventeenth and eighteenth centuries, Lower Second for Translation and bare Upper Seconds for the rest.

Another person I liked and admired in my first year was Martin Lightfoot. After Prelims I was very flattered when he called on me and asked me if I would like to be on the committee of the English Club. I had regularly attended meetings of the club, which was run by Lightfoot and his friends in Downing. One speaker was Karl Miller, on literary journalism. In the discussion Lightfoot said that he didn't like Frank Kermode but, unlike most literary journalists, 'at least he had a mind.' I noted this at the time as an example of naive Leavisite arrogance. Miller of course took him apart. I subsequently heard, however, that Miller liked him, and it was this encounter that launched him on his career in publishing. The last time I saw him, in 1968 or 1969, he told me that universities were a backwater.

Although I liked Lightfoot and other men in his year at Downing, I and my Clare friends had no contact whatever with our immediate Downing contemporaries. I can only recall two of them, who always went around together, in a permanent condition of white-faced tension. I suppose that they epitomized the betrayal, according to Leavis, of his followers in the schools by Downing, when Shapira was passed over in favour of Vickers.

When I returned to Cambridge for my second year I was very excited. Mason was installed as the Leavis Lecturer and I thought that the *Scrutiny* era was about to be recreated; there was talk of a summer school to be run by Leavis and Mason. But there was also talk, among us undergraduates, as early as October 1965, of Mrs Leavis hating Mason and possibly jeopardizing the Leavis-Mason relationship. In the autumn term of that year the first issue of *The Cambridge Quarterly* appeared, carrying Leavis's essay on *Anna Karenina*, but also the promise, 'for future publication', of '*Scrutiny*'s failure with Shakespeare' by J.M. Newton. This was to appear in the second issue, and Newton was already giving the lectures that were to be published with the title 'Henry James's Spiritual Disease'.

Not surprisingly this was a very difficult time for Robin Leavis; not only was he caught between his parents and his supervisor, but his closest friends were exuberantly and aggressively in favour of the *Quarterly* 'gang' (as his mother called them). At one point two of us went to Newton's house to declare our faith in him. It did not help matters that, like his mother, Robin disliked Lawrence, who was more or less a God to the rest of us. Among our group such matters were not discussed in a dispassionate academic manner but with a violent, quasi-religious intensity. One was defined by the authors one admired, by how and why one admired them. A Clare undergraduate who had gone up to read Classics thought of changing to English, but was put off because we seemed so 'committed'. Needless to say, just as, at school, we had continued the lessons in the café, so now there was no division between work and social life. Literature, or matters related to it, occupied nearly all our waking hours; if we discussed film (we were for some reason especially devotees of the Italian film director Antonioni) or art or music, it may have been more amateurishly, but it was with the same intensity and critical rigour (or what we thought was critical rigour) with which we approached writing.

Despite all the conflict, I had lunch at the Leavis house in November. On this occasion, which may have been the last, Leavis was in York. For the same reason, there were no more supervisions for Cambridge undergraduates. Mrs Leavis told us that she had been refused a fellowship at Newnham, through the machinations, she said, of Muriel Bradbrook. L. C. Knights came badly out of this story: according to Mrs Leavis, because it was the Faculty that hindered the appointment, he was the ultimate court of appeal, and refused to intervene.

Throughout this year I was busy working for the English Club. The President was Kevin Sheerin, a Downing man in the year above me whom Leavis held in high regard. Apart from the American poet Ed Dorn, invited at the suggestion of the one non-Leavisite member of the committee, the speakers were predictable: W. W. Robson on Browning, Morris Shapira on *Henry V*, Andor Gomme on the Baroque, Harold Coombes on 'Maturity Considered', Peter Coveney on a topic I don't remember and D. W. Harding on 'Women's Fantasy of Manhood: a Shakespearean Theme'.

Most significantly, however, at the beginning of term, we had Mrs Leavis to give her celebrated paper on *Wuthering Heights* and *Jules et Jim*. For this meeting we had an enormous audience and, since people had to join the Club to get in, we greatly increased the membership – mostly with people who never came again. There was, if I remember rightly, some acrimonious misunderstanding about her taxi fare. She also attended most of the meetings throughout the year, and I think Leavis himself attended at least the Harding talk.

On one occasion I was in Kevin Sheerin's room when one of the Downing men in my year turned up, characteristically white-faced. There had been a flare-up over Brian Vickers, and some Downing men wanted to send a letter to *The Times* which was allegedly libellous. This man called Sheerin a traitor because he would not sign the letter. Sheerin was a Catholic. He once reported a conversation with Vickers in which the latter had offered his services as a moral adviser, and Sheerin had replied that 'some of us have our own arrangements for that, thank you.' He was rather distanced, if not from literature, then certainly from the passions of Cambridge English. Once when I used the expression 'literary people' he said, 'Do you mean people made of paper?'

Each week I attended Mason's Italian classes, in which we studied the language by reading *L'Inferno* and, later, listening to Mozart libretti. Mason struck me as immensely worldly, even a little corrupt, and a complete contrast in personality to Leavis.

In retrospect it was during this year that my conception of myself as a 'Leavisite' began to slacken, though it did so only slowly and I would probably not have rejected the title even when I took up a lectureship in Sheffield in 1970. A major factor in this was the disillusionment produced by the acrimony over *The Cambridge Quarterly* and the Lectureship.

After December 1965 I stopped keeping a diary, so my memories of the remainder of my time at Cambridge are more impressionistic. I do, however, have documentary evidence of the climactic episode in my relations with the Leavises, which occurred in the summer of 1966. My friends and I took over the English Club for the following year. We set about planning the programme, and naturally we invited both the Leavises. We received a formal, if rather messy, refusal from Leavis, but our invitation to Mrs Leavis provoked a letter condemning the activities of the Club in the previous year. She alleged that there was no serious discussion of papers, and that the majority of the audience seemed just to come to be entertained. She associated this with the allegation that Mason's lectures as Leavis Lecturer consisted of 'putting on an act'.

In reply to this letter I wrote that the English Club, as an official Faculty society, had come under attack from the Faculty for having degenerated into a clique, and that in the preceding year we had countered this attack by attracting the largest ever membership, mainly because of her lecture. I remarked (rather contradictorily) that subsequent audiences were much smaller and more like the kind of discussion group of which she approved. Graham Bradshaw, as Secretary of the Club, also sent a letter.

She wrote again, telling me that the Faculty were right in their allegations, except that the 'clique' was not a 'Leavisite' one but part of the 'gang' who had usurped the name of Leavis for purposes antithetical to everything he stood for. She derided the papers given in the previous year by Robson, Shapira and Gomme, significantly excluding Harding and Coveney (who were not members of the 'gang') as 'serious lecturers' whose papers were poorly attended. She also complained that the text of an earlier paper that she had delivered at the Club was borrowed and copied for students without her permission by Shapira. This letter concluded with an insistence that Graham and I call on her.

It is a long time since I previously read these letters, and they now seem to me more reasonable than they did at the time. It is perfectly true that we exploited her name to increase the membership of the Club. It is also true that we were a clique, though I have no memory now of the Faculty pressure to which I referred in my letter. A form of election had been gone through, and three of us were returned unopposed. There was, however, an election for Vice-President, with one of our group running against a perfectly nice man from Christ's. The rest of us lobbied for our friend and I remember solemnly taking the ballot box to the Christ's man's room to demonstrate that he had lost. I burn with shame when I remember this episode, since anyone in a normal state of mind would have invited him to join the committee anyway. I think he was a year junior to us and would have provided continuity. What made the episode even more shameful was that the 'successful candidate' took a year out and never took up his position, but we still did not invite the Christ's man on to the committee.

Graham and I presented ourselves at the Leavises' on a Sunday afternoon. Both of them were present at the interview. Mrs Leavis sat with her back to the window, Leavis a little further off in a corner. I was positioned uncomfortably close to Mrs Leavis, Graham discreetly a little behind me. We were subjected to what I felt to be a violent verbal assault, though it may be that I would now feel it to be more reasonable, like the letter. I remember only a few details however. One related to John Newton. In his lectures on James he had described Ralph Touchett in *The Portrait of a Lady* as 'wet'. This had been reported to Mrs Leavis and she had seized on it as a central and characteristic item of Newton's critical vocabulary: 'James is wet! Hopkins is wet!' I also remember her telling Graham and me that we had 'no spiritual manners'. Leavis intervened once, in conciliation, to say that he was 'sure we were personally innocent in the matter'. I must have protested that not all the speakers in the previous year had been members of the *Quarterly* clique and that someone, perhaps it was Andor Gomme, had not written in the *Quarterly*. Mrs Leavis replied that he had written in *Delta*, and that was just as bad.

She claimed to derive much of her information from 'people who, being senior to yourselves, have some standards to judge by.' This is I think mainly a reference to an American whom we believed to be the Leavises' main source of information about Mason's and Newton's lectures. This was the time of Vietnam and like many American students this man was desperate about the draft and was extremely intense and neurotic, even in comparison with us.

After this meeting I could not imagine that Mrs Leavis would ever speak to me again, and I was astonished and embarrassed when, meeting me in the street, she behaved as if nothing had happened. Again this behaviour now strikes me in a different light – what could be more natural than for a sixty-year-old woman to tear a strip off a twenty-year-old boy and then treat him indulgently? Later, when I was a research student, and applying for research fellowhips, she was asked by one of the colleges to read the chapters of my thesis that I submitted and she was, via Robin, quite complimentary about them, saying that I was a 'natural academic, in the good sense' and even forgiving me for disagreeing with her husband about *Hard Times* on the grounds that this was tactically necessary. However, that meeting about the English Club remains one of the most unpleasant experiences of my life.

After all that, I'm afraid that we did not run the Club very well. I can remember virtually nothing about Club events during my final undergraduate year, except for a sparsely attended talk by nice Harry Coombes on T. F. Powys, and a visit by four Oxford poets to which no-one at all came.

During my final undergraduate year I attended weekly Latin classes conducted by Mason, reading Catullus and Lucretius, and a number of meetings organized by Mason and held in Ronald Gray's rooms in Emmanuel, to hear papers on Shakespeare. Of these the one I remember most distinctly was by J. C. F. Littlewood on *Coriolanus*, read *in absentia* by Shapira, which identified the hero with Leavis by saying that Coriolanus might have said 'I was, and knew I was, Rome, the essential Rome, in spite of Rome.'

In my Part Two exams I wrote on Tolstoy, Lawrence and George Eliot for the Novel paper, Shakespeare, Euripides and Strindberg for the Tragedy paper, Tennyson and Clough, Arnold and Ruskin, Dickens and Gaskell for the Special Period. I also remember writing on censorship for the general paper. I must have done some other papers too, but I have forgotten them. I had followed my rather ordinary Prelims performance with an Upper Second in Part One, but I must have worked more effectively for Part Two, because I got a First. Among my circle of friends there was an affectation of despising Tripos results (not entirely unjustified, considering the barbaric way in which the Tripos was examined). We were particularly hostile to what we called 'working for a First', something that we supposed successful examinees did cynically and mechanically. Having imbibed Leavis's view of himself and his circle as outsiders, and of serious academic work as unofficial, done on the margins of the institution, we did not identify our teachers – particularly Newton – with the institution at all, and thought of the examiners as an alien and hostile body. Despite this I was, of course, delighted with my results, which transformed my prospects and earned me three years' funding for research.

This was the end of us as a group. I was the only one who stayed at Cambridge and when I went back up in the Autumn of 1967 it was to a largely new, more healthily varied circle of friends. I moved into a flat with an Egyptologist (my schoolfriend John Ray, now Reader in Egyptology at Cambridge), a Persian scholar, an economist and a highly intelligent and cultured group of scientists, some of whom were pupils of Francis Crick. This environment was, ironically, much more like the liberal ideal of a university than my undergraduate years had been.

My research supervisor was Raymond Williams, whom I liked and respected, but with whom I had virtually no real intellectual engagement. Nevertheless, my contact with him, slight as it was, played a part in loosening my Leavisite affiliation, as did my later contact with Empson in my first year at Sheffield, where I was appointed to a Lectureship in English. Among literature students I had a new set of contacts at Trinity, for whom Leavis and Mason were certainly significant presences, but who had a more distant and relaxed sense of their importance. Some of these people were devotees of Northrop Frye and for the first time, really, I experienced critical debate with people who were hostile to Leavis.

I married, and during my last year as a research student my wife and Mrs Leavis happened to be hospitalized in Addenbrookes at the same time. I once gave Leavis and Robin a lift there in our old Y-type MG with running-boards, leather upholstery and chrome headlamps. This is perhaps my favourite Leavis memory.

Looking back on my undergraduate years, and the events I observed and in a sense lived through, it seems clear to me now that they represented the death-throes of the Leavis movement. But it did not seem like that at the time. The arrival of Mason in Cambridge seemed to me and my friends to be a new beginning – as it seemed to Leavis, too, before the catastrophe. And, indeed, Leavis himself was to publish, between 1965 and his death, as many books as he did during the whole of his previous career. There were no hints evident to us, then, of the developments that were soon to make Leavis look archaic, though, before I left Cambridge, my contemporary Stephen Heath put on a series of lectures entitled 'Introduction to Semiology' – the first time I saw the word. Over the years that followed Mason's work began to look marginal, Newton became increasingly eccentric and the *Cambridge Quarterly* a sideshow run, indeed, by a clique, that had no very obvious reason for existing. No doubt I would have been better prepared for the life to come at Roland Barthes's seminars in Paris, but it was still a privilege, in one's formative years, to be close to the centre of a major cultural movement, even in its decline.

Reader's Guide and Notes

Richard Storer

F. R. Leavis: A Reader's Guide

Leavis has been well-served by bibliographers. The standard guide for many years was D. F. McKenzie and M.-P. Allum, *F. R. Leavis: A Check-List 1924–1964* (London: Chatto & Windus, 1966). This was supplemented in 1980 by William Baker's 'F. R. Leavis 1965–1979 and Q. D. Leavis 1922–1979: A Bibliography of Writings by and about them' (*Bulletin of Bibliography* 37 [1980], pp. 185–208). The indispensable work is now William Baker, M. B. Kinch and John Kimber, *F. R. Leavis and Q. D. Leavis: An Annotated Bibliography* (London: Garland, 1989). This offers a comprehensive listing of all Leavis's published works, plus an extensive listing of writings about him, up to 1984. It also provides a 'Chronology of Exchanges', enabling the reader to trace the stages in the arguments in which Leavis was involved, and check-lists of Leavis's writings on Eliot and Lawrence.

To list below all Leavis's original publications – books, articles and letters – would simply be to replicate the work of the Garland editors. So I have taken the opportunity here to arrange Leavis's work on a slightly different principle. The listing below encompasses all Leavis's published works, but does not specify individual items which were later collected in books either compiled, edited or sanctioned by Leavis himself. In other words, it lists the books first, and then those fugitive items which remained unavailable in book form during Leavis's lifetime. Though there are some details it cannot register (for example changes made between journal and book) I hope this design may yield some fresh insights into Leavis's approach to publication and re-publication.

As far as writings about Leavis are concerned, again the best approach seems to be to work with and from the Garland bibliography. Baker, Kinch and Kimber list and summarise over 1,000 books, articles and reviews which discuss F. R. Leavis – and their work only goes up to 1984. The short selection from their listing which I offer in Part 2 of this

Guide cannot pretend to be more than a personal selection of the works I have found most interesting, but I have tried to include the important books and the essays to which are most often cited in discussions of Leavis, plus some of the essays to which Leavis himself responded. Part 3 is offered as a provisional supplement to the Garland bibliography, listing items mostly published since 1984. In some of these items the discussion of Leavis is fairly brief or subordinate to the main topic – but in all of them he is treated seriously as a significant figure in the history of criticism, 'English' or education.

This seems the best place to mention two other items which do not find an obvious slot in a Reader's Guide. The BBC film, 'The Last Romantics', written by Nigel Williams and directed by Jack Gold, was broadcast on BBC-2 on Sunday 29 March 1992. And Ian Holm's impression of Leavis's voice in the 1960s, in this film, may be compared to a tape recording of Leavis himself, lecturing on 'T. S. Eliot and the life of English Literature' at Cheltenham in 1968, in the National Sound Archive (T4296W).

I WRITINGS BY F. R. LEAVIS

Books and Pamphlets by F. R. Leavis to 1978

Mass Civilization and Minority Culture. Cambridge: Minority Press, 1930. [Also reprinted in *For Continuity* and *Education and the University* (2nd edition: 1948)]

D. H. Lawrence. Cambridge: Minority Press, 1930.

New Bearings in English Poetry: A Study of the Contemporary Situation. London: Chatto & Windus, February 1932.

How To Teach Reading: A Primer for Ezra Pound. Cambridge: Minority Press, 1932.

(With Denys Thompson) *Culture and Environment: The Training of Critical Awareness.* London: Chatto & Windus, January 1933.

For Continuity. Cambridge: Minority Press, 1933.

Revaluation: Tradition and Development in English Poetry. London: Chatto & Windus, October 1936.

Education and the University: A Sketch for an 'English School'. London: Chatto & Windus, November 1943.

The Great Tradition: George Eliot, Henry James, Joseph Conrad. London: Chatto & Windus, November 1948.

New Bearings in English Poetry: A Study of the Contemporary Situation. New edition with Retrospect. London: Chatto & Windus, 1950.

The Common Pursuit. London: Chatto & Windus, January 1952.

D. H. Lawrence: Novelist. London: Chatto & Windus, September 1955.

Two Cultures? The Significance of C. P. Snow. The Richmond Lecture, 1962. With an essay on Sir Charles Snow's Rede Lecture, by Michael Yudkin. London: Chatto & Windus, October 1962.

Scrutiny: A Retrospect. Cambridge: Cambridge University Press, 1963.

'Anna Karenina' and Other Essays. London: Chatto & Windus, November 1967.

(With Q. D. Leavis) *Lectures in America.* London: Chatto & Windus, January 1969.

English Literature in Our Time and the University. The Clark Lectures, 1967. London: Chatto & Windus, November 1969.

(With Q. D. Leavis) *Dickens the Novelist.* London: Chatto & Windus, October 1970.

Gerard Manley Hopkins: Reflections After Fifty Years. The Second Annual Hopkins Lecture. London: The Hopkins Society, 1971.

Nor Shall My Sword: Discourses on Pluralism, Compassion and Social Hope. London: Chatto & Windus, July 1972.

Letters in Criticism. Edited with an Introduction by John Tasker. London: Chatto & Windus, May 1974.

The Living Principle: 'English' as a Discipline of Thought. London: Chatto & Windus, September 1975.

Thought, Words and Creativity: Art and Thought in Lawrence. London: Chatto & Windus, August 1976.

Books edited or introduced by F. R. Leavis

Towards Standards of Criticism: Selections from 'The Calendar of Modern Letters' 1925–1927. Chosen and with an Introduction by F. R. Leavis. London: Wishart, 1933.

Biaggini, E. G. *English in Australia: Taste and Training in a Modern Community.* Foreword by F. R. Leavis. Melbourne: Melbourne University Press, in association with Oxford University Press, 1933.

Determinations: Critical Essays. Introduction by F. R. Leavis. London: Chatto & Windus, June 1934.

Biaggini, E. G. *The Reading and Writing of English.* Preface by F. R. Leavis. London: Hutchinson, 1936.

Mill on Bentham and Coleridge. Introduction by F. R. Leavis. London: Chatto & Windus, November 1950.

Bewley, Marius. *The Complex Fate: Hawthorne, Henry James and Some Other American Writers.* Introduction and Two Interpolations by F. R. Leavis. London: Chatto & Windus, 1952.

Twain, Mark. *Pudd'nhead Wilson: A Tale.* Introduction by F. R. Leavis. London: Zodiac Press, 1955.

Conrad, Joseph. *Nostromo: A Tale of the Seaboard.* Foreword by F. R. Leavis. Signet Classics. New York: New American Library, 1960.

Eliot, George. *Daniel Deronda.* Introduction by F. R. Leavis. New York: Harper, 1961.

Eliot, George. *Adam Bede.* Foreword by F. R. Leavis. New York: New American Library, 1961.

James, Henry. *Selected Literary Criticism.* Edited by Morris Shapira. Preface by F. R. Leavis. London: Heinemann, 1963.

Bunyan, John. *The Pilgrim's Progress.* Afterword by F. R. Leavis. New York: New American Library, 1964.

Eliot, George. *Felix Holt, the Radical.* Introduction by F. R. Leavis. Everyman's Library. London: Dent, 1967.

Coveney, Peter. *The Image of Childhood.* Revised Edition. Introduction by F. R. Leavis. Peregrine Books. Harmondsworth: Penguin Books, 1967.

A Selection from 'Scrutiny'. Compiled by F. R. Leavis. Prefatory by F. R. Leavis. Two Volumes. Cambridge: Cambridge University Press, 1968.

Towards Standards of Criticism: Selections from 'The Calendar of Modern Letters' 1925–1927. Chosen and with Introductions (1933 & 1976) by F. R. Leavis. London: Lawrence and Wishart, 1976.

Books containing a substantial collection of items by F. R. Leavis

Bentley, Eric, ed. *The Importance of 'Scrutiny': Selections from 'Scrutiny: A Quarterly Review'.* New York: George W. Stewart, 1948.

Coombes, H., ed. *D. H. Lawrence: A Critical Anthology.* Harmondsworth: Penguin Books, 1973.

Items not collected or reprinted in books listed above

'The Relationship of Journalism to Literature: Studied in the Rise and Earlier Development of the Press in England'. Unpublished Ph.D thesis, University of Cambridge, 1924.

[Untitled] Review of Osbert Sitwell, *England Reclaimed,* and F. R. Higgins, *The Dark Horse,* in *The Cambridge Review,* 18 November 1927, p. 114.

[Untitled] Review of Augustus Ralli, *Critiques,* in *The Cambridge Review,* 24 February 1928, p. 285.

[Untitled] Review of G. H. W. Rylands, *Words and Poetry,* in *The Cambridge Review,* 6 June 1928, p. 510.

[Untitled] Review of Edmund Blunden, *Retreat,* in *The Cambridge Review,* 12 October 1928, p. 20.

[Untitled] Review of Shane Leslie, *The Skull of Swift,* in *The Cambridge Review,* 18 January 1929, p. 199.

'T. S. Eliot: a Reply to the Condescending', *The Cambridge Review,* 8 February 1929, pp. 254–256. [later collected in *Valuation in Criticism and other essays*]

[Untitled] Review of *Cambridge Poetry 1929,* in *The Cambridge Review,* 1 March 1929, pp. 317–318.

[Untitled] Review of Richard Aldington, *Death of a Hero,* in *The Cambridge Review,* 25 October 1929, p. 61.

'More Gothick North', *The Cambridge Review,* 8 November 1929, p. 100.

'Green Fields', *The Cambridge Review*, 15 November 1929, p. 118.

'T. F. Powys', *The Cambridge Review*, 9 May 1930, pp. 388–389.

'On D. H. Lawrence', *The Cambridge Review*, 13 June 1930, pp. 493–495. [later collected in *Valuation in Criticism and other essays*]

[Untitled] Review of *Cambridge Poetry 1930*, in *The Cambridge Review*, 16 May 1930, pp. 414–415.

[Untitled] Review of Katherine Mansfield, *Novels and Novelists*, in *The Cambridge Review*, 28 November 1930, p. 169.

'Intelligence and Sensibility', *The Cambridge Review*, 16 January 1931, pp. 186–187. [later collected in *Valuation in Criticism and other essays*]

[Untitled] Review of W. H. Auden, *Poems*, in *TLS*, 19 March 1931, p. 221.

'The Influence of Donne on Modern Poetry', *The Bookman* 79 (March 1931), pp. 346–347. [later collected in *Valuation in Criticism and other essays*]

'Criticism of the Year', *The Bookman* 81 (December 1931), p. 180.

'Poetry in an Age of Science', *The Bookman* (April 1932), p. 42.

'Poetry-Lovers, Prosody and Poetry', *The Spectator*, 14 May 1932, pp. 705–706.

[Untitled] Review of W. H. Auden, *The Orators*, in *The Listener*, 22 June 1932, p. 906.

'This Age in Literary Criticism', *The Bookman* 83 (October 1932), pp. 8–9.

'"Lord, What Would They Say . . .?"', *Scrutiny* I.3 (December 1932), pp. 290–291.

'An American Lead', *Scrutiny* I.3 (December 1932), pp. 297–300.

'Resolute Optimism, Professional and Professorial', *Scrutiny* I.3 (December 1932), pp. 300–301.

'More Lawrence', *Scrutiny* I.4 (March 1933), pp. 404–405.

'Dostoevsky or Dickens?', *Scrutiny* II.1 (June 1933), pp. 91–93.

[Untitled] Review of Peter Quennell, *Aspects of Seventeenth-Century Verse*, and Elizabeth Holmes, *Henry Vaughan and the Hermetic Philosophy*, in *Scrutiny* II.1 (June 1933), pp. 108–109.

'Battles Long Ago', *Scrutiny* II.2 (September 1933), pp. 202–204.

'English Letter', *Poetry* 43 (January 1934), pp. 215–221.

'English Letter', *Poetry* 44 (May 1934), pp. 98–102.

'Auden, Bottrall and Others', *Scrutiny* III.1 (June 1934), pp. 70–83.

[Untitled] Review of C. E. M. Joad (ed.), *Manifesto*, *Scrutiny* III.2 (September 1934), pp. 215–217.

'Shelley's Imagery', *The Bookman* 86 (September 1934), p. 278.

'Marianne Moore', *Scrutiny* IV.1 (June 1935), pp. 87–90.

'English Letter', *Poetry* 46 (August 1935), pp. 274–278.

'Hugh MacDiarmid', *Scrutiny* IV.3 (December 1935), p. 305.

'Doughty and Hopkins', *Scrutiny* IV.3 (December 1935), p. 316.

[Untitled] Review of Richard Heron Ward, *The Powys Brothers*, in *Scrutiny* IV.3 (December 1935), p. 318.

'The Orage Legend', *Scrutiny* IV.3 (December 1935), p. 319.

[Untitled] Review of Michael Roberts (ed.), *The Faber Book of Modern Verse*, and I. M. Parsons, *The Progress of Poesy*, in *Scrutiny* V.1 (June 1936), pp. 116–117.

[Untitled] Review of Richard Eberhart, *Reading the Spirit*, in *Scrutiny* V.3 (December 1936), pp. 333–334.

'The Marxian Analysis', *Scrutiny* VI.2 (September 1937), pp. 201–204.

'Advanced Verbal Education', *Scrutiny* VI.2 (September 1937), pp. 211–217.

'The Recognition of Isaac Rosenberg', *Scrutiny* VI.2 (September 1937), pp. 229–234.

'The Fate of Edward Thomas', *Scrutiny* VII.4 (March 1939), pp. 441–443.

'Hart Crane From This Side', *Scrutiny* VII.4 (March 1939), pp. 443–446.

'Arnold's Thought', *Scrutiny* VIII.1 (June 1939), pp. 92–99.

'The Function of the University', *Scrutiny* VIII.2 (September 1939), pp. 208–209.

'Critical Guidance and Contemporary Literature', *Scrutiny* VIII.2 (September 1939), pp. 227–232.

'Pope on the Upswing', *Scrutiny* VIII.2 (September 1939), pp. 237–240.

'Hardy the Poet', *Southern Review* 6 (Summer 1940), pp. 87–98. [later collected in *The Critic as Anti-Philosopher*]

[Untitled] Review of B. Ifor Evans, *A Short History of English Literature*, in *Scrutiny* IX.2 (September 1940), pp. 180–181.

'Education and the University (II): Criticism and Comment', *Scrutiny* IX.3 (December 1940), pp. 259–270.

[Untitled] Review of T. S. Eliot, *East Coker*, in *The Cambridge Review*, 21 February 1941, pp. 268–270.

'An American Critic', *Scrutiny* XI.1 (Summer 1942), pp. 72–73.

'Landor and the Seasoned Epicure', *Scrutiny* XI.2 (December 1942), pp. 148–150.

'The Liberation of Poetry', *Scrutiny* XI.3 (Spring 1943), pp. 212–215.

'Little Gidding', *Scrutiny* XII.1 (Winter 1943), p. 58.

'Catholicity or Narrowness?', *Scrutiny* XII.4 (Autumn 1944), pp. 292–295.

'Meet Mr Forster', *Scrutiny* XII.4 (Autumn 1944), pp. 308–309.

'Comments: Henry James and the English Association; *The Times Literary Supplement*; An Irish Monthly; *The Kenyon Review* and *Scrutiny*; For Whom Do Universities Exist?', *Scrutiny* XIV.2 (December 1946), pp. 131–137.

'Henry James's First Novel', *Scrutiny* XIV.4 (September 1947), pp. 295–301. [later collected in *Valuation in Criticism and other essays*]

'The Teaching of Literature (III): the Literary Discipline and Liberal Education', *Sewanee Review* 55 (1947), pp. 586–609. [later collected in *Valuation in Criticism and other essays*]

'Critic and Leviathan: Literary Criticism and Politics', *Politics and Letters* 1.2–3 (Winter-Spring 1948), pp. 58–61.

'L. H. Myers and the Critical Function: Rebuke and Reply' *Scrutiny* XVI.4 (Winter 1949), pp. 330–333.

'Poetry Prizes for the Festival of Britain, 1951', *Scrutiny* XVI.4 (Winter 1949), pp. 333–335.

'The Legacy of the "Twenties"', letter to *The Listener*, 29 March 1951, pp. 502–503.

'Saints of Rationalism', *The Listener*, 26 April 1951, p. 672.

'Lawrence and Eliot', *Scrutiny* XVIII.2 (Autumn 1951), pp. 139–143.

'The Approach to James', *The Listener*, 6 December 1951, p. 987.

'The State of Criticism: Representations to Fr Martin Jarrett-Kerr', *Essays in Criticism* 3 (April 1953), pp. 215–233.

'The Critical Forum: The State of Criticism', *Essays in Criticism* 3 (July 1953), pp. 364–365.

'The "Great Books" and a Liberal Education: Must All Free Men Read Them – Or Be Slaves?', *Commentary* (September 1953), pp. 224–232. [later collected in *The Critic as Anti-Philosopher*]

'The Perfect Critic', letter to *The Manchester Guardian*, 21 October 1953, p. 4.

'*Scrutiny*', letter to *The Manchester Guardian*, 23 December 1953, p. 4.

'Correspondence', *Scrutiny* XIX.4 (October 1953), p. 330.

'A History of Switzerland', letter to *TLS*, 2 September 1955, p. 509.

'The Tone of the Critic', letter to *TLS*, 4 May 1956, p. 269.

'Literary Studies: A Reply', *Universities Quarterly* 11 (November 1956), pp. 14–25. [later collected in *Valuation in Criticism and other essays*]

'The Critic's Task', *Commentary*, July 1957, pp. 83–86.

'Polish Master of English Prose', *The Times*, 3 December 1957, p. 11.

'Lacking *Scrutiny*', letter to *TLS*, 8 May 1959, p. 273.

'How Far Short of True Greatness?', *The Guardian*, 8 April 1960, p. 13.

'A Note on the Critical Function', *Literary Criterion* 5.1 (Winter 1961), pp. 1–9.

'Done for Lawrence?', *The Guardian*, 24 March 1961, p. 15.

'The Two Cultures?', letter to *The Spectator*, 16 March 1962, p. 335.

'The Oxford Tradition', *The Spectator*, 2 August 1963, pp. 150–151.

'*Scrutiny*', letter to *The Spectator*, 8 November 1963, p. 597.

'Scrutinising the Classics', letter to *TLS*, 28 May 1964, p. 455.

'Correspondence', letter to *The Cambridge Review*, 7 November 1964, pp. 103 & 105.

'Valuation in Criticism', *Orbis Litterarum* 21 (1966), pp. 61–70. [later collected in *Valuation in Criticism and other essays*]

'T. S. Eliot and the Life of English Literature', *Massachusetts Review* 10 (Winter 1969), pp. 9–34. [later collected in *Valuation in Criticism and other essays*]

'Eliot and Pound', letter to *TLS*, 28 August 1970, p. 951.

'Wordsworth: The Creative Conditions', in *Twentieth-Century Literature in Retrospect*, pp. 323–341. Edited by Reuben Brower. Cambridge, Massachusetts: Harvard University Press, 1971. [later collected in *The Critic as Anti-Philosopher*]

'Henry James and Dickens', letter to *TLS*, 19 March 1971, p. 325.

'Reply to Noel Annan', *The Human World* 4 (August 1971), p. 65.

'F. R. Leavis Discusses *Xenia*, by the Italian Poet Eugenio Montale', *The Listener*, 16 December 1971, pp. 845–846. [later collected in *The Critic as Anti-Philosopher*]

'Justifying One's Valuation of Blake', *The Human World* 7 (May 1972), pp. 42–64. [later collected in *The Critic as Anti-Philosopher*]

'A Message from Dr F. R. Leavis' *Literary Criterion* 10.2 (Summer 1972), p. 1.

'Memories of Wittgenstein', *The Human World* 10 (February 1973), pp. 66–79. [later collected in *The Critic as Anti-Philosopher*]

'Questions of Tone', letter to *TLS*, 9 November 1973, p. 1372.

'Verbicide', letter to *TLS*, 31 May 1974, p. 586.

'"Believing In" The University', *The Human World* 15–16 (May-August 1974), pp. 98–109. [later collected in *The Critic as Anti-Philosopher*]

'Who Will Lead Against Inflation?', letter to *The Times*, 1 August 1974, p. 15.

'F. R. Leavis', letter to *TLS*, 5 December 1975, p. 1475.

'F. R. Leavis', letter to *TLS*, 19 December 1975, p. 1516.

'Mutually Necessary', *New Universities Quarterly* 30.2 (Spring 1976), pp. 129–151. [later collected in *The Critic as Anti-Philosopher*]

'Eliot's Permanent Place', *Aligarh Journal of English Studies* 2 (October 1977), pp. 125–143.

Books and pamphlets published after Leavis's death

Reading Out Poetry and Eugenio Montale: A Tribute. Together with the proceedings of a commemorative symposium on Leavis held at the Queen's University of Belfast, with Lord Boyle of Handsworth as Guest Speaker. Belfast: The Queen's University of Belfast, 1979.

The Critic as Anti-Philosopher: Essays and Papers. Edited by G. Singh. London: Chatto & Windus, 1982.

Valuation in Criticism and Other Essays. Edited by G. Singh. Cambridge: Cambridge University Press, 1986

More Letters in Criticism by F. R. Leavis and Q. D. Leavis. Edited by M. B. Kinch. Bradford-on-Avon: M. B. Kinch, privately printed, 1992.

2 WRITINGS ABOUT F. R. LEAVIS TO 1984: A SELECTION FROM THE GARLAND BIBLIOGRAPHY

Anderson, Perry. 'Components of the National Culture', *New Left Review* 50 (July-August 1968), pp. 3–57.

Annan, Noel. 'The University and the Intellect: The miasma and the menace', *TLS*, 30 April 1970, pp. 465–468.

Baldick, Chris. *The Social Mission of English Criticism 1848–1932*. Oxford: Clarendon Press, 1983.

Bateson, F. W. 'The Function of Criticism at the Present Time', *Essays in Criticism* III.1 (January 1953), pp. 1–27; and 'Correspondence: The Responsible Critic', *Scrutiny* XIX.4 (October 1953), pp. 317–321.

Belsey, Catherine. 'Re-Reading the Great Tradition'. In *Re-Reading English*, pp. 121–135. Edited by Peter Widdowson. New Accents series. London: Methuen, 1982.

Bergonzi, Bernard. 'Leavis and Eliot: The Long Road to Rejection', *Critical Quarterly* 26.1–2 (Spring/Summer 1984), pp. 21–43.

Bilan, R. B. *The Literary Criticism of F. R. Leavis*. Cambridge: Cambridge University Press, 1979.

Black, Michael. 'The Third Realm: An expository essay on *Scrutiny*', *The Use of English* XV.4 (Summer 1964), pp. 280–288, and XVI.1 (Autumn 1964), pp. 21–31.

Boyers, Robert. *F. R. Leavis: Judgment and the Discipline of Thought*. London: University of Missouri Press, 1978.

Cain, William E. *The Crisis in Criticism: Theory, Literature, and Reform in English Studies*. London: Johns Hopkins, 1984.

Cox, C. B. '*Scrutiny*: A Revaluation', *The Spectator*, 25 October 1963, pp. 531–2, and 22 November 1963, p. 666.

Filmer, Paul. 'Literary Study as Liberal Education and as Sociology in the Work of F. R. Leavis'. In *Rationality, Education and the Social Organization of Knowledge: Papers for a reflexive sociology of education*, pp. 55–85. Edited by Chris Jenks. Routledge Direct Editions. London: Routledge & Kegan Paul, 1977.

French, Philip. *Three Honest Men: Edmund Wilson, F. R. Leavis, Lionel Trilling: a critical mosaic*. Manchester: Carcanet New Press, 1980.

Greenwood, Edward. *F. R. Leavis*. Writers and their Work. Harlow: Longman, for the British Council, 1978.

Hayman, Ronald. *Leavis*. London: Heineman, 1976.

Holderness, Graham. 'Lawrence, Leavis and Culture', *Cultural Studies* 5 (Spring 1974), pp. 85–110.

Jacobson, Howard; Terry, Chris; and Jewel, P. J. *Dr F. R. Leavis: The Ogre of Downing Castle and other stories*. Oxford: Oxonian Press, 1963.

Lawford, Paul. 'Conservative Empiricism in Literary Theory: A Scrutiny of the Work of F. R. Leavis', *Red Letters* I (1976), pp. 12–15 & II (1976), pp. 9–11.

Lerner, L. D. 'The Life and Death of *Scrutiny*', *The London Magazine* 2.1 (January 1955), pp. 68–77.

Lucas, F. L. 'English Literature'. In *University Studies: Cambridge 1933*, pp. 259–294. Edited by Harold Wright. London: Ivor Nicholson & Watson, 1933.

MacKillop, Ian. 'F. R. Leavis: A Peculiar Relationship', *Essays in Criticism* XXXIV.3 (July 1984), pp. 185–192.

Mathieson, Margaret. *The Preachers of Culture: a study of English and its teachers*. Unwin Education Books series. London: George Allen & Unwin, 1974.

McCallum, Pamela. *Literature and Method: towards a critique of I. A. Richards, T. S. Eliot and F. R. Leavis*. Dublin: Gill and MacMillan, 1983.

Mulhern, Francis. *The Moment of 'Scrutiny'*. London: New Left Books, 1979.

Musgrave, P. W. 'Scrutiny and Education', *British Journal of Educational Studies* XXI.3 (October 1973), pp. 253–276.

Narasimhaiah, C. D., ed. *F. R. Leavis: Some Aspects of His Work*. Mysore: Rao & Raghavan, 1963.

Poole, Roger. 'Life *versus* Death in the later criticism of F. R. Leavis', *Renaissance and Modern Studies* 16 (1972), pp. 112–141.

Putt, S. Gorley. 'Technique and Culture: Three Cambridge Portraits'. In *Essays and Studies 1961*, pp. 17–34. London: John Murray, 1961.

Robertson, P. J. M. *The Leavises on Fiction: An Historic Partnership*. London: Macmillan, 1981.

Snow, C. P. 'The case of Leavis and the serious case', *TLS*, 9 July 1970, pp. 737–740.

Steiner, George. 'Men and Ideas: F. R. Leavis', *Encounter* 18.5 (May 1962), pp. 37–45.

Strickland, Geoffrey. *Structuralism or Criticism? Thoughts on How We Read*. Cambridge: Cambridge University Press, 1981.

Thompson, Denys, ed. *The Leavises: Recollections and Impressions*. Cambridge: Cambridge University Press, 1984.

Walsh, William. *F. R. Leavis*. London: Chatto & Windus, 1980.

Watson, Garry. *The Leavises, the 'Social', and the Left*. Swansea: Brynmill, 1977.

Wellek, Rene. 'Literary Criticism and Philosophy', *Scrutiny* V.4 (March 1937), pp. 375–383; and 'Correspondence: Literary Criticism and Philosophy', *Scrutiny* VI.2 (September 1937), pp. 195–196.

Williams, Raymond. *Culture and Society*. London: Chatto & Windus, 1958.

Wright, Iain. 'F. R. Leavis, the *Scrutiny* movement and the Crisis', in *Culture and Crisis in Britain in the Thirties*, pp. 37–65. Edited by Jonathan Clark, Margot Heinemann and Carole Snee. London: Lawrence and Wishart, 1979.

3 FURTHER WRITINGS ABOUT F. R. LEAVIS TO 1995: A SUPPLEMENT TO THE GARLAND BIBLIOGRAPHY

Annan, Noel. *Our Age: The Generation That Made Post-war Britain*. London: Weidenfeld and Nicolson, 1990; paperback edition, London: Fontana, 1991. [See Chapter 20: 'The Deviants – F. R. Leavis', pp. 426–449]

Ball, Stephen. 'English for the English since 1906'. In *Social Histories of the Secondary Curriculum: Subjects for Study*. Edited by Ivor Goodson. London: Falmer Press, 1987.

Ball, Stephen; Kenny, Alex; and Gardiner, David. 'Literacy, Politics and the Teaching of English', in *Bringing English to Order: The History and Politics of a School Subject*, pp. 47–86. Edited by Ivor Goodson and Peter Medway. Lewes: The Falmer Press, 1990.

Barnett, Ronald. *The Idea of Higher Education*. Buckingham: SRHE & Open University Press, 1990.

Barrett, Cyril. 'Wittgenstein, Leavis, and Literature', *New Literary History* 19.2 (Winter 1988), pp. 385–401.

Bell, Michael. *F. R. Leavis*. Foreword by Christopher Norris. Critics of the Twentieth Century series. London: Routledge, 1988.

Belsey, Catherine. 'Anti-Imperative: Questioning the Old Order', *PN Review* 48 (1985), pp. 26–27.

Bergonzi, Bernard. *Exploding English: Criticism, Theory, Culture*. Oxford: Clarendon Press, 1990.

Brewer, Derek. 'Yes, But . . .', *The Cambridge Review*, January 1985, pp. 25–29.

Brooke, Christopher N. L. *A History of the University of Cambridge: Volume IV, 1870–1990*. Cambridge: Cambridge University Press, 1993.

Carter, Ian. *Ancient Cultures of Conceit: British University Fiction in the Post-War Years*. London: Routledge, 1990. [See Chapter 10 'Dark Days and Black Papers', pp. 215–258]

Chainey, Graham. 'The other Leavises', *The Cambridge Review* (January 1985), pp. 7–9.

Collini, Stefan. *Public Moralists: Political Thought and Intellectual Life in Britain*. Oxford: Clarendon Press, 1991.

Coombes, John E. *Writing from the Left: Socialism, Liberalism and the Popular Front*. London: Harvester Wheatsheaf, 1989. [See 'Bloomsbury and *Scrutiny*: A note on English literary politics in the 1930s', pp. 30–37]

Cordner, Christopher. 'F. R. Leavis and the Moral in Literature', in *On Literary Theory and Philosophy*, pp. 60–81. Edited and Introduced by Richard Freadman and Lloyd Reinhardt. New York: St Martins, 1991.

Cox, Brian. *Cox on Cox: An English Curriculum for the 1990s*. London: Hodder & Stoughton, 1991. [See pp. 75–77: 'The Leavis Tradition']

Davies, Chris. 'The Conflicting Subject Philosophies of English', *British Journal of Educational Studies* XXXVII.4 (November 1989), pp. 398–416

De La Mothe, John. *C. P. Snow and the Struggle of Modernity*. Austin: University of Texas Press, 1992.

Dean, Paul. 'Meeting in Meaning: Leavis, Language and the GCSE', *The Use of English* 39.2 (Spring 1988), pp. 21–29.

Dixon, John. *A Schooling in 'English': Critical episodes in the struggle to shape literary and cultural studies*. Milton Keynes: Open University Press, 1991.

Doyle, Brian. *English and Englishness*. New Accents series. London: Routledge, 1989.

Eagleton, Terry. *Literary Theory: An Introduction*. Oxford: Basil Blackwell, 1983. [See Chapter 1: 'The Rise of English', pp. 30–38]

Felperin, Howard. *Beyond Deconstruction: The Uses and Abuses of Literary Theory*. Oxford: Oxford University Press, 1985. [See Chapter One: 'Leavisism Revisited']

Freadman, Richard; and Miller, Seumas. *Re-Thinking Theory: A critique of contemporary literary theory and an alternative account*. Cambridge: Cambridge University Press, 1992. [See Chapter Two: 'Two Paradigms of Literary Theory', pp. 34–50]

Gervais, David. 'Literary Criticism and the Literary Student', *English* 41 (Summer 1992), pp. 149–161.

Gregor, Ian. 'F. R. Leavis and The Great Tradition', *Sewanee Review* 93.3 (Summer 1985), pp. 434–446.

Gross, John. *The Rise and Fall of the Man of Letters: Aspects of English Literary Life since 1800*. London: Weidenfeld & Nicolson, 1969. Reissued with an Introduction and Afterword. Harmondsworth: Penguin Books, 1991.

Hamilton Eddy, David. 'A forgotten embarrassment of riches', *THES*, 24 April 1992, pp. 15 & 18.

Hartman, Geoffrey. 'Placing Leavis', *London Review of Books*, 24 January 1985, pp. 10–12.

Hawkes, Terence. 'Take Me To Your Leda', *Shakespeare Survey* 40 (1988), pp. 21–32.

Hawkes, Terence. 'The Institutionalization of Literature: The University'. In *Encylopaedia of Literature and Criticism*, pp. 926–937. Edited by Martin Coyle, Peter Garside, Malcolm Kelsall and John Peck. London: Routledge, 1990.

Houghton, R. L. 'What for – what ultimately for? The Leavises in the sixties and seventies', *The Cambridge Quarterly* XVII.1 (1988), pp. 66–67.

Houghton, Robert (R. L.). 'Morris Shapira and the Downing English School', *London Magazine* 30.1–2 (April/May 1990), pp. 19–33.

Hughes, Eamonn. 'Leavis and Ireland?', *Text & Context* 3 (Autumn 1988), pp. 112–32.

Kearney, Anthony. 'Leavis on Eliot: Personality versus Intelligence', *The Use of English* 40.3 (Summer 1989), pp. 59–67.

Keys, Kevin. 'F. R. Leavis: the development of a critical vocabulary'. Unpublished Ph.D thesis, University of Edinburgh, 1984.

Kinch, M. B. 'F. R. Leavis's "Poetry and the Modern World"', *English Studies* 69.1 (February 1988), pp. 55–71.

Kinch, M. B. '"Saying Everything at Once"? The Prose Style of F. R. Leavis', *English Studies* 73.6 (December 1992), pp. 517–27.

Lu, Jian-De. 'F. R. Leavis: His Criticism in Relation to Romanticism'. Unpublished Ph.D thesis, University of Cambridge, 1989.

MacCabe, Colin. 'The Cambridge Heritage: Richards, Empson and Leavis', *Southern Review* 19.3 (November 1986), pp. 242–249.

MacKillop, Ian. 'F. R. Leavis', *The Cambridge Quarterly* XX.3 (1991), pp. 258–264.

MacKillop, Ian. *F. R. Leavis: A Life in Criticism*. London: Allen Lane, 1995.

McCleery, Alastair. 'Naughty Old Leavis', *THES,* 13 September 1991.

Mulhern, Francis. 'English Reading', in *Nation and Narration*, pp. 250–264. Edited by Homi K. Bhabha. London: Routledge, 1990.

Needham, John. 'Leavis and Language', *PN Review* 48 (1985), pp. 23–25.

Needham, John. 'Leavis and the Post-Saussureans', *English* 34 (Autumn 1985), pp. 235–250.

Newton, K. M., ed. *Twentieth-Century Literary Theory: A Reader*. Basingstoke: Macmillan, 1988. [See 'Leavisite Criticism', pp. 65–73]

O'Hear, Anthony. 'The University as a Civilizing Force', in *Higher Education into the 1990s: new dimensions*, pp. 17–28. Edited by Sir Christopher Ball and Heather Eggins. Milton Keynes: SRHE and Open University Press, 1989.

Parrinder, Patrick. 'Jolly Jack and the Preacher', *London Review of Books*, 20 April 1989, pp. 14–15.

Parrinder, Patrick. *Authors and Authority: English and American Criticism 1750–1990*. Basingstoke: Macmillan, 1990.

Robinson, Ian. 'F. R. Leavis the Cambridge Don', *The Use of English* 43.3 (Summer 1992), pp. 244–254.

Samson, Anne. *F. R. Leavis*. Modern Cultural Theorists. Hemel Hempstead: Harvester Wheatsheaf, 1992.

Scherr, Barry. 'Leavis's Revolt against Eliot: The Lawrence Connexion', *Recovering Literature* 15 (Summer 1987), pp. 37–104.

Selden, Raman. *Practising Theory and Reading Literature: An Introduction*. Hemel Hempstead: Harvester Wheatsheaf, 1989. [See Chapter 1: 'Moral Criticism (F. R. Leavis): John Bunyan', pp. 19–24]

Selden, Raman; and Widdowson, Peter. *A Reader's Guide to Contemporary Literary Theory*. Third Edition. London: Harvester, 1993. [See Chapter 1: 'New Criticism, Moral Formalism and F. R. Leavis', pp. 10–26]

Simons, Michael; and Raleigh, Mike. 'Where we've been: A brief history of English Teaching', *The English Magazine* 8 (1981), pp. 23–28.

Snow, Philip; Annan, Noel; Black Michael; Rose, Steven; and Steiner, George. 'Symposium: The Two Cultures Re-visited', *The Cambridge Review*, March 1987.

Storer, R. G. 'English, Education and the University: An Historical Study of the Work and Significance of F. R. Leavis'. Unpublished Ph.D thesis, University of Sheffield, 1993.

Strickland, Geoffrey. 'Great Traditions: The Logic of the Canon'. In *Encyclopaedia of Literature and Criticism*, pp. 696–707. Edited by Martin Coyle, Peter Garside, Malcolm Kelsall and John Peck. London: Routledge, 1990.

Widdowson, Peter. 'W(h)ither "English"?'. In *Encyclopaedia of Literature and Criticism*, pp. 1221–1236. Edited by Martin Coyle, Peter Garside, Malcolm Kelsall and John Peck. London: Routledge, 1990.

Willinsky, John. 'Literary Theory and Public Education: The Instance of F. R. Leavis', *Mosaic* 21.3 (1988), pp. 165–177.

Wilson, Keith. 'Academic Fictions and the Place of Liberal Studies: A Leavis Inheritance'. In *University Fiction*, pp. 57–73. Edited by David Bevan. Rodopi Perspectives on Modern Literature 5. Amsterdam: Rodopi, 1990.

'Correspondence' [on the Leavises], *The Cambridge Quarterly* XV.1 & XV.3 (1986).

'Distaste for Leavis', Letters to *London Review of Books*, 8 November 1990 – 24 January 1991.

Notes

Full publication details for all Leavis's books are given in 'F. R. Leavis: A Reader's Guide'. They are referred to by title only in the notes below and, unless otherwise stated, the page numbers given are those of the original editions.

INTRODUCTION

1. Noel Annan, *Our Age: The Generation That Made Post-War Britain* (London: Fontana, 1991), p. 435.
2. F. R. Leavis, '"English" – Unrest and Continuity', *TLS*, 29 May 1969, p. 570; reprinted in *Nor Shall My Sword*.
3. F. R. Leavis, *English Literature in Our Time and the University*, pp. 66 & 67.
4. F. R. Leavis, 'Keynes, Spender and Currency-Values', *Scrutiny* XVIII.1 (June 1951), pp. 45–56.
5. F. R. Leavis, *Education and the University*, pp. 110 & 47.
6. F. R. Leavis, *Education and the University*, p. 44.

CHAPTER I: LEAVIS AS CRITIC OF NEW POETRY

1. 'Saints of Rationalism', *The Listener*, 26 April 1951, p. 672.
2. See 'Retrospect 1950' in *New Bearings in English Poetry* (new edition: 1950), pp. 215–238.
3. *The Cambridge Review*, 12 October 1928, p. 20; see also *New Bearings*, pp. 66–68.
4. 'Green Fields', *The Cambridge Review*, 15 November 1929, p. 118.
5. 'T. S. Eliot: a Reply to the Condescending', *The Cambridge Review*, 8 February 1929, pp. 254–256; [Untitled] Review of *Cambridge Poetry 1929*, in *The Cambridge Review*, 1 March 1929, pp. 317–318.
6. [Untitled] Review of *Cambridge Poetry 1930*, in *The Cambridge Review*, 16 May 1930, pp. 414–415.
7. 'Poetry-Lovers, Prosody and Poetry', *The Spectator*, 14 May 1932, pp. 705–706. The books Leavis reviewed were: Anne Page, *The Little Drum*; Alan Mulgan, *Golden Wedding*; Anna de Bary, *Verses*; Dorothy Wellesley, *Jupiter and the Nun*; John Appleby, *Morning Mist*; A. Abrahams, *Poems*; Julian Huxley, *The Captive Shrew*; R. C. Trevelyan, *Rimeless Numbers*; William Plomer, *The Fivefold Screen*; William Jeffrey, *The Golden Stag*.

8. See 'Auden, Bottrall and Others', *Scrutiny* III.1 (June 1934), p. 76.

9. [Untitled] Review of W. H. Auden, *Poems*, in *TLS*, 19 March 1931, p. 221; [Untitled] Review of W. H. Auden, *The Orators*, in *The Listener*, 22 June 1932, p. 906; see also John Haffenden (ed.), *Auden: The Critical Heritage* (London: Routledge & Kegan Paul, 1983), pp. 88–91 & 100–1.

10. 'English Letter', *Poetry* 43 (January 1934), pp. 215–221.

11. 'English Letter', *Poetry* 44 (May 1934), pp. 98–102.

12. 'Auden, Bottrall and Others', *Scrutiny* III.1 (June 1934), pp. 70–83.

13. 'English Letter', *Poetry* 46 (August 1935), pp. 274–278.

14. 'Hugh MacDiarmid', *Scrutiny* IV.3 (December 1935), p. 305.

15. 'Marianne Moore', *Scrutiny* IV.1 (June 1935), pp. 87–90.

16. See 'The Recognition of Isaac Rosenberg', *Scrutiny* VI.2 (September 1937), pp. 229–234.

17. 'The Fate of Edward Thomas', *Scrutiny* VII.4 (March 1939), pp. 441–443.

18. 'Hart Crane From This Side', *Scrutiny* VII.4 (March 1939), pp. 443–446.

19. [Untitled] Review of T. S. Eliot, *East Coker*, in *The Cambridge Review*, 21 February 1941, pp. 268–270.

CHAPTER 2: LEAVIS AS READER OF *Daniel Deronda*

1. 'George Eliot (IV): *Daniel Deronda* and *Portrait of a Lady*', *Scrutiny* XIV.2 (December 1946), pp. 102–131, reprinted in *The Great Tradition* (1948), which included as an appendix, '*Daniel Deronda*: A Conversation by Henry James'.

2. 'George Eliot's Zionist Novel', *Commentary* 30 (October 1960), pp. 317–325, reprinted as the Introduction to George Eliot, *Daniel Deronda* (New York: Harper, Academy Library, 1961) and in *Valuation in Criticism* (1986).

3. 'Gwendolen Harleth', *London Review of Books* 4.1 (January,1982), pp. 10–12: also published in *The Critic as Anti-Philosopher* (1982). [But see below: Chapter 3, Note 4]

4. All page references in this essay are to the 1878 Blackwood edition used by Leavis himself: 'GE' is found on the following pages: 19, 48, 57, 59, 62, 63, 67, 77, 109, 115, 124, 130, 145, 240, 271, 283, 323, 354, 372, 374, 384, 418, 420, 424, 450, 468, 488, 502, 504, 506, 507, 514, 516, 542, 551, 562, 563, 564, 565, 601, 602, 606, 607, 609.

5. F. R. Leavis, *The Great Tradition*, p. 96.

6. F. R. Leavis, *The Great Tradition*, p. 84.

7. F. R. Leavis, *The Great Tradition*, p. 96.

8. See Raman Selden, *A Reader's Guide to Contemporary Literary Theory* (Brighton: Harvester, 1985), pp. 112–13.

CHAPTER 3: LEAVIS AND `GWENDOLEN HARLETH´

1. F. R. Leavis, *The Great Tradition*, p. 122.

2. F. R. Leavis, 'George Eliot's Zionist Novel', in *Valuation in Criticism*, p.64.

3. The economical note on Mordecai (p. 309) suggests how much information the new reader of *Gwendolen Harleth* would have been missing: 'Mordecai, the Zionist who turns out to be the long-lost brother of Mirah Lapidoth, the young Jewess whom Deronda, having rescued her from the Thames, falls in love with and, in the last chapter of *Daniel Deronda*, marries.'

4. The Introduction was published first in the *London Review of Books*, 21 January–3 February 1982, pp. 10–12, and then in *The Critic as Anti-Philosopher* (1982). The two texts are slightly different, and neither corresponds to the final text as it would have appeared in *Gwendolen Harleth* – and as it is now to be found in the Bodley Head file. The two published versions seem to be based on different copies of Leavis's typescript made *before* he agreed to certain changes with The Bodley Head. For example, the sentence 'The astringency of the creative genius can be wholly unreductive and is in any case free from superiority' was significantly changed by Leavis to: 'The astringency of the creative genius is never petty, vain or malicious; it expresses the perspicacity and the profound common sense of generous insight.' Several rather tortuous sentences were also simplified. The *London Review of Books* text does not contain these changes, but it does include the final section which was added by Leavis in June 1974. The version which appears in *The Critic as Anti-Philosopher* includes neither. One or two phrases in this version have also been doctored to make the essay read like a proposal rather than the Introduction to a completed project: where Leavis wrote 'It has nevertheless turned out to be after all possible . . . I make the penultimate chapter . . . It had to go in . . .' the doctored version reads 'It should nevertheless be possible . . . I should make . . . It would have to be included.' In the context of the book as a whole this does make better sense.

5. Leavis's terms for the two parts in his Introduction. As usual, Francis Mulhern is the most acute commentator on this issue: 'Leavis's critique of George Eliot furnished a remarkable practical demonstration of the chief methodological feature of Leavisian criticism: the dualism of "recognition" and "explanation" . . . If *Daniel Deronda* constituted the extreme case of Eliot's artistic achievement, Leavis's readiness to dismember the novel was the logical terminus of his own methodological dualism' (*The Moment of 'Scrutiny'*, pp. 257, 259). Mulhern was aware of the proposed Bodley Head edition from Ronald Hayman's *Leavis*, which refers to it briefly (p. 76): 'When a publisher invited him to do the work of extrication for himself, he rose to the challenge, but *Gwendolen Harleth* never appeared in the bookshops, so his theory has not been put to the ultimate test.'

CHAPTER 7: *Education and the University*

Because one function of this chapter is to document the relation of *Education and the University* to its source texts in *Scrutiny*, I have provided a slightly more cumbersome set of parallel references below than would otherwise be necessary. Where no relevant parallel with *Education and the University* exists, however, and the context is fairly clear, I have given the page reference in brackets in the text itself.

1. F. R. Leavis, *Education and the University*, p. 7.
2. Pound's *How to Read* was published as a book in 1931, but originally appeared as a series of articles in the *New York Herald Tribune Books* in 1929. A reference to Leavis appears in a letter from Pound to John Drummond, dated 18 February 1932: 'What is Leavis? He recently sent me his "Primer"' (D. D. Paige [ed.], *The Selected Letters of Ezra Pound 1907–1941* [London: Faber & Faber, 1950], p. 246). But it is rather difficult to make this date fit the evidence on Leavis's side – unless the 'Primer' Pound received was a very early draft. Leavis's letters to Ronald Bottrall refer to him finishing *How To Teach Reading* in October 1932, and the pamphlet actually quotes from a *Scrutiny* article ('What's Wrong With Criticism?') published in September 1932. The Chatto & Windus Archive reveals that Leavis offered *How To Teach Reading* to Chatto & Windus in November 1932, having offered it first to Harmsworth, Pound's publisher. When Chatto & Windus also declined it, he arranged for it to be published by the Minority Press in Cambridge. The pamphlet is usually dated 1932, but a Minority Press advertisement in *For Continuity* actually describes it as published in early 1933.
3. F. R. Leavis, 'An American Lead', *Scrutiny* I.3 (December 1932), pp. 297–301. For the book itself and the background to Meiklejohn's project see Alexander Meiklejohn, *The Experimental College* (London: Harper & Bros, 1932), pp. 329–49; G. C. Sellery, *Some Ferments at Wisconsin, 1901–1947: Memories and Reflections* (Madison: University of Wisconsin Press, 1960), pp. 9–34; and Bruce Kimball, *Orators and Philosophers: A History of the Idea of Liberal Education* (New York: Teachers College Press, Columbia University, 1986).
4. See particularly '"The Literary Mind"', *Scrutiny* I.1 (June 1932), pp. 20–32; and 'Intelligence and Sensibility', Leavis's review of Empson's *Seven Types of Ambiguity* in *The Cambridge Review*, 16 January 1931, pp. 186–7.
5. *Education and the University*, p. 38.
6. F. R. Leavis, 'Why Universities?', *Scrutiny* III.2 (September 1934), p. 117.
7. 'Why Universities?', pp. 119–21; reprinted in *Education and the University*, pp. 22–4, with one or two minor changes and additions: Leavis amended 'faculties' to 'powers', for example; and turned the 1934 question 'But what reason can anyone show for being exhilarated by the hopes of revolutionaries?' into a statement: 'in our time only the very naive have been able to be exhilarated by the hopes of revolutionaries.'
8. 'Why Universities?', p. 130; *Education and the University*, pp. 29–30.
9. 'Why Universities?', p. 121; *Education and the University*, p. 25.
10. 'Why Universities?', p. 122; *Education and the University*, p. 26.
11. 'Why Universities?', p. 123; *Education and the University*, p. 27; quoted from Meiklejohn, *The Experimental College*, xv.
12. 'Why Universities?', p. 125; *Education and the University*, p. 28.

13. 'Why Universities?', p. 131.

14. 'After Ten Years', *Scrutiny* X.4 (April 1942), p. 327; reprinted as a quotation in *Education and the University*, p. 30. Leavis did retain the first sentence from the 'Why Universities?' passage quoted, however: '. . . their function, fully performed, comprises so much more than any talk of education can suggest'. But after 'education' he inserted 'or research and scholarship' – evidently more aware in 1943 than in 1934 that more than one limiting misconception of the function of a university was possible.

15. 'Why Universities?', pp. 126–8; *Education and the University*, pp. 44–6.

16. *Education and the University*, p. 51.

17. 'The Spens Report: A Symposium-Review', *Scrutiny* VIII.3 (December 1939), pp. 242–56; the opening paragraphs were reprinted as a quotation in F. R. Leavis, 'Education and the University (IV): Considerations at a Critical Time', *Scrutiny* XI.3 (Spring 1943), p. 162; *Education and the University*, p. 15. *Scrutiny* VIII.3 is unique among the 76 issues of the journal in containing no article, review or comment signed by F. R. Leavis.

18. F. R. Leavis, 'Education and the University: Sketch for an English School', *Scrutiny* IX.2 (September 1940), p. 103 (referred to below as 'Sketch'); reprinted in *Education and the University*, p. 42. It is worth noting that the original title of this article differed slightly from its counterpart in *Education and the University* ('A Sketch for an "English School"') and was *not* numbered as the first in a series, although it is cited in this way in the Leavis bibliographies and the *Scrutiny* index.

19. 'Sketch', p. 101; *Education and the University*, p. 40.

20. These events are briefly described by Boris Ford and Frank Whitehead in Denys Thompson (ed.), *The Leavises: Recollections and Impressions*, pp. 111 and 143–4; and were referred to by Leavis himself in *Education and the University*, p. 47.

21. 'Sketch', p. 103; *Education and the University*, p. 41.

22. Meiklejohn, *The Experimental College*, xiii.

23. 'Sketch', p. 106; *Education and the University*, p. 48.

24. 'Sketch', pp. 106–7; *Education and the University*, p. 48.

25. 'Sketch', p. 104; *Education and the University*, p. 43. Whether Leavis was right to interpret the foundation of the Cambridge English Tripos in this somewhat mythical way is of course a large controversial subject in itself. In his only detailed account, in the Introduction to *English Literature in Our Time and the University* (1969), pp. 11–24, Leavis seems intent on re-routing the 'Cambridge English' tradition through Forbes and Chadwick (Cambridge figures representing History and 'Anthropology') rather than Quiller-Couch (representing Oxford, Classics and Belles-Lettres). But it is arguable that Quiller-Couch and others had a much more significant role in determining the ethos of the new 'School' than Leavis was willing to admit. The different accounts of the origins of 'Cambridge English', particularly as a form of liberal education, are discussed in more detail in my Ph.D thesis, *English, Education*

and the University: An Historical Study of the Work and Significance of F. R. Leavis (1993). Barry Cullen explores the philosophical background to 'Cambridge English' in Chapter 8 of this book.

26. 'Sketch', p. 112; *Education and the University*, p. 55.

27. Quoted in F. R. Leavis, 'Education and the University (II): Criticism and Comment', *Scrutiny* IX.3 (December 1940), pp. 259–60. Further references to this article are given in the text.

28. 'Sketch', pp. 114–5; *Education and the University*, p. 59.

29. F. R. Leavis, 'Education and the University (III): Literary Studies', *Scrutiny* IX.4 (March 1941), p. 311; *Education and the University*, p. 73. Other parts of this ghostly 'appreciation and analysis' book – known as *Judgment and Analysis* to Chatto and Windus, who waited in vain for it for over thirty years – were published in *Scrutiny* and eventually collected in *The Living Principle*.

30. T. S. Eliot, 'The Christian Conception of Education', in *Malvern 1941: The Life of the Church and the Order of Society: Proceedings of the Archbishop of York's Conference* (London: Longman's, Green & Co, 1941), pp. 206 & 208. This essay is reprinted in T. S. Eliot, *The Idea of a Christian Society and other writings* (Second edition, London: Faber & Faber, 1982), pp. 148–158. The sentence Eliot attributed to Brooks Otis was in fact Leavis's own, quoted from 'Why Universities' (pp. 120–1) in 'Sketch' (pp. 101–2).

31. F. R. Leavis, 'Education and the University: Considerations at a Critical Time', *Scrutiny* XI.3 (Spring 1943), p. 166; *Education and the University*, p. 19. Although it pre-dated it by six months, this final article in the 'Education and the University' series was in effect reprinted *from* the text of the completed book, and presented by Leavis as such.

32. F. R. Leavis, 'Eliot's Later Poetry', *Scrutiny* XI.1 (Summer 1942), p. 71; *Education and the University*, p. 103.

33. 'Eliot's Later Poetry', p. 71; *Education and the University*, p. 104.

34. The information in this paragraph is based on the relevant files in the Chatto & Windus Archive at the University of Reading Library. During the war Leavis's contact at Chatto and Windus was Harold Raymond rather than Ian Parsons.

35. See F. R. Leavis, 'The Teaching of Literature (III): Literary Discipline and Liberal Education', *Sewanee Review* 55 (1947), pp. 586–609; and 'The "Great Books" and a Liberal Education: Must All Free Men Read Them – Or Be Slaves?', *Commentary* (September 1953), pp. 224–32. Both essays were more explicit than *Education and the University* in their bias towards Oxford and Cambridge (one reason, probably, why Leavis was reluctant to reprint them in the 1960s, after he had transferred his allegiance to a 'new' university at York).

36. F. R. Leavis, 'Critic and Leviathan: Literary Criticism and Politics', *Politics and Letters* 1.2 (Winter 1947–Spring 1948), pp. 59–61. On *Politics and Letters*

see Alan O'Connor, *Raymond Williams: Writing, Culture, Politics* (Oxford: Basil Blackwell, 1989), pp. 11–12.

37. Quoted in Storm Jameson, *Journey from the North* , II (London: Collins and Harvill, 1970), pp. 297–8.

38. F. R. Leavis, 'Two Cultures? The Significance of Lord Snow', in *Nor Shall My Sword: Discourses on Pluralism, Compassion and Social Hope* (London: Chatto & Windus, 1972), p. 63. This lecture was given at Downing College on 28 February 1962 and reprinted in *The Spectator* and a separate Chatto & Windus volume in the same year (the original title referred to 'C. P. Snow', of course).

CHAPTER 8: THE IMPERSONAL OBJECTIVE: F. R. LEAVIS, THE LITERARY SUBJECT AND CAMBRIDGE THOUGHT

1. Francis Mulhern, *The Moment of 'Scrutiny'* (London: NLB, 1979).

2. I. A. Richards, *The Meaning of Meaning* (London: Routledge, 1923), pp. 4–6.

3. Richards had been a friend of Eliot's since 1920, and had tried to persuade him to become a member of the English school at that time. Although he was not successful in this, Eliot did agree to give some lectures in 1922 and 1924. See I. A. Richards, 'On T.S.E.' in *The Man and His Work*, ed. Allen Tate (London: Penguin pb., 1967), p. 3; also T. S. Eliot, *The Varieties of Metaphysical Poetry*, ed. R. Schuchard (London: Faber, 1993), p. 5.

4. 'It seems to me that he would have every reason to hope for a distinguished philosophical career in this country . . .' Bertrand Russell to Charlotte Eliot, 3 December 1915, in *The Letters of T. S. Eliot*, volume I 1898–1922, ed. Valerie Eliot (London: Faber, 1988), pp. 122–123.

5. T. S. Eliot, *The Varieties of Metaphysical Poetry*, p. 5.

6. There seems to have been a pronounced element of professional rivalry in Richards's relationship with his philosophy colleagues; *The Meaning of Meaning* was persistently critical of the logic-based epistemology of Russell and Wittgenstein. Richards was particularly dismissive of Wittgenstein's thought. Cf. *The Meaning of Meaning*, pp. 253–255; see also I. A. Richards, *Selected Letters of I.A.Richards* (Oxford: Clarendon Press, 1990).

7. T. S. Eliot did not accept this interpretation of his poem, nor did he accept the cultural meanings that Richards placed upon it. This is evident from a lengthy debate the two conducted through the latter part of the 1920s. Some instances of this exchange are indicated in J. P. Russo, *I. A. Richards: His Life and Work* (London: Routledge, 1989), p. 760.

8. Cf. F. R. Leavis, *The Living Principle*, p. 64.

9. F. R. Leavis, 'Memories of Wittgenstein', in *The Critic as Anti-Philosopher*, p. 143.

10. Ian Robinson, one of FRL's sincerest admirers, criticized him for his attitude to philosophy departments and, by implication, his view of Wittgenstein. See *The Human World*, 15–16, May–August 1974, pp. 109–110.

11. *The Living Principle*, p. 62; and pp. 57–62.

12. Rene Wellek, 'Literary Criticism and Philosophy', *Scrutiny* V.4 (March 1937), pp. 375–384; F. R. Leavis, 'Literary Criticism and Philosophy', *Scrutiny* VI.1 (June 1937), pp. 59–71; Wellek, 'Letter', *Scrutiny* VI.2 (September 1937) pp. 195–7; cf. also *The Critic as Anti-Philosopher*, pp. ix–x.

13. Wyndham Lewis, *Men Without Art* (Santa Rosa: Black Sparrow Press, 1934), p. 60. Further page references are given in brackets in the text.

14. T. S. Eliot, *The Sacred Wood* (1920: this edition London: Methuen, 1960), p. 56.

15. Eliot, *The Sacred Wood*, p. 117.

16. Michael Bell has some pertinent comments in his *F. R. Leavis* (London: Routledge, 1988), pp. 66–67.

17. 'T. S. Eliot – A Reply to the Condescending', *The Cambridge Review*, 8 February 1929; 'F. R. Leavis's "English Poetry and the Modern World"', tr. M. B. Kinch, *English Studies* 69.1 (February 1988), pp. 55–71. (The original was published in France in October 1930 under the title: 'La Poesie Anglaise et le Monde Moderne: Etude de la Situation Actuelle'.)

18. Although there is little extant to show that Richards's importance was comparable to that of Eliot's at this time, it is evident, inferentially, that Richards's influence on Leavis had already been formative over a range of important topics such as those of language and poetic truth, the centrality of poetry, the nature of the poet, and, pre-eminently, the nature of the cultural crisis.

19. F. R. Leavis, 'T. S. Eliot – A Reply . . .', pp. 254–5.

20. Cf. I. A. Richards, *Principles of Literary Criticism* (London: Routledge, 1924), pp. 289–295.

21. F. R. Leavis, 'English Poetry and the Modern World', p. 63.

22. F. R. Leavis, *New Bearings in English Poetry*, p. 113. Further page references are given in brackets in the text.

23. Bell, *F. R. Leavis*, p. 64

24. Bell, *F. R. Leavis*, p. 67

25. Bell, *F. R. Leavis*, p. 67

26. See F. R. Leavis, *A Selection from 'Scrutiny'* (1968), pp. 1–47.

27. Bell, *F. R. Leavis*, pp. 35, 36.

28. Lyndall Gordon, *Eliot's New Life* (Oxford: Oxford University Press, 1988), p. 31.

29. F. R. Leavis, *Two Cultures? The Significance of C. P. Snow*, p. 28.

30. F. R. Leavis, 'Mutually Necessary', *New Universities Quarterly* 30.2 (Spring 1976); reprinted in *The Critic as Anti-Philosopher*, p. 196. Further page references are given in the text.

31. F. R. Leavis, *The Great Tradition*, p. 7.

32. T. S. Eliot, *The Sacred Wood*, p viii.

33. The critic, as Leavis latterly saw him, has to become, as an extension of his

task of making literature available, an 'anti-philosopher', a not wholly serious term but one which points in a wholly serious direction.

CHAPTER 9: LEAVIS AND POST-STRUCTURALISM

1. Antony Easthope, *British Post-Structuralism Since 1968* (London: Routledge, 1988), pp. 207–8 & 172.
2. Catherine Belsey, *Critical Practice* (London: Methuen, 1980), p. 7. It is only fair to note that Belsey's critique of Leavis is quite summary and she gives a more sustained one in her 'Re-reading the Great Tradition' in Peter Widdowson (ed.), *Re-Reading 'English'* (London: Methuen, 1982), pp. 121–135. Nevertheless, her analysis of *Daniel Deronda* in that article is based on the conception of Leavis she articulates in *Critical Practice*.
3. F. R. Leavis, 'Valuation in Criticism', in *Valuation in Criticism*, p. 278.
4. Belsey, *Critical Practice*, p. 13.
5. F. R. Leavis, 'Henry James and the Function of Criticism', in *The Common Pursuit*, p. 225.
6. F. R. Leavis, 'Tragedy and the Medium', in *The Common Pursuit*, p. 130.
7. F. R. Leavis, 'Valuation in Criticism', p. 281.
8. F. R. Leavis, 'The Pilgrim's Progress', in *'Anna Karenina' and Other Essays*, p. 46.
9. Belsey, *Critical Practice*, p. 46.
10. Belsey, *Critical Practice*, p. 52.
11. F. R. Leavis, 'Standards of Criticism', in *Valuation in Criticism*, p. 246.
12. For a discussion of the relation between meaning and significance, see E. D. Hirsch, *The Aims of Interpretation* (London: Chicago University Press, 1976) p. 8.
13. Belsey, *Critical Practice*, pp. 53–54.
14. Belsey, *Critical Practice*, p. 55
15. William Empson, 'I. A. Richards and Practical Criticism', *Argufying: Essays on Literature and Culture*, ed. J. Haffenden (Iowa: University of Iowa Press, 1987) p. 194.
16. F. R. Leavis, 'Standards of Criticism', p. 250.
17. Samuel Hynes, *The Auden Generation: Literature and Politics in England in the 1930s* (London: Pimlico, 1976) p. 66.
18. F. R. Leavis, 'Mass Civilization and Minority Culture', in *Education and the University*, p. 158.
19. 'Under Which King, Bezonian?', in *Valuation in Criticism*, p. 43
20. T. S. Eliot, quoted by Leavis in 'Mass Civilization and Minority Culture', p. 158.
21. Walter Pater, 'Style', in *Essays on Literature and Art,* ed. Jennifer Uglow (London: Everyman, 1990), p. 74.
22. F. R. Leavis, 'Towards Standards of Criticism', in *'Anna Karenina' and Other Essays*, p. 224.

23. 'To make a . . . point one has to use key words in special senses which one must rely on the context to define', F. R. Leavis, *The Living Principle*, p. 34. Such a remark should put paid to any lingering notion that Leavis regards 'the' meaning of words as fixed and absolute.

24. F. R. Leavis, 'Thought, Meaning and Sensibility: the Problem of Value Judgment', in *Valuation in Criticism*, p. 285.

25. Steven Best and Douglas Kellner, *Postmodern Theory: Critical Interrogations* (London: Macmillan, 1991), p. 21.

26. Belsey, *Critical Practice*, p. 60.

27. Belsey, *Critical Practice*, p. 44.

28. Belsey, *Critical Practice*, p. 4.

29. Terry Eagleton, *Literary Theory: An Introduction* (Oxford: Basil Blackwell, 1983), p. 31.

30. Easthope, *British Post-Structuralism*, p. 211.

31. See, for example, F. R. Leavis, *Nor Shall My Sword*, pp. 105, 107 and 109.

32. F. R. Leavis, '"English", Unrest and Continuity', in *Nor Shall My Sword*, p. 110.

33. See Maurice Kogan, 'Universities Under the Axe', in *Guardian Education* 18, 1994, pp. 6–7.

34. Michael Tanner 'Mutually Necessary: A Rejoinder', *New Universities Quarterly* XXX.3 (Summer, 1976), pp. 313–323; and M. B. Kinch, '"Saying Everything At Once?" The Prose Style of F. R. Leavis', *English Studies* LXXIII.6 (Winter 1992), pp. 517–22.

35. It would be unfair to claim that all post-structuralist writing is equally difficult. It is easier to read Foucault, for example, than Lacan. 'Difficulty', however, is intrinsic to post-structuralism, due mainly to its focus on how the structure of language complicates its use to make claims regarding logic, reason or truth.

36. F. R. Leavis, 'Luddites? or There is Only One Culture', in *Nor Shall My Sword*, p. 97.

37. 'Our sense of . . . Leavis would benefit from a fuller understanding of just what view or views of English history and literature he took himself to be challenging since his early work is these days too simply regarded as a familiar form of cultural conservatism, without its original, oppositional and dissident . . . character being properly recognised.' Stefan Collini, *Public Moralists: Political Thought and Intellectual Life in Britain 1850–1930* (Oxford: Clarendon Press, 1991), p. 370.

38. See Sigmund Freud, *Civilization and its Discontents*, trans. Joan Rivière, revised and newly edited by James Strachey (London: Hogarth Press and the Institute of Psychoanalysis, 1979). All further references to this work, and to F. R. Leavis, *Mass Civilization and Minority Culture*, as reprinted in *Education and the University*, are given in brackets in the text.

39. C. L. Mowat, *Britain Between The Wars: 1918–1940* (London: Methuen, 1955) p. 392; also pp. 379–93, 402–406.

40. For a discussion of the relation between money and language, see Allen Hoey, 'The Name On the Coin: Metaphor, Metonymy and Money', in *Diacritics* XVIII.2 (Summer, 1988) pp. 26–37.

41. Leavis defines 'the minority capable of appreciating Dante, Shakespeare, Donne, Baudelaire [and] Conrad' as 'the consciousness of the race' (*Mass Civilization*, p. 144). He also quotes with approval Norman Angell's comment that 'rationalised second thought' should seek to constrict and modify 'more primitive feelings and impulses' (p. 148). Finally, Leavis talks about a 'critically adult public' (p. 159) implying the existence of an uncritical, infantile one. Metaphor and consciousness come together in all these instances. Moreover, although Leavis would understand by consciousness the capacity for 'un-prompted, first hand judgement' (p. 143) his basic model of 'critical adult' versus uncritical, infantile or 'rationalised second thought' versus 'primitive feelings' is in many ways parallel to the Freudian distinction between consciousness and unconsciousness. His metaphors of consciousness, in other words, extend the term beyond any definition he gives of it.

42. R. Paget, quoted by Leavis in *Mass Civilization* (p. 167).

43. Freud locates the origin of civilisation first in the adoption of an erect posture and then in the killing of the father (*Civilization and its Discontents*, pp. 36, 68). He favours the latter explanation rather than the former which is relegated to a footnote. However, it is difficult to see how the killing of the father can establish civilisation since the father is already head of a 'civilisation'. Indeed, it is this fact which causes his siblings to band together and kill him. Leavis too presents a number of different causes for the 'plight' of civilisation claiming that each one is the only one. First 'it is enough to point to the machine' to 'support . . . the belief that the modern phase of human history is unprecedented' (*Mass Civilization*, pp. 145–6) then the condition of civilisation is attributed to the absence of 'an informed and cultivated public' (p. 156) before finally being explained in terms of 'a concourse of signals . . . bewildering in their variety and number' (p. 158).

44. See Roman Jakobson, 'Two Types of Language and Two Types of Aphasia Disturbance', in Roman Jakobson and Morris Halle, *Fundamentals of Language* (New York: Moulton Publishers, 1956), pp. 69–76.

45. Lyotard invokes the category of the sublime to signify the effect which that which escapes complete representation has upon us. See Jean Francois Lyotard, *The Different: Phrases in Dispute*, trans. Georges Van den Abeele (Manchester: Manchester University Press, 1988), pp. 151–81.

46. For an overview of the establishment of consumer culture, see Garry Cross, *Time and Money: The Making of Consumer Culture* (London: Routledge, 1993); also Daniel L. Le Mahieu, *A Culture for Democracy: Mass Communication and the Cultivated Mind in Britain Between the Wars* (Oxford: Clarendon, 1988).

47. 'The 1930s looked up . . . to the Charles Atlas types with their built up or building up bodies', Valentine Cunningham, *British Writers of the Thirties* (Oxford: Oxford University Press, 1988), p. 165.

48. Norman Angell, quoted by Leavis in *Mass Civilization*, p. 148.

CHAPTER 10: LEAVIS ON LAWRENCE

1. K-numbers cited in the text refer to the very useful check-list of all Leavis's writings on Lawrence (and on Eliot) given in M. B. Kinch, William Baker and John Kimber, *F. R. Leavis and Q. D. Leavis: An Annotated Bibliography*. Full publication details of all Leavis's writings will also be found in this work, though I have provided enough information here for all the texts I discuss to be easily traced. In the Lawrence list in the *Annotated Bibliography* K1 and K2 should actually be transposed, since Leavis's pamphlet was an expansion of material which appeared earlier in the year as a *Cambridge Review* article.

2. F. R. Leavis, 'The Living Lawrence', *The Listener*, 5 October 1932, iv–vii.

3. F. R. Leavis, 'D. H. Lawrence – the Novelist', *The Listener*, 29 September 1949, pp. 543–544.

4. I have argued this case in my book on *Sons and Lovers* in the 'Landmarks of World Literature' series (Cambridge 1992). My argument is that the restoration of the substantial portions which Edward Garnett deleted reveals a structure which takes the book out of the category 'autobiographical document' and gives it the impersonality – to use that term – which critics such as Mark Schorer and J. C. F. Littlewood thought it lacked.

5. 'A Coping Stone', Letters to *TLS*, 5 & 19 April, 3 May, 1957.

6. F. R. Leavis, 'Romantic and Heretic?', *The Spectator*, 6 February 1959, pp. 196–7.

7. F. R. Leavis, 'The New Orthodoxy', *The Spectator*, 17 February 1961, pp. 229–30.

8. F. R. Leavis, 'Lady Chatterley', Letter to *The Spectator*, 3 March 1961, pp. 291–2.

9. F. R. Leavis 'Lawrence After 30 Years', reprinted in H. Coombes (ed.), *D. H. Lawrence: A Critical Anthology* (1973).

Index

An asterisk indicates a reference to a passage or passages by the author named that was discussed by Leavis in his lectures on 'Appreciation and Analysis' (See Chapter 6).